COLONIAL RECKONING

Duke University Press   Durham and London   2023

LOUIS A. PÉREZ JR.

Race and Revolution in
Nineteenth-Century Cuba

COLONIAL RECKONING

© 2023 DUKE UNIVERSITY PRESS. All rights reserved
Project Editor: Ihsan Taylor
Designed by Aimee C. Harrison
Typeset in Whitman and Anton by Westchester Publishing Services

Library of Congress Cataloging-in-Publication Data
Names: Pérez, Louis A., Jr., [date] author.
Title: Colonial reckoning : race and revolution in nineteenth-century Cuba / Louis A. Pérez, Jr.
Other titles: Race and revolution in nineteenth-century Cuba
Description: Durham : Duke University Press, 2023. | Includes index.
Identifiers: LCCN 2023005411 (print)
LCCN 2023005412 (ebook)
ISBN 9781478032007 (paperback)
ISBN 9781478020684 (hardcover)
ISBN 9781478027584 (ebook)
Subjects: LCSH: Nationalism—Cuba—History. | Spanish-American War, 1898. | Cuba—History—1810–1899. | Cuba—History—Revolution, 1895–1898. | Cuba—Relations—Spain. | Spain—Relations—Cuba. | BISAC: HISTORY / Caribbean & West Indies / Cuba | SOCIAL SCIENCE / Black Studies (Global)
Classification: LCC F1783 .P38 2023 (print) | LCC F1783 (ebook) | DDC 972.91/05—dc23/eng/20230607
LC record available at https://lccn.loc.gov/2023005411
LC ebook record available at https://lccn.loc.gov/2023005412

Cover art: William Allen Rogers (1854–1931), *Battle of Desmayo, Spanish American War*, 1899. Courtesy of Superstock / Alamy Stock Photo.

Contents

vii		Acknowledgments
1		Introduction: Rethinking the Paradigms of National Formation
11	1	Something to Fear
40	2	Half Defeated upon Arrival
97	3	To Confront Impossible Odds
169	4	Neither Victor nor Vanquished: Reckoning Deferred
195		Notes
265		Index

Acknowledgments

It is not often that a book a long time in the writing preserves the memory of its origins. This is such a book. It was first imagined in 2002, in the Estadio Latinoamericano in Havana, during a baseball game between the host team Los Industriales against the visiting Cienfuegos Elefantes, as the home-team supporters heckled the fans rooting for the visiting Cienfuegos club, hurling at them verbal epithets, "¡Guerrilla!" How odd. . . .

A book completed over the span of a score of years cannot but have accrued many debts of gratitude. I owe much—actually, almost everything—to the archivists, librarians, and curators of the great repositories of records who discharge the solemn custodial responsibility of the organization, maintenance, and preservation of manuscript collections, records, books, periodicals, newspapers, photographs, and maps. In Cuba, a very special appreciation is extended for the support and collaboration of the staffs who often work under execrable conditions to preserve the stuff of *patrimonio nacional*, the women and men of the Archivo Nacional de Cuba, the Instituto de Literatura y Lingüística "José Antonio Portuondo Valdor," the Instituto de Historia de Cuba, the Instituto Cubano de Investigación Cultural "Juan Marinello," and the Unión de Escritores y Artistas de Cuba. I am especially grateful to the staffs of the Biblioteca Nacional "José Martí" for their assistance in locating some of the images that appear throughout the book, including many of the photographs and the editorial cartoons. Many of the latter reveal the raw racism with which the colonial regime sought to sustain its authority and suggest too the ways that the premise of racial animus insinuated itself into the popular imagination. In the United States, I have been a beneficiary of the collaborative disposition of the staffs of the National Archives and the Library of Congress in Washington, DC. Access to the special collections and manuscript divisions of several university libraries has been indispensable, including the Cuban Heritage Collection at the University of Miami, the Special and

Area Studies Collections at the University of Florida, the American Heritage Collection at the University of Wyoming, and last—but always first—Wilson Library and Davis Library at the University of North Carolina at Chapel Hill, and especially the interlibrary loan staff at Davis.

And the legion of debts to friends and colleagues . . . over the years they extended unconditional forbearance to listen to the hum—and sometimes to the drone—of a work in progress, the ever-changing avenues of inquiry, and the new directions and the new redirections, over and over again, sometimes in conversation, often by way of correspondence, and occasionally by way of reading and rereading multiple drafts, often of the same chapters. The give-and-take, the clash of arguments, and the convergence of agreements—all of it—contributed mightily to what may be good on the pages that follow. A special thanks to José Abreu Cardet, María del Carmen Barcia, Cecilia Bermúdez García, Reinaldo Funes Monzote, Nuria Gregori Torada, the late Jorge Ibarra, Rebecca J. Scott, Eduardo Torres-Cuevas, José Vega Suñol, José Viera Linares, Oscar Zanetti, and especially to the late Francisco Pérez Guzmán, in whose company I shared the experience of the Los Industriales–Cienfuegos baseball game. A special acknowledgment of gratitude to Beatriz Riefkohl Muñiz, who read drafts of chapters in various stages of (in)completion—all to be made better and always so much. I benefited greatly from the wisdom of my friend and colleague Joseph Glatthaar, whose knowledge of military history served to inform many of my perspectives on the nature of warfare in the nineteenth century. I am indebted to Karen Fisher for a careful reading of the completed manuscript—and for all the improvements that such a careful reading produced. I wish also to convey my thanks to Teresa Chapa, Brianna Gilmore, and Bonnie Lucero for timely assistance and frequent improvised collaborations.

I cannot overstate my appreciation for the encouragement and enthusiasm with which Gisela Fosado, editorial director at Duke University Press, embraced this project. Her engagement with the ideas of this book made for a perfectly delightful collaboration. A particular note of gratitude to members of the staff of Duke University Press for their thoughtfulness and helpful assistance during the final stages of production: a special acknowledgment of appreciation to Alejandra Mejía, Ihsan Taylor, Aimee Harrison, and Emily Estelle.

Deborah M. Weissman was perhaps the first person to learn of my puzzlement over the Cienfuegos–Los Industriales baseball game. Her support sustained the years of inquiry that followed, from the last pitch at the Estadio Latinoamericano to the first pitch to Duke University Press.

And to end to where almost everything begins: to express an enduring *cariño* and *aprecio* to Fidel Requeijo and Gladys Marel García, who, alas, were of little assistance in unpacking the meaning of the taunts hurled at the fans of the Cienfuegos Elefantes but who in every other regard provided insight into everything else in Cuba. I am the grateful beneficiary of their unstinting generosity and unfailing friendship for the better part of the last forty years.

LAP
Chapel Hill, NC

INTRODUCTION

Rethinking the Paradigms
of National Formation

Cuban narratives of national liberation long ago assumed discernible forms of received wisdom, something of a settled epistemology akin to an article of faith: those foundational chronicles to which successive generations of historians are heir, into which they are more or less socialized, and to which they are mostly disposed to accede. The liberation narratives appear credible, certainly, as a matter of custom and convention, told and retold, remembered and recounted, and in the aggregate have served as stories deployed to inform the premise of *lo cubano*.

Liberation narratives are especially susceptible to discursive forms of conceit, of course. They are in part myths, at times swooning to heights of lore and legend—a people infatuated with the "glorious legends" of their past, Santiago Rey offers—produced by historical actors at the time, for practical reasons, and reproduced by historians thereafter, often for reasons no less practical.[1] The myths possess an internal logic of their own, as indeed myths often do, expanding fully into belief systems, mostly because they idealize those attributes that a people most like about themselves. Achievements to commemorate, virtues to emulate, values to live up to: all fundamental to the foundation myths. "La historia como identidad," pronounced Miguel Barnet.[2] What is there not to like?

It could hardly be otherwise, of course: the remembrance of heroic sacrifice and Homeric struggle, noble leaders and notable deeds. No moral ambiguity here. The indignation of an aroused people driven to take history into their own hands was a matter of collective resolve, coming together in common purpose fully persuaded of the righteousness of their claim to a nation of their own: women and men, young and old, black and white, Cubans of means and of modest origins alike—together—over successive generations, giving themselves unconditionally to the idea of Cuba Libre as a means of being, belonging, and becoming. Sublime leaders, many of whom perished in the process, were lifted aloft in the swell of apotheosis, thereupon transformed into martyrs, models, and metaphors: Carlos Manuel de Céspedes, Ignacio Agramonte, José Martí, Mariana Grajales, and Antonio Maceo, among many others—"magnificent examples of virtue for Cuban youth to imitate," exulted Matías Duque.[3] They gave meaning to *lo cubano*. They fixed the standard of how Cubans should live and set the purpose for which Cubans should die. Invitation to martyrdom in exchange for the prospects of everlasting life. "To die for the *patria* is to live forever," promises the Cuban national anthem.

This is seductive stuff, possessed of an appeal often difficult to resist. The historiography of the nineteenth century is rich with the memorialization of liberation as a collective experience from which the normative determinants of nationality have assumed meaning. The narratives tend to hew closely to the proposition of history as a source of resilience and a means of redemption, a past to look up to and live for, at once didactic and instrumental, history as a metaphysics worthy of the protagonists for whom dedication to the idea of the sovereign nation was, in the words of writer Lisandro Otero, "associated with moral duty."[4] The master narrative of the nineteenth-century liberation project closes in on itself and allows little possibility for alternative outcomes, tending instead to subordinate the contingencies of history to the privilege of hindsight.

The heroic narratives of national liberation do in fact bear a measure of verisimilitude, of course. How true the historic chronicles may be—or not—is often less important than the role they play. Narratives endowed with instrumental purpose are used to explain the origins of the nation and to serve the needs of the people who deploy them. To understand the nineteenth-century wars of liberation, historian Jorge Ibarra explained as his purpose for writing *Historia de Cuba* (1971), implied the need "to call attention to the continuity of this historical process with the socialist revolution."[5] To serve notice: the revolution had a history.

At least as important as the truths included and remembered, however, are the truths excluded and forgotten, denied entrée into the foundational narratives of the nation, often feared as a threat of destabilizing the presumption of clarity upon which the normative determinants of nationality rest: a people—perhaps properly so—disinclined to admit moral ambiguity into the meaning of their past. The silences, anthropologist Michel-Rolph Trouillot wrote in a different context, in those historiographies are "heavily guided by national—if not always nationalist—interests."[6]

The liberation project spanned much of the nineteenth century, pursued principally in the form of thwarted conspiracies and short-lived uprisings, as failed filibustering expeditions and ill-planned annexationist plots, and as a successions of wars: the Ten Years' War (1868–78), the Little War (1879–80), and the War for Independence (1895–98). Years during which enmities deepened and settled into sharply defined markers of fixed estrangement: ill will between the colony and the metropolis, among social classes and within the privileged classes, between Cubans and Spaniards, among Cubans themselves, between blacks and whites. All in all, cultural distinctions, ethnic divisions, and racial differences often found expression in the form of spasms of violence and thereupon settled into a politics of virulent intensity.

The nineteenth century was a time of visceral animus, of hate extending outward and inward into the sensibility of a people at war among themselves. Some lived with the fear of loss and displacement; others lived with the fact of loss and displacement. Living daily life in close proximity with one another, close enough for them to understand they were the source of each other's fears—and the object of each other's hatreds. Circumstances that could not but act to distill hatred into a raw force for political change—or not—animosities taking deep root over the span of nearly one hundred years, burnished deeply into the temperament of a people through the violence of chattel slavery, rebellion and repression, resistance and subjugation. An arrangement of checks and balances of enmities—in its own right—served fully as a system of governance to hold in place a colonial regime long past its time.

The expansion in the population of people of color—both enslaved Africans and free people of African descent—as a consequence of sugar production after Saint-Domingue changed everything. Census data for 1792 indicate the presence of an estimated 85,000 enslaved Africans and 54,000 free people of color. This population more than doubled to 199,000 and 114,000 respectively by 1817, and doubled again to 436,000 and 153,000 in 1841.[7] In no other Spanish colony was the local economy so fully dependent on the labor of enslaved people. In no other Spanish colony did enslaved Africans constitute so large a part of the population. In no other Spanish colony did the total African-descended population expand to constitute a majority.[8]

The presence of a vast population of enslaved people upon whom the producing classes depended but from whom they also needed protection acted relentlessly to shape much of the history that would follow. The loyalty of the Ever-Faithful Isle often had less to do with heartfelt fealty than with pragmatic expedience. Colonialism was an arrangement of security and stability, of course, but also was a strategy to defend the racial hierarchies upon which chattel slavery and the exercise of white privilege depended. To live with an interior knowledge of the iniquity of chattel slavery, however, with and among vast numbers of African-descended people, was also to live with the specter of retributive justice. "The whites of the island of Cuba," Félix Varela warned as early as 1822, during the restoration of the liberal 1812 Constitution in Spain, "do not cease to congratulate themselves for having overturned the old despotism and having recovered the sacred rights of free men. And do they expect that the natives of Africa will remain passive spectators to these emotions? Their rage and despair will oblige them to choose between liberty and death."[9] Planter José Luis Alfonso did not fail to discern ominous portents in the slave uprisings of the 1840s. "Are we to be surprised that enslaved men rose up to fight for their liberty?" Alfonso asked rhetorically. "With each passing day we discern greater determination among them, with a deepening tendency to rebel and claim their rights through force."[10]

To interrogate anew the experience of liberation implies the need to situate the matter of race relations at the center of the colonial reckoning in the nineteenth century as context for almost everything else. The fear of the expanding presence of people of color—free and enslaved—reached deeply into the cosmology of white, a presence to keep at bay and hold in check, a colonial status quo sustained by fear, a pervasive disquiet that settled into a condition of daily life during most of the nineteenth century. Time enough for fear to acquire a proper history, kept alive as a result of recurring acts of rebellion and allegations of conspiracies, thereupon to confirm the worst fears of a fearful people. A restive criollo patriciate and an overbearing *peninsular* officialdom, representatives of the producing classes, including planters, manufacturers, merchants, and industrialists, all, in sum, whose well-being was implicated in sugar and slavery, lived with fear: fear of the abolition of slavery, of the emancipation of the enslaved, of the rebellion of the enslaved, of race war, of black suffrage, and inevitably a fear that extended into a dread of Cuban independence—for the same reason.[11] Political change seemed almost always to implicate populations of color, almost always perceived as a threat to prevailing racial order—that is, almost always everything. There was perhaps no more effective means through which to uphold the logic of colonialism than the specter of social dissolution attending independence. Early in the nineteenth century—and long thereafter—among the beneficiaries of an enduring status quo, the proposition of sovereignty became synonymous with black ascendancy.

To address the colonial reckoning of the nineteenth century implies the need to acknowledge ambiguity and complexity in the process of liberation, to work through contradictions and contingencies, to address anomalies that were often as incompatible as they were incongruent. The *independentista* project spanned the lifetime of three successive generations over the course of the nineteenth century, circumstances that could not but allow for the entrée of disparate voices and divergent visions, changing with the times as the times changed, changing too as an ever-expanding separatist coalition changed. The idea of Free Cuba evolved over the course of time, often as a matter of pragmatic adaptation, haltingly, and advancing in fits and starts, expanding—or contracting—to accommodate competing ideological formulations and reconcile conflicting strategies of liberation, almost always as practiced efforts to cobble together a political consensus into an executable military plan of action. The liberation purpose was transacted by way of opportunistic alliances and within principled coalitions, among the well-meaning and the mischievous, as hastily improvised uprisings and well-prepared plots.

Cuba Libre meant different things to different people, differences that often coexisted incongruously and unresolved within an ever-changing paradigm of national liberation. For the time being—at the time—as a matter of practical necessity over the short run, it was enough that something of a consensus formed around the necessity to obtain the independence of Cuba from Spain, a unanimity of purpose and unity of interests to which almost all other differences were purposely subordinated.

But the differences persisted, and they accumulated: differences over competing visions of nation and contested meanings of nationality, indeed often over the very plausibility of the proposition of Free Cuba. Separation from Spain did not always mean sovereignty for Cuba. Political fault lines etched deeply across the physiognomy of the *criollidad*, fissures often as deep as they were wide, among advocates for home self-rule within the colonial system, supporters of annexation to the United States, and proponents of national sovereignty, between Cubans on the island and Cubans in the emigration, between—as Carlos Loveira would memorialize—the *generales y doctores*.

But it was more complicated still. In fact, vast numbers of Cubans remained loyal to *la madre patria* to render vital service to Spain, criollos Melchor Loret de Mola would later characterize as "the type of Hispanicized Cuban" (*el tipo del cubano españolizado*), Cubans whose needs accommodated easily to the benefits of colonialism.[12] The collaboration of Cubans with the colonial regime was an essential facet of Spanish governance, to confer political legitimacy in times of peace and enhance military capacity during times of war. During the final decades of the nineteenth century, Cubans of means and education enrolled in the leadership of the Autonomist Party to seek home-rule/self-government authority within the framework of the colonial system, and especially to navigate between the known constraints of colonialism and the unknown consequences of independence. Other Cubans served the colonial government with arms, through service in the *milicias*, recruited by Spain as a way to share the responsibility for stability, to render support in the maintenance of internal security, to contain slave rebellion and recapture escaped slaves, to defend the island against external filibustering expeditions and combat internal separatist uprisings. Service as officers in the *milicias* offered the well-to-do young men of creole families access to official positions of authority, perhaps too a pathway to upward mobility within colonial officialdom. Many thousands of Cubans of color similarly filled the ranks of the *batallones de pardos y morenos*, also as a matter of career options and a means of livelihood in an environment of otherwise limited opportunities.[13]

Nowhere perhaps did Cubans render greater service in defense of Spanish colonial sovereignty than in the role of paramilitary auxiliary forces known variously as guerrillas, *guerrilleros*, and *contra-guerrillas*, organized to assist *peninsular* army units in the suppression of the colonial insurgencies between 1868 and 1898. The view of the guerrilla in the service of a counterrevolutionary project appears as an anomaly, most assuredly, for in the modern imagination the proposition of guerrilla/guerrilla warfare serves to denote a method of war associated most commonly with armed resistance, with the weak against the strong, with wars of national liberation. Certainly the weight of the historiography of the nineteenth-century wars of independence tends to favor descriptions of the guerrilla and guerrilla warfare as the method of war waged by the Cubans against the Spanish government.

No doubt a correct modern description of the operational facets of the Cuban way of war. But in Cuba—at the time—and on both sides, *guerrilla* meant something very different. The word *guerrilla* derived its original sensibility from the campaign of irregular—"small war"—paramilitary operations sustained by Spanish armed resistance against the occupation of Spain by the Grande Armée of Napoleon. The Spanish resistance fighters performed heroically in collaboration with the Duke of Wellington during the Peninsular War in what would become known as Spain's war of independence (1808–14). All due credit owed to the guerrillas, reported British Captain T. Sydenham:

> [The Spanish guerrillas] obliged the French to fortify themselves in every village and town in the country; they harassed the parties who were through the provinces either to subsist themselves, or to procure supplies from the enemy's magazines.... They intercepted convoys of provisions and stores; they rendered the communications of the enemy very difficult and hazardous, and often cut them off for weeks together; and finally, they assisted in keeping alive the spirit of resistance against the invaders.[14]

The guerrillas in Spain had acquitted themselves honorably. They had redeemed the nation, and henceforth the persona of the guerrilla was invoked with respect and reverence. It was not a designation Spain would bestow upon the Cuban *insurrectos*, who were variously characterized as outlaws, traitors, criminals, and arsonists—but never as guerrillas. Guerrillas in Cuba were the *nativos de la isla*, as the Spanish were wont to say, practiced in the ways of paramilitary warfare, in this instance, in the methods of counterinsurgency—in the contemporary vernacular—in defense of Spanish colonial rule. Both Spanish authorities and Cuban *insurrectos* understood guerrillas to be Cubans in the service of Spain.

Spanish army commanders in Cuba arrived early at an understanding of the character of warfare in the middle latitudes of the New World. This was not warfare between opposing armies engaged in set-piece battles. On the contrary, these were wars waged against unseen combatants supported by populations of visible noncombatants. The nineteenth-century insurgencies in Cuba foreshadowed the twentieth-century colonial wars of national liberation between the colonized and the colonizer, in settings where distinctions between combatants and noncombatants rarely revealed themselves with discernible clarity. The enemy in Cuba was everywhere, the Spanish army command understood—and acted accordingly.

Spain waged a new kind of war, given to adjustments of tactical methods and adaptation of strategic purpose—continually—against combatants and noncombatants alike, of course, but also to contend with an insufferable climate and an unfamiliar topography. The insurgencies of nineteenth-century Cuba suggest new dimensions to environmental history, to understand a European soldiery waging war in equatorial latitudes within a special kind of meteorology, enclosed within dense, luxuriant rain forests, with the sun constantly at a near-vertical position by noon, and the seasonal cycles of relentless torrential rains. Unbearable temperatures. Impenetrable jungles. Impassable marshlands. And mosquitoes. And disease. A combination that wreaked havoc on what had been among the mightiest mobilizations of European combat soldiers in the New World. No small truth was contained in the observation offered in 1873 by physician Félix de Echauz, chief of the Sanitation Corps of the Spanish army in Cuba, that "the principal enemy we face in Cuba is not the *insurrecto* but the climate."[15]

Spain conducted ferocious wars in Cuba, deploying a different kind of violence, costly to the Cubans, of course. But also costly to Spanish soldiers. The results of the wars were ghastly. An estimated 200,000 women, men, and children perished between 1868 and 1878. Perhaps as many as 500,000 women and men—mostly Cuban civilians—lost their lives between 1895 and 1898. The estimates of death among Spanish soldiers were staggering. Perhaps as many as 150,000 dead between 1868 and 1878 and another 100,000 dead between 1895 and 1898—deaths due mostly to disease.

The colonial wars were waged principally between and within populations of shared cultural systems and similar moral tenacities, protracted affairs stretching into years, countless military operations mostly without consequences, wars fought with the settled conviction that victory—or perhaps better said, that defeat—had less to do with outcomes of battles than with the need to deplete the morale and weaken the resolve of the enemy. The type of conflict that often develops into something of a personal matter, thereupon sustained with deepening hatreds that often act to transform the conduct of war into campaigns of reprisal and revenge.

Peninsular army commanders understood the need for the assistance of *los nativos de la isla*. Many tens of thousands of Cubans, black and white, often including former *insurrectos* who defected to Spain (*presentados*), acclimated to and familiar with the interior habitat of the insurgency (*la manigua*), served variously as *prácticos* to guide Spanish military columns and as mobile cavalry units to carry the war to the *mambises*. *Los nativos* did indeed render important service. Some of the most significant losses suffered by the *mambises* were inflicted in operations conducted by guerrilla units. The Spanish assault against the encampment of San Lorenzo in 1874 where Carlos Manuel de Céspedes was killed was based on the intelligence provided by *presentado* Ramón Jacás serving as *práctico*.[16] In 1870 the guerrillas of Cinco Villas mounted the attack against General Antonio de Armas, who was captured and subsequently executed.[17] Operations that resulted in the capture of General Julio Sanguily in 1871 were directed by a unit of two hundred guerrillas.[18] General Augusto Arango was killed in guerrilla operations led by Lieutenant Ramón Recio—"*un mal cubano*," decried Vidal Morales y Morales.[19] Antonio Maceo fell mortally wounded at Punta Brava in battle with guerrilla forces under the command of Doroteo de Peral.

To examine the role of the Cuban guerrillas is to arrive at a fuller appreciation of Spanish capacities to sustain years of punishing losses, and this offers a far more nuanced understanding of the workings of Spanish colonialism and the success of Spanish military operations—success in this instance to mean the ability to forestall the always-looming prospects of defeat. It is perhaps impossible to understand the resilience of the Spanish army in the face of frightful losses of life without attention to the vital assistance rendered by Cubans on behalf of *peninsular* military operations.

To accommodate the presence of the guerrillas within the historiography of the nineteenth century also acts to complicate the liberation narratives and to problematize further the liberation process. The moral clarity so long a hallowed feature of the historiography of Cuba, in fact, does not correspond exactly to the varieties of the Cuban experience as lived. The heroic historical narratives have tended to efface the complexities of the profound social transformations in which not all Cubans were transformed equally. In fact, the wars for independence were also armed conflicts between Cubans, wars without quarter assuming the unforgiving intensities that so often accompany civil wars.

The first-person experiences as remembered and recorded by the *mambises*, that is, the protagonists themselves, have served historians well, mostly a combination of personal correspondence, memoirs, diaries, field journals, autobiographies, and reminiscences written by the men and women who committed to posterity a record of their presence, to insert themselves as party to and participants in the outcomes to which they contributed: an act of agency, in its own right, to claim the role of protagonist in their own history. To see the past through their eyes, in their own words, to see what they observed and to read what they wrote, even if encumbered with an imperfect and incomplete understanding of the forces acting to shape the course of events, is to be situated inside the experience of armed engagement. They often failed to appreciate the significance of what they saw or misrepresented the importance of what they observed. It bears remembering, too, that these texts are profoundly skewed, always favoring the voice of participants with the gift of letters: access to the past through the privilege of literacy, perhaps among the most inexorable filter of inequality.

Considered separately and apart, the first-person liberation chronicles seldom rise above realms of the anecdotal, as historians often caution, texts in the form of personal observations and individual experiences that may—or may not—have significance to matters beyond the gaze of the observer. In the aggregate, however, they are transformed into something else, into a body of evidence, to suggest the presence of patterns, perhaps to point to tendencies and draw attention to trends, to allow for the possibility of inference, always as a matter of a tentative construct, of course, through which to suggest the plausibility of a hypothesis.

In fact, however, the memory of participants has not always found a welcoming space within the normative provenance from which the heroic historical narratives have been assembled. There is something subversive about the honesty of the first-person memoir that has often inclined historians to mute the range of the *mambí* voice. On the matter of the guerrillas, the historiography is conspicuous for its silence, recalling Ernest Renan's adage that "the essence of a nation is that all individuals have many things in common, and also that they have forgotten many things."[20] It was not that the guerrillas were forgotten, however. They were made forgettable. The historiographical silences are especially noteworthy in light of the prominence given to the guerrillas in almost all the memoirs, reminiscences, and autobiographies of the *mambises* themselves, those first-person accounts that served to chronicle the character of the war and the characteristics of the combatants.

The guerrillas pass through Cuban historiography mostly in silence, a subject that rarely rises above the status of a footnote. The formidable and indeed prodigious history of the Ten Years' War by Ramiro Guerra y Sánchez, *Guerra de los Diez Años, 1868–1878* (1950), in every regard rich with detail in its reach and sweeping in its scope, offers but scant reference to the presence of the guerrillas.[21] The magisterial four-volume history by Herminio Portell Vilá, *Historia de Cuba en sus relaciones con los Estados Unidos y España* (1938–41), is all but silent on the matter of guerrillas, as is the prodigious scholarship of Emilio Roig de Leuchsenring, Jorge Ibarra, and Eduardo Torres Cuevas.[22] The thoughtful essay by Juan Luis Martín, "El combatiente cubano en función de pueblo," mentions briefly the recruitment of blacks in the service of guerrilla units.[23] Among the most notable exceptions is Fernando Portuondo del Prado, who acknowledged the participation of nearly thirty thousand *guerrilleros insulares*, "mostly peasants for whom no part of the interior countryside was unknown." Portuondo offered pointed reference to the wave of rural repression unleashed by troops of Spanish General Valmaseda in Oriente—*la cresciente de Valmaseda*—during the Ten Years' War as "accompanied by excellent creole guides."[24] Years later, on the occasion of the First National Congress of History in 1942 in Havana, Jorge Juárez y Sedeño chided the assembled Cuban historians for having failed to remember *las guerrillas de los batallones, las guerrillas locales, las guerrillas volantes, las guerrillas especiales, las guerrillas de Camajuaní, la guerrilla de Matanzas*, and *la guerrilla Cuba Española*.[25]

Difficult indeed to accommodate the presence of the many tens of thousands of Cubans as guerrillas without lacerating the historical sensibility of *lo cubano*, perhaps as many as one hundred thousand Cubans, suggested Miguel Varona Guerrero, a member of General Máximo Gómez's staff.[26] Years later, in 1941, geographer Salvador Massip would offer a rueful acknowledgment: "It is sadly known that the number of *guerrilleros* was far greater than the number of *insurrectos*."[27] The history of national liberation is murky indeed. Free Cuba was a contested construct all through the nineteenth century, a contest that persisted and reached deep into the twentieth century, circumstances that invite reexamination of the narratives of liberation. If the revolution has a history, so too most assuredly does the counterrevolution.

To admit the presence of Cubans who defended Spanish colonial sovereignty into the master narrative of national formation does not diminish the authenticity of the liberation narratives, of course. The credibility of the liberation chronicles will endure, for in the end they include truths that do indeed stand up well to close scrutiny. Rather, to address the presence of the guerrilla is to add complexity to the narrative of a century-long struggle against colonialism, a way to interrogate anew the multifaceted social dimensions and multiple political aspects of a complex drama of national formation, to appreciate some of the incongruities and inconsistencies of life as lived, and thereupon to arrive at a deeper understanding of the history that followed.

SOMETHING TO FEAR

The people who have something to fear in Cuba, including the great property owners and the commercial classes, know full well the dangers that a Constitution based on liberty and equality [i.e., independence] poses to their person and property. These words that sound so melodious to our ears are in Cuba words of extermination and death. The existence of the African race in Cuba, which forms half the population ... is and will forever be an obstacle to the principles that prevail in enlightened nations with a homogenous population.
—José Ahumada y Centurión, *Memoria histórico política de la Isla de Cuba, redactada de orden del Señor Ministro de Ultramar* (1874)

The fear which the Cubans have of the blacks is the most secure means which Spain has to guarantee her domination over this island.
—Spanish Premier José María Calatrava (1836)

I am certain that the proponents of independence would [seek to] obtain the support of almost all the African-descended people.... But let us suppose that we would possess sufficient means to mount a glorious resistance and that we would emerge triumphant: most certainly all our mercantile relations would have come to an end, with agriculture entirely destroyed, as well as a large part of both the white and black population.... The Island of Cuba, whose commerce is worthy of such esteem the world over, would remain reduced to country of poor fishermen until another great power would seize it and secure the advantage that Spain failed to obtain.
—Félix Varela, "Memoria que demuestra la necesidad de extinguir la esclavitud de los negros en la Isla de Cuba, atendiendo a los intereses de sus propietarios" (1822)

At no point did [the inhabitants of Cuba] think of affiliating with the revolutionary flag unfurled in the other countries of [Latin] America. Public peace continued uninterrupted, save a number of insignificant and isolated uprisings of people of color that were almost instantly suppressed with the creoles [*los hijos del país*] registering the most active role in the suppression of the revolts. . . . Fear was everywhere.
—Mariano Torrente, *Bosquejo económico político de la Isla de Cuba* (1852)

The idea of sovereign nationhood seized hold of the New World imagination early: a powerful idea indeed, thereupon to plunge the Atlantic colonial systems into disarray and dissolution. The nineteenth century was the time of the nation in Latin America, a time in which the idea of the nation-state gained ascendancy as the principal means through which to transact a collective destiny. An idea lifted aloft in the swoon of romantic sentimentality, to be sure, but an idea also possessed of powerful instrumental value, an idea endowed with the capacity to summon popular mobilization as a means of collective agency. The Latin American wars for independence waged against Spain in the name of freedom and liberty were most commonly articulated as demands for self-determination and national sovereignty, that is, for a people for whom the hope of remedy for colonial oppressions was invested in the promise of a nation of their own.

Almost everywhere. But not Cuba.

It seemed as if history had bypassed Cuba. Certainly the criollos of Cuba shared many of the same grievances that had contributed to the discontent of criollos on the mainland. The Cubans too—at least in private—brooded among themselves in grudging resentment over the arbitrary excesses of an overbearing Spanish colonial officialdom and an overreaching Spanish burgher class, at the practices of impunity and patterns of corruption, at the deeds of misconduct and the acts of maladministration: all settled customs that so often compromised the interests of *los nativos de la isla*. "The restrictions and denial of political rights, the exclusion of Cubans from all forms of official positions, and the taxes," Gaspar Betancourt Cisneros decried. "Neither Cubans of our time nor those who follow us have any reason to expect from Spain anything other than chains, injustice, and unconscionable and unrelieved corruption."[1]

Nor were the criollos of Cuba unreceptive to the prerogatives of sovereignty, of course. Indeed, the possibility of an expanded exercise of self-government in defense of self-interests was not without its appeal. "If there exists on the island of Cuba the general impulse for independence from Spain," writer Félix Tanco offered, "it is not for the purpose of delivering the island from the state of oppression and misery in which it finds itself. It is, rather, so *that the creoles can replace the Spanish as rulers, and leave everything else exactly as it is.*"²

A discontent with the general state of affairs, most assuredly: but not with everything. In fact, self-interest was deeply implicated in the status quo, in the greater need to leave everything else as it was, for which the Cubans were persuaded that acquiescence to an odious Spanish presence was the necessary concession of the Faustian exchange. "There is hardly a Cuban who does not covet and desire independence," observed Jacinto de Salas y Quiroga in 1840. "But it does not go beyond a passive desire." Salas y Quiroga continued:

> Between the desire to have and intending to have [*entre desear tener e intentar tener*] there is a terrible distance. . . . The Cubans desire independence but they will not bestir themselves to possess it, because at the moment it is suicide. . . . The day that the cry for independence is heard in Havana will signal the ruin of the island. Commerce will flee, industry will end, and all the paths to prosperity will be blocked. In sum, the island is lost.³

The status quo was not without its advantages. A new economy was in the making. Revolution in Saint-Domingue in 1791 had visited calamity upon the French colony, with years of civil strife and war, followed by the collapse of what had been among the most productive sugar regions in the Western Hemisphere: an estimated 800 sugar plantations, producing an annual average of 71,000 tons of sugar, were razed; nearly 3,000 coffee estates, yielding more than 30,000 tons of coffee annually and accounting for almost two-thirds of the world supply, ceased to produce. Production descended into disarray, and eventually into demise. The plantations passed into various states of ruination: harvests diminished, production decreased, exports declined, planters departed.

The downfall of sugar production in Saint-Domingue was a windfall for sugar producers in Cuba. The law of supply and demand wreaked its inexorable havoc on the world markets: supplies dwindled, demand increased, prices soared—all in all, more than adequate incentive to bestir planters in Cuba to expand sugar production.⁴ "The loss of Santo Domingo," one official report summarized, "raising to extraordinary heights the price of sugar and coffee, excited private [planter] interests which, protected by the government and local authorities, quickly committed to the development of this important branch of Cuban agriculture."⁵ Thus it was that Cubans plunged headlong into the history that followed.

A time of dazzling prosperity and the amassing of great fortunes. The hinterlands surrounding the towns and cities—mostly in the western and central jurisdictions— developed rapidly into vast expanses of flourishing agricultural enterprises, a mixture of sugar plantations and coffee estates, orchards and groves, small vegetable farms and livestock ranches. The number of coffee estates (*cafetales*) increased from two in 1774 to 108 in 1802, to 586 in 1804, more than doubling to 1,315 by 1806, and almost doubling again to 2,067 by 1827, more than half of which (1,207) were located principally in Pinar del Río, Havana, and Matanzas and accounting for more than 75 percent of Cuban production.[6] The number of farms (*fincas*) increased almost fivefold, from 7,580 in 1778 to 34,798 in 1827 and increasing again to nearly 50,000 in 1846.[7] Of the total number of *fincas* in 1827, fully 75 percent—26,194 out of 34,978—were located in the western and central zones.[8] Abiel Abbot visited new agricultural zones around Guanajay southwest of Havana in 1828, taking note of "twelve coffee estates on the road, most of them extensive; two large sugar estates, three more were in sight; two vegas of tobacco, one of ten acres, and the other of two; seven large potreros, or pastures for cattle, two of them very large; forty farms of small extent.... In all these directions there is high cultivation."[9]

But it was mostly about sugar. There was something of an inexorable tenacity about the way that sugar established its grip in Cuba: it seized hold and held sway. Vast swaths of lands of all types—farms, fields, and forests—were plowed under to prepare for sugar.[10] The land passed into sugar production at an accelerated pace: an estimated 1,700 acres annually in the 1790s, to 3,500 acres by the 1810s, and reaching 13,000 acres by the 1840s. The number of sugar mills in Cuba almost doubled from 529 in 1792 to 1,000 in 1827, and increased again to 1,442 in 1846, and again to 2,400 mills by 1860.[11] Production output increased at an exponential pace: 17,000 tons of sugar in 1791 doubled to 37,000 tons in 1810, and doubled again to 60,000 tons in 1823, thereafter to swell to 165,000 tons in 1836 and 223,000 tons by 1850—by which time, historian Franklin Knight correctly noted, Cuban sugar production was "the most advanced the world had ever experienced."[12]

It was not, hence, so much that history had bypassed Cuba. It was, rather, that Cuba had been overtaken by another history. Sugar changed almost everything, which is to say that almost everything had something to do with sugar, to which almost everything was subordinated, and for which nothing was spared. The importance of sugar, observed Ramón de la Sagra in 1831, was due "to the consequences that its prosperity or its decline ha[d] on all classes of society."[13]

The imperative of sugar governed almost all facets of the colonial political economy. Nothing seemed to matter more, or matter more immediately. A dense network of mutually reinforcing practices, policies, and polities—interlocking, interacting, and interdependent—ordered and arranged to accommodate the needs of property and production. Sugar not only determined the purpose of the land and the purpose of production; it also lay claim to the purpose of public policy. "It is true," observed Jacinto de Salas y Quiroga in 1840, "that in matters of industry, the government . . . is nothing more than the oil that facilitates the movement of the [sugar] machinery."[14] It could hardly have been otherwise, of course. The solvency of colonial administration was deeply implicated in the success of sugar production. Revenues produced by sugar exports filled the coffers of an appreciative Royal Exchequer, who henceforth would act with uncommon solicitude in behalf of sugar production. Sugar seized hold securely, historian Manuel Moreno Fraginals correctly noted, and to "an extraordinary extent" resulted in the "abandonment of all that did not have something to do with sugar, directly or indirectly."[15] The needs of sugar served to inform the very raison d'être of Spanish administration, thereupon to influence almost all decisions bearing on the conduct and content of public policy as the overriding consideration to which decisions of colonial governance were subject.

New capital investment transformed production systems, transforming, too, land tenure forms, property relationships, and especially labor systems. Sugar had summoned into existence complex production modes dependent on the coerced labor of newly enslaved Africans on a scale unprecedented in the nineteenth century. Enslaved Africans arrived in Cuba in vast numbers, many tens of thousands of young women and men, in seemingly endless waves of human cargo. Between 1792 and 1817, the enslaved population of Cuba more than doubled, from 85,000 to 199,000; and between 1817 and 1841, it doubled again, from 199,000 to 436,000—by which time, too, enslaved Africans accounted for nearly half the total population of Cuba.[16] "An indisputable material strength of blacks over whites," warned José Ferrer de Couto, "in an obviously dangerous proportion."[17] All in all, "sufficient indications unto themselves," cautioned the *Revista Bimestre Cubana* in 1832, "to understand that we find ourselves gravely ill" (*nos hallamos gravemente enfermos*) and raising the specter that "death may surprise in the very midst of the apparent felicity we are enjoying" (*la muerte puede sorprendernos en medio de la aparente felicidad que gozamos*).[18]

In fact, the Cuban producing classes understood that to "replace the Spanish as rulers" implied a direct threat to everything else exactly as it was. They recoiled in horror at the spectacle of disorder and disarray occasioned by the New World wars for independence—Saint-Domingue, of course. But also the rebellion of Indians and mestizos in Mexico, to which Lucas Alamán bore witness as "assassination and plunder, cries of death and desolation."[19] And the *castas* of Venezuela and the Indians of Peru. The wars of independence in South America had released powerful destructive forces, acts of depredation and campaigns of desolation—"war without quarter," Simón Bolívar had proclaimed—total war indeed, in which the practice of pillage and plunder served as cost-effective methods of warfare. Precious little was spared. Little survived. What had been the result of the "shattering of the bonds of loyalty"? The Havana weekly *La Concordia Cubana* posed the portentous interrogative in 1823—and answered, "The destruction of our communities; wives transformed into widows; innocent children transformed into orphans; shattered and divided families; the countryside razed; the homes of the wealthy reduced to ashes; the roads awash with human blood; the prostrate resident of all the towns succumbing to hunger."[20]

A war for independence in Cuba could hardly be contemplated. "Independence would be barbaric," Domingo del Monte warned, the onset of "complete social dissolution" that "would release on the island ferocious instincts. As a result of what has transpired in the civil wars of Spanish America . . . it is possible to foresee the horrors and the abominations that would occur on this island under similar circumstances."[21] The price of independence, the producing classes feared, far exceeded the cost of colonialism. "Under our present circumstances," José Antonio Saco predicted in 1848, "the political revolution will necessarily be accompanied by the social revolution, and the social revolution is the complete ruin of the Cuban people" (*la raza cubana*).[22]

But there was more. The cause of independence in South America had summoned to arms divergent political constituencies and diverse social coalitions bearing a variety of grievances and advancing an assortment of remedies, a call to war informed by a purpose of another kind: propounding new freedoms as redress to old oppressions, including—and especially—the abolition of slavery as a matter of republican constitutionality writ large. Unthinkable in Cuba.

Slavery was not debatable. Abolition was not negotiable. That the pursuit of independence as an end implied the necessity to end slavery as a means foreclosed any likelihood of creole mobilization to challenge Spanish colonial rule. The internal logic of sugar production had developed fully within and entirely dependent upon the premise of chattel slavery. The producing classes understood well the need to accommodate themselves to their circumstances as aggrieved subjects of colonial rule as a condition necessary to sustain the subjugation of enslaved Africans. Slavery, Domingo del Monte commented bluntly, "is the cause of our political oppression."[23]

But it was more complicated still. At least as important as the need to protect slavery was the need for protection against slaves. The island was filling with many tens of thousands of newly enslaved Africans—intractable, undisciplined, resentful, and with memory of sequestration—even as New World slavery was under assault from within and without. A war of independence in Cuba, one presumptively between *peninsulares* and criollos, the Cubans feared, threatened to shatter the solidarities upon which enforcement of colonial racial hierarchies was transacted. Whites at war with each other implied a diminished capacity of whites to sustain violence against blacks. To live with the specter of slave rebellion as a condition of daily life, Spanish engineer Anastasio de Arango commented in 1825, had rendered criollos permanently susceptible to "their overwrought imagination as a result of the terror of the horrific and bloody effect of fear of an insurrection of blacks."[24] José Antonio Saco brooded over the implications of a breach between criollos and *peninsulares*, in which case "whites divided among themselves would provide the blacks the opportunity for a general uprising."[25] Richard Madden learned of white angst during a midcentury visit to Cuba: "The great apprehension [of an independence movement] that was entertained was of the slaves,—of their taking advantage of the revolution to get rid of all the whites, both Spaniard and Creoles."[26] Perhaps no less likely: *peninsulares* or criollos, forced to confront the prospects of an imminent defeat, would be tempted to summon the enslaved population to arms as allies to rescue a flagging cause. "Cuba to rise up in rebellion?" Domingo del Monte asked rhetorically. "In this instance, the Spaniards and creoles would engage in combat across the fields of Cuba, and which ever side perceived itself faltering would necessarily appeal for support among the ranks of the blacks of the sugar plantations, and in return offer freedom for their support."[27]

The producing classes understood well the political economy of colonialism, an environment of their own making, of course, but appreciated even more how deeply their well-being depended upon leaving everything else as it was. On some matters, *Diario de la Marina* editor Dionisio Alcalá Galiano noted, "Cubans [*los hijos del país*] were in absolute agreement with the Spanish," adding, "The fear that slavery would be adversely affected as a result of political turmoil constitutes one of the principal sources of stability upon which we can rely [and] the consequences of which underwrites our sovereignty in Cuba.... *Quieta non movere* is our motto."[28] The producing classes also understood that self-government could not but threaten to invite havoc upon self-interests, and indeed that the need to defend the latter could not but exceed the capacity of the former, that the colonial system that sanctioned the practice of official malfeasance, to which they were victim, was one and the same that sustained the prevailing racial hierarchies, to which they were beneficiary, and that—finally—the consensus to which producers had subscribed, if only as an act of passive acquiescence, implied the need for political subservience as a means of economic well-being. "The Creoles are bitterly displeased with the Spanish government, and they have reason for being so," observed Fredrika Bremer during her midcentury visit to Cuba. "They wish universally to be liberated from the Spanish yoke, but are themselves too weak to undertake their own liberation; and they fear the negroes, who, on the first occasion, would rise against them."[29]

The producing classes understood—most of all—the anomaly of their circumstances: they had summoned into existence a vast enslaved labor force upon which their well-being depended while at the same time having called into being the social forces capable of their destruction. "The *peninsulares* as well as the Cubans," José Ahumada commented tersely, "have looked upon slavery and the existence of this race among them as a condition necessary for their well-being, without failing to recognize that grave danger that this condition presents."[30] José Antonio Saco dismissed outright the prospects of a successful slave uprising, certain that "blacks in Cuba, left to their own devices, cannot destroy the white race or establish mastery over the island, as occurred in Santo Domingo." Rather, Saco was more concerned with consequences of a white victory over blacks: "This is the very victory we should avoid, for it will result in our ruin. The victims who will fall under the shrapnel of our cannons will be our own slaves, and our fields will suddenly be deprived of the only labor that makes them prosperous. We will have to weep over our misery in the very fields of triumph."[31]

The calculus of colonialism was not complicated. "The enlightened criollos," Domingo del Monte warned, "wealthy and virtuous, the ones who would be mostly likely to render the idea of independence into a dangerous undertaking if they were so moved, know full well—and better than the authorities of the Island—the consequences that would befall their country attending political disorder and popular revolution.... They would lose their homes, their wealth, the vitality of the countryside, and their country."[32] José Antonio Saco was lucid about the Cuban condition:

> The Cubans, enticed by the extraordinary prices attained [by sugar] in the markets of Europe, multiplied their sugar estates.... And although the sight before their very eyes of the catastrophe [of Saint-Domingue] should have restrained them, or at least have made them more circumspect, the prosperity of the moment blinded them to the dangers of the future.... In the midst of the terror caused by the destruction of Saint-Domingue, in the thick of the flames of that inferno, they still longed for blacks, believing that without them there could be no prosperity for Cuba.[33]

The dread of black rebellion insinuated itself into the cosmology of white, something of a visceral fear informed by an abiding suspicion that generalized into an abhorrence of any popular mobilization that included people of color within its ranks. "There was not a single planter in Cuba," observed historian Roland Ely, "who did not live with the terror that might befall the plantations."[34] A powerful source of white solidarity, of course, to which other sources of white discord were subordinated. A community of interests: whites "united and unified with respect to the African race," commented Jacinto de Salas y Quiroga in 1840, warning, "The present opulence and prosperity of the island of Cuba is bought at the price of its coming misfortune."[35] Something of a presentiment of disaster had insinuated itself into a collective criollo state of being, "docile or puerile," Richard Madden discerned in 1853, a timidity that "yielded to the old natural instinct of fear and self-preservation, which is common to all the residents of the white class in the island of Cuba."[36] Poet-novelist Gertrudis Gómez de Avellaneda recalled her father living with fear, always wishing to return to Spain, fearful, she wrote, "that Cuba would share the same fate of the neighboring island [Saint-Domingue], the prey of the blacks," and imploring her mother "to leave for Spain with the children." A fear that Avellaneda would later inject into her novel *Sab* through the utterances of Don Carlos: "The Cubans always fearful [*siempre alarmados*] after the horrifying recent example of a neighboring island."[37]

The producing classes thus reconciled themselves to the known certainties of misgovernment to avoid the dreaded uncertainties of self-government. "The wealthy Cubans and residents," Captain General Francisco Dionisio Vives understood, "fully informed of the disastrous consequences of emancipation, are persuaded of the efficacy of remaining under the shadow of a government dedicated to peace, security, and other benefits afforded by His Majesty the King."[38] Charged with the task of security of the island, engineer Anastasio de Arango offered sardonic commentary on the character of the Cuban producing classes. "The nature of these inhabitants," Arango observed in 1825, "is one of docility":

> Agriculture and commerce have enabled vast fortunes. [Planters] have produced an agile progress, first to live in comfort and secondly to acquire great wealth. When men obtain the means of subsistence with such ease, as has occurred on this fertile soil, they assume a flexible and docile character. That is why the structure of this country in no way resembles ... those of [Latin] America, for nowhere are found in greater numbers the capitalists or landowners that are found in Cuba.... It is this combination of interests that has served to maintain tranquility on the Island of Cuba and prevented the contagion of disorder [*el contagio desorganizador*] that has devoured the other provinces of America.[39]

Aspirations of self-government were subordinated—like almost everything else—to the imperative of sugar. Grievances against colonial administration notwithstanding—and there were many—the producing classes understood that Spanish sovereignty offered the best guarantee of stability and security, that is, the best protection of property and prosperity. "Our union with Spain," planter José del Castillo observed, "does not depend exactly on the will or force of Spain. It does depend on the interest and the will of the most influential part of our population, upon the love of our aristocracy . . . of its own self-interest, on its physical and moral existence."[40]

The continuity of everything else as it was, in sum, depended on the maintenance of a precarious balance of social forces, an equilibrium obtained principally through a collaboration of convenience between the criollo producing classes and the *peninsular* colonial officialdom, joined together to protect production systems so very much implicated in the defense of chattel slavery and upon which the colonial revenue stream depended. "The island of Cuba cannot exist without its dependence on Spain," *La Concordia Cubana* recited as the prevailing conventional wisdom and asked, "What would become of the island of Cuba if by some misfortune it were to cut its connection to Spain?" And answered: "It would disintegrate immediately into anarchy."[41] A grudging loyalty of the Ever-Faithful Isle to Spanish governance as a means to sustain the status quo, something of a colonial covenant, a compact through which to guarantee mutual interests. To render fealty to Spanish sovereignty as long as Spain rendered protection to the interests of sugar. Those who had compromised themselves in defense of the status quo, scoffed Félix Varela, had done so "in behalf of profit, not out of love of Spain or loyalty to the king."[42] This was not a happy creole patriciate, in fact, living between the Scylla of a feared race war and the Charybdis of abuses of colonial governance. "How very sad it is to live here," Miguel de Aldama brooded in 1844. "We have arrived at such a deplorable state of affairs that no one can live in tranquility, there are no guarantees, . . . everything is overwhelmed under the weight of tyranny and ignominy."[43]

An uncommon consensus settled upon the overlapping colonial networks from which Spain claimed moral warrant to govern, within expanding cohorts of interests among planters and proprietors, between the professions and the vocations, among the purveyors of trade and commerce, the merchants, manufacturers, financiers, brokers, and jobbers, and the multiple recipients of state subsidies and subventions, including newspapers, the Catholic Church, and a far-flung bureaucracy—all of whom to a lesser or greater extent participated in and were beneficiaries of the well-being derived from sugar and slavery. In this sense, Cuban needs and Spanish interests converged, and—for much of the nineteenth century—were mostly one and the same. This was not a complicated syllogism. Cuban support was vital for the continuity of Spanish colonialism. Spanish defense of slavery was essential for the Cuban support. Spanish defense of the prevailing racial hierarchies was essential to the defense of colonialism.

And the obvious and the necessary: the expansion of sugar production and the increase of the population of enslaved Africans had summoned the need for new internal security arrangements. New needs served to expose some of the more egregious oversights of colonial administration, to set in relief what the colonial officialdom did not know about the physiognomy of the island. Which implied too the need for precise information and accurate knowledge of terrain and territory, of the interior landscapes and internal landforms, of dimensions of distance and details of habitat, about the density of the population and the types of land tenure, without which the requirements of internal security would be impossible to ascertain. Colonial administration had dedicated little sustained attention to the physical topography and political geography of the island. For too long, the *Revista Bimestre Cubana* acknowledged, "the governors of the Island have been anxious to possess precise geographical and topographical knowledge of this country for the purpose of preparing a plan for defense," but without success, resulting in an "absolute lack of knowledge about the country" and an inability "to measure distances with even the slightest degree of accuracy [of scale]."[44] Plans "to organize a system of general interior defense," Ramón de la Sagra warned in 1831, required "the most minimum information to sustain a plausible basis of a system of defense," noting too that topographical knowledge was "limited to inexact descriptions, vague and incomplete reports, and data gathered without a systematic methodology and lacking also discernible objectives."[45]

All through 1820s and 1830s, colonial authorities set about the task of assembling new knowledge about the physical geography of the island, about the contours of the interior topography, "to gather," in la Sagra's words, "all the information necessary for defense and public security, reaching into the most remote points of the Island."[46] New methods of cartography and new ways of mapping took hold of the official imagination, advances variously celebrated as efficient, scientific, and modern: new knowledge summoned in the service of new security requirements.[47] Scores of surveyors, cartographers, and topographers dispersed into the interior to prepare new maps and gather new knowledge of the interior geography of the island, all collected with the imagined user—and purpose—in mind. The principal cities were mapped with scrupulous attention to detail. New topographical surveys identified the principal agricultural enterprises, including haciendas, *hatos*, *ingenios*, *vegas*, *cafetales*, and *ranchos*; land surveys were prepared with attention to road networks, bridges, ports, and wharves, and natural topography, including mountains, creeks, rivers, lakes, swamps, and bays.[48]

Colonial authorities understood too the need to gather demographic information on the island, to take the measure of the population, its regional density and geographic distribution, and especially the racial composition of the expanding population and the comparative ratio of whites to blacks—free and enslaved—gathered as usable knowledge from which to fashion the strategic calculus of internal security.[49]

Census after census, a total of six population censuses in 1792, 1817, 1827, 1841, 1846, and 1861, and periodic *informes*[50]—as well as frequent local population surveys (*padrones*) and a series of agricultural censuses, published and unpublished—combined to offer powerful testimony to the careful attention dedicated to the demographic transformations attending the expansion of sugar and slavery.[51] Spanish colonial authorities were "devoted census watchers," historian Robert Paquette commented.[52]

Attention turned increasingly to the need to enhance the internal security infrastructure. Existing roads and highways serving production zones were repaired, widened, and extended. Priority was given to the construction of a central highway (*camino central*) and new secondary roads. New roads linked the centers of sugar production in the interior to provincial capitals and port cities, to improve overland communications systems to accommodate systems of trade and commerce through which to service sugar.[53] Railroad networks expanded accordingly. By midcentury, more than four hundred miles of railroad connected the production zones principally in the western regions with port cities, in service, historians Oscar Zanetti and Alejandro García correctly noted, of "its main—and practically only—export product: sugar."[54]

Jurisdictional units across the island were reorganized into more efficient units to administer, smaller and more geographically coherent jurisdictions through which to increase the weight of an official presence. Existing lines of political administration were redrawn, new boundaries of civil-military jurisdiction adapted and adjusted to correspond to changing population centers and expanding production zones. Three new military jurisdictions (Occidental, Central, and Oriental) served as the provincial units of administration, with a total of twenty military subdivisions. The Occidental Department was organized into eleven districts, and included Havana, Jaruco, Matanzas, Langunillas, Macuriges, Güines, Quivicán, Palacios, Filipinas, Guanajay, and Quemados. The Central Department encompassed five districts: Trinidad, Jagua, Villa-Clara, Sancti-Spíritus, and Puerto Príncipe. The Oriental Department was divided into four districts, including Santiago de Cuba, Bayamo, Holguín, and Baracoa.[55]

All more or less tending to enhance the security capacities within the vital production zones of the interior hinterland of the western regions, which were also the principal sites of concentration of the enslaved plantation labor forces (*dotaciones*). Captain General José G. de la Concha emphasized at midcentury the importance of expanding "points of fortifications in the interior as well as storage centers and hospitals to support army operations." New barracks were constructed, designed to serve as much as sites of acclimatization for new *peninsular* recruits as for points of strategic deployment of troops in important production zones.[56] Old forts were repaired and new ones were constructed; attention was given to maintaining military posts fully provisioned with arms, ammunition, and military supplies throughout the west. De la Concha called official attention to the absence of adequate road systems in the eastern third of the island, urging in 1851 the construction of an extended *camino central*, "the utility of which has at all times been recognized by all governors," and cautioned, "In my view, a *camino central* is a matter of the greatest urgency for the defense of the island. Without roads the movement of military forces is impossible in a country in which the rainy season renders the natural roadways impassable to traverse and the rivers impossible to cross."[57] De la Concha's concerns passed unaddressed.

Sugar and slavery had transformed the security requirements of the island, a heightened awareness of the changed contingencies upon which the Spanish claim to sovereignty depended: less to confront perils from without than to contain threats from within. For much of the previous three hundred years, Cuba had loomed large in the strategic calculus of empire, imagined almost from the outset of the Enterprise of the Indies as something of a bulwark to shield the interior mainland domains against unwelcome outside trespass from rival seaborne European powers—that is, frontline defenses against maritime threats tending to require the allocation of resources for the fortification of littoral zones and armed garrisons deployed among the important coastal cities.[58]

Sugar and slavery changed everything. The Spanish claim to sovereignty in Cuba was henceforth very much a matter of looking inward, to address threats perceived to originate inside the island, from within the extended networks of the many hundreds of sugar estates, from among the many tens of thousands of enslaved Africans distributed across miles of the distant interior hinterland. "It is necessary not to lose sight of the fact," Félix Varela had warned, "that the white population of Cuba resides almost entirely in the principal towns and cities, while the countryside can be said to belong to the blacks."[59]

A threat to the prevailing order of things originating from within the island implied adaptation of internal security arrangements, to recruit from within the *criollidad* on the island—"*naturales del país*," historian Fernando Redondo Díaz indicated—volunteers for colonial militias (*milicias disciplinadas*).[60] Criollos who could be counted upon to defend Spanish sovereignty as a matter of self-interest against the expanding population of color. The participation of *naturales del país* in matters of internal security was designed to relieve Spain of the cost of a permanent military presence on the island—"guarantees of inestimable value," pronounced Ramón Just—and offset the delays of distance from Spain.[61] Slow communication and even slower transportation served to underscore the importance of the presence of local militia units, insisted government attorney Vicente Vázquez Queipo, to respond to "unforeseen attacks and disturbances that may arise."[62] Local *milicias* also served as a way to reduce the exposure of Spanish soldiers to the baneful effects of the climate of the island.[63] Creole recruits were far more desirable than *peninsular* troops, Jacobo de la Pezuela insisted, for the Cuban "is far better prepared to withstand the ferocity of the sun that enriches his luxuriant land, is far more familiar with the hidden recesses of the landscape than *peninsular* units, is far better prepared to live off the land, and is more accustomed to the variations of the climate."[64]

Criollos welcomed service in the *milicias*, an opportunity to advance their interests, a way to mobility and career opportunity, to aspire to official status commensurate with social standing. "The uniform of the militia of Cuba," commented General Antonio de Letona, "is held in high esteem as a means of a career within the state."[65] Officers were recruited from among prominent creole families, among whom—recalled one militia veteran—were "the surnames of the oldest, distinguished, and wealthiest families of Cuba," drawn to an opportunity for livelihood and the prestige of a career in arms and with accompanying emoluments and privilege.[66] The principal officers of the Havana militia, Jacobo de la Pezuela commented at midcentury, were "always from the most notable and well-established families" (*las familias más notables y arraigadas*), while a *milicia* company deployed in Cuatro-Villas was commanded by a colonel who was "almost always some distinguished planter of the country" (*casi siempre algun hacendado distinguido del país*).[67] The *milicia* of Cuba, Dionisio Alcalá Galiano wrote in 1859, "has had and should always have an officer corps . . . consisting of well-established men" (*hombres de gran arraigo*). Alcalá Galiano recalled two commanders of the battalion in which he served who "represented a minimum capital of six million *pesos*, hence hardly to be suspected of revolutionary tendencies."[68] For many of the young men of the expanding *criollidad*, José Antonio Saco noted, the militia "offered a promising career in arms" as an alternative to the priesthood, jurisprudence, and medicine.[69] Service within the enlisted ranks of the militia provided Cubans of modest means—"*los desheredados de la fortuna*," observed Spanish Major Leopoldo Barrios y Carrión—with an opportunity for security and livelihood.[70] "For most of them," historian Allan Kuethe correctly noted, "the distinctions offered by their privileges and the honor of the uniform was enough to sustain their interest in weekly drills during normal times. They mastered military skills in impressive numbers and performed effectively when called upon."[71] Authorities also draw upon recruits from within the expanding population of free people of color, also with service in the battalions of *pardos* and *morenos* promising status and security. "The militia of color," historian Rafael Duharte Jiménez indicated, "offered blacks and mulattos concrete benefits that resulted in social prestige: military privilege, the right to bear arms, pensions, and privileged priority for certain public positions. Indeed, the officers of the *batallones* obtained the right to use the title *don* before their names."[72]

The security of the western zones of production commanded the attention of Spanish colonial administration as a matter of common sense, self-evident, self-explanatory. An obligatory deference to the imperative of sugar, to address the logic of production and attend to the logistics of security. Very much about the need to concentrate material resources and military assets at the sites of the most productive sugar estates and the concentration of enslaved labor: that is, the economy upon which the claim of Spanish sovereignty depended. The west accounted for more than 90 percent of Cuban sugar production in 1860 (461,000 tons out of a total of 508,000 tons).[73] Production on this scale, of course, also accounted for the presence of the vast majority of the *dotaciones*. Of the total 371,000 enslaved Africans in 1860, almost 86 percent (319,000) were located in the western jurisdictions of Las Villas, Matanzas, and Havana.[74]

Deployment of military units could not but respond to the demographics of sugar production. The determinants of internal security developed around a complex system of interdependent but counterpoised military units, including an estimated sixteen thousand *peninsular* troops deployed at midcentury in Cuba, consisting principally of infantry, cavalry, and artillery units, almost 60 percent (9,500) of them located in the western jurisdictions.[75] A carefully calibrated tactical distribution of soldiers "to maintain tranquility in the countryside" (*mantener la tranquilidad de los campos*), the military mission stipulated.[76] Militia units were also deployed in the west as a "national militia," José Antonio Saco wrote approvingly, distributed "in rural Cuba to contain the slaves."[77] The authorized strength of militia units included battalions *milicias disciplinadas* deployed in Havana and distributed among Cuatro-Villas, Puerto Príncipe, Santiago de Cuba, and Bayamo. Early in the nineteenth century, the *milicias* had expanded to nearly 29,000 recruits distributed between urban centers (*compañías urbanas*) and throughout the interior (*compañías rurales*), divided between infantry units (*milicias de infantería*) and cavalry (*milicias montadas*) (see table 1.1).[78] Militia units were distributed "to prepare for whatever great defense need may arise to maintain permanently the submission of the *dotaciones* of the great estates," Jacobo de la Pezuela noted, to avert the conditions that overtook Saint-Domingue at the end of the eighteenth century.[79] Creole militia units deployed principally to address the threat of black rebellion. "An efficient cavalry for the protection of the country against the insurrection of the blacks," John Wurdemann offered.[80] Abiel Abbot took note of the presence of militia units as early as the 1820s, a militia that was "always armed," and concluded that "wherever there is a numerous slave population, there is danger.... The best security of the island against the horrors of St Domingo, is this armed militia."[81] Anastasio de Arango emphasized the need to expand the capacity for internal security through the recruitment of a local soldiery. "It is indispensable," Arango exhorted in 1825, "to dedicate a part of the white population to maintain order and tranquility in the countryside, with sufficient resources to suffocate at its origins any insurrection of blacks."[82]

Colonial authorities dedicated studied attention to internal security arrangements. An official assessment of military preparedness in 1844 expressed confidence in the comparative ratio of military personnel vis-à-vis the population: one regular soldier for every forty-five men of color and thirty-two whites. A ratio, authorities were certain, that compared favorably with Jamaica, for example, that had one regular soldier for eighty-four inhabitants of color and nine whites. The Cuban ratio, attorney general Vicente Vázquez Queipo was certain, was "sufficient to contain the slave population [*contener la población esclava*] ... as well as preserve order and tranquility within the

Table 1.1 Militia Deployment (ca. 1804)

	MILITIA RECRUITS
Milicias Disciplinadas: Infantry	
Havana	1,442
Puerto Príncipe	721
Milicias Disciplinadas: Cavalry	
Havana and its jurisdiction	517
Rural Milicias	
East of Havana and Matanzas	7,995
West of Havana	5,688
Extramuro Havana	5,368
Cuatro-Villas	2,640
Puerto Príncipe	1,728
Santiago de Cuba	2,412
Total	28,511

SOURCE: Alexander Humboldt, *Ensayo político sobre la Nueva España*, trans. Vicente González Arnao (2nd ed., 5 vols., Paris, 1827).

white population."[83] A decade later, Joseph Dimock reported learning that for "every four white men on the island there is one soldier."[84]

But it was also true that the producing classes were rarely assuaged. A restive colonial polity ever mindful of an expanding population of color during a time of increasing abolitionist sentiment and—more important—at a time of an accelerating frequency of New World slave rebellions: in Barbados (1804, 1816, and 1824), Brazil (1822), British Guiana (1823), Jamaica (1795, 1824, and 1831), and Antigua (1831). Slave uprisings in Cuba increased in number and expanded in kind: no fewer than twenty revolts during the early decades of the nineteenth century, mostly notably in Trinidad (1812); in Matanzas (1825); in Wajay (1830); in Matanzas again and in Macuriges, Jaruco, and Havana (1835); in Cienfuegos and Cárdenas (1837)—"revolts that became increasingly concentrated in the west-central districts of the island," historian Aisha Finch noted.[85] A number of short-lived and localized disturbances occurred among the western *dotaciones*, Captain General Francisco Dionisio Vives reported in 1832. But "the distribution of the army across the territory," Vives hastened to add, "and the new warrant conferred on the rural militias . . . and the vigilance of the government contributed to keeping them under control and maintaining public security."[86] An uprising of enslaved Africans outside Havana in 1836, Captain General Miguel Tacón commented, "offers new proof of the danger to public order," and it was only the strategic location of infantry units "that crushed the seditious intent at its inception."[87]

Early revolts during the 1820s and 1830s were not uncommon, born principally of grievances localized within individual estates, often short-lived spontaneous but violent affairs characterized by widespread destruction of property and followed by flight. During the 1840s, however, the character of rebellions changed: in Cárdenas an uprising in 1843 of the *dotación* of the Alcancía plantation expanded onto the neighboring estates of La Luisa, La Trinidad, Santa Rosa, Las Nieves, and La Aurora; in 1843 a revolt of the *dotación* of the Triunvirato estate in Matanzas was joined by the enslaved workers on the Acana estates, thereupon to march on La Concepción, San Miguel, San Lorenzo, and San Rafael estates—to form an "invading mass" (*masa invasora*), wrote planter Miguel de Aldama.[88] "The slaves on this occasion were not satisfied with burning the cane fields and fleeing into the mountains as they have in the past," Domingo del Monte commented. "Rather, they murdered six whites and proceeded to neighboring estates with the intention of encouraging the *dotaciones* to rise up in rebellion and proclaimed liberty for all blacks [*toda la raza de color*]. It is necessary to understand that these uprisings have very different origins and a very different character from all their predecessors." A very different character indeed: "The insurrections have become more frequent, and have assumed a more alarming character. Instead of being provoked by the severity of treatment by some administrator or overseer as before, whom the blacks wished to be rid of, they are the result of a settled conviction among the slaves of their own rights and the rights of their race." Warned del Monte, "The blacks . . . threaten the political and social existence of the colony. The Island of Cuba is in imminent danger of being irremediably lost not only to Spain but to the white race and to the entire civilized world."[89]

Unsettling portents, Domingo de Aldama feared: "the first symptoms of a grave debacle that will attack the body social and may even destroy it."[90] A presentiment of disaster settled uneasily over the planters, who were not reluctant to communicate their fears to Captain General Leopoldo O'Donnell:

> These uprisings that previously were isolated, and whose destruction and death were limited principally to the sites in which they occurred, today assume a menacing character . . . as a result of their frequency, as a result of their planning, and as a result of coordination of conspiracies among slaves of a great many different plantations at the same time. The idea of emancipation and hopes for a previously unknown happiness have spread among these aroused individuals and no doubt is the cause of the scope of the disorder that represent such a grave danger to the country. . . . It is hence necessary to maintain a physical force to contain their bellicose spirit and to punish with an iron fist the horrendous crimes to which they lend themselves.[91]

Colonial authorities did indeed respond to slave uprisings with an "iron fist"—through a "vigorous employment of force," commented José Ahumada y Centurión.[92] A display of strength and a demonstration of efficiency: a comforting confirmation that planter confidence in the security capacity of Spanish colonial administration had not been misplaced. Rumors of a far-flung plot in 1844—La Escalera, as the conspiracy became known—however, changed everything. La Escalera plunged the colonial officialdom and producing classes into panic amid allegations of a conspiracy said to have implicated many thousands of the enslaved and free people of color distributed among 186 sugar plantations in twenty-five districts spanning the jurisdictions of Havana, Matanzas, and Cárdenas.[93] "A calamitous event," recalled Pedro Antonio Alfonso, a conspiracy whose reach appeared to have risen fully to the scale of Saint-Domingue.[94] "The far-reaching scope of the horrendous conspiracy which involved our plantations," planter Miguel del Aldama anguished in early 1844, "is day by day becoming apparent. The entire island was implicated and if it had not been discovered by the hand of God, the fields of all the sugar plantations would have been reduced to ashes."[95] John Wurdemann, visiting Matanzas in 1844, was told that "all the horrors of the San Domingo massacres were to have been repeated. Many of the whites were to have been flayed and broiled while alive, and with the exception of the young women, reserved for a worse fate, all, without discrimination of age or sex, were to have been massacred."[96] A vast conspiracy among people of color—free and enslaved—informed with a different motive, organized for a different purpose, pronounced the military commission convened to investigate the conspiracy. "Plans for the extermination of all whites with the intention of conquest and mastery of the country," Captain General Leopoldo O'Donnell reported to Madrid.[97] "All our confidence resides in wise government measures and in the force and discipline of our army," Gaspar Betancourt Cisneros wrote to a friend.[98]

Colonial authorities responded with dispatch and ruthless intent to prosecute and execute the accused conspirators. But still, a disquiet insinuated itself into a body social that would not be easily dissipated without demonstrable official measures, principally in the form of an expanded military presence.[99] "It does not require much forethought," nearly one hundred merchants, property owners, and planters from Matanzas petitioned O'Donnell, "to anticipate the consequences of the preponderance of the combined population of color, free and enslaved," and continued:

> Hopefully, the horrific example of Haiti so nearby will not be repeated, but one should never ignore the experience, so as to avoid a second edition of a similar work. The slave race [*la raza esclava*], Your Excellency, has already revealed a marked tendency to rebellion in just this year alone.... The countryside of the island, and principally the jurisdiction of Matanzas, populated by 60,000 slaves, demands your attention with protection and security.[100]

But fear was not confined solely to the threat of a single mass slave insurrection that would plunge the island into conditions of generalized civil strife. Sporadic uprisings, too, warned José Antonio Saco, "repeated here and there, are sufficient to destroy credit and confidence, thereupon to cause emigration, capital will take flight, agriculture and industry will rapidly decline, public rents will diminish . . . and result in a state of continuous alarm." With an inevitable outcome, Saco predicted: "Until we arrive at a terrible denouement."[101]

Rumors that La Escalera involved the complicity of members of the battalions of *pardos* and *morenos* resulted immediately in the disbanding of the militias of color.[102] The producing classes had long looked warily upon the deployment of militias of color. Whites could draw a distinction between the desirable service of blacks to defend the island against external threats, on one hand, and the armed presence of blacks to defend against race war, on the other. "The interior security of the island is compromised with the establishment of the militias of free men of color," Arango y Parreño had warned as early as 1792:

> Militias of blacks and mulattos [in Cuba] are unknown in the neighboring colonies.... The *batallones* of free blacks and mulattos were organized upon the creation of the militias. These men, accustomed to hard work, frugality, and subordination, are without doubt some of the best soldiers in the world. The establishment of this force, considered militarily and from the perspective of external security, was a necessary recourse in those times. But today at a time when there are sufficient numbers of whites, the interior security of Cuba should not be placed at risk. The armed *batallones* are not the ones that pose the greatest risk. It is the veterans, mustered out of service who retired to the countryside, that in my judgment present the most formidable threat.[103]

The training and arming of free men of color, potentially to make common cause with the enslaved population, could not but arouse fear and foreboding among the producing classes. The "very barbarism" of *pardo* and *moreno* troops, Félix Varela was certain, in the ordinary course of events, made them incapable of rebellion. But blacks in uniform, he warned, were to be considered "an enemy power" (*una potencia enemiga*), for "the best soldier is the most barbarous one."[104]

In fact, the colonial officialdom increasingly cast a suspicious gaze upon the loyalties of *los naturales de la isla*, and especially of the officers of the militias, most of whom emerged from the ranks of the prosperous *criollidad*.[105] "Indigenous militias to whom was entrusted the preservation of public order," one official recalled the independence movements in South America, "were among the first to deploy their arms against the interests of the Metropolis. Something similar would occur on the island of Cuba if we were to make the mistake of admitting Cubans [*los hijos del país*] into its [military] garrisons."[106] Creole loyalty to Spain could not be presumed.

Colonial governance depended largely on the need to balance competing—and often conflicting—interests among the multiple colonial constituencies. This was especially true with military units. Internal security arrangements tended increasingly to favor recruitment from within the loyalist *peninsular* population in Cuba, Spanish-born residents from the multiple regional communities of Catalans, Asturians, Galicians, Andalucians, and Canary Islanders, among others.[107] The Cuerpo de Voluntarios—"a militia of *peninsulares*," suggested Fernando Padilla Angulo—was recruited from among manufacturers, industrialists, merchants, the "best established men in all the cities," as officers and their employees and dependents as soldiers: "in discharge of an uncompromising resolve of loyalty, a noble patriotism of the sons of Spain [*hijos de Iberia*], and the conviction that as long as there exists in Cuba Voluntarios the unity of national integrity [*la integridad nacional*] will prevail."[108] At the time of its organization, the authorized strength of the Cuerpo de Voluntarios numbered nearly eight thousand officers and men, all of whom, Captain General Federico Roncali explained, were to be exclusively of *peninsulares*, "for I have no confidence in providing arms to the creoles" (*naturales*).[109] The *milicias* and Voluntarios developed as two separate military entities, both presumptively united in the defense of the colonial status quo but also divided by mutual suspicions: *milicias* made up almost entirely of creoles and the Voluntarios almost all *peninsulares*.[110]

The producing classes had summoned a history with no exit. The internal logic of sugar and slavery could work only within the larger premise of colonialism, that is, within those exchanges through which interests were transacted as reciprocities of loyalty. Eminently instrumental, often a matter of expediency and convenience, of course, but for the producing classes the defense of Spanish sovereignty represented the strategy of choice as the principal means through which to defend self-interests. But Spain also had interests very much implicated in the status quo: Cuba as a source of colonial revenues, most assuredly, but at least as important, a determination to retain possession of Cuba as a function of a psychology of *patrimonio* and the defense of the dignity of sovereignty; Cuba as a matter of national honor to sustain national integrity, for which Spain was more than adequately disposed to sacrifice almost everything, including—and if necessary—the interests of the producing classes.

All through the mid-nineteenth century, Spain confronted recurring threats to its sovereignty. The idea of annexation to the United States gained currency among important representatives of the producing classes, including Cristóbal Madán, José Aniceto Iznaga, Alonso Betancourt, Domingo del Monte, Miguel de Aladama, José María Sánchez Iznaga, Francisco de Frías (count of Pozos Dulces), José Luis Alfonso, and Gaspar Betancourt Cisneros: Cubans who looked upon the genius of American political institutions with admiring approval, institutions that enabled an accommodation between democratic ideals and chattel slavery. "It is an irrefutable fact," pronounced Domingo del Monte, "that the United States of America [has] . . . enjoyed the greatest political liberty since its founding, and still they have slaves."[111] Annexation promised the producing classes an opportunity to expand slavery and gain untrammeled access to new markets, as well as the opportunity to exercise greater local self-rule in defense of self-interests. "Annexation is not a sentiment," explained Gaspar Betancourt Cisneros; "it is a calculation. It is more: it is the obligatory law of necessity, the sacred duty of survival."[112]

It happened too that at about the same time, the Americans had succumbed to the rapture of Manifest Destiny, to which they gave themselves unabashedly in spasms of expansionist outbursts: the annexation of Texas, a war with Mexico, filibustering expeditions to Central America, and of course the always-covetous gaze toward Cuba. In 1848, President James Polk offered Spain $100 million for Cuba, without success. Six years later, President Franklin Pierce raised the purchase offer to $130 million, also without success. At about the same time, US ministers to Spain, France, and England met in Ostend, Belgium, and issued a manifesto publicly exhorting the United States to renew its offer to purchase the island. If Spain declined the American offer, the Ostend Manifesto warned, "then, by every law, human and divine, [the United States] shall be justified in wresting it from Spain, if we possess the power."[113]

Annexationist conspiracies spanned the midcentury and included three ill-fated filibustering expeditions organized by Narciso López: in Manicaragua (1848), Cárdenas (1849), and Bahía Honda (1851).[114] Other annexationist plots followed, one in Puerto Príncipe (1851) organized by Joaquín de Agüero; a short-lived revolt by Isidro Armenteros in Trinidad (1851); an annexationist conspiracy organized by Ramón Pintó in Havana (1854); and an ill-fated Baracoa expedition from the United States under Francisco Estrampes and Juan Enrique Félix in 1854. "The seed of rebellion [*gérmen de la rebelión*] remains," Captain General José G. de la Concha warned the Spanish minister of state in mid-1854, "and it is necessary for Your Majesty's government to remember that our foreign enemies [*nuestros enemigos exteriores*] are presently working without rest to foment revolt."[115]

Annexationist sentiment flourished especially in the region of Puerto Príncipe in the Centro Department. De la Concha had dedicated studied attention to the demographics of the Centro jurisdiction, "a department which in my judgment is one of the most dangerous points on the island." With a total population of 114,954 whites, including 5,305 *peninsulares* and 109,649 *criollos*, Spaniards accounted for 4.6 percent of the total white population, as compared to the west, where *peninsulares* represented 15.8 percent of the population (38,682 out of 244,109), data from which de la Concha inferred a far greater potential for emboldened *criollos* to act on their discontent. But it was the population of color that aroused de la Concha's concern. The population of color in Centro—free and enslaved—totaled 81,100 inhabitants, accounting for 4.1 percent of the total population of the department, standing in stark comparison with the population of color in the west of 289,507 and representing 54 percent of the total population. Whites in the Centro Department, de la Concha surmised, did not share the same fear of blacks as whites in the west, where enslaved Africans were deemed to be the "enemy of both *peninsulares* and *criollos* and served as a restraint [*freno*] to contain the proponents of change and disorder":

The fear, hence, that the colored race instills in those who would otherwise contemplate the tortuous road of revolution [*la tortuosa senda de la revolución*], does not appear to be as intense in Puerto Príncipe as it is in Havana. One must further keep in mind that with the exception of the districts of Trinidad and Cienfuegos, Puerto Príncipe does not have the colossal sugar mills as in the west, each one representing immense sums of capital, and whose ruin would be the likely outcome in the event of a war resulting from the difficulty in maintaining control of the masses of slaves that make up each *dotación*. Thus, in Puerto Príncipe one does not find the powerful *freno* that revolutionaries confront in other regions of the island.[116]

The annexationist swell in Cuba happened to crest during years of domestic political unrest in Spain. The Spanish revolution of 1854 plunged *la madre patria* into crisis, with military *pronunciamientos* and political intrigue joined with regional conflicts and armed uprisings across the peninsula, all in all, circumstances that acted to limit the Spanish capacity to deploy armed forces in sufficient numbers to defend the island against a feared US assault. "This government," Prime Minister José María Calatrava acknowledged, "can send no force from Spain to oppose any attempt that may be made on the Island. If what is there proves insufficient there will be no remedy."[117] As early as 1849, Captain General Federico de Roncali had informed Madrid that the colonial government possessed insufficient numbers of naval war vessels and inadequate quantities of arms and ammunition, and that while Cuba could mobilize a militia of thirty thousand troops, it possessed an inventory of a mere six thousand rifles.[118]

But colonial authorities in Cuba were not without assets to deploy and advantages to exploit. In the absence of sufficient military force, intendant Mariano Torrente suggested, "there remained always, as a matter of last resort, the option to recruit volunteers from among people of color [*reclutar voluntarios de la gente de color*], who have been continually loyal to the Spanish throne [*constantemente fieles al trono español*], and who would be ever more so from the moment we would appeal to their enthusiasm to expel the invaders from our profaned soil. There is no doubt they would volunteer by the thousands and commanded by Spanish officers would introduce terror and confusion in the ranks of the enemy."[119] De la Concha planned accordingly. "There is the belief in the United States," de la Concha surmised, "given the success obtained by [US] arms in the war with Mexico, that the conquest of the island would be a relatively easy undertaking. Nothing could be further from the truth." He continued:

> They have not taken into consideration that Cuba is garrisoned by a large well-organized and well-disciplined army. . . . But it is not only the army that would

defend Cuba, for on its behalf would rally another force no less dedicated, consisting of Spaniards, many of whom are experienced in waging partisan warfare [*hacer la guerra de partidarios*]. . . . And finally, in the eventuality of such a war, the government could rely on the population of color among whom exists a sentiment of respect and veneration toward the king of Spain. Full confidence in the sentiment of people of color has persuaded me that, if circumstances were to acquire urgency . . . I would not have hesitated to rearm the battalions of *pardos* and *morenos*, not to bring upon the inhabitants of Cuba the horrors that were visited upon the unfortunate Santo Domingo, but because I was profoundly persuaded that among the people of color would be found a new powerful force to defend the monarchy.[120]

Spain to summon people of color in defense of its sovereignty, indifferent to the fears of the producing classes—on the contrary, as retribution for the mischief of the producing classes. In 1854, in the aftermath of the López expeditions and the short-lived annexationist plots, Captain General Juan Pezuela and his successor de la Concha revived the militias of *pardos* and *morenos*, in response, de la Concha acknowledged, to "the discovery of a vast conspiracy in the interior [of the island] that relied upon a large-scale expedition prepared in the United States."[121] Pezuela was categorical: "Taking into consideration the loyalty, the suffering and the zeal with which *pardo* and *moreno* volunteers have on multiple occasions defended the Spanish flag, the very flag we are committed to defend at all costs in Cuba, I have determined, with the authorization of the queen, to revive the former military corps of free men of color."[122] The armed *milicias de color* were organized into sixteen companies consisting of equal numbers of *pardo* and *moreno* units, deployed across the full length of the island (see table 1.2).[123] Unlike the previous units of *pardos* and *morenos*, the newly reconstituted militia was organized as an auxiliary force of the regular *peninsular* army.[124] In addition, three *milicia* units were subsequently organized in 1858 in the military department of Guantánamo, composed of resident "*mestizos* and *pardos* of the jurisdiction," dedicated specifically to the task of the "pursuit and capture of runaway and fugitive slaves" (*cimarrones y apalencados*).[125]

But it was more complicated, for the organization of *milicias* of color implied a purpose of far more portentous reach. Spain would serve notice: the militias of color would be deployed against the disaffected producing classes. "When the government, or its followers, has come to fear some rising of the [white] Cubans," Alexander Jones reported learning in 1851, "their first threat has been that of arming the colored people against them for their extermination."[126] US Consul William Robertson described an unsettled mood in Havana, with creoles looking warily upon the "large number of blacks to be organized and armed" and fearing the consequences,

Table 1.2 Distribution of *compañias de pardos y morenos* (1855)

Pardo and Moreno Companies	
Havana	33
Matanzas	11
Trinidad/Sancti-Spíritus	1
Villa-Clara/Remedios/Cienfuegos	1
Puerto Príncipe	11
Bayamo	1
Santiago de Cuba/Manzanillo/Baracoa	12
Total	70

SOURCE: *Diario de la Marina*, August 9, 1855.

as logical as necessary, to wit: that the moral influence of superiority which to this time, had served as a guaranty for the peace and safety of the whites will disappear like smoke; and the black race having acquired a moral superiority to, or at least an equal moral influence to that of whites... will cause that their material and moral strength produce or bring on their emancipation, and as a necessary consequence the Africanization of Cuba.[127]

At about the same time, from the US Legation in Madrid, First Secretary Horatio Perry forwarded a confidential report to President-Elect Franklin Pierce, detailing "personal knowledge" gathered in the course of "three years in immediate contact with the men who rule this country." Spain would "defend the Island of Cuba to the last effort of her power," Perry reported learning, and was prepared "to organize & equip regiments of blacks in Cuba under Spanish officers, and turn their arms against the Creole whites," and warning, "*Spain is resolved, in the last resort—if all the ordinary resources of War should fail her—to emancipate the black population of Cuba and to give them arms.*"[128] Developments that traveler Maturin Ballou corroborated during his midcentury visit to Cuba:

> An order has recently been issued by Pezuela, the present governor-general, for the enrolment of free blacks and mulattoes in the ranks of the army, and the devotion of these people to Spain is loudly vaunted in the captain-general's proclamation. The enlistment of people of color in the ranks is a deadly insult offered to the white population of a slave-holding country—a sort of shadowing

Something to Fear 35

forth of the menace, more than once thrown out by Spain, to the effect that if the colonists should ever attempt a revolution, she would free and arm the blacks, and Cuba, made to repeat the tragic tale of St. Domingo, should be useless to the Creoles if lost to Spain.[129]

US Special Agent Charles Davis, dispatched to Cuba on a confidential fact-finding mission in 1854, confirmed Spanish plans to mobilize an armed population of color—free and enslaved—to defend Spanish sovereignty. "Convinced that her feeble power had not strength sufficient to maintain her dominion at so great distance by the influence of the bayonet alone," Davis wrote, Spanish authorities "believed that the dread of an insurrection of [blacks] would prevent the Cubans from an attempt at Revolution."[130]

Colonial governance required Spanish authorities to calibrate the structural tensions wreaked by sugar and slavery, to exploit contradictions and use conflicting interests. Perhaps no better way to contain the mischief of the producing classes, whose capacity for agency was in any case circumscribed by dependence on *peninsular* governance, on one hand, and fear of black rebellion, on the other. "It is the policy of the court of Madrid to keep the island of Cuba in her dependence," observed British Consul David Turnbull in 1840; "and this, it is supposed, can only be done effectually by the salutary terror inspired by the presence of a numerous, half-savage negro-population. The existence of such a population seems at once to justify and require the presence of a *peninsular* army."[131]

Something of a relentless reciprocity joined the needs of the producing classes with the interests of the colonial officialdom, a shared well-being implicated in the premise of chattel slavery as a matter of common purpose, if for different reasons: for the producing classes as a means of production, for the officialdom as a means of sovereignty—that is, the defense of chattel slavery as the means through which the logic of colonial governance was transacted and the loyalty of the producing classes exacted. Gaspar Betancourt Cisneros understood well the government "idea that the blacks are the means to subjugate the island of Cuba" and recounted, "A magistrate of the [Puerto Príncipe] Audiencia indicated to me that to suppress the slave trade [*la trata*] and promote white immigration would be to deliver the first and second tolling of the bells of independence."[132]

Certainly Spanish authorities were not unaware of the practiced opportunism of which the producing classes were capable, and learned adeptly to exploit creole fear as a usable method of colonial governance. "The property owners who are dedicated to *la madre patria*," Captain General Dionisio Vives recognized as early as 1825, "will persist [in their allegiance] without deviation as long as they are beset by the fear of losing or risk the loss of their slaves, which constitutes the most compelling foundation of their fortunes."[133] Spanish Prime Minister José María Calatrava was more succinct: "The fear of the negroes is worth an army of 100,000 men, and . . . will prevent the whites from making any revolutionary attempts."[134] In defense of *patrimonio*, and as last resort, Spain was not unwilling to visit havoc upon the producing classes. The defense of slavery as a condition of creole support of Spanish sovereignty was turned on its head, with Spain threatening to ruin the producing classes with the abolition of slavery as a means to foreclose annexation. "The opinion of the majority of the sons of this land" (*la mayor parte de los hijos de este suelo*), Captain General Federico Roncali explained to Madrid in 1849 in a confidential communication, "is opposed to the continued rule of the metropolis. The spirit of Spanish nationality is in decline. But they recognize too that it is impossible to constitute an independent nation and have set their goal of annexation to the United States." The threat that the *hijos de este suelo* feared most, Roncali understood, was the threat to the continuance of slavery "as the principal base of the wealth of the country" and the "imminent danger that the island and the vast private fortunes would be at risk at the slightest sign of disorder or disturbance." Among the "considerable sources of power that Spain relied upon to defend this island," Roncali explained, was—"as last resort"—the threat to abolish slavery. He continued:

> The interest [of the producing classes] in preserving their fortunes and in developing the rich crops from which their wealth originates cannot but oblige the wealthy inhabitants of the country to fear the first hint of conflict which may act to weaken the subjugation of slaves or threaten emancipation. From which I infer that the preservation of slavery is the restraint [*freno*] that through fear and self-interest will serve to keep in submission the great majority of the white population. But if in the event that a foreign war and internal disturbance should threaten [Spanish] sovereignty over the island, what should be the conduct of the captain general toward slavery? . . . I am convinced that this terrible weapon [emancipation] which the government holds in its possession could as last resort prevent the loss of the island, and that if the inhabitants are persuaded that it will be used they will tremble and renounce every illusion rather than bring upon themselves such an abomination. . . . The freedom of all the slaves on a day of such grave peril, proclaimed by Her Majesty's representative in these territories, would reestablish control and even strengthen possession, based as it would be on the very class that is suppressed. . . . But if this final measure proved insufficient . . . the victors would inherit a Haiti instead of the rich and prosperous Cuba. The spurious sons [will] have brought down upon themselves a calamity of complete ruin.[135]

The editor of *Diario de la Marina*, Dionisio Alcalá, who enjoyed the confidence of Captain General Roncali, later wrote of "our shared maxim" during the disturbances of the 1850s, and the determination that "Cuba would be either African or Spanish and fully resolved to realize our threats":

> If the moment of supreme crisis had arrived, we would certainly have seen ourselves obliged fearlessly to carry out the ultimate recourse, and fight to the death or prevail with a rifle in one hand and the incendiary torch in the other, and with the terrible word of "emancipation" on our lips. This desperate resolution . . . can be clearly explained and justified by many reasons. . . . If even the weakest and most cowardly of the hunted animal often tends to turn against its pursuers when cornered . . . it seemed to us very natural that we seek in our hour of ruin the delicious pleasure of vengeance [*el sabroso placer de la venganza*] that was available to us with such ease within our reach.[136]

"It is necessary to bear very much in mind," Gaspar Betancourt Cisneros brooded, "that a mere stroke of the pen [*una plumada*] will bring ruin to Cuba."[137]

Emancipation would also have most assuredly dampened American enthusiasm for annexation, Spain understood, for midcentury US expansionist designs were in large measure an extension of the deepening sectional dispute in the United States, with the South seeking to increase the number of slaveholding states and the belief that the acquisition of Cuba was essential for the survival of slavery. "If the Anglo-American annexationists covet the island," José G. de la Concha explained, "it is principally due to the institution of slavery."[138] The abolition of slavery in Cuba would immediately negate the appeal of annexation: the desire to add another slave state. "In the event that the fortune of a war with the U. States should turn against [Spain] in Cuba," Horatio Perry warned President-Elect Pierce from Madrid,

> as I have no doubt at all it would, then will the torch be put to the magazine and victors & vanquished be blown up together. Should a war with the United States break out at present, *this great blow of negro emancipation may be looked upon as certain in the circumstances referred to.* . . . A violent transfer of the sovereignty of Cuba, and especially anything like negro emancipation or the arming of the blacks—which would inevitably accompany a contest now—would be the ruin of certain vast possessions in the Island.[139]

Special Agent Davis could hardly conceal his alarm, predicting that the "savage races" would "destroy at one blow the productions of the Island and place in the hands of the incendiary the lighted torch and . . . deliver the knife to the assassin. . . . They would attack the whites they hate and whose superior civilization they fear, and would not rest until [they] destroyed them or forced them to leave the Island." Warned Davis:

> [The] inevitable immediate result will be the destruction of the wealth of the Island, a disastrous bloody war of the races, a step backwards in the civilization of America—and, in a commercial view, an immense loss to the United States; it being one of the best markets for their produce—and in a political view its loss would be incalculable as it would be a never ending source of embarrassments and danger to the whole Union.[140]

Consul Robertson in Havana agreed: "The liberation of all the Africans . . . would lead to the destruction of all discipline. . . . The natural consequence of this state of things would be that the Island would be entirely in the hands of the colored population, the whites would have to abandon it or be sacrificed. That this condition of the Island would affect the interests of the Union cannot be a matter of conjecture."[141]

Spanish authorities seized upon the creoles' lack of choice with skill. Members of the producing classes who aspired to and conspired for annexation as a way to defend slavery were forced to confront the very fate they sought to avoid. They were subjugated by the very conditions of subjugation they had created. "It is asserted that [the government] is privately not unwilling to see the island filled with wild Africans," Fredrika Bremer reported learning during her midcentury travels in Cuba, "because the dread of the unrestrained power of these, if they should one day emancipate themselves, restrains the Creoles from rebellion against a government which they can not do other than hate. Government oppresses the slave-owners, the slave-owner oppresses the slave."[142]

HALF DEFEATED UPON ARRIVAL

2

The following day, only minutes after having commenced their march [in Puerto Príncipe], our guerrillas encountered enemy forces, but in such large number that for a moment they found themselves completely surrounded, to such an extent that the "valiant soldiers" of Cuban liberty called out "¡Al machete!" But our *guerrilleros* answered with an enthusiastic "¡Viva España!" and forced the enemy to retreat.
—*Diario de la Marina* (January 31, 1871)

A European army deployed to fight in tropical zones without a careful plan for hygiene and corresponding sanitary services is half defeated immediately upon its arrival.
—Gonzalo Reparaz, *La guerra de Cuba: Estudio militar* (1896)

There was in that struggle [Ten Years' War] true heroism on both sides, for it is necessary to do justice to everyone. . . . The qualities that the enemy possesses cannot be denied, all the more so when that enemy is our son [*ese enemigo es hijo nuestro*], and those qualities are the very same that he has inherited from us.
—Leopoldo Barrios y Carrión, *Importancia de la historia de las campañas irregulares y en especial de la guerra de Cuba* (1893)

All the Armies will perish and our independence will thus be guaranteed forever in our virgin Jungles, where death in the dress of Aurora sallies forth to receive with loving care [*recibir cariñosamente*] the adventurers who arrive with the intent of slaughtering us.
–José Enríquez Collado to Félix Figueredo (March 22, 1877)

The long-feared uprising did indeed originate from among the far-flung sugar plantations. But the uprising initiated on the estate of La Demajagua on October 10, 1868, was not the result of the discontent of slaves but rather the disaffection of slave owners, among representatives of the very producing classes from whom Spain had obtained the moral warrant to govern Cuba. Families of means with status and standing, to be sure, but floundering in a vertiginous warp of downward mobility, representatives of a provincial gentry in hard times, with dwindling assets and diminishing fortunes—"long neglected, parochial, and impoverished," historian Hugh Thomas offered.[1] Well-to-do families well imbued with a sense of entitlement, but living with the brooding disquiet that often attends the onset of a presentiment of demise. No ready way out and no apparent way up—other than the hope that things would be better in a nation of their own. Planters Carlos Manuel de Céspedes, Jaime Santiesteban, Pedro Figueredo, and Francisco Vicente Aguilera, among others, were joined by ranchers Manuel de Quesada, Vicente García, and Salvador Betancourt Cisneros—a total of thirty-seven conspirators—obtaining popular support among scores of small farmers in the countryside, from members of the professions and among the vocations in the cities, from rural laborers and urban workers and among vast numbers of free men of color, including Antonio Maceo, Guillermo Moncada, and Flor Crombet, as well as recently emancipated slaves, almost all of whom bore in some form grievance against the circumstances of the status quo.[2]

Never before had Spain confronted as formidable a challenge to its sovereignty in Cuba as the ten years of protracted war that ensued. All through the first half of the nineteenth century the threat to the prevailing order of things was associated principally with the expanding population of color, and especially among the *dotaciones* of hundreds of thousands of enslaved Africans and their descendants, concentrated principally within the production zones of the west, accounting for nearly 86 percent of the total of enslaved people on the island, distributed mostly among the estates that produced 90 percent of Cuban sugar.[3]

The political calculus of internal security settled into arrangements deemed to be as self-evident as they were self-explanatory. It could hardly be gainsaid, of course, for indeed therein lay the political economy of colonialism: the well-being of Cuban production systems in the west as the overriding logic of Spanish sovereignty, which implied too the presence of well-mapped topographies and well-surveyed terrains, of serviceable transportation networks and usable communication systems, and occasioning too—of course—the strategic and well-planned deployment of military units. All in all, modes of reciprocities through which the affluence of the producing classes sustained the continuance of colonial administration—and vice versa.

No such ties of reciprocity linked the well-being of the producing classes of the east with the interests of colonial administration in Havana. On the contrary, the reach of Spanish solicitude seemed always to have ebbed thin upon reaching the distant eastern jurisdictions—and with commensurately thin ties of fealty rendered to colonial administration.[4] The rural economies of the east languished, with sparse cartography and scarce land surveys, with insufficient transportation networks and inadequate communication capacities.[5] "Backward," Captain General Camilio Polavieja once scoffed.[6] Perhaps. But the east was also a region where discontent flourished unchecked, something of a chronic condition deemed mostly without consequences and unworthy of official attention.

The call for independence issued with the pronouncement of the Grito de Yara summoned the multiple sources of Cuban discontent into an armed mobilization of enormous force in the name *la nación integral*. "When a people reach the extreme point of degradation and misery," the signatories of the Manifesto of La Demajagua proclaimed on October 10, 1868, "such as we find ourselves, no one can reproach them for reaching for arms to emerge from a state of such opprobrium." In the weeks and months that followed, an estimated five thousand Cubans across the east reached for arms in response to the call of "¡Viva Cuba! ¡Muera España!"[7]

The rebellion overwhelmed *peninsular* military garrisons almost everywhere across the eastern jurisdictions, extending from Nuevitas to Baracoa along the north coast, and from Manzanillo to Santiago de Cuba in the south, and up to Bayamo and Las Tunas inland. Sparsely garrisoned army posts and inadequately defended towns and cities across Oriente and Camagüey passed easily under insurgent control, including Bayamo—the third-largest city in Oriente—as well as Guisa, Baire, Cascorro, Jiguaní, El Cobre, Palma Soriano, Santa Rita, and Guáimaro, even as the *insurrectos* lay siege to the cities of Manzanillo, Holguín, Gibara, and Las Tunas.[8]

The overriding mandate of colonial governance—the necessity to protect sugar production of the west as the logic central to the premise of Spanish sovereignty—had given scant attention to conditions in the east. It was not, hence, that Spain had failed to prepare for the possibility of rebellion. On the contrary, for much of the nineteenth century the Spanish army had been on something of a war footing as the principal purpose of its deployment in Cuba. It was, rather, that Spain had prepared for a rebellion of another kind, with different characteristics, against a different enemy, in a different region. An army totaling 16,000–18,000 officers and men, units of infantry, cavalry, and artillery, was positioned principally as an armed bulwark against the *dotaciones* of the great estates, a garrison presence distributed mostly within the production zones of the west.⁹ An eminently successful military presence, to be sure: in the year of Yara, the great sugar estates of the west produced a record harvest of 750,000 tons, what was then the largest crop in the history of Cuba.

There is little evidence to suggest that Spain had prepared for the possibility of an armed rebellion on the scale and scope of 1868. The lack of foresight was compounded by the absence of oversight. Official military rolls were themselves often a fiction, largely embezzlement arrangements through which to defraud the Royal Exchequer. This was an army much of whose authorized strength existed principally on paper as a budget line item, padded payrolls with fictitious military personnel and misappropriated funds. The actual number of *peninsular* troops available for military operations in 1868 did not surpass 6,000–8,000 officers and men.¹⁰ Three years before Yara, General Antonio de Letona, the military commander of Oriente, had warned against the diminishing number of troops stationed in Cuba—without effect.¹¹ The presence of sufficient military forces in Cuba, Lieutenant Colonel Francisco de Moya later insisted, "would have ended the insurrection immediately, without danger, without sacrifices, without costs."¹² The limited operational capacity of the Spanish army was circumscribed further by seasonal circumstances. Jacobo de la Pezuela estimated in 1863 the size of the army to number 24,000 troops, 80 percent of whom he deemed unable to serve as an "effective force" (*fuerza efectiva*) due to "yellow fever and other endemic fevers to which the garrisons are subject from April through October."¹³

The lack of an "effective force" was only part of the problem. The colonial budget was in disarray, and disbursements of all types were in arrears, a condition not unrelated to deepening budgetary crises in Spain that threatened *la madre patria* with economic collapse. "The resources of the government are so far exhausted," US Minister Daniel Sickles reported from Madrid in September 1869, "and its credit so low, that it is now using the reserves appropriated to the payment of the interest on the public debt due in December and must soon suspend specie payments altogether."¹⁴

Depleted inventories of military supplies and aging equipment made everything worse. Not only too few soldiers but also too few resources, what Spanish Major Leopoldo Barrios later described as "the ridiculously small number of military personnel [and] the absolute scarcity of materiel."¹⁵ Deplorable conditions within the soldiery, reported Colonel Luis Fernández Golfín as early as 1866, included insufficient supplies, inadequate diet, salaries in arrears, and widespread demoralization due to the "monotony of daily life and the illnesses produced by the tropical climate."¹⁶ The outbreak of the insurrection, General Francisco de Acosta y Albear acknowledged in 1875, found colonial administration without "the most minimum plan of operations and [without] absolutely everything needed to wage war, including arms and ammunition"—"the island in a complete state of military helplessness," recalled former Voluntario Eugenio Antonio Flores.[17] All at a time of chronic political instability and civil strife in Spanish realms: the "Grito de Lares" in Puerto Rico on September 23, 1868, and the "Glorious Revolution" deposing Queen Isabella II in Spain on September 30, 1868.

Something had gone terribly wrong, colonial authorities understood—"a moral disaster," pronounced Lieutenant Colonel Francisco J. de Moya.[18] That poorly armed and loosely organized insurgents had seized important population centers across the eastern third of the island, thereupon to extend mastery over vast swaths of the interior countryside, suggested conditions of incompetence at the highest levels of colonial administration—developments, Emilio Soulère wrote with understated candor, that implied the need "to confess that our leadership left much to be desired."[19] General Francisco Acosta y Albear was among the many Spanish officers to realize that "the insurrection, which began ineptly and almost without vigor, expanded and strengthened, with us being the principal factor in its development."[20] All in all, an incomprehensible turn of events and inadmissible challenge to national integrity (*la integridad nacional*).[21] "Loyalist forces, caught by surprise, disorganized and without arms, could do nothing to contain the insurrection," *La Voz de Cuba* acknowledged, and continued: "The jurisdictions of the eastern department passed almost completely under the control of the insurgents. The small military detachments of the interior population centers withdrew to their respective provincial capitals. Santiago de Cuba and Puerto Príncipe found themselves isolated and blockaded by the rebels and gravely threatened."[22] Yara revealed the tenuous military presence of colonial authority, of course, but it also revealed a previously unimaginable military reach of political discontent.

Yara served to confirm the worst fears of a polity living under the pall of race war. Vast numbers of men of color had indeed enrolled in the armed ranks of Free Cuba, within the officer corps and among the soldiery, thereupon to set the salient sociology of the insurrection in sharp relief. The social composition of Yara could not but reflect the demographic habitat of the uprising. The insurrection expanded across the eastern jurisdictions and reached into the many hundreds of *caseríos*, *aldeas*, *pueblos*, *villas*, and *ciudades* of the east in which the population of color represented a preponderant presence.[23] The 1862 census recorded a population of color—free and enslaved—in Oriente accounting for more than half the total inhabitants (135,570 out of 255,919). In some jurisdictions, most notably Santiago de Cuba and Guantánamo, people of color made up more than 70 percent of the total population.[24]

Certainly enslaved Africans seized the occasion of the fog of war to flee chattel bondage. As a military matter, insurgent assaults against the plantations almost always implied a corresponding commitment to manumission. But as a political matter, the Cuban leadership addressed the subject of abolition with guarded ambiguity, an ambiguity that in the ensuing years diminished as the participation of blacks in the rebellion expanded.[25] The degree to which enslaved Africans enrolled in *insurrecto* ranks is not clear. Historian Franklin Knight suggested that the "reluctance" of slaves to join the insurrection was due to their "confidence in an ultimate victory of the metropolitan government . . . [and] they remained unconvinced that a Creole victory would significantly ameliorate their servile condition."[26] Rebecca Scott, on the other hand, posited that "as long as the rebellion represented abolition, however nominal and compromised, those slaves who could do so had reason to flee their masters to the insurrectionist lines."[27]

The number of slaves who joined the rebellion is not clear. Some did. Many did not. But it was not the number of slaves, exactly, joining the uprising that aroused alarm. Rather it was the act—the example.[28] Certainly large numbers of free Cubans of color had enrolled in the insurrection in sufficient numbers to confirm the worst fears among the producing classes and within the colonial officialdom. Authorities were quick to call attention to the demographics of disorders, of course—and not without mischievous intent: an attention designed purposely to arouse alarm among the population upon whose support Spanish sovereignty depended, to exploit racial disquiet as a means to discredit the *independentista* project.

But Yara posed a deeper if perhaps less immediately discernible threat to the prevailing order of things. The plausibility of Spanish sovereignty was inscribed in the promise of security, a commitment that had assumed the form of received wisdom: namely, that the threat to the well-being of the producing classes originated principally from the expanding population of color, free and enslaved. And more: that security of life and property was itself a condition best obtained by preserving the status of people of color within prevailing social arrangements and racial hierarchies—in sum, the defense of racial privilege as a means through which to transact Spanish claims to power. A culture of colonial governance had formed around a fragile consensus between *peninsulares* and criollos, a compact of sorts, drawn less out of conviction than from convenience, less from choice than from necessity, a convergence of strategies of material self-interest and political self-preservation, always fraught with internal tensions, to be sure, but not without shared benefits. Representatives of the producing classes, historian María del Carmen Barcia Zequeira suggested, were "immersed in a complex social process through which they were joined together and transformed."[29] Former editor of *Diario de la*

Marina Dionisio Alcalá Galiano was certain that bonds shared between *"el partido español"* and *"el partido criollo"*—"the perfect and indisputable community of material interest"—served to guarantee the solidarity of whites, dedicated to "the security to enjoy the fruits of their labor at the lowest possible cost and to reduce to the most minimum possible [all] obstacles to exercising their intelligence and industry.... If the production of the island expands, if commerce increases and its scope expands, we would all rightly rejoice, given that we are all participants in the wealth thus created."[30] They mingled in the corridors of power and privilege, brought together in the pursuit of shared interests through powerful associations, including the Sociedad Económica de Amigos del País, the Real Consulado de Agricultura y Comercio, and the Junta de Fomento. Something of a recognition of a pragmatic necessity: *peninsulares* and criollos sharing together the privilege of whiteness, but otherwise often riven by competing interests, wary of each other, to be sure, but more wary of the perils ascribed to the expanding population of color, and encumbered with collective racial anxieties of sufficient magnitude so as to render the efficacy of social cohesion an arrangement as obvious as it was obligatory.

Therein lay the political circuitry through which colonial solidarities were transacted as a matter of existential urgency from which the logic of Spanish governance assumed the form of self-evident truths. *Peninsular* authorities often to warn criollos of the folly of the *independentista* aspirations, predicting that blacks would seize upon the occasion of a war for independence against Spain to organize a race war against all whites—*"el desbordamiento de los negros,"* many feared. "Let the Cubans be under no illusions," Vicente García Verdugo, government attorney of the *audiencia* of Puerto Príncipe, cautioned criollos in 1869: "If they have pretensions, if they presume to maintain in obedient submission 400,000 slaves, it would not be as a result of their own resources, nor the result of their moral and material resources, but to the protection that Spain provides. The day that the black and white races confront each other, do the Cubans really believe that they will not be irrevocably overrun [*irremisiblemente arrollados*] by the onslaught of the blacks?" Adding: "The independence of Cuba would result in anarchy followed by the domination of the black race."[31] A year into Yara, Nicolás Azcárate recoiled in horror at the thought of independence, surely to plunge Cuba into "the abyss of a race war," and warned that "the revolution cannot ignore the blacks; and in the face of the possibility— in the face of that great possibility—the result will be a long and devastating war leading to the extermination of the white race in Cuba."[32] What would happen in Cuba, asked the weekly *El Voluntario de Cuba* in 1870, if the "least industrious, least educated, least intelligent, least virtuous, and least honorable were to prevail?" And answered: "The Island of Cuba, abandoned by Cubans and Spaniards to whom the *insurrectos* have vowed a hatred to the death, abandoned by the Spanish government, would not be able to establish itself as a republic such as exists in South and Central America. The black slaves whom the *insurrectos* have not yet dared to declare emancipated will thereupon emerge the most powerful and far stronger than the whites, and would easily seize control of the entire country, transforming it into a new Santo Domingo."[33] The fate of a free Cuba, warned Juan Güell y Ferrer, "will not be the one of the Republics of the Continent, which with frequent dissension and disorders nevertheless preserved the [white] race. It will be like Santo Domingo."[34] The outcome of independence, Federico Ordas Avecilla predicted: "Horrors! Bloody internal wars. The emigration of Spaniards. The flight of capital and credit. . . . And masses of blacks demanding participation in the government and hordes of bandits dominating the countryside."[35] Nicolás Pardo Pimentel warned of the doom certain to follow, predicting that independence would "reduce [Cuba] to the condition of Santo Domingo. . . . When 100,000 wild beasts will obtain their liberty and our race will disappear, the forests will be set ablaze as in Port-au-Prince, and the Island will become a desert and a mound of ruins," adding:

> Who is it that asks for independence of Cuba? Some thousands of adventurers, fools, or traitors. That is what constitutes the army of insurrection, but not whites, not Spanish. . . . If it were possible to imagine the triumph of that idea, the first consequences would be the immediate emigration of the white population that could save itself from the cataclysm. Then with the evacuation of the army and navy, followed by the mass uprising of the blacks [*la subvelación en masa de los negros*], slaughter, fire, extermination. That is what the independent Island of Cuba would look like.[36]

"If not Spanish the Island of Cuba will be black, necessarily black," warned José Ahumada.[37] Oft-repeated and well-rehearsed admonitions were something of a practiced recitation to warn of the race war surely to eclipse aspirations to independence. The specter of Haiti cast a long shadow deep into the nineteenth century.

Yara changed everything. The colonial officialdom had transacted the power of governance principally as broker among multiple constituencies bound together by way of overlapping and interdependent affinities of privilege, "a perfectly woven mesh of economic and political interests," commented historian Consuelo Naranjo Orovio.[38] These were not especially noteworthy networks of shared interests, of course, for indeed they were endowed with a self-evident wisdom with a self-serving purpose as the inner logic of colonial administration. Spanish sovereignty in Cuba was sustained from within, a condition perhaps not always readily apparent in times of order and stability, but always understood as a moral system upon which the status quo depended, itself deeply inscribed in the dread of the deluge surely to follow: principally in the form of affinities of whites, solidarities of fear as a matter of existential urgency. "The immediate result of a declaration of independence," warned *Diario de la Marina* in 1872, "would be a destructive bloody civil war."[39] All in all, networks of multiple beneficiaries of sugar and slavery bound together in common political purpose through which the legitimacy of Spanish sovereignty was sustained and the well-being of the producing classes secured.

The community of common interests fractured in 1868, to expose discernible fissures within a long-standing unity of purpose. The rebellion organized by white Cubans of means, among prominent representatives of the producing classes—even if a downwardly mobile patriciate—in concert with Cubans of more modest origins, black and white, a constituency into which the formerly enslaved were more or less admitted, thereupon implied the emergence of an alternative polity, one taking form around the idea of a sovereignty of another kind, advancing a notion of nationhood vested in the proposition of self-government. Yara shattered the premise of *peninsular*-criollo unity, a solidarity for which defense against the population of color was deemed necessary, dealing also and at the same time a body blow to the raison d'être of Spanish sovereignty.[40] Not everywhere, of course. Nor among everyone. October 10 had summoned a new convergence of social forces in defense of a new political vision, revealing what historian Julio Le Riverend suggested as "the capacity of the Cuban people to embark upon its own destiny."[41] The historic fear that disaffected criollos rising up in arms against loyalist *peninsulares*—that is, whites at war with whites—would provide the occasion for blacks to rise up in rebellion against whites was put to rest. Perhaps the most important moral Antonio Saco drew from Yara was that "free and enslaved blacks remained quiet and acted only within the parameters of the war, and most of them were conscripted into participation by whites themselves."[42]

Ten years of war produced a new paradigm of sovereignty from which Spain was excluded, and more: into which to consolidate an emerging biracial and multiclass alliance in the pursuit of an independent nation, which implied also—and especially—the inclusion of Cubans of color as party to and participants in the formation of a new nation. The war served to create new participatory spaces, opened new opportunities for mobility, and offered new domains of agency, to advance the premise of a new nationality informed with the promise of inclusion and the possibility of community, a process, historian Ramiro Guerra y Sánchez suggested, resulting in "the definitive creation and consolidation of Cuban nationality."[43] There would be no going back.

After Yara, within the multiple *independentista* constituencies among criollos of means, among the many thousands of white women and men who invested themselves in the proposition of Free Cuba, the population of color was no longer perceived as an adversary to be feared but an ally to be recruited. This is not to suggest, of course, that the producing classes embraced the proposition of a biracial, multiclass coalition as a way to national sovereignty. They did not. Not in 1868. Not in 1895. Perhaps not ever. But the paradigm of a socially inclusive mobilization as the catalyst of a new nationality drew into its premise vast numbers of participants and served to consolidate an expanding social amalgam around which the *independentista* project assumed a plausible means of nationhood. The specter of race war that had long acted to stall the separatist purpose—and indeed had served too as the principal unifying source of the colonial consensus from which Spain derived the claim to sovereignty—had begun to lose the capacity of coherence. The moral inferred from Yara, historian Ada Ferrer suggested, was that an *independentista* rebellion "could succeed without generating racial upheaval."[44] Ten years of war served to draw the population of color into the logic of the sovereign nation, to participate in and make demands of a national project as a means of remedy of accumulated grievances, where the idea of *el negro* was subsumed into the ideal of *el cubano*. "To arms!" Antonio Maceo exhorted Cubans of color. "Ask for nothing as black, everything as Cuban."[45] Blacks as agents of the nation served to inscribe the purpose of racial equality into the promise of nationality. Cuban history was forever changed.

Yara deeply offended Spanish sensibilities. The Cuban call to arms raised the specter of national disintegration, an assault on the nation, a struggle between *lo español* and *lo cubano*, between *la integridad nacional* and *la nación integral*. Cubans had revealed themselves as "enemies of national integrity" (*los enemigos de la integridad nacional*), *peninsulares* decried—"the Island of Cuba is an indissoluble part of the Spanish Nation," *La Voz de Cuba* proclaimed—and worse: they threatened the indivisibility of Spanish nationality.[46] The Cubans had declared war "against Spanish nationality" (*contra la nacionalidad española*), decried *Diario de la Marina*.[47] "On the island of Cuba," *Diario de la Marina* thundered, "exists only one legitimate nationality, purchased with Castilian blood and validated over the course of centuries. This nationality is Spanish [*esta nacionalidad es la española*]. . . . One can easily contemplate attacks against political parties and men, but attacks against the Nation are repugnant and horrendous."[48] Cuba was as much a part of Spain as Andalusia and Catalonia, insisted the weekly *El Voluntario de Cuba*.[49] The *insurrectos* were "enemies of our nationality," decried the Madrid daily *El Imparcial*.[50] "To abandon [sovereignty over] Cuba is to accept the dismemberment of the nation" (*aceptar la desmembración de la patria*), pronounced Emilio Soulère.⁵¹ Simply put, the cause of the Cuban nation implied the demise of the Spanish nation. "When the Yara rebellion pronounced the shouts of 'Death to Spain,'" *La Voz de Cuba* warned,

> the traitors who launched the uprising did not call for the death of one political faction or other. They did not proclaim death to Isabel II, or death to Prince Alfonso, or death to Charles VII.... No. This is not what they proclaimed. What they said was "Death to Spain!" And since this call for death having been directed toward the communal homeland [*a la patria común*] is necessarily directed to all the political parties of the nation and to all the men on the island of Cuba who identify with these political parties, all of us feel equally threatened.... The call for death issued by the traitors was against Spain and all Spaniards.... The attack was against everyone equally, because it was against *la patria comun*, it was directed against the nationality [*a la nacionalidad*].⁵²

The insurrection was "an act of madness" (*un acto de demencia*), scorned Vicente García Verdugo, "for Cuba is a province of Spain ... forming an integral part of its territory in which, by right, there are neither Cubans nor *peninsulares*, only Spaniards.... Cuba does not exclusively belong to Cubans. It belongs to Spain and all Spaniards."⁵³ Cuba "*is not a colony*," thundered Antonio Porrua; "*it is a province of Spain.*"⁵⁴ Accounts of successful Spanish military operations against *insurrectos* after 1868 were often celebrated explicitly as victories for "the cause of our nationality" (*la cause de nuestra nacionalidad*).⁵⁵ The duty of *los buenos españoles, los españoles honrados,* and *los verdaderos españoles,* as the loyal *peninsulares* often described themselves, was "to maintain the honor of the flag, to conserve the civilization and the culture that our forefathers brought to this undiscovered island."⁵⁶ The island of Cuba, *La Voz de Cuba* bristled in 1873, "hardly more than fifty years ago, was an uncivilized country [*un país inculto*], a vast desert with a population of scarce importance":

> A country without productive capacity that in order to subsist needed annual alms from the viceregal exchequer of Mexico ... to make up for what the country did not produce. And in these few years, the island of Cuba has progressed in its population, in its agriculture, in everything that makes for the development of a country. Proportionally more than any country on earth, it has become the most prosperous, the richest, and the most coveted place in the world. This is an accomplishment that cannot be disputed and that no one can deny.... All owed to those who arrived from the Peninsula to work.⁵⁷

Far-flung *peninsular* populations across the island drew together to close ranks in defense of *la integridad nacional*. The cause of *Cuba española* forged a solidarity of uncommon intransigence around an uncompromising defense of *la madre patria*. A resident population of 116,000 Spaniards, distributed principally in Havana and in provincial capitals, included the women and men of the Spanish *casinos* and regional societies, within the Catholic Church and among members of civic clubs, guilds, and business circles, representatives of important sectors of the economy as hacendados and industrialists, as merchants and retailers, in the trades and artisanal production, and the vast number of workers in their employ.[58] Pronouncements from colonial officials and sermons from Catholic priests summoned *los buenos españoles* to the defense of *la madre patria*. The enactment of *españolismo* assumed the form of political rallies and street demonstrations as events of daily occurrence. "We will not permit this land to be ripped from the bosom of our nation," Juan de Almansa vowed, insisting that "the Spaniards who are on this island will never be defeated, will never give up, and will never be sold out. Cuba will be Spanish or we will abandon it only after being converted to ashes."[59] Commitments of patriotic generosity, celebrated acts of faith in the form of collective financial contributions and individual donations, raised tens of thousands of pesos in support of the Spanish war effort among "*los peninsulares intransigentes*," observed José Ramón Betancourt.[60]

The Spanish population across the island assumed something of a war footing. *Peninsulares* enrolled in the expanding ranks of the Cuerpo de Voluntarios by the many thousands, as many as thirty thousand by early 1869 and subsequently expanding to more than sixty thousand officers and men.[61] Spaniards of means were appointed as officers to command Spaniards of modest origins recruited as soldiers, an armed citizenry organized as the frontline defenders of *la integridad nacional*. "Spanish above all else" (*español sobre todo*) was the *peninsular* watchword.[62] "Upon the outbreak of the insurrection," Spanish journalist Gil Gelpi y Ferro wrote in 1870, "and in view of the scarcity of troops and the inevitable delay in the arrival of reinforcements from the Supreme Government in Spain, everyone recognized the need to organize battalions of Voluntarios."[63] *Peninsulares* did not hesitate. "The resident *buenos españoles* in Cuba," exulted Evaristo Martín Contreras in 1876, "understood immediately the duty they were obliged to honor to *la madre patria* in those critical moments."[64]

Decisive developments. Voluntarios may have indeed saved the colonial regime from collapse in 1868. "A critical situation was averted as a result of the enthusiasm and patriotism of the resident *peninsular* population of our Island," acknowledged General Adolfo Castellanos.[65] The Voluntarios rarely conducted field operations against the *insurrectos* but instead assumed the task of garrison duty, an armed presence to guarantee order and stability, deployed principally in towns and cities across the island—"from Havana to the smallest hamlets," Ramiro Guerra y Sánchez correctly noted—thereupon to enhance the operational capacities of the *peninsular* army for service in the disaffected zones of the east.[66] The Cuerpo de Voluntarios "is devotedly-loyal to the preservation of the connection between the island and Spain," US Consul Edward Plumb observed from Havana in 1869:

> There is little doubt it is due to the presence of [Voluntarios], in the early part of the present year, and since, that the island has been saved to the mother country. This organization now numbers probably upwards of forty thousand men, well organized, armed, and equipped, and now considerably accustomed to the exercise of arms. They hold all the ports and all the towns, and they have a stake and interest to defend, for they are residents here; they are connected with the commerce and industry of the island, and they expect and desire to remain here. They are not government employees. Their officers are generally men of some position and wealth, as are also very many in the ranks. They have no idea of submitting to, or being ruled by, the Cuban portion of the population. It may be doubted whether all the Cubans in arms within the island number half as many; nor have they the means, the organization, or the arms of the volunteers.[67]

At least as important, the Voluntarios also served as an instrument of political intimidation. A "coarse and crude people," recalled Spanish Captain Nicolás Estévanez, "who in the large cities, and especially in Havana, did nothing but disrupt public order with their abuses, demands, and crimes."[68] Dolores María de Ximeno remembered the Voluntarios as "caring men of households, kind in their private lives, loving fathers of families, who were transformed into lunatics upon the donning of that [Voluntario] uniform."[69]

Not all Cubans had broken faith with Spain, of course. Most did not. But many did, and in sufficient numbers to provoke *peninsular* wrath against criollos by virtue of their being Cuban. Yara aroused a collective fury of indignation among *los buenos españoles*, rising fully to the level of visceral animus and vindictive malice toward all criollos. "Here a deadly hatred exists between the Spaniards and Cubans that is growing stronger day by day," reported US Vice-Consul Richard Gibbs from Nuevitas in late 1868: "There is no half way, no room for compromise; ninety-five out of every hundred of the natives are heart and soul in the rebellion, if not bodily. I don't care how neutral a man may be, how loyal he may be, how his interests may incline him to peace, the very fact of his being a native-born is enough in the eyes of the bigoted Spaniard to make him an enemy."[70] Spaniards bore a "great hatred and bitterness against the Cubans," reported US Consul Edward Plumb from Havana in mid-1869. "They believe only in severe measures against the Cubans, or the insurgents, which are considered here as almost identical terms."[71] Years later, Antonio Reyes Zamora would remember the Voluntarios in Cuba as "irreconcilable enemies [and] ferocious fanatics against Cubans" who acted as an "unyielding bulwark against all compassion and against any measure that could have humanized the war so as not to become a war of extermination.... They had no sympathy toward Cubans and did not recognize the reach of their hatred toward Cubans."[72] The Voluntarios attacked the *milicias disciplinadas*, demanding—and obtaining—the disbandment of all creole militia units. The proposition of units of armed creoles was no longer plausible.[73] In early 1869, Voluntarios directed an aroused wrath against criollos in the capital and rampaged on the streets of Havana with the cries of "¡Viva España con honra!" to attack known sites of creole social gatherings, including the Villanueva Theater and the Louvre café, and plundered the home of reformist Miguel Aldama. All through early January, Voluntario mobs lay siege to Havana from within. "Those who have been a model of subordination and discipline," *Diario de la Marina* offered feeble criticism of the Voluntarios, "who have been dedicated to order and respect for the principle of authority, cannot fail to uphold such honorable traditions, they cannot cease to be what they have always been."[74] Two years later, yielding to Voluntario demands, the government charged University of Havana medical students with desecrating the tomb of Gonzalo Castañón, previously the director of the newspaper *La Voz de Cuba*. Eight students were found guilty and executed by firing squad.[75]

In ways not immediately apparent, new stress points had traced out fault lines along which the colonial consensus would fracture.[76] Criollos and *peninsulares* would no longer look upon each other in the same way. The enmity assumed structural form after the war with the emergence of new political alignments: *peninsulares* in the Partido Unión Constitucional representing the intransigence of *los buenos españoles* in defense of *Cuba española*, the reformist criollos in the Partido Liberal (Autonomist) pursuing colonial reforms and home rule, and the separatist Cubans abroad pursuing independence through the Partido Revolucionario Cubano.[77]

Colonial authorities responded indecisively to the early days of Yara, in part the result of the administrative confusion to which Captain General Francisco Lersundi succumbed, in part due to the logistical difficulties hampering Spanish counteroffensive military operations. In early 1869, Lersundi launched a full-scale military assault in the east, a combined expeditionary force of some four thousand infantry, artillery, and cavalry troops under the command of General Blas Diego de Villate (Conde de Valmaseda), a campaign of pacification meant to end the insurrection through the deployment of force in a single counteroffensive operation. Nothing left was left to chance. "Disposed to assemble all the means required," commented Gil Gelpi, "so as to make certain that with that campaign the pacification of the Island would be completed."[78]

The outcome of the Spanish military operations was never in doubt. Within weeks Valmaseda had defeated the main insurgent armies defending Bayamo, inflicting as many as two thousand casualties among the Cubans.[79] The insurgents had been routed and Bayamo recaptured.

Spanish military operations had registered decisive results, Valmaseda exulted, a success of sufficient magnitude to prompt pronouncements of a quick victory and predictions of an early peace. Certainly these were the expectations that shaped the triumphalist hubris informing government announcements all through 1869 and into early 1870. "Pacification will be completed in the coming months," Valmaseda exulted confidently in January 1870.[80] A series of well-organized and well-executed military operations, Captain General Lersundi was satisfied, had scattered the insurgent forces into disarray and defeat.[81] "The insurrection is enclosed inside a circle of iron," *Diario de la Marina* proclaimed days after the recapture of Bayamo, "one that is tightening every day. Its efforts are desperate and its death is imminent." And one week later: "Reports from Oriente encourage us to believe that peace will soon be restored to the island."[82] The insurrection "is in crisis," the government was certain. "Its so-called army has fractured into insignificant bands and does not dare to confront the [army] columns."[83]

There seemed to be something of a tragic inevitability to the course of events after 1869. A moment of "exaggerated confidence," Justo Zaragoza would later acknowledge.[84] Not altogether unforeseeable, to be sure, but perhaps even the benefit of foresight would not have altered the outcome. Insurgent forces dislodged from the cities dispersed into the countryside, in flight and in scattered retreat beyond the reach of *peninsular* army units: "fractured into insignificant bands."

But that was the problem. Military authorities had regained control of the cities, but in so doing lost control of the countryside. The implications were not long in revealing themselves. "Far from having ended the civil war on the Island," reported a resident Spanish journalist at the time, "the capture of Bayamo has had no importance or influence in the subsequent course of events."[85] In fact, it did. The capture of Bayamo expelled insurgents from the city, who thereupon "dispersed into the forests and mountains," remembered Luis Lagomasino.[86] In the weeks and months that followed, the reach of the revolt expanded in scope: across the complicated political geography of the eastern third of the island, into the dense inner recesses of the rural interior—the *manigua*—inside the remote mountain folds and within the impenetrable woodland habitat, the *monte*, of Oriente—"the luxuriant forests,"

Franklin Knight aptly wrote—and onto the expansive plains of Camagüey.[87] "Instead of diminishing," a disheartened Emilio Soulère lamented, "the insurrection expanded, and the political skies of Cuba darkened." Colonial authorities had erred, Soulère understood: "The *insurrectos* would separate into small groups [*fraccionar*], subdivide their forces . . . to reappear later with new vigor and new energy."[88] Everything changed after 1869. What began as a rebellion expanded into an insurgency, for in dispersing into the rural interior of the east, the Cubans expanded the radius of operations, in the process drawing ever-larger numbers of recruits into *insurrecto* ranks. "Cities depopulated so as to join the ranks of the insurrection," recalled Spanish Colonel Ramón Domingo de Ibarra.[89] The insurgency had expanded to an estimated ten thousand *insurrectos*, a formidable armed multitude rendered all the more formidable as small mobile units possessing familiarity with the interior habitat that would serve as the principal theater of war for nearly a decade. Insurgent armies moved about almost at will: Vicente García in the region of Tunas, Calixto García in Holguín, Antonio Maceo in Santiago de Cuba, Ignacio Agramonte in Camagüey, Máximo Gómez in Guantánamo. In April 1869 in a gesture of audacity, Cuban delegates representing various insurgent army commands convoked a full-fledged Constituent Assembly in Guáimaro, Camagüey, to promulgate a new constitution and proclaim the establishment of the Republic-in-Arms under the presidency of Carlos Manuel de Céspedes.[90] "In the early days," Spanish commander Leopoldo Barrios recalled, "apart from the group that launched the insurrection, true combat units [*verdaderos núcleos combatientes*] did not exist, and indeed we could also affirm that there hardly existed combatants." By early 1869, however, Barrios acknowledged, "the insurgency began inexorably to expand from its rudimentary origins."[91] Years later Captain General José G. de la Concha could not but look upon the course of events of 1869 with regret. "At the beginning of 1869," he recalled in his *memoria*, "the thousands of men who had rallied behind the insurgent flag abandoned the population centers to take up life in the countryside [*habitar los campos*], thus providing the insurgent element with immense support and great strength which in no small way contributed to sustaining the war."[92]

The insurrection had entered a new phase. *Insurrecto* armies dispersed across the eastern interior, adapting to and expanding into an environment well-suited for irregular warfare, to develop the capacity to sustain perhaps indefinitely a protracted war of attrition. The insurgency expanded in a display of demonstrable staying power, seemingly poised with the capacity to enlarge its scope—certainly seeking to extend its scope—beyond the confines of its eastern provincial origins.

And therein lay the danger. A brooding disquiet settled over colonial authorities who did not fail to discern the implications of an insurgency that expanded amorphously but not purposelessly, sustained by the logic of expansion as a tactical imperative through which to weaken the Spanish claim to sovereignty. The proposition of the Invasion (*la Invasión*)—to expand the disruptive reach of war into the production centers of the west—loomed large in the strategic vision of Cuban warfare: a calculus described by historian Francisco Ponte Domínguez as a "thesis" (*la tesis invasora*), the "general desire to extend the war across the entire island."[93]

The tactical impulse of the insurrection could not but seek to expand westward, as a matter of destination and design, as indeed it was inevitably required to as a purpose intrinsic to the logic of the insurgency: as a means of national liberation to expand beyond the geography of the marginal economies of the east to carry the war into the productive west, to disrupt production and interrupt commerce, to introduce havoc into the principal sources of colonial revenues. "Under no circumstances," José Manuel Mestre exhorted, "can we consent that Spain continue to extract from our country and obtain from our receipts the resources to wage war against us."[94] A simple formulation, actually: to reduce the productive capacity of Cuba to the point of rendering the island not worth fighting for. And perhaps also, at the same time, to obtain recruits into the armed ranks of Cuba Libre from among the hundreds of thousands of enslaved Africans in the western jurisdictions. "It was necessary to secure the triumph [of the insurrection]," wrote Eduardo Machado Gómez in 1874, "by advancing into the West, destroying by surprise the great sugar plantations of Colón and Cárdenas, summoning the slave labor force to war, and with that multitude armed with machetes, to carry fire, desolation, and panic to the very doors of Havana."[95] In fact, most of the populations of the west experienced Yara hardly at all, a distant war happening somewhere else. Certainly residents of the western jurisdictions, in Havana and the provincial capitals, were rarely inconvenienced by the ten years of war. A remote faraway disturbance having little to do with the daily life of *habaneros*. "In Havana," Spanish Captain Nicolás Estévanez recalled of his arrival on the island in 1871, "one would never have known that there was a war going on. The *paseos* were animated with people, the cafés crowded with patrons, the theaters filled with audiences, businesses in brisk activity, and the port crowded with ships."[96]

The insurgent leadership understood well the moral systems summoned to inform the political economy of colonialism, and understood too that the sources of the colonial authority lay in Spain's capacity to defend property and protect production, without which the logic of Spanish sovereignty was untenable. Insurgent operations against the economy implied the need to wage war beyond the defensive capacities of the Spanish army. To lay siege to trade and commerce, against isolated bridges and culverts, against miles of unprotected railroad tracks and vast stretches of unguarded telegraph lines: in sum, war against property and production—against sugar, that is—as the method to assail Spanish sovereignty at its source.[97] Máximo Gómez was lucid about the task at hand:

> A single *ingenio* set ablaze acts to alarm [the Spanish] more than a battle lost: they replace the soldiers who die in the campaign easily, for Spain is extravagant [*pródigo*] with the blood of its sons. The *ingenio* set ablaze remains permanently destroyed, and buried within its ashes is the *españolismo* flaunted by the owner. I am persuaded that the burning of 100 *ingenios* in Las Villas and Colón would contribute more to the triumph of the Revolution than the loss of 100,000 Spanish soldiers as a result of combat and disease.[98]

That Spain seemed untroubled by mounting casualties of war was also noted by the US minister in Madrid, Daniel Sickles, who commented in 1869 on the "willingness" of Spain to "sustain annual losses for the army in Cuba . . . from 10,000 to 15,000 men."[99]

Colonial authorities were indeed alive to the larger strategic purpose of Cuban arms, mindful too that failure to protect property and production boded ill for the plausibility of Spanish sovereignty. The *peninsular* army command deployed substantial numbers of troops to defend production sites, within the eastern jurisdictions, of course, but especially in the western zones, a decision not without operational consequences, for troops deployed to protect property reduced in equal numbers troops available for field operations.[100] In sum: tactical purpose in function of the political calculus of colonialism. "The concentration of our forces [centered] attention on the security of our cities and zones of agricultural production," Spanish General T. Ochando recalled at war's end, "which if destroyed would entirely deplete the Island of all its resources. Public opinion reflected the justified fears of the hacendados, demanding above everything else the defense of the rural estates."[101] During the 1871–72 sugar harvest (*zafra*), an estimated six thousand Spanish troops were deployed for garrison duty on the sugar estates.[102] *New York Herald* correspondent James O'Kelly visited the Esperanza estate near Ti-Arriba and recorded the presence of a small army detachment, noting that "for the most part [local sugar mills] are defended by a really respectable force."[103] Sugar mattered.

Perhaps the most ambitious effort to contain the insurgency in the eastern jurisdictions involved the construction of a physical barrier between the disaffected zones in the east and production centers of the west. The fortified trench—*la trocha*—in

Camagüey extended from Morón on the north to Júcaro on the south: a necessity, Captain General Cándido Pieltain insisted, "given that on the other side of this line lay exposed Las Villas and the Occidental department, where the most productive estates are located."[104] To "impede the passage of the *insurrecto* forces into Las Villas," explained Leopoldo Barrios, "a territory of far greater wealth [than Camagüey], and where the attack on property would have profoundly disturbed public morale and reduced public revenues."[105] Constructed principally through the labor of enslaved Africans levied from the *dotaciones* of local plantations, the *trocha* cleared an expanse of thirty miles of land enclosed within dense wire fencing.[106] It was defended with a total of thirty-three forts and blockhouses spanning intervals of every five hundred meters and linked with telegraph service, garrisoned with five thousand troops and supported with mobile artillery units transported north to south along a narrow-gauge railroad track.

The efficacy of the Júcaro-Morón *trocha* was a matter of continuous debate within the Spanish army command. *Insurrecto* forces often breached the *trocha*, of course, mostly in the form of short-lived armed forays into the west, there to conduct random assaults on the sugar estates, periodic breaches that were a reminder of the importance of containing the insurgency within the eastern departments. The imperative of the political economy of colonialism had inscribed itself deeply into the calculus of Spanish military planning. "An invasion from Oriente," General T. Ochando understood, "would not only have readily obtained ... sufficient local resources to sustain operations, but would also have rendered our already weakened condition even more precarious as result of overriding necessity to protect the vast and invaluable property."[107] For many years, Tesifonte Gallego insisted later, the *trocha* was "the bulwark of the *Patria*" (*el baluarte de la Patria*).[108]

The insurgency stretched into ten years of desultory warfare, a war mostly of offensive raids and forays, of defensive ambush and skirmish, with few memorable battles and many forgotten clashes, military operations confined mostly within the 23,000 square miles that made for the jurisdictions of the eastern third of the island. The war in Cuba lasted almost as long as the wars of independence in South America earlier in the nineteenth century. All the while, all through the ten years, boatloads of young Spanish conscripts arrived in Cuba, continuously, to defend *la integridad nacional*, successive waves of reinforcements, at random intervals and in irregular numbers: 46,000 troops by 1870, to which was added another contingent of 40,000 troops in 1871–73; an additional 42,000 soldiers arrived in 1874–75, with nearly 60,000 soldiers arriving during the final phase of the war in 1876–78. Over the span of the ten years of war, an estimated 200,000 Spanish soldiers had served *la madre patria* in

Cuba, an army that exceeded the total number of Spanish troops deployed in South America between 1808 and 1824.[109]

Spanish authorities coming to terms with the implications of the changing nature of warfare in Cuba: confounded by an enemy determined to avoid set-piece battles, an enemy preferring instead engagements of ambush and acts of sabotage, given to assaults against transportation networks and communication systems, favoring the destruction of property and the disruption of production. "The enemy flees in all different directions," Colonel José de Chessa complained, "without daring to show his face even once to our brave soldiers."[110] How to wage war against an elusive enemy that practiced what military authorities described as "*el sistema de fraccionamiento*," whereby insurgent forces dispersed into ever smaller units, thereupon, one officer recognized, "making it extremely difficult [*sumamente difícil*] for any one operation to have importance in defeating the enemy"?[111] Lieutenant Colonel Antonio Ortiz complained during military operations near Manzanillo that insurgent forces "divided into small groups [*pequeñas fracciones*] better to elude engagements with the forces that pursued them."[112] Government officials in Spain were no less exasperated and certainly no better informed, lacking also an understanding of the tactical logic of the Cuban way of war. "Only roving bands," Spanish Prime Minister Juan Prim complained to US Minister Daniel Sickles in Madrid in mid-1869, "who fly when they are pursued, and who have never been found in numbers sufficient to give or accept battle."[113] Given to committing acts that authorities readily denounced as deeds of lawlessness attributed to brigands and bandits, lacking political significance and without military consequences. Easy to discount. Easier to discredit. "The only *insurrectos* who remain in the field," Valmaseda commented scornfully in January 1870, "are some runaway slaves [*cimarrones*] and criminals."[114] The war in Cuba, Gonzalo Reparaz pronounced, was not really a military campaign but "the pursuit of bandits writ large." Errors of judgment that military authorities would soon regret.[115] General T. Ochando was among the many commanders later to rue the failure to "have given the insurrection all the importance it deserved."[116]

Spain faced insurmountable challenges. Troops engaged in operations deep in the *manigua* frequently outdistanced their supply lines. Quartermaster, commissary, ordnance, and medical supplies were transported into interior encampments by way of convoys of pack mules and oxen-pulled wagons (*carretas*) over roads often hardly wider than footpaths. "Impassable during the rainy season," Alexander Humboldt had pronounced almost sixty years earlier.[117] Spanish military operations could not extend too far or remain away too long from regional bases of supplies. "Overland transports were scarce and virtually useless," Captain General Cándido Pieltain acknowledged, noting that the rivers during the time of the summer rains were transformed into torrential floods over which there were no bridges.[118] "In the eastern half of the Island," Leopoldo Barrios remembered years later, "there hardly existed roads, and what did exist were dirt roads created over time through repeated use [*caminos naturales*], without any pavement or building materials."[119] The absence of an interior transportation network in the east made everything worse. Spanish officer Fabián Navarro was incredulous. "In the entire department," he bemoaned, "there does not exist a single meter of highway other than a small stretch of road linking Gibara with Holguín."[120] The "part of island that rebelled," General Adolfo Castellanos recalled, "is entirely without highways. . . . During the time of the rains, which can last for half the year, the roads are transformed into terrible conditions, overrun with a profusion of creeks and rivers . . . of such velocity and width as to make crossings almost impossible, making it especially difficult for army columns transporting ill and wounded soldiers, rations, munitions, mules, and medical supplies."[121]

Eastern interior cities—Puerto Príncipe, Las Tunas, Holguín, and Bayamo—from which Spain mounted military operations out into the surrounding hinterland depended upon the arrival of scheduled convoys for supplies, and a precarious dependency it was. "The management of the convoys was one of the principal enemies of our campaign in Cuba," acknowledged Gonzalo Reparaz. "It required the escort of thousands of men who otherwise should have been engaged in the pursuit of the enemy. The grueling demands of convoy operations also resulted in illnesses that required hospitalization. And in the end, the mightiest efforts notwithstanding, munitions and provisions always arrived late and in poor condition and together with a poor diet increased the number of illnesses . . . causing many surrenders."[122] It was with a barely concealed hint of demoralization that General T. Ochando described the full dimensions of the tasks confronting the Spanish army:

> Those who are familiar with a convoy of 100 wagons, each one dragged along by six oxen in a country with no roads, over waterlogged terrain and saturated with recent rains, needing often to cross gullies and the deep channels produced by the creeks during the rainy season, or crossing in single file the densely tangled thicket, would not be surprised that an experienced enemy with foreknowledge of these expeditions days in advance . . . would be able to concentrate forces and take advantage of the opportune moment to attack these convoys that often stretched out three miles, often causing considerable harm at little cost to themselves.[123]

Supply lines stretched tenuously into the interior of the eastern third of the island. Military convoys traversing a distance of seventy miles from Puerto Príncipe to Las

Tunas were always subject to ambush and attack.[124] A total of 210 miles separated Puerto Príncipe and Bayamo, connected by the Camino Real in which, General Antonio López de Letona learned, during the summer rains, "horses engaged in mail service sink submerged and remain almost totally buried." Convoys from the port city of Manzanillo serving Bayamo, Jiguaní, Veguitas, Bueycito, and Cauto Embarcadero rarely escaped ambush. Supply convoys between Puerto Príncipe and Bayamo often involved an eight- to ten-day march, López de Letona added, "in which military escorts were vulnerable "to a well-designed ambush, well-prepared and well-executed at any number of points of arduous passage at which the troops are exposed as targets of well-aimed gun fire with impunity."[125] The railroad between the port of Nuevitas in the north and Puerto Príncipe in the interior south, one of the principal military supply lines into an important theater of operations, was subject continuously to ambush and sabotage, including destruction of rail stations, bridges, ties, rails, and railcars—"always at the mercy of the enemy," acknowledged Valmaseda in 1875.[126] Transportation over a distance of forty-five miles of rail often required three or four days to complete.[127]

The city of Bayamo posed an especially difficult logistical challenge. Bayamo depended principally upon supplies from Manzanillo, a distance of thirty miles. But distance was not the problem. Topography was. The thirty miles traversed five rivers (Buey, Babatuaba, Jucaibama, Mabay, and Bayamo), all of which flooded into impassable swampland during the seasonal rains, rendering convoys of *carretas* all but impossible. "The *carretas* were immobilized in the mud," recalled one Spanish officer. "At times even the yoke of eight or ten oxen was insufficient to extricate the *carretas*, only to sink again at another point." And perhaps worse still: "The enemy has magnificent and multiple vantage points with which to ambush the convoys."[128] *Insurrecto* Francisco Estrada y Céspedes wrote of one such ambush to his wife in March 1875: "We attacked the convoy from Bayamo to Cauto. We seized 37 *carretas* and some 300 mules and horses, all weighed down with important supplies. They suffered 140 dead and 80 prisoners, who were released unconditionally. We seized an ocean of rifles and ammunition and an infinite variety of provisions."[129]

Spanish logistical capacities were constantly compromised by the inability to sustain supply lines, which in turn imposed severe limitations on the range of Spanish military operations. "Exhausted troops," wrote historian Luis Navarro García, "in pursuit of insurgent bands lacking guides, limiting incursions to short duration as a result of the absence of supplies in the countryside, and each column unable to carry rations to sustain operations longer than four days."[130] Spanish soldier Teodorico Feijóo recalled "a withering day-long march and skirmish encounters, not being able to eat because the rains were so heavy that we were unable to maintain a fire with which to cook, even under improvised shelters."¹³¹ Tenuous logistical networks rendered depleting marches necessary. General Adolfo Jiménez Castellanos remembered:

> Prior to the outbreak of the insurrection the army in Cuba lacked adequate means of transportation to supply foodstuffs, munitions, etc. . . . Columns on operations could carry only six or eight days of rations, resulting in the need to return to population centers once the rations were consumed, for the army lacked points of support at which to leave soldiers who were ill or wounded and secure a resupply of footwear, clothing, and ammunition. Operations were reduced to marches from one *pueblo* to another, or to range across the countryside for six or eight days, usually to return to the original point of departure.¹³²

Logistical support that was often unreliable was also almost always insufficient. Shortages of supplies and scarcity of equipment were experienced as chronic conditions. Soldiers dependent on marching rations faced continuously life-threatening shortages of food. Army physician Ramón Hernández Poggio would later write of the "disastrous effects that the scarcity of food had on the soldiers," never more debilitating than the shortages of food for soldiers hospitalized in field hospitals.¹³³ "Neither officers nor soldiers," Major Leopoldo Barrios wrote of conditions after 1868, "had the knowledge to operate in the fields of Cuba, nor adequate uniforms, nor adequate arms, nor sufficient rations, nor ambulances, nor any of the conditions necessary to have undertaken the prosecution of and defeat of the insurgents."¹³⁴

Military equipment and supplies that were inadequate and insufficient were also often inappropriate and ill adapted to warfare in the middle latitudes of the New World. Materials distributed from existing inventories of military supplies in Spain were designed principally for combat of a different sort in a different place. Troops were clothed in uniforms ill suited to a tropical climate and provided with equipment ill fitted for irregular warfare. "The uniforms were not appropriate to the type of field operations required by the military campaign," Barrios complained.¹³⁵ As late as 1873, five years into the war, General Juan Montero Gabuti, the commander of the Spanish army in Cuba, denounced persisting shortages of every type. "It can be said without fear of contradiction that the troops here lack uniforms and equipment," Montero Gabuti complained, noting that the fabric of uniforms was ill adapted to the rigor of the Cuban campaign: "It is impossible not to recognize the necessity for light fabric due to the climate."¹³⁶

A disquiet settled over the Spanish army command, weary of futile operations against an elusive enemy concealed within the impenetrable habitat of the *manigua* and *monte*: all the ways the advantages of a superior army were neutralized and negated.

2.1 *Insurrectos* in the *manigua*, depicting the density of the tropical rain forest. SOURCE: LA ILUSTRACIÓN ESPAÑOLA Y AMERICANA 16 (JANUARY 1, 1872).

Spanish military operations in the *manigua* produced a special kind of psychic dread among *peninsular* soldiers, a war where visibility implied vulnerability, something of a condition of defenselessness that made for the terror of the *manigua*. "One must not think of the *manigua* as some woods," Emilio Soulère explained, "but a thick and intricate forest where between the palm trees grow thousands of crawling plants and thickets of vines, with bushes and shrubs that reach almost seven feet to form a dense compact. All an impenetrable network, where a trail constructed today by way of the machete has disappeared a day later."[137] The *manigua* consisted of "dense vegetation formed with trees and thickets," recalled General Adolfo Castellanos, "with an abundance of thorns and impenetrable vines."[138]

Warfare within the habitat of the dense vegetation of the *manigua*, with a limited line of sight and a shortened arc of fire, offered the *insurrectos* an unparalleled advantage of concealment. "The enemies of Spain sustain themselves," journalist Gil Gelpi y Ferro conveyed the exasperation of Spanish commanders, "by dispersing and hiding or choosing to concentrate at some select point." Army units "passing a mere 100 steps from the *insurrectos* without being able to see them," Gelpi understood, was "sufficient evidence of the great difficulties attending the prosecution of the war against the rebels within virgin forests [*los bosques virgenes*], in the most rugged and the least populated terrain of the island of Cuba."[139]

Nor were the *montes* of Cuba similar to the forests of Europe: not the temperate stands of mostly deciduous woodlands, but the shady canopy of dense tropical trees, entangled within impenetrable undergrowth and fallen trees, masses of brambles and vines, and exposed root systems, and soldiers, horses, and wagons mired in marshland, swamps, and waterlogged terrain. "Nature itself appeared decidedly to have joined the insurgency," concluded Eugenio Antonio Flores.[140] Leopoldo Barrios recalled the *monte*:

> It is difficult to provide an image of the tropical forests. They are characterized not only by a density of trees but also by an abundance of reeds, climbing vines, and other parasitical growths. The ground is covered with undergrowth of weeds and brambles which attain great height and thickness.... It is impossible to travel through the *monte* of the island without the need constantly to open trails with a machete or with an axe if wagons are in transit.[141]

The principal advantage of the *insurrecto*, Barrios understood, was "lush vegetation" (*la vegetación exuberante*) of the *monte* and *manigua*. The *peninsular* army could not sustain war in Cuba, Barrios concluded. "Every time Spanish troops mounted an attack in this terrain, they suffered a defeat. The enemy understood that his fortress was in the *monte* and *manigua*."[142]

There seemed to be little glory in a war waged in the *monte* and the *manigua*. There seemed to be no war. An army depleting its resources and exhausting its soldiers in operations conducted within a remote habitat against an elusive adversary, always scanning the impenetrable landscape in futile hope of sighting an invisible foe, waging war against an enemy perceived as inferior, mostly bands of loosely organized and lightly armed insurgents who declined to engage except in ambush. "Those *insurrectos* inflict much damage without having the courage to defend their ideas in the field of battle," scorned Manuel in the stage play *El gorrión* (1869) by Luis Martínez Casado.[143] "A traitorous war of surprises and ambushes," Lieutenant Colonel Francisco J. de Moya complained.[144] "They limit their engagements to ambushes,"

Lieutenant Antonio del Rosal despaired. "They know the *monte* well [*grandes conocedores del monte*] in which they find ready refuge, avoiding combat every time they wish. They are rarely encountered unless they wish to be found."[145] General Francisco Acosta y Albear was lucid about the nature of the insurgency: "The vitality of the armed insurrection... emanates entirely from the accurate and prompt information [the *insurrectos*] have concerning our forces and movements and the facility with which they disperse and concentrate [*dispersarse y reunirse*], to appear in territory abandoned by our columns and disappear where our forces concentrate. This system results in the fatigue and exhaustion of our troops, causing infinite casualties related to illness.[146] General Antonio López de Letona wearied at waging war against an elusive enemy, "knowing full well that if he does not wish to be found, he will not be found," of conducting "operations against an invisible enemy who never presents a target to attack, who is never surprised at any point because the entire country protects him [with intelligence information], and whose method of warfare is designed to provoke marches and the movement of troops as a way to decimate them through illness resulting from the climate." Writing in midsummer 1869, Letona was blunt: "To abuse the troops by knowingly subjecting them to constant and futile operations is not only incompetence. It is criminal."[147]

The chagrin extended widely across the Spanish army command. An elusive enemy resorting to ambush as a method of offense and practicing concealment as a means of defense, perhaps a cowardly enemy, an adversary seeming always to operate beyond reach and out of range: in the end, an unworthy adversary engaged in unprincipled warfare. "Whoever has an idea of Nature in the tropics," Juan Escalera recalled his military service in Cuba, "would understand the difficulties one confronts pursuing an enemy who constantly flees and has at his disposal so many different ways to hide." Escalera yearned for battle: "We desired so much to see him face to face, to engage him in serious and decisive action, for we were fully persuaded that we would render the enemy into complete defeat."[148] The thousands of soldiers who served as armed escorts of the convoys into the interior experienced war as a condition of onerous drudgery, harried and harassed by unseen assailants, "without fame and glory," one dispirited officer complained, "only an abundance of soggy undergrowth, malaria, and yellow fever, many dying with only the shouts of cart drivers and the bellowing of the oxen ringing in their ears."[149]

There was no glory in a war against traitors and cowards: a war "sustained from the inaccessible mountains and impenetrable thicket of the *manigua*," decried José de Granda, "a war of traps [*asechanzas*] and ambush [*emboscadas*] against our brave troops... without ever daring to fight face to face."[150] José Alvarez Pérez was fully persuaded that the Cubans "lacked the courage to wage a real war," while General Pedro de Zea scoffed at the "hordes of black savages who avoided combat when they did not have a ten to one advantage."[151] Angel Chaves recalled the eagerness with which he anticipated deployment to Cuba, to confront "that degenerate race of traitors" (*aquella degenerada raza de traidores*) who had "visited dishonor upon the nation," for "surely the hordes who valued only ambush and only accepted battle when they were one hundred percent certain of victory could hardly be considered valiant." Chaves was disappointed: "Instead of the great battles of war that I had dreamed of, I found myself subjected to continuous marches that depleted our strength, not by enemy bullets but from the harshness of a land that with the same cunning of its inhabitants distributed death in every pool of water."[152]

The Cubans did not even look like soldiers. Lieutenant Antonio del Rosal recalled preparations for military operations against "ferocious, semi-savage men wielding machetes," all "nearly naked [*casi desnudo*] black men," and adding, "It is known by all that the war sustained in Cuba . . . is distinguished by its ferocious character, inevitably to be attributed to the fact that we are dealing with an enemy that is mostly black and mulatto, and whose state of savagery is notorious."[153] Colonel Francisco de Camps recalled a conversation with a fellow officer, recovering from wounds suffered in an ambush, who pronounced, "This is not war. I do not wish to fight entangled within the dense foliage [of the *manigua*], unable to see enemy forces under the command of a mulatto 'general.' When I heal I will return to Spain. I have not

2.2 An *insurrecto* ambush of a Spanish convoy in the *manigua*. SOURCE: LA ILUSTRACIÓN ESPAÑOLA Y AMERICANA 16 (MARCH 16, 1872).

dedicated my life to professional preparation in order to fight soldier to soldier with a shirtless African" (*batirme de militar á militar con un africano que no lleva camisa*).[154]

Spanish commanders struggled to overcome the disadvantages of an unfamiliar operational environment, often a matter of seeking to understand what they did not know, at other times seeking to render the accumulated experience of asymmetrical warfare into a usable narrative order, or worse: to arrive at an understanding of the tasks at hand only to discover they lacked the resources to complete their mission. The war settled into something of a stalemate, with the island divided along ominous geopolitical lines. The Spanish controlled important cities and ports in the east. But the Cubans controlled almost everything in between, and by controlling almost everything in between had compromised the security of vital lines of communication and transportation among far-flung Spanish positions. "The rebels have increased in numbers," Walter Goodman recorded in his travel journal while visiting Santiago de Cuba in the early 1870s. "They have occupied all the districts which surround our town, destroyed the aqueduct, cut the telegraph wire, and intercepted the land mails to Havana. There is now no communication with the capital, save by sea."[155] As late as the final years of the war, Spanish control of the island was precarious. Recalled General T. Ochando: "With our forces thus concentrated to attend to the security and protection of invaluable property, we controlled only the towns and terrain upon which we stood. The rest of the Island was 'Cuba Libre,' wholly unfamiliar to us, covered with dense forests, without roads, and where the enemy encamped at will, rarely disturbed by our forces."[156]

The Spanish army command faced the daunting task of conducting military operations in the inhospitable habitat, knowledge of which remained confined mostly to the local population: "A topography about which exists an insuperable ignorance," colonial administration acknowledged, a "lack of knowledge of the mountainous regions as well as the entire topography of this province."[157]

Years of official indifference had rendered the lands of the east something of a terra incognita, unknown and unfamiliar, a vast, unmapped topography and uncharted terrain, without adequate road networks and lacking serviceable means of communication, and a population very much isolated from the west. One nationality, as the Spanish were wont to say, perhaps, but the east was a foreign country. "Not withstanding a population of such importance," observed Fabián Navarro during the war, "the inhabitants of this region not merely failed to receive but actively resisted the advance of education and progress. There hardly exists in the entire department any means of communication other than the steamships that serve the coastal cities."[158] General Antonio de Letona could only despair over the security implications of fragile communication systems and backward transportation networks. Three years before

Yara, Letona could only hope for divine beneficence, since "we are unable to rely on these resources, we are obliged to rely on God for the loyalty of the country."[159] The Spanish army "lacked any idea of the conditions and elements required to undertake the campaign necessary in Cuba," Leopoldo Barrios recalled. "Neither officers nor soldiers had any experience in the countryside of the Island, which constituted an absolute necessity given its special topography."[160] Usable maps of the eastern interior, to scale, did not exist. Officers often lacked knowledge of the terrain in which they were ordered to conduct military operations.[161] Journalist Antonio Pirala, an indefatigable chronicler of the war, understood the implications of "the vast expanse of the territory of the war zone, its topographical conditions, and the necessity to search out the enemy in such dispersed small groups distant even among themselves ... and at points where Spanish forces could not easily communicate with themselves." Pirala understood too the nature of the insurgency, recognizing that the war was not a matter of combat, that rare indeed were the occasions of battle, whereupon the Cubans "would disperse instantly and the object of our pursuit would disappear. More than fight them, it was necessary to hunt them down."[162]

A *peninsular* army dispatched to Cuba to wage a special kind of war was unprepared, without officers properly trained and adequately experienced for a colonial insurgency. Circumstances that readily invited denunciations of incompetence and ineptitude. "The authorities and officials who occupied leadership positions were carelessly selected," Leopoldo Barrios tersely insisted years later.[163] Journalist Antonio Pirala agreed, denouncing "the scarcity of competent officers [*jefes hábiles*] to direct operations [and] resulting in some disastrous results."[164]

Perhaps. But it was just as likely that the capacities of Spanish officers were circumscribed by the culture of their formation and the tradition of their professional education, trained to wage war by way of strategic, operational, and tactical conventions of European warfare, all of which were of limited value in Cuba. Newly graduated academy officers were especially prone to errors in judgment and mistakes in command.[165] Colonial insurgency was a type of warfare unfamiliar to most Spanish officers. "It was a war without front lines," historian Juan Luis Martín correctly emphasized.[166] Artillery was of limited use in the *monte*. Bayonets were of no value in the *manigua*. In close-quarter combat the machete possessed far greater versatility than the bayonet.[167] Colonel Francisco de Camps y Feliú, military commander of Holguín, early acknowledged the plight of the Spanish army. "The war in Cuba is of a very specialized nature," Camps recognized. "Artillery is useless in the *manigua*, and long-range arms are of little value in the forests, as the views of distances are very much reduced; that is to say, cannon and rifles of such value in Europe are of no advantage in close-quarter combat." Camps understood that the Spanish command had failed to comprehend the nature of warfare in Cuba. "The war on the island of Cuba is a difficult fight" (*una pelea difícil*), he brooded, "especially one in which good officers have much to learn," adding:

> I fear that European tactics will be of little value in Cuba.... The battalions cannot fight with the same precision as in Europe. Artillery cannot fire with the same accuracy.... Bayonet charges are nearly impossible due to the scattered nature of dispersed enemy units within densely overgrown terrain [*el fraccionamiento del enemigo en terrenos enmaniguados*].... The secret of the war in Cuba is found in the *manigua*, and it is necessary never to lose sight of the fact that 4,000 *insurrectos*, for example, have more importance than 40,000 [soldiers]. The invulnerability [of the enemy force] is in its small size [*pequeñez*]. The destruction of this small unit in a short time is the problem that our generals must resolve, totally disregarding the organization, the tactics, and the great military maneuvers executed in recent wars of Europe.... A military chief possessed of knowledge of this country and the customs of its inhabitants is worth more—much more—than a well-educated chief who had never set foot on the densely overgrown terrain [*terreno enmaniguado*].[168]

The ways of Old World warfare had rendered a superior army an inferior combat force. Spanish commanders continued to wage the type of war for which they had been trained. Infantry units conducted military operations encumbered with rifles fitted with bayonets, while cavalry units burdened with excess equipment and consisting principally of horsemen armed with lances and sabers were ill prepared to engage the mobile horsemen of the insurgent cavalry. "Our cavalry is inferior to that of the enemy," General Francisco de Acosta y Albear acknowledged grudgingly, "not for the lack of courage but because the arms, equipment, and saddles are not adequate for that type of war," all too often "forcing our units to retreat in disorganized fashion."[169] Leopoldo Barrios complained that "there were cavalry units still equipped with lances.... The infantry was equipped with bayonets and lacked machetes which were absolutely indispensable in the countryside campaign on the Island."[170] Between 1873 and 1874, Spanish cavalry units suffered costly defeats at the hands of the *insurrecto* horsemen: at Cocal del Olimpo, Sacra, Palo Seco, Naranjo-Mojacasabe, and most notably at Guásimas, where the Spanish suffered more than a thousand casualties.[171] All engagements in which Spanish soldiers were reported as having been "sliced to pieces" (*acuchillado*) by machete-wielding *insurrectos*, Spanish journalist Gonzalo Reparaz wrote—what José G. de la Concha would later acknowledge to have been "the disastrous campaign of 1873."[172]

The accounts of cavalry encounters had unsettling effects on Spanish soldiers. Emilio Soulère wrote of Spanish reversals in 1873 having produced "consequences that could not have been more pernicious. The collapse of army morale was so great that our soldiers could no longer bear the thought of confronting the machete-wielding *insurrectos*."[173] Major Leopoldo Barrios was succinct: "Let us admit honestly, our cavalry before the war, based upon models of old Europe, did not respond nor could it have responded to multiple missions required in Cuban operations."[174]

Spanish commanders conducted military operations with a sense of dread. Without the aid of guides (*prácticos*) to escort army columns into the interior, there was often no way in—and sometimes no way out. "What despairs me is that I do not have a single guide," General Sabas Marín bemoaned. "I am going completely blind [*voy completamente a ciegas*]. The enemy is encountered purely by chance. . . . If I had a guide familiar with this land I would mount some surprise attacks at night, but now it is impossible."[175] Spanish commanders faced the task of military operations within a population of 265,000 inhabitants stretched across the interior geography of Oriente, dispersed in scattered population clusters among isolated *caseríos*, *aldeas*, *villas*, *pueblos*, and *ciudades*, some with origins as *palenques* of runaway slaves, among rural communities by tradition and temperament hostile to the presence of colonial authority, a population of a "particular character and independence in its way of life" (*en su modo de vivir*), noted a census enumerator in 1841.[176] The army command could not but contemplate the prospects of recurring operations in the *manigua* with deepening misgivings, operations, General López de Letona complained, that "have always caused the loss of blood and have no importance except as a result of the sacrifice they have caused."[177]

Almost everything—impenetrable terrain, inhospitable topography, and unreliable lines of supply—conspired against Spanish soldiers in pursuit of an elusive enemy on lands populated by a people disposed to kill them. The insurgents "avail themselves of the services of individual sympathizers in all the localities their forces operate," General Acosta y Albear brooded during an occasion of rueful candor:

> For their communications they rely on the advantage provided by topography of the island . . . which is divided with inaccessible mountain ranges that extend from Cape San Antonio to Maisí Point [i.e., from one end of the island to the other]. . . . Within these mountains enemy bands take refuge to organize and regroup within ranges of densely forested zones. . . . These are people of admirable frugality, and the little they need with which to survive, by virtue of the habits of the country people, can be obtained from forests. They are very patient men with a great capacity to resist fatigue, who can undertake extraordinary marches on

foot or, like the best horsemen in the world, using the horses they acquire along the way and can scatter and disperse upon being pursued.... Is it not worthy of admiration that with only 8,000 or 10,000 men they can counteract our much larger army? If this enemy could be forced into continuous combat, we would have long ago disposed of him. But having on his side so many favorable advantages acquired as a result of experience and used with great effect, the only way to defeat him is to enclose him in a limited territory [*territorio limitado*], to be deprived of all sorts of resources and in which many columns, each sufficiently strong, would confront the enemy in combat.[178]

Spanish commanders dwelled at length—often incessantly—on the powerlessness of their circumstances, where mighty efforts produced mostly meager results. "Spain counts upon a powerful veteran army in Cuba," army chief of staff General José Riquelme bemoaned in 1872, "in possession of all necessary resources and aided by 60,000 Voluntarios." Riquelme could only sigh: "All the forts, military installations, towns, villages, hamlets, haciendas and farms, are in our possession. There is no place our soldiers cannot enter and enter with ease. Yet 4,000 to 5,000 *insurrectos* have our battalions in check; they live almost always in the forest, poorly dressed, without rest, without a hut in which to shelter themselves, and disposed only to take advantage and attack the enemy opportunistically."[179] José G. de la Concha wearied at military campaigns in the vastness of the eastern jurisdictions, where the population lived off the land effortlessly and which "pose great difficulties when it becomes necessary to engage the *insurrecto* bands in combat and pursue them by the traces of the trail they leave behind," to be drawn into the "extensive and dense forests, which often oblige a march of a single file stretching into large distances and vulnerable to attacks."[180]

Certainly Spanish military authorities could fashion a narrative to approximate the combat environment to which they were subject. "Ill-conceived marches in Cuba have caused us far more harm than the bullets and machetes of the rebels," Gonzalo Reparaz acknowledged.[181] The marches and countermarches took a frightful toll. "Those campaigns were extraordinarily difficult for the soldier who marched continually hungry and thirsty," Juan Escalera remembered, "in an environment where even the protection offered by the cover of shade failed to provide relief from the sun that threatened to reduce us to ashes."[182] Antonio Serra Orts was among the Spanish reinforcements who arrived in Cuba in 1875 and quickly learned about "the system" of Cuban warfare: "Avoid contact with the [Spanish troops]; tire the soldier so as to fill the hospitals with sick soldiers, exhaust Spain through prolongation of the war, and incur the constant and necessary costs in men, supplies, and war material."[183] Serra Orts was correct. General Máximo Gómez understood well: "The army of the

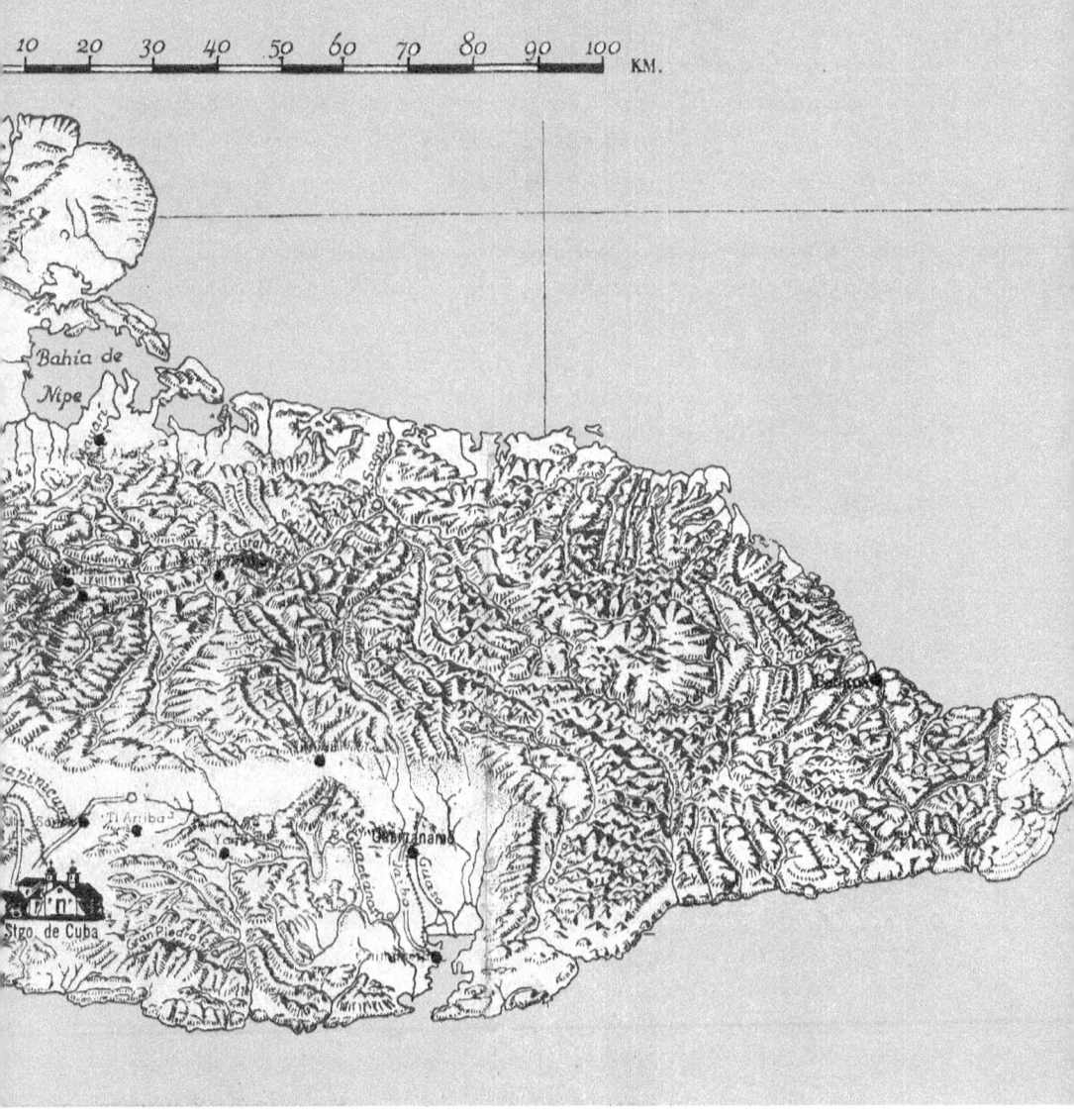

2.3 Oriente Province, ca. 1870s. SOURCE: http://www.latinamericanstudies.org.

enemy daily consumes itself in appalling marches and countermarches, and what bullets and machetes cannot achieve will be accomplished by the climate."[184]

Climate indeed. Everything was made intolerably worse by an insufferable climate, a condition aptly memorialized by novelist Anselmo Suárez y Romero in *Francisco* (1875) as "that time of year when the sun begins to suffocate the inhabitants of Cuba with heat."[185] Climate wreaked havoc on the ranks of the Spanish soldiery, sapping physical endurance and depleting collective morale. "The first enemy against which one must fight," *La Voz de Cuba* acknowledged, "is the climate, which favors the insurrection."[186] New recruits were especially susceptible to heat prostration upon arriving to Cuba.[187] "Never in my life had I experienced such an asphyxiating heat as that day in June," Captain Nicolás Estévanez recalled of his arrival to Santiago de Cuba.[188] Climate also caused problems in the maintenance of ammunition and supplies, resulting in the deterioration of rations, provisions, and ordnance, all compounded, of course, by the uncertainties of tenuous supply lines—and every now and again a hurricane: in October 1870, September 1873, September 1875, and October 1876.

Climate presented woes of another kind. Early spring through late autumn were the months of the seasonal rains and the accompanying episodic flooding, day after day, often for weeks at a time. "Every day," Eugenio Antonio Flores recalled, "at 3 p.m., with mathematical precision, the torrential downpours began, which ended approximately at 5 p.m., when the blistering sun reappeared." Flores long retained anguished memories of thirty-eight consecutive days of rain.[189]

The summer rains appear to have produced something of a culture shock to Spanish commanders. "He who has not seen it rain in Cuba has no idea what a biblical deluge must have been like," commented Gonzalo Reparaz.[190] Long days and nights of unyielding heat and unrelenting humidity. Spanish commanders could only look upon the prostration to which their troops succumbed with resigned despair. "The suffering [Spanish] army in Cuba," General Francisco de Acosta y Albear recalled in his memoirs, "subject to privations of every type, exposed to the inclemency of the tropical climate and lacking the means to attend to the pernicious consequences of climate, without rest to pursue the enemy across the floodplains, over nearly inaccessible forests, wading daily across flooding rivers, and enduring incessant fatigue ... was guided solely by its love of the Nation and consciousness of duty."[191]

But everything was worse than it appeared. The months of the seasonal rains and unrelieved heat were also the time of the mosquito, and of disease and illness, and inevitably a time of staggering mortality rates. Tropical illness, sickness, and infectious diseases ravaged the ranks of the Spanish army. Death arrived in many forms: yellow fever, malaria, dysentery, cholera, tuberculosis, smallpox, typhus, and heatstroke. Spanish soldiers often succumbed to yellow fever within days of their arrival in Cuba.[192] Illness often traveled along the very routes of convoy supply lines and transportation networks. In 1870 a virulent cholera outbreak was linked to a battalion of Spanish troops arriving by rail in Nuevitas after weeks of field operations in Puerto Príncipe.[193] And almost always everything was exacerbated by chronic malnutrition and vitamin deficiencies, producing conditions, historian Luis Navarro García suggested, that contributed "to the weakness of the soldiers, who lived in condition of anemia, rendering them vulnerable to all types of ailments," and where "a simple scratch or a simple abrasion would develop into sores and infections requiring months of treatment."[194]

The adversities to which Spanish soldiers were subject resulted in a frightful loss of life. Military operations were hampered by chronic conditions of inadequate medical attention and insufficient medicines, a scarcity of trained health care personnel and a shortage of hospitals and infirmaries. "The number of hospitals was insufficient for the number of patients," General Francisco de Acosta y Albear complained in 1873, "and many patients were released prematurely to make room for others; soldiers still convalescing were deployed with convoys in operations when they should have been in the hospital for another 15 to 30 days with proper nutrition. The infirmaries lacked everything."[195]

Spanish soldiers withered in plain view. Between 1869 and 1872 Ramón Hernández Poggio served as army physician attached to the principal military hospital in Havana and subsequently assigned to a number of field encampments, including occasional service with army columns on interior front lines. His accounts of Spanish military operations make for sober reading. "An implacable war," Hernández Poggio remembered, "where military tactics of the great armies were powerless to engage an enemy that depended solely on surprise and malice in its form of combat, and dispersing when he was deprived of advantage," where Spanish "troops scorched by the burning rays of the tropical sun marched in the rainy season, attired with light uniforms soaked through to the skin, over trails that had been transformed into immense lagoons, and whose only place of rest in the evening was the saturated grounds of the open field."[196] Hernández Poggio was especially critical of the marches, the deployment of army columns on four- or five-day military operations exposing soldiers to hardships of the climate, fatigue, hunger, and inevitably disease and tropical illness. He recounted his experience with a column of five officers and 107 soldiers operating south of the Sierra Maestra in October 1876:

> The column undertook the march over a wholly unfamiliar and rugged terrain, without the assistance of a guide, the reason why this unit lost its way in the immense and dense forests; unable to locate a usable road, suffering all kinds of

privations over the course of four days of operations, and without adequate food supplies; struggling against the heat and the torrential downpours occasioned by thunderstorms, on a terrain difficult to traverse as a result of the accumulated rainwater, and always with the preoccupation of a surprise ambush from the insurrectionary forces. Almost all troops succumbed to malnutrition, malaria, and a variety of endemic fevers.[197]

Climate and disease often combined to bring Spanish military operations to a complete halt. "The great mortality among the Spanish forces, rainy weather, and bad roads," US Vice-Consul C. H. Bithorn in Manzanillo reported tersely in the summer of 1869, "impede all military operations."[198] Federico Parreño Ballesteros recalled his military service in Cuba: "It is 10 a.m., the time of the terrible heat in these latitudes. The countryside seems to succumb to a still languor in response to a blistering temperature. The breeze is also stilled, as if the radiance of the sun scorched its wings.... The rarefied air suffocates. The silent soldier advances slowly... his body bathed in sweat that soaks his clothing."[199] Captain General Cándido Pieltain suspended operations in the summer of 1873 to enable the army to prepare for an "energetic defense" in the autumn, specifically "to economize for the time being all those operations that have as their objective to discover [the enemy's] most hidden camps, and which demand difficult marches and incessant movements," noting that "the season we are presently passing through, with its excessive rigor in this dreadful climate, requires the need to care for the health and lives of our valiant soldiers."[200] Simply put, Pieltain could not conduct military operations:

> The climatic conditions and the terrain of Cuba . . . obstruct our ability to conduct large-scale offensive operations during long periods of the year. From April to October Cuba is in the season of rains and storms . . . with the alarming onset of endemic and deadly illnesses that serve to fill the hospitals and clinics and decimate the European population. . . . Yellow fever, malaria, cholera, tetanus, dysentery, and deadly fevers are all fearsome enemies to expose troops in their operations as they march across swampy terrain . . . to suffer the pernicious consequences of those sudden tropical downpours, of the daily withering sun to which they succumb.[201]

"Much sickness prevails among the newly arrived Spanish troops," US Vice-Consul A. E. Phillips in Santiago de Cuba reported in 1870, "who find it impossible to endure the climate. It is estimated that fifty percent of the Spanish volunteers from sickness are put *hors du combat*; the hospitals are full to overflowing.... It is impossible for any force that Spain can send to exterminate the rebel force, owing to the climate and topography of the country."[202]

The Cuerpo de Sanidad Militar operated a total of thirty-eight military hospitals in Havana and in the provincial cities, as well as scores of field hospitals and temporary infirmaries located in the interior at or near sites of military operations. Over the course of ten years of war, hundreds of thousands of Spanish soldiers and sailors were admitted—often repeatedly—to hospital facilities across the island.[203] In one year alone, in 1874, the military hospital of Havana received fifteen thousand soldiers stricken with cholera, yellow fever, and smallpox.[204] It must be presumed that at any given time between 1868 and 1878, significant numbers of Spanish soldiers were rendered unfit for military operations. Colonel Luis Otero y Pimentel recalled the need to transfer in 1874 more than four hundred soldiers deemed unfit for military service from Nuevitas to Havana hospitals.[205]

The Spanish army could not sustain military operations in the *manigua*. "Notwithstanding the care that I devote to the health of my troops," General Antonio López de Letona despaired early in the war, "battalions of 800 men have been reduced to 350–400 soldiers as a result of yellow fever, cholera, and dysentery. Every single day of operations reduces my troops by ten percent, who I cannot leave behind en route, with an attending loss of 8 men for each stretcher and who are irremediably condemned [*irremisiblemente condenados*] to death if they remain in these conditions for any more than four or five days."[206] Juan Escalera remembered the toll of the tropics during one military operation: "The first day, 35 stricken soldiers died. On the second day, another 42. On the third, 43. Those of us who survived looked as if we belonged more to the world of shadows than the real world [*pertenecíamos más bien al mundo de la sombra que al mundo real*]; we were not men, we were ghosts."[207] Over the span of five months from 1869 to 1870, seventy officers and seven hundred troops of the San Quintín battalion perished.[208] Of the additional 82,500 troops deployed to Cuba in 1874, US Consul Caleb Cushing in Madrid reported learning, some "36,412 have succumbed in the field or from disease, leaving only a nominal force of say 46,000 (many of whom must be invalids) for present service of the government."[209]

But it was at the level of the field hospitals and infirmaries located in the distant war zones of the interior that the grim mortality of the Spanish soldiery was laid bare. Physician Hernández Poggio was appalled at conditions in the encampments in the east, situated in "dense thickets and extensive forests, where sunlight never reached resulting in a constant dense humidity," all of which served to transform the encampments into breeding grounds for "terrible and deadly illnesses among those soldiers." Hernández Poggio added, "Conditions having no less fatal consequences: the quality and the quantity of available water. If efforts were made to establish encampments in the vicinity of rivers and creeks, the waters were generally muddy and slow flowing, bearing decaying vegetable matter, dead animals, by-products of sugar production, all organic matter . . . creating sites of putrification."[210]

The registries of the field hospitals in the eastern jurisdictions provide somber testimony of places far away and a time long ago, where the appalling loss of life assumed fully the condition of a daily normal. Day after day, scribbled entries chronicled the deaths of scores of soldiers, mostly young recruits between late adolescence and their early twenties, deaths attributed variously to yellow fever, malaria and its most virulent form *fiebre perniciosa*, dysentery, typhoid, cholera, and chronic diarrhea, as well as a host of miscellaneous illnesses, including anasarca, hepatitis, acute bronchitis, atopic fever, enteritis, tuberculosis, anemia, pleurisy, and deaths attributed to heart attack, "infection," and—occasionally—wounds suffered in combat. Wounded and weakened soldiers, returning from days of military operations, entered makeshift hospitals with an assortment of infirmities and in varying stages of illness, near collapse, often with fevers and suffering from gangrene, to be treated by physicians with limited field-care experience, working under execrable conditions and scarcities of all types. Scores perished as a result of postoperative infections.[211] And always, Captain General Cándido Pieltain commented with understated candor, operations beset with shortages of personnel and lacking "the desirable quantities of supplies."[212]

Army physician Santiago Ramón y Cajal served at two Spanish field hospitals at Vista Hermosa and San Isidro during 1874–75, both located near zones of Spanish military operations in Camagüey Province. The Vista Hermosa facility, the future Nobel Prize winner recalled years later, consisted "of an enormous wooden barracks, with a palm-thatched roof and 200 beds filled with soldiers sick with malaria and dysentery, all from the columns engaged in military operations in Camagüey." Vista Hermosa was located within the "miasma of the swamps" and subject continuously to a relentless onslaught of insects: "We were surrounded by clouds of mosquitos. In addition to the *anopheles claviger* mosquito, the common carrier of the malarial protozoan, we were constantly besieged by the nearly invisible sandfly [*jején*] and an army of innumerable fleas, cockroaches, and ants. Our beds were enveloped by vast waves of parasitic life, which devoured our provisions and tormented us at all times." Ramón y Cajal discovered conditions of widespread alcohol abuse among the army physicians of the hospital encampment, a condition that "more than yellow fever could be considered the best ally of the Cuban insurgents." Subsequently transferred to San Isidro, Ramón y Cajal learned that two-thirds of the physicians and nurses were themselves ill and unable to care for patients, with a chronic shortage of medicines and food supplies. And almost everywhere along the supply chain of Cuerpo de Sanidad Militar, from the highest levels of authority to the field infirmaries, was pilfering, embezzlement, graft, and corruption: from the military pharmacies in Havana, to provincial distributors in Puerto Príncipe, to the hospital administrators at Vista Hermosa and San Isidro.[213] General Emilio Mola Vidal later recalled these years with pained candor, remembering "the multitude of men deployed without the slightest idea [of their mission], without adequate arms and equipment," adding, "In Cuba our military incapacity was made manifest, reaching shameful extremes in every aspect [of the campaign], especially with regard to the care of military personnel. Medical service, for example, was so deficient that the terrible yellow fever decimated entire expeditionary battalions. Quartermaster services did not exist, which obliged the troops to live off the land."[214]

Estimates of the mortality of Spanish soldiers in Cuba are incomplete and vary widely, but in almost every instance the estimates tend toward a staggering loss of life due principally to disease and tropical illness. Spanish Surgeon General José Clairac estimated a total of 65,000 deaths due directly to smallpox, yellow fever, and cholera.[215] Journalist Antonio Pirala estimated that Spain had deployed to Cuba a total of 175,000 troops, nearly 100,000 of whom had perished during the war, without including an additional 11,000 troops disabled in the war and another 14,000 soldiers who returned to Spain in various stages of illness; of the 100,000 soldiers who perished in Cuba, Pirala suggested, 8,112 died as a result of combat (*resultas de las acciones de guerra*) and 91,112 perished as a result of illness.[216] Lieutenant Colonel Francisco de Moya insisted that 120,000 men had perished: 8 out of every 100 soldiers due to combat, 92 out of every 100 as a result of illness.[217] "Death has depleted your ranks more, much more," Captain General Joaquín Jovellar acknowledged publicly to army officers and soldiers at the end of the war, "infinitely more in the encampments and on the grim marches than in combat. You have been battered by the climate." Jovellar estimated that of the total of 290,000 soldiers to have served in Cuba, 80,000 had perished.[218] US Minister Daniel Sickles calculated a loss of 60,000 troops during the first four years of the war.[219] Colonels Francisco de Camps y Feliú and Luis Otero y Pimentel and Major Leopoldo Barrios estimated a total of 200,000 deaths.[220]

Historians similarly offer different estimates. Luis Eugenio Togores calculates that of the total of 181,040 soldiers deployed to Cuba, 88,513 perished as a result of disease and illness, with another 25,122 troops repatriated with chronic illnesses and infirmities.[221] Historian Eladio Baldovín Ruiz determined that a total of 57,495 soldiers perished: 3,469 as a result of military operations, 54,086 the result of illness and disease.²²² Andreas Stucki indicates a total of 145,884 deaths, of which 133,555 were attributed to illness.²²³

A consensus does emerge: many tens of thousands of Spanish soldiers perished in the *manigua*. "Cuba will forever be called the horrific cemetery of the Spaniards" (*el espantoso cementerio de los españoles*), brooded Lieutenant Colonel Luis Otero y Pimentel years later.²²⁴

Years of war took their toll on Spanish officers and men in other ways. The loss of morale and motivation further weakened war-weary troops. Incidents of alcoholism and desertions were on the rise. Pay was in arrears, in some instances up to as many as five months overdue.²²⁵ Captain General Cándido Pieltain arrived in Cuba in 1873, five years into the war, and was horrified to discover the disarray into which the Spanish army had plunged. Pieltain recorded a catalog of problems: "Careless recruitment, poor training, the lack of adequate acclimatization and instruction, chronic fatigue, a deterioration of military discipline, inadequate food supplies, inadequate means of overland transportation, carelessness in matters related to uniforms, lack of proper arms, divisive rancor, resentment, and rivalries among military commanders due to disparities in pay, the abandonment of best practices—all in the face of an astute and almost always invisible enemy."²²⁶ Many were boys, Adolfo Jiménez Castellanos later lamented, "hardly more than adolescents, who succumbed readily to illness and were incapacitated for military service.... They received no training either in Spain or in Cuba, for the conventional wisdom held that their comrades would teach them everything they needed to know.... They were often sent into the field without even target practice."²²⁷

There seemed to be no way to register increments of Spanish military success, such as they were, in part because there was no defined front line, in part because there was no discernible enemy. The insurgency had been contained principally in the remoteness of the eastern jurisdictions, to be sure, but it persisted with demonstrable capacity to sustain itself—perhaps indefinitely, some Spanish commanders feared—and always a threat to expand beyond the confines of its provincial origins. A fear not unfounded. As late as 1875, Máximo Gómez crossed the *trocha* into Las Villas at the head of a combined infantry and cavalry force of nearly a thousand troops, proclaiming that "the operations to which preference will be given will be the destruction of the estates that serve to provide benefits to the enemy, principally the sugar estates."²²⁸

A campaign against an elusive enemy given to ambush and flight, thereupon to dissolve into the *manigua*, produced its own logic of warfare, a way to act out and act upon the weariness of military operations seeming often as senseless as they were useless. The enemy was not to be seen anywhere, or perhaps the enemy was everywhere, in plain sight: within the scores of rural communities in the interior, among the farms and fields, within the *pacífico* population that was perhaps not so pacific. Valmaseda had carried the war deep into the interior, operations that served to plunge rural communities of eastern Cuba into disarray and extended the convulsions of the conflict into the countryside. He declared the eastern rural interior a proscribed space, posting in 1869 a proclamation to the "inhabitants of the countryside," warning that "all men above 15 years of age found outside the confines of their *fincas* without justified reason" were to be summarily executed. Every uninhabited home would be razed; every home that did not display a white flag "as a signal that its occupants desired peace" would be reduced to ashes. Women who were not living in their own homes or the homes of relatives were to be "reconcentrated into the towns of Jiguaní or Bayamo, where maintenance [would] be provided. The women who [did] not present themselves [would] be forcibly relocated."[229] Something of a total war against the rural population, what *insurrecto* commander Melchor Loret de Mola recalled as "a bloody iniquitous war without quarter, of extermination against the Cubans."[230] "A war of extermination," US Vice-Consul A. E. Phillips in Santiago de Cuba agreed.[231]

Spanish wrath was increasingly directed against the rural population of noncombatants, often indiscriminately but not haphazardly, acts of tactical purport and punitive retribution sustained with single-minded resolve: all in all, part of a studied strategy of reconcentration of the rural population devised by General Valmaseda's chief of staff Colonel Valeriano Weyler, designed to deprive the insurgency of support and sustenance, laying waste to the rural economy, against fields and farms, against the herds of livestock and the patches of cultivation, families dislocated and households disrupted.[232] One official report of Spanish military operations in the Sierra Cubitas in Camagüey against *insurrecto* commander Salomé Hernández Villegas offers insight into the character of pacification:

> Forces under the command of Lieutenant Colonel José Bergel reconnoitered scrupulously all of the Cubitas mountain range, to the most remote and impenetrable points, and successfully dispersed the inhabitants of the sierra from their hideouts, and scattered the band of Salomé Hernández that fled in many different directions.... The result of the operations has been to have cleaned the Cubitas mountains not only of the enemy but of its inhabitants [*ha sido haber quedado limpia no solo de enemigos sino de habitantes*], having destroyed all their food supplies and crops, and destroying too what supplies they had accumulated in reserve, seizing arms and ammunition ... and burning 19 *ranchos*, 153 *bohíos*,

two encampments each with more than 100 *bohíos*, 27 *estancias*, and seizing 24 horses with saddles and bridles.²³³

The war settled into a dismal stalemate, a desultory warfare of skirmishes and ambushes, of futile marches and failed operations. An army of some 150,000 officers and men by the early 1870s was deployed principally in the eastern third of the island, seemingly mired in continuous military operations without consequences. The deployment of additional tens of thousands of *peninsular* troops, year after year, it seemed, to no effect. "There was no reason for Spain to fear the loss of the island," historian Luis Navarro García correctly wrote of the middle years of the war, "but it was not at all clear how and when the conflict would be brought to an end."²³⁴

Few indeed were the Spanish commanders who failed to develop an appreciation of the complexity of the war in Cuba, to understand that the mere continued presence of armed insurgents retaining the capacity to mount even limited military operations signified a moral defeat. "Merely our permanence in the fields of the revolution," *insurrecto* commander Serafín Espinosa y Ramos was persuaded, "wherever we may have been, represented an important service to the *patria*, for it demonstrated to the government of Spain our determination to persevere to the end with victory or death, notwithstanding the adversities and the miseries."²³⁵

Nor did Spanish commanders fail to understand that Cubans in arms were not the only enemies: indeed, to realize that Cubans in arms were not even the principal enemies.²³⁶ The real enemies were the *manigua*, the *monte*, and the mosquito. And malaria, yellow fever, and smallpox. And the malaise of demoralization that coursed its way through the ranks and into the officer corps—all circumstances interrelated, of course, but also all conditions mostly beyond the immediate reach of remedy. And all the while casualties continued to mount.

A consensus settled within the Spanish army command during the early 1870s, conveyed in official communiqués and in personal correspondence, remembered and recorded as anguished memoirs, something of a recognition that things were going poorly—and not getting better. A time of disheartening duress given coherent narrative structure, articulated as doctrinal musings in the form of acknowledgment of the limits of Spanish capacities: the recognition of a stalled war, a stalemate that was tantamount to defeat, the army command coming to understand that Spain could not sustain indefinitely a war in the form of a standstill. A vast Spanish army fought to a draw by loosely organized and lightly armed colonial insurgents. How utterly incongruous. "The war could not continue in the direction that it was taking without leading to catastrophic consequences," Antonio Pirala feared.²³⁷

These were years of sober realization of the realities of a war that would not yield to the received wisdom of conventional warfare, of Spanish commanders learning what they did not know and unlearning what they knew, and a paradigm shift to accommodate the possibility of tactical adjustment and strategic adaptation. "None of this," Major Leopoldo Barrios later acknowledged, "developed in any clear manner during the early months of the war... but rather evolved as an organic and logistical facet of operations."[238] They came to recognize the need to enlist the services of Cubans in the *manigua* and the *monte*, Cubans who possessed habitat knowledge, with an understanding of the ways of the rural interior and familiarity with the landscape of the insurgency, to conduct reconnaissance and surveillance, to gather intelligence—"persons familiar with the terrain and accustomed to the privations attending life in the wilderness," *Diario de la Marina* insisted—adapted to the climate and endowed with the physiology of the tropics to fend off the illnesses that visited havoc upon Spanish soldiers.[239] Cubans to serve as *prácticos*: "a man very knowledgeable" (*muy conocedor*), wrote Lieutenant Antonio del Rosal, "not only of the terrain but also of the traces [*rastros*] left behind by persons and animals that traverse across the *monte*, from which he deduces their number and many other details."[240] *Prácticos* in the company of *peninsular* army units, familiar with the local fauna and flora, also to teach Spanish troops how to live off the land, to sustain themselves with foodstuffs in the *manigua* from local fruit trees and plants.[241] Spain would train, equip, and pay Cubans to enroll in the service of Spain against the *mambises*. "Given the unique character of the country and the war in which we were engaged," Captain General Cándido Pieltain remembered, "one of the most urgent necessities recognized from the very outset of the earliest operations was the need to rely upon on numerous, intelligent, and loyal *prácticos* who would escort the troops with security through the labyrinths of the forests and *manigua*, where the enemy was constantly stalking to take advantage of our inexperienced soldiers."[242]

Guerrillas, *guerrilleros*, and *contra-guerrillas* were the names given to Cubans recruited into service with the Spanish army, to engage the *mambises* on their own terms, to operate within the densities of the *manigua* and the *monte*, with knowledge of the terrain and familiarity with the topography. New modes of military operation, new methods of warfare, new agents of war. "Entire nights passing through ambushes after long marches," *Diario de la Marina* described the new warfare in one account of guerrilla operations in Remedios, "deprived of provisions and having to search for the supplies of the enemy for their own use; to encamp in their miasma-infected strongholds and endure all types of privations and exhaustion."[243] To recruit soldiers "hardened and formed by the withering fatigue of the campaign," José de Granda insisted, "who are able to endure the rigor of the tropical climate, [who recognize] that the enemy is astute and refuses to be defeated."[244] Leopoldo Barrios came to understand the implications of "an irregular struggle" (*una lucha irregular*), including "soldiers selected who demonstrated a special aptitude":

> One of the details that stood out was [our] ignorance of the geographic topography of the country. As a result, more than in any other country, all the forces engaged in operations needed the constant assistance of guides, without whom they could hardly take a step outside the confines of the towns to which they were deployed. These guides were peasants [*guajiros*], sometimes white, other times black, who more or less steadfastly were taken into the service of the troops. The necessity of their service was of such dire and necessary urgency as to require officially the appointment of one or more guides to each corps and column in operations.[245]

"It is without reservation," General José Riquelme pleaded with Captain General Francisco de Ceballos in 1872, "that I assure Your Excellency that the complete organization of these *contra-guerrillas* is an objective of the greatest importance to which we must attend, even if it were to require the cost of great sacrifice," and added:

> The *contra-guerrillas* are called upon to seek out the enemy that refuses to engage in combat and rouse them out of their positions; to discover their operations and surround their encampments and to make impossible the movement of small groups that act in search of foodstuffs and livestock. In a word, to subject them to a state of siege in their own territory. The *contra-guerrillas* discover and follow their trails, make it difficult for the enemy to recruit men who dwell in the *monte*, investigate the remote corners where they care for their wounded and ill, and give notice to the columns on operations when their numbers are insufficient. When they march with the columns, they always assume the position of vanguard and cover the flanks. . . . They are advanced sentinels against the enemy, they seek out livestock for our troops and serve as guides and scouts. But that is not all: assigned in a timely fashion and with the necessary knowledge they aid the detachments, protect overland communications and telegraph, and at any given moment can mobilize 600–800 men at a given point, to which they are transferred with rapidity and without fatigue.[246]

The formal establishment of an armed auxiliary—as "a regular and homogenous organization"—was completed in 1872 with the organization of three guerrilla units: *guerrillas volantes*, *guerrillas locales*, and *guerrillas de batallón*, each designed to respond to the "peculiarities" of the insurgency:

> In the special war of Cuba, where it is necessary to pursue an enemy who always refuses to engage in combat except on those occasions in which he enjoys the

advantage of numbers and position, it is necessary to deploy troops well adept at stalking the trails and who can mount attacks as quickly as they can effect retreats.... It is necessary also that they be ideally suited to pursue the enemy's reconnaissance patrols assigned to gather livestock, maintain communications between encampments and, in sum, to attend to all other indispensable tasks. The experience of more than three years has demonstrated that no other units perform these tasks better than the *contra-guerrillas*.[247]

Guerrillas volantes were deployed within specified zones of operation, required to possess knowledge of the character and customs of members of the community (*convecinos*) as well as familiarity with the terrain in which they operated. The ranks of the *guerrillas locales* included local residents—"*todos hijos del país*," commented General Adolfo Jiménez Castellanos—assigned to guard the communities from which they were from, to protect local agricultural production and defend local economies.[248] The *guerrillas de batallón* were assigned to *peninsular* battalions and organized as combat units and deployed in military operations as *prácticos*, in reconnaissance and surveillance, and as escorts to protect the flanks and the forward positions of Spanish columns.[249] "The presence of good guerrillas allows for a thorough reconnaissance of the field," General Francisco de Acosta y Albear explained, "without the necessity to tire the troops with useless marches."[250] Guerrillas conducted nighttime military operations in the *manigua*, led by experienced *prácticos*, and wreaked havoc on insurgent encampments. "A great number of Cubans have fought on our side," General Ochando exulted, "organized into companies of... *guerrillas locales* and *guerrillas de batallón*, demonstrating great valor and constancy... and giving evidence of an indisputable loyalty to the Spanish cause," adding:

> They have struggled tirelessly, on their own and with our columns, to which they have rendered inestimable cooperation, offering constantly invaluable service in matters of exploration and reconnaissance.... The *hijos de Cuba*, finally, have been also among the innumerable guides for our columns, possessed of deep knowledge of the lands, the mountains, their resources and what the enemy would need, without which many of our operations would have been difficult to complete and would have resulted in meager results.[251]

"It is necessary," the General Order of May 1873 stipulated, "to rely always on the service of good *prácticos*, who escort the troops with total security and under the conditions that the nature of operations require."[252]

The Spanish army command initially organized a total of thirty-five units of *guerrillas locales* and twenty-nine units of *guerrillas volantes*, with an estimated total of

Table 2.1 Authorized Strength of Guerrillas, ca. 1876

GUERRILLAS VOLANTES

Division I (Puerto Príncipe)	1,250
Division II (Tunas)	375
Division III (Bayamo)	625
Division IV (Bueycito/Vicana Cañizal)	1,405
Total	3,655

GUERRILLAS LOCALES

Division I

Guanaja	57
Magarambomba	115
Caobillas	115
San Gerónimo	115
Santa Cruz	115
Cascorro	115
Minas	115
Total	747

Division II

Las Tunas	80
San Andrés	125
San Agustín	125
Fray Benito	150
Cuaba	125
Yareyal	100
Velasco	80
Maniabon	125
Guamo	50
Salados	80
Total	1,040

(continues)

Table 2.1 cont'd

Division III

Bayamo	60
Baire Arriba	60
Laguna Blanca	60
Yara	100
Bueycito	60
Guias de Ampudia	120
Cauto	80
Total	**540**

Division IV

Sagua	100
Jamaica	50
Yeguas	50
Caney	50
Palma	100
Remanganaguas	50
Cobre	50
Ti-Arriba	50
Línea de Puertos	50
Demajayabo	50
Dos Caminos	50
Total	**650**
Total	**6,632**

SOURCE: José L. Riquelme, *Contestación a la memoria publicada por el Sr. Marqués de La Habana sobre su último mando en Cuba* (Madrid, 1876).

6,600 officers and soldiers (see table 2.1).[253] Guerrilla recruits received monthly stipends ranging between 45 and 60 pesos for officers and 15 and 30 pesos for soldiers—"well-paid," Barrios wrote—with allotments of daily rations and assigned horses, saddles, and arms.[254] An estimated 1,000 *guerrillas de batallón* were assigned to serve with *peninsular* army units operating in the eastern jurisdictions. Military authorities subsequently expanded the guerrilla units with an additional cavalry unit—*guerrillas montadas*—to conduct joint operations with the Spanish cavalry: a "product of necessity," Major Leopoldo Barrios conceded, "required by circumstances, a small group of irregular cavalry that emerged with the name of *guerrillas montadas*, organized much later and taking form slowly."[255] The *guerrillas montadas*—"in imitation of the enemy," commented Emilio Soulère—were assigned to specific tasks within the battalion.[256]

> The name *guerrillero* in the Cuban campaign served to designate groups of select soldiers who demonstrated a special aptitude, also providing the army columns specialized services, generally comparable to what a light cavalry offers larger units. That is to say, similar to its modern form.... They serve as the antennas of columns in operation, inserting themselves between the columns in making contact with the enemy, hiding their presence or movements through diversionary actions, drawing fire to themselves and serving as messengers and constant contacts among the columns and population centers occupied by our troops.[257]

"Magnificent mounted *guerrillas*" (*magníficas guerrillas á caballo*), exulted Spanish Lieutenant Colonel Eusebio Sáenz, "who as often undertake machete charges into battle as assaults with swords and rifles."[258] "With the services of the guerrillas the country can be pacified," a confident General Francisco de Acosta y Albear predicted in 1872, at about the same time that José Ferrer de Couto celebrated "the Cuban forces that have these past four years defended the Spanish flag in Cuba with sustained resolve."[259]

Guerrilla units expanded all through the 1870s, although precise numbers are difficult to ascertain. *Insurrecto* General Eusebio Hernández estimated a total of 36,000 Cubans had served as guerrillas during the war. Historian José Luciano Franco calculated a total of 30,000 Cubans had enrolled in the ranks of the guerrillas.[260] Historian Santiago Perinat agrees, suggesting that at the height of the insurgency, the *insurrecto* forces never surpassed 7,000 officers and men, while the number of Cubans in guerrilla service reached 30,000.[261]

A complicated picture emerges from the fields of insurgent Cuba during the 1870s. The character of the insurrection had changed. Midway into the ten years, the Cuban purpose had veered unabashedly toward an antislavery stance—and not unrelated: ever-increasing numbers of blacks within the insurgency and a greater proportion of insurgent officers. *New York Herald* correspondent James O'Kelly visited the encampment of Calixto García to report that "about one-third of the fighting men are white, and the majority of the other two-thirds are of color other than black, all shades of brown predominating."[262] José Luciano Franco indicated that by 1874–75, the insurgent forces consisted of an estimated eight thousand troops, "the majority of whom were black."²⁶³ White *insurrecto* commanders also perceived the expanding presence of blacks—at times, not without chagrin. "The size of the army has diminished to such an extent," Ignacio Mora confided to his campaign diary in mid-1873, "that two-thirds of them are blacks from the coffee estates and sugar mills, that is to say, savages who live better off in the war than on the estates of their masters." And a year later: "The insurrection is reduced entirely to men of color, brutalized by slavery, and a small number of white peasants."²⁶⁴

Accounts of a preponderance of soldiers of color within the ranks of the insurgency are difficult to corroborate. Certainly anecdotal observations and first-person accounts tend to confirm an expanding participation of blacks. Certainly too the perception gained wide currency by the mid-1870s, from within the insurgency and from the outside. Nor perhaps does it matter that the changing demographics of the insurgency cannot be confirmed, for the perceptions can indeed be verified, and it was on the basis of these perceptions that the protagonists of the war arrived at an understanding of the social reality from which their choices were determined.

The colonial officialdom had more than passing interest in drawing attention to the expanding prominence of blacks in the insurgency, of course, for it served to corroborate the ever-present threat of *el desbordamiento de los negros* from which Spanish authorities advanced the claim to govern. "The immense majority of the *insurrectos* I saw," Lieutenant Antonio del Rosal wrote in 1873, "were blacks and mulattos. . . . There were large numbers of black officers, even chiefs and generals."²⁶⁵ The "insurrection is almost a race war," General Francisco de Acosta y Albear warned in 1875.²⁶⁶ José Alvarez Pérez, returned to Spain after service in Cuba, could attest personally to the ferocity of the war resulting from "confronting an enemy consisting mostly of blacks and mulattos who waged a notoriously savage campaign."²⁶⁷ Captain General José G. de la Concha was apocalyptic. "The immense majority of the *insurrectos*," de la Concha warned, "consisted of blacks [and] mulattos and it was apparent . . . that Máximo Gómez depended upon elements of color in order to transform a war that had commenced by proclaiming the independence of Cuba into a race war."²⁶⁸ The moral was not difficult to divine: more than ever, the Spanish presence was necessary to defend the racial hierarchies upon which the prevailing order of things depended. The Madrid daily *La Epoca* made the point explicitly:

> Within the colored race [*la raza de color*] an estimated 300,000 are African by birth, who have come to adulthood in a savage state and remain yet to be completely civilized. They do not possess even the small amount of civilization that the American slaves possess. With this material it would have been impossible to construct a nation, and if Spain had seen itself obliged to withdraw, the white

race would have fallen victim to the savage passions of these barbarians. Cuba would have been converted into a second Saint-Domingue.[269]

Colonial authorities had long deployed the specter of race war as a usable narrative device to sustain the claim of Spanish sovereignty, of course. But it was more complicated. The army command understood the sociology of the insurgency, and understood too that the perception of an insurgency having sustained itself principally through the expanding presence of *insurrectos* of color implied something more than useful propaganda fodder. It also suggested a way to redress the balance of social forces that had brought the war to a near standstill, to develop the means through which to incorporate into the loyalist polity—in a manner of speaking—the population of color in defense of the colonial regime. Yara had accelerated the debate over the abolition of slavery in Cuba. The ambiguous antislavery position of the *insurrecto* leadership was met by an equally timid Spanish abolition project in the form of the Moret Law, an effort by Spain, historian Rebecca Scott suggested, "to capture the apparent moral high ground from the insurgents and to win gratitude from freed slaves and free people of color."[270] Among the provisions of the Moret Law included freedom granted to all children born of enslaved mothers, the establishment of the *patronato* as an apprenticeship transition toward freedom, and Article III declaring free all slaves having served in defense of Spanish sovereignty.

By the early 1870s, authorities had arrived at an understanding of the advantage of recruiting Cubans of color into Spanish service. An anomalous politics, to be sure: Captain General José G. de la Concha having fomented racial animus for political ends and at the same time practicing racial solicitude for military purposes. De la Concha returned to Havana to resume the captaincy general in 1874, and almost immediately revived the battalions of *pardos* and *morenos*. An insurgency sustained principally by an expanding presence of blacks, as the Spanish themselves had propounded, suggested an opportunity to weaken the insurgency by accommodating within the interstices of the fractured colonial polity the presence of blacks in military service. With the pending abolition of slavery, Antonio Pirala commented, "it was necessary to count upon the support and commitment of that race ... all of which counseled the expansion of the *tropas de color* and its definitive organization as an integral part of the permanent army of the Island."[271]

Colonial authorities organized a total of eight battalions of *pardos* and *morenos*, each consisting of 750 soldiers commanded by officers accorded the same considerations as commanders in the Spanish army, with the same pay, privileges, rations, and status as their counterparts in the *peninsular* army.[272] The army command also organized companies of slaves (*libertos*) levied from the *dotaciones* across the island, mostly to undertake manual labor attending to the needs of Spanish encampments and military operations. "Our lives settled into giving orders to blacks," Juan Escalera recalled of the arrival of a *liberto* company to his unit, "to complete the work that previously had been entrusted to us."²⁷³

Spanish authorities were pleased with the results. "Large numbers of blacks and mulattos have enrolled in our ranks," General T. Ochando reported, "as much as volunteer soldiers as *guerrilleros*, in the battalions of *milicias de color*, as free men and as workers.... The entire island is covered with their military [public] works, *trochas*, towers, forts, barracks, hospitals, warehouses, bridges, roads, and telegraph lines."²⁷⁴ Ochando noted that "all the warehouses for foodstuff and supplies, hospitals, and barracks to aid troops in military operations were constructed by *milicias de color*, "whose experience with the resources of the forest for these types of works allowed for efficiency and economy."²⁷⁵ In the novel *Misterios de Cuba* (1893), writer Francisco Ortiz offered a vivid scene of

> a small group of whites, blacks, and mestizos which, although armed for war for the defense of the country, did not correspond to any established class of permanent militia; both in its uniform and in its arms, the difference was notable. Some of the men who made up this group mounted horses atop pack saddles, others were on foot barefooted.... These armed groups were organized to fight the insurrection, commanded by improvised chiefs, and Juan Pérez was one of these officers who operated within that topography with his squadron as a guide.... The guerrilla [unit] that Juan Pérez commanded consisted of ten to twelve horsemen, most of them poorly mounted and ill-dressed but well-armed.... The men of Pérez's squadron consisted of dedicated soldiers, mostly countrymen [*hombres del campo*], mulattos and blacks who had signed up for the campaign.²⁷⁶

Not a new politics, of course, for the premise of the battalions of color had antecedents early in the nineteenth century. But in 1874, *pardos* and *morenos* were summoned to military service with a new urgency. The establishment of the *milicias*, de la Concha insisted, was "of the greatest military and political importance," a way "to rectify the ill-conceived policies toward the *gente de color* who formed the majority of the insurgent bands, for among them love of Spain had also been the dominant sentiment."²⁷⁷ That the new battalions of *pardos* and *morenos* might act to encourage defections among the *insurrectos* of color, and thereby deplete the insurgent ranks, seemed to promise another advantage: "To deplete the rank and file of the insurrection of the class of free blacks as well as slaves," de la Concha argued, to offer amnesty and thereupon "to grant a general pardon and admit the *insurrectos* of color into the *milicias* and in the companies of *libertos*, preserving in them the positions they had attained in the insurrection, and those who had been slaves to remain free."[278]

The *insurrecto* leadership observed these developments with deepening disquiet, understanding the larger implications of Spanish policy and appreciating too the significance of the shifting balance of social forces. "The spies and contacts in Puerto Príncipe indicate that 1,000 blacks have arrived in the city," Ignacio Mora noted in his diary in mid-1874, "and that Concha is expected to arrive with another 4,000." Mora pondered the implications:

> Today that force does not have any importance. But later on those blacks will have an important and transcendental impact. The blacks who have entered in the military service [of Spain] have been mobilized hastily. Bestialized [*envilecidos*] by slavery, accustomed to work and privation, [military] service offers them a better life, and as a result of the force and punishment to which they have become accustomed, they can develop into soldiers who can withstand the fatigues attending the unhealthy climate, its humidity, its heat, its torrential rains—all those things we were counting upon to befall the Europeans.[279]

A studied examination of the landscape of the war during the middle years of the 1870s fails to reveal the point at which the momentum of the insurgency faltered into an irreversible decline. The stalled war had also taken a toll among the *mambises*. "The war goes well," Francisco Estrada y Céspedes confided to his wife from Camagüey in 1873, "every day filled with higher hopes, but my love they persist only as hopes, so high that one tires of hopes." And again two years later: "We are weary of living this miserable life, so filled with privations, separated from our loved ones, separated from you, who I love so much."[280] Weary and worn-down officers and men were increasingly inclined to abandon a cause that had failed to fulfill expectations. "Panic and demoralization" in the mid-1870s, Enrique Collazo remembered.[281] Many who previously had enjoyed a life "of comfort and the advantages of civilization," Melchor Mola recalled in 1893, wearied of the "semisavage life in the *manigua*."[282] Surrenders began in the mid-1870s. *Presentados* they were called by the Spanish—having "presented" themselves in arranged surrenders to the *peninsular* military authorities, including demoralized *insurrectos* abandoning the *manigua* to accept offers of pardon, amnesty, and clemency.[283] "Diez de Octubre!" Ignacio Mora brooded on the occasion of the anniversary of Yara in 1874. "Memorable date for the Island of Cuba and for Spanish domination! . . . The overriding question was whether Cuba could sustain a war with Spain. And the passage of six years have proven that not only was it possible to wage war with advantage but also to defeat Spain. But to achieve [victory] it was necessary that Cubans accept the war and commit themselves to the greatest extent possible. It has not been thus."[284]

Defeat was a matter of a process, cognizance of which revealed itself slowly among different insurgent commands, often imperceptibly until the very end, and even then, in 1878, many—most notably Generals Ramón Leocadio Bonachea and Antonio Maceo—refused to concede defeat. Insurgent ranks diminished, morale declined, supply lines dissolved. Awareness of defeat arrived in the form of small increments of time: easy to deny, difficult to demonstrate. Domingo Méndez Capote recalled these final years, a time of an "extremely difficult and unsustainable situation," circumstances that produced "a fundamental change in the mood, in the spirit, and in the sentiments that had inspired unimaginable sacrifices among Cuban separatists."[285]

In this environment, the impact of the guerrillas must be considered decisive. "The results of this new way to combat the insurrection were not long in coming," historian Fernando Redondo Díaz affirmed. "*Insurrecto* bands went from pursuing to being pursued."[286] Armed engagements during the final years of the war assumed mostly the form of encounters between guerrillas and *mambises*, a war fought principally between Cubans, and one that acquired, historian Ramiro Guerra y Sánchez correctly noted, "the character of intense ferocity with the expansion of the guerrillas."[287] In Camagüey, Tomás Estrada Palma reported, the enemy had limited operations to "incursions," that is, "limiting himself to deploying guerrillas to assault the family farms, and practicing theft, plunder, and murder."[288] Published accounts of military operations seemed mostly about guerrilla units: the Séptima Guerrilla of Las Villas, the Guerrilla of Morón, the Guerrilla of Santa Cruz del Sur, the Contra-guerrilla of Laguna Blanca, the Guerrilla de La Trocha, the Contra-guerrilla de Remanganaguas, the Guerrilla Local of Luisa.[289] Antonio Serra Orts remembered military operations in Oriente as Spanish troops established encampments in the interior, and dispatched columns into the *manigua* escorted by guerrillas "to reconnoiter the woods and places where the enemy could have been hiding." The conflict, Serra Orts observed, had become "less a war than a true man-hunt" (*una verdadera cacería de hombres*).[290]

The war had taken a decisive turn. The *insurrectos* in Oriente had dispersed, reported one Spanish observer in early 1878, "and hardly exchange gunfire [and] no longer engage in combat."[291] The conflict seemed to have settled into a desultory pursuit of war-weary insurgent armies. "Our operations consisted principally to search without rest even the most remote locations," Spanish Major Barrios recalled the final months of 1877, "in search of enemy groups who were not disposed to combat due to their small numbers, who had moved into settlements with women and children, and who had no choice but to succumb to our troops."[292] Operations aided and abetted "with good guerrillas [*buenas guerrillas*] in the zones of operation," making it "possible to reconnoiter in every regard without necessity of tiring the troops with useless marches, preserving them for the moment to concentrate them at a useful point or when with certainty the presence of the enemy or the trail of the enemy was known," adding, "No expense is too great to obtain their services and the service of scouts and spies, of which we have never had enough."²⁹³

Spanish commanders uniformly recognized the contributions of guerrilla units in bringing the insurgency to an end. "The experience of more than three years," General Cándido Pieltain acknowledged in 1879, "has come to demonstrate that no force rendered more important service than the guerrillas and *contra-guerrillas* of battalions, *volantes*, and *locales*," adding:

> In that unique struggle, in which we were obliged to pursue and seek out an enemy that refused to engage in combat except in those circumstances where he enjoyed the advantage of numbers and position, [the guerrillas] were of the greatest value, even more so given the lack of secure intelligence.... The individuals who formed these units were required to be informed in the pursuit of the enemy scouts, gather livestock into the encampment of columns, maintain communication among the detachments on operations, and a thousand other tasks that regular troops were unable to discharge.²⁹⁴

"In the jurisdiction of Manzanillo, Bayamo, and Jiguaní," reported General Luis Prendergast in 1877, "the *guerrillas volantes* are the forces that have constantly sustained our flag. They also discharge an important role in operations conducted in Santiago de Cuba [and] Guantánamo."²⁹⁵ Guerrillas had the capacity "to range over great distances," General Adolfo Jiménez Castellanos feared, "and to remain sufficiently strong to conduct reconnaissance operations in the forests and *manigua*. They conducted daring operations in which their audacity, agility and valor almost always resulted in the best outcomes." In sum, Jiménez Castellanos pronounced, "the guerrillas are indispensable."²⁹⁶

Spanish army units appeared to have attained something of combat parity with the *mambises*, deploying guerrillas throughout the *manigua* with efficiency as a matter of expertise and experience. "The services rendered by guerrillas were so excellent and with such positive results," Major José Ignacio Chacón wrote several years later, "that *insurrectos* were thus stalked by the mobility of the guerrillas and surrendered in large numbers."²⁹⁷ Cuban commanders also recognized these circumstances. "If Spain had not appealed to the treasonous assistance rendered by the traitors," General Calixto García commented in late 1878, "the Spanish would never have been able to defeat us by force of arms."²⁹⁸

The effectiveness of the guerrillas increased with the addition of newly arrived *presentados*, bearing fresh intelligence and current information on insurgent forces and their operations, their encampments and arsenals. Many were incorporated directly into the service of *peninsular* units. "I have in my ranks," General Francisco de Acosta y Albear reported as early as 1871, "200 men who previously participated in the insurrection . . . and who have fought and spilled enemy blood."[299] Alejandro Urquiza organized a two-hundred-man guerrilla unit in Sancti-Spíritus in 1875 consisting principally of *presentados*.[300] Former *insurrecto* Lieutenant Colonel José Boitel similarly organized a guerrilla unit consisting entirely of former *insurrectos*.[301] Juan Escalera recalled the many hundreds of *presentados* who subsequently joined guerrilla units and provided "excellent results."[302] The *presentados* "knew perfectly well the zones of operation," Cándido Pieltain recounted; "our columns . . . were led directly to the enemy and less frequently subject to ambushes and surprise attacks."[303] Cuban insurgent commander Francisco de Arredondo y Miranda despaired over the ascendancy of the Spanish army in Camagüey, noting, "we Cubans found ourselves in terrible conditions . . . precipitating numerous surrenders of valuable men, who thereupon served the Spanish government in the formation of *guerrillas movilizados*, who caused us a great deal of harm, and who by serving as *prácticos* penetrated the *montes* attacking the *ranchos*, robbing and assassinating the inhabitants."[304] *New York Herald* correspondent John O'Kelly visited the town of Ti-Arriba in 1874, with a population "almost wholly composed of colored volunteers . . . nearly all men who had been insurgents, but had surrendered from various causes, and now were in arms against their ancient comrades." O'Kelly wrote of the service of *prácticos* "leading the Spaniards to points they could never reach without their assistance, for these men have the same wonderful instinct, or power, of finding their way in a forest . . . a power rivaling the sense of scent in animals."[305] The guerrillas, Colonel Francisco de Camps recalled, were indispensable in discharging multiple tasks of the Spanish war effort, as "the cart drivers of the convoys and the *practicos* at the vanguard of the columns," adding, "They are totally ignorant of military arts, but possess an instinct for the art of war. Astute in searching for the enemy, they prepare ambushes with skill, and anticipate the weakness of the enemy. . . . They have been brilliant in following the trail of the enemy."[306] Ramón Roa recalled years later being pursued by "an enemy guerrilla unit that had scented my tracks" (*había husmeado mis huellas*).[307]

The war came to an end slowly. By 1877, the insurgent forces had dispersed in desultory fashion into the *manigua*. Newly appointed Captain General Arsenio Martínez Campos arrived in Cuba in 1877 in the company of an additional twenty-five thousand troops.[308] But he did not arrive to wage war but to arrange peace, to offer, one commentator indicated, "a policy of conciliation," to end a war with something of a recognition that it could not continue.³⁰⁹ Martínez Campos understood, Emilio Soulère wrote, "that it was not possible to continue with a system of war that was slowly depleting our treasury and devouring our men. He understood that the immense advantage held by the enemy was not only the climate, in his impenetrable forests and dense *manigua*, but in the mode of warfare."³¹⁰ Peace was an arduous process, Martínez Campos acknowledged, with little usable intelligence and having to deal with a "mulatto who was a mule driver and today is a General," adding, "This can hardly be called a war. It is a hunt in a climate that is deadly to us . . . against *hijos del país* who have become accustomed to a savage life [*á la vida salvaje*], who go about naked or almost naked, having the sensibility of wild animals."³¹¹ Spain committed to administrative and political reforms, offered generous cash bounties together with pardons and amnesty to insurgent Cubans, extended pardons to Spanish army deserters, and promised freedom to all previously enslaved Africans who had enrolled in the ranks of the insurgency. The Spanish army, historian Luis Eugenio Togores Sánchez wrote of the last months of the war, "had pacified Oriente and Camagüey almost without combat."³¹² Not exactly correct: almost without combat of Spanish soldiers.

TO CONFRONT IMPOSSIBLE ODDS

3

The Spanish soldiers were very much embarrassed by the natural difficulties of the country and their lack of familiarity with these difficulties and the country itself. They dared not leave their positions without the guidance of someone born in the country. The recruiting of these guides became one of the problems of their life. Each day it became more difficult to recruit the guides; they feared the insurgents and were haunted by visions of the reprisals which they feared might follow any great victory of Gomez's army. The insurgents had declared that any Cuban found by them serving in the ranks of the Spanish army should be hanged.
—Baron J. Antomarchi, "Life with the Cubans" (1898)

But to fight the traitors
in the dense *manigua*
and to fight against that climate
that poisons the body
is to confront impossible odds
—Vicente Moreno de la Tejera, *Los dramas de la guerra* (1897)

No one better than the natives of a country in war [*los naturales de un país en guerra*] know how to adapt to the conditions of the terrain, making a virtue of necessity, and render the utensils and tools of work into combat arms with which to defend their rights, their aspirations, and their liberty.
—"Aumentan las guerrillas," *El Correo Militar* (June 7, 1897)

In a single family—and there have been many cases—some brothers have joined the [Spanish] army and others joined the *mambises*. Sons of Spaniards who always defended their *patria* have gone into the *manigua* against the wishes of their parents. Others, sons of former *insurrectos*, fight alongside Spanish troops.
—Ricardo Donoso Cortés, *Cuba española: El problema de la guerra* (1896)

The enemy were not of the regular Spanish forces, but of a corps of guerrillas, native-born Cubans, who preferred the flag of Spain. They were all men who knew the craft of the woods and were all recruited from the district.... Each seemed to possess an individuality, a fighting individuality, which is only found in the highest order of irregular soldier. Personally they were as distinct as possible, but through equality of knowledge and experience they arrived at concert of action. So long as they operated in the wilderness they were formidable troops. It mattered little whether it was daylight or dark, they were mainly invisible. They had schooled from the Cuban insurgent to Spain.
—Stephen Crane, "The Sergeant's Private Madhouse" (1899)

The war came to an end in 1878, unceremoniously, only one hundred miles from where it began: a pact of peace concluded in the remote *caserío* of Zanjón. Or perhaps the war did not come to an end at all. Much of the historiography of the last fifty years propounds a narrative arc whose downward slope serves to enclose a "long history" of the *independentista* project: a thirty-year war (1868–98), with the years between 1878 and 1895 rendered as a time of a fruitful truce, an interlude of *una tregua fecunda*.[1]

But neither was it much of a truce. In the years that followed Zanjón, *independentista* uprisings were as commonplace as they were short-lived. The Little War (La Guerra Chiquita), launched in August 1879, ended in September 1880.[2] Another uprising in 1885 came to nothing in a matter of months. A rebellion in September 1890 ended in November of the same year. An uprising in January 1892 sputtered to an end in days. A revolt in October 1894 foundered and failed in weeks.

The uprising in February 1895 began no less inauspiciously, in Baire, in Oriente. Baire was among the many towns and cities across the island poised to rise together in rebellion on February 24, the first Sunday of Carnival. A very well-planned conspiracy, in fact. But almost everywhere, in Havana, in Matanzas, in Santa Clara and Camagüey, and in the many smaller towns and cities in between, a well-planned conspiracy resulted in an ill-executed plot. Thus it was that news of an uprising in the remote foothills of the Sierra Maestra mountains aroused little official concern in Havana. "Everyone believed that it was a disturbance of no importance," Emilio Reverter Delmas acknowledged in 1897. Short-lived distant disorders of no significance, colonial authorities convinced themselves; outlaw bands engaged again in random acts of depredation.[3] Disorder dismissed and disregarded: "The insurrection did not at first promise to be serious," planter Edwin Atkins recalled.[4] Years later, General José Lachambre, the Spanish commander in Oriente, would look back on February 1895 with persistent bewilderment. "The government was, in fact, taken by surprise," Lachambre remembered, "and was quite unprepared to meet such a formidable revolution, and this condition very seriously increased and intensified by the fact that almost the entire population, especially the rural population, including that of the small villages and towns, was with the insurrection."[5]

The populations of familiar place names—Santiago de Cuba, Bayamo, Holguín, Manzanillo, Guantánamo, Las Tunas, Jiguaní, and El Caney—added their voices to the *grito* of Baire, populations not dissimilar to the *orientales* who rose in rebellion in 1868, and indeed many who had risen in 1868 rose up again in 1895: women and men, rural workers and urban laborers, farmers and field hands, Cubans of the professions and from among the vocations.[6] Within weeks of the *grito* of Baire an estimated four thousand *orientales* had taken to the *manigua*.[7] Vast numbers of Cubans of color again enrolled in the ranks of the insurgency, with perhaps among the most notable differences in 1895 being a far larger presence of officers of color in positions of military command: Antonio and José Maceo, Jesús Rabí, Flor Crombet, José Guillermo Moncada, Quintín Bandera, and Agustín Cebreco, among many others.[8] Slavery had ended in 1886, but the moral systems and social practices through which the premise of enslavement was transacted persisted—persisted and deepened, precisely because slavery had ended. At the time of Baire, African-descended people constituted fully one-third of the total population of Cuba, approximately 529,000 out of 1.6 million inhabitants, the vast majority of whom continued to experience conditions of daily life within the hierarchies of race through which the Spanish colonial administration had sustained the logic of governance. For many tens of thousands of women and men of color, the liberation project promised entrée into an emerging national community based on, exhorted Antonio Maceo, "the unshakeable foundation of equality before the law."[9] Cubans now spoke of a "redemptive revolution" (*la revolución redentora*), implying something of an egalitarian project, "with all, and the good of all," as José Martí had envisioned, sharing more in common with the wars of national liberation of the twentieth century than with the post-Enlightenment independence wars of the nineteenth, a movement of far greater complexity in the 1890s than in the 1860s, attracting a larger diversity of social constituencies bearing a wider range of political grievances. The difference between Yara and Baire, Máximo Gómez explained, was that the former originated from "the top down, that is why it failed; this one surges from the bottom up, that is why it will triumph."[10]

The insurgency early assumed something of a life of its own, a relentless expansion, to seize hold across the full length of Oriente within months—from Baracoa in the east to Las Tunas in the west; from Mayarí and Holguín in the north to Santiago de Cuba and Guantánamo on the south. Small Spanish army detachments—"often little more than a thatched-roof hut with four soldiers and one corporal," commented Antonio Díaz Benzo—rendered vulnerable in far-flung isolation across the interior, withdrew in retreat.[11] "The insurgents are practically in possession of the Province of Santiago," the British consul reported in June 1895. "The Government troops scarcely move out of the towns and villages where they have planted themselves."[12] Spanish army units withdrew to the security of towns and cities. "The countryside is ours," Antonio Maceo exulted in August 1895.[13] A token military presence suffered years of chronic conditions of official indifference. "Ill-trained, underpaid and underfed troops," historian Octavio Avelino Delgado wrote, "inadequate weapons, deficient sanitation, and an almost total ignorance of the terrain which was to become the theater of operations."[14]

This time the insurgency would not be contained in the east. It expanded outward—westward, to be precise—gaining new recruits, amassing more arms, and gathering offensive momentum all along the way: a movement so very mindful of the need to carry the war into the west to assail colonialism at its source. In July 1895, the Spanish army suffered a humiliating defeat at Peralejo, in Oriente. "The battle was difficult," Captain General Arsenio Martínez Campos cabled Madrid. "I miscalculated the size of enemy force. It was three times larger than I thought. A difficult battle fought on highly disadvantageous terrain."[15] Weeks after Peralejo, *insurrecto* columns under the command of Antonio Maceo—now designated as the Ejército Invasor—passed into Camagüey. In September, at Jimaguayú in Camagüey, the advancing *insurrecto* armies paused long enough to convene a Constituent Assembly to proclaim a Republic-in-Arms and promulgate the Constitution of Jimaguayú. In October, Máximo Gómez crossed the Júcaro-Morón *trocha* into Las Villas at the head of a cavalry force of three thousand troops.[16] "Until now," Spanish journalist Fernando Gómez reported from Santa Clara in December 1895, "the revolution has not encountered any obstacle to slow its expansion. The insurgent wave expands every day with the expectation of success."[17] With worse to come: battles at Mal Tiempo, in Las Villas, and at Coliseo, in Matanzas—on December 15 and December 23, respectively—the Spanish army suffered two more jolting defeats. After Coliseo, Martínez Campos withdrew from field operations and retreated to Havana. Increasingly, his contact with reality dimmed until it became no more.

The Cubans continued westward into Matanzas, and by early January 1896 had reached the Havana suburb of Hoyo Colorado—"ten minutes from Havana," journalist Emilio Reverter Delmas wrote in appalled disbelief.[18] Two weeks later, 1,600 mounted troops of the Ejército Invasor entered the town of Mantua in Pinar del Río, the westernmost extremity of the island. "At the end of 1895," José Miró Argenter—Maceo's chief of staff—recorded in his field diary, "within a mere ten months, the Revolution has extended its banner across the great theater [of operations] in the West."[19] The insurgents of 1895 had accomplished in ten months what the *insurrectos* of 1868 had failed to achieve in ten years: to carry the war into the production centers of the west.[20] The invasion had been completed. Everything was different.

Spanish authorities were in a state of dazed disbelief. Something had gone very wrong. The Spanish garrison in Cuba in 1895, a total of some seventeen thousand soldiers, deployed principally in the production zones of the west, with a mere two thousand soldiers in Oriente, proved inadequate to contain the insurgency—a "great scarcity of military forces," Ricardo Donoso Cortés commented in 1896.[21] "In Cuba there hardly existed anything that could be called an army," decried Gonzalo Reparaz in September 1895. Reparaz moved freely with confidence among the senior Spanish army commanders and could be relied upon to convey military sentiment throughout the war. "The neglect was of such magnitude," he added, "that in Santiago de Cuba, the capital of the most rebellious province, it was not possible to mobilize more than a few dozen soldiers at the outbreak of the insurrection."[22]

Spain hastened to send reinforcements, and indeed *peninsular* recruits arrived in Cuba by the tens of thousands all through 1895. Voluntarios were mobilized. Within six months of Baire, Spain had deployed an additional sixty thousand troops to the island. To the seventeen thousand soldiers in Cuba at the outbreak of the insurrection, Madrid added another 100,000 troops by early 1896, to increase again to nearly 193,000 by the end of the year (see table 3.1).[23] A massive mobilization of infantry (159,419), followed by cavalry (5,617), artillery (3,143), engineers (3,535), and sailors (2,590).[24]

A formidable deployment of combat troops, to be sure, arriving in a timely fashion, but—to the astonishment of many—still unable to contain the advance of the invasion. The reaction in Madrid was one of disbelief. Almost no one able to understand

3.1 Church blessing of Voluntarios Urbanos in Havana preparing for operations.
SOURCE: LA ILUSTRACIÓN ARTÍSTICA 15 (JULY 13, 1896).

the failure of Spanish military operations in Cuba. "How is it possible that having in Cuba more than 100,000 men, our generals cannot oppose a concentration of 10,000 *insurrectos*?" asked *El Heraldo de Madrid* with a mixture of incredulity and incomprehension.[25] "We are at a loss to explain the success of the *insurrectos*," editorialized *La Correspondencia de España*, "who have passed from Oriente to Camagüey, and from Camagüey to Las Villas, from Matanzas to Havana to Pinar del Río.... How is the inexplicable explained?"[26] An army of more than 100,000 soldiers, a perplexed Emilio Reverter Delmas later pondered, with "everyone naturally asking: 'where is it and to what purpose was such a large army put?' ... It was truly sad. We were watching it and not believing it." (Lo estábamos viendo y no lo creíamos.)[27] Spanish Captain Cristóbal Reina y Massa could hardly contain his indignation:

> If an army of some 150,000 men, equipped with all the necessary requirements to wage war, commanded by officers who have studied the profession of arms, supported by a nation that spares nothing in its behalf, is powerless to dominate a rebellion of several thousand poorly armed bandits, without a shadow of disci-

Table 3.1 Deployment of Spanish Troops, March 1895–November 1896

	SOLDIERS
March 8–23, 1895	8,802
April 1–19	7,252
April 26–May 8	3,418
May 20–June 10	2,668
June 18–July 11	9,193
July 31–September 10	26,835
October 5–November 30	24,170
December 10–January 28, 1896	8,667
February 12–April 10	21,463
April 20–July 21	7,246
July 25–November 10	36,836
November 19–30	17,801
Two battalions from Puerto Rico	1,450
Total deployment to Cuba	**175,801**
Troops stationed in Cuba in February 1895	17,000
Total troop strength in November 1896	**192,801**

SOURCE: "La semana militar," *La Correspondencia de España*, January 28, 1897.

pline ... with little or no munitions of war, obliged to sustain itself through theft and live in continuous risk: if such an army cannot subdue such a rebellion, what purpose do modern armies serve?[28]

The war had expanded beyond Spanish military capacities, which implied too a failure to recognize the changing character of the Cuban purpose, changes that were both cause and consequence of the invasion. The speed with which the insurgency had expanded was surpassed only by the scope it had attained. Certainly early military operations in Oriente were reminiscent of the campaign of 1868–78, warfare conducted in the hostile habitat of the *manigua* against "an enemy who never shows his face," *La Epoca* acknowledged; military operations under impossible circumstances, in a war that could not be sustained.[29] Within one year of the invasion, "our forces [in the east] suspended military operations," reported Emilio Reveter Delmas, "for at the very moment they evacuated any given point, it was immediately occupied by the rebels."[30]

Nothing seemed to have changed since Yara. Unconventional warfare in an unfamiliar terrain—again. Overland transportation was almost impossible. Spanish soldier Manuel Corral recalled the execrable conditions of the roads: "hardly more than passages flattened by wagons through repeated use, with no attention to upkeep, without bridges, transformed into marshland during the rainy season into which horses, oxen, and wagons would sink and where even foot traffic was often impossible"—all of which rendered Spanish columns and convoys vulnerable to ambush.[31] "Fate surely does not favor us," rued Spanish Lieutenant Enrique Piqueras Causas, "for there are enemy [forces] all around us but we never encounter them."[32] The Cuban way of war, *insurrecto* Comandante Manuel Arbelo explained, obliged Spanish troops operating in the *manigua* "to expect that with every step, the Cubans would appear, who up to that moment had been invisible, thereupon to release a volley of shots, only to disappear again in order to find another favorable location from which to attack."[33]

3.2 View of convoy of Viñales, First Battalion of Valencia, 1896. SOURCE: *LA ILUSTRACIÓN ESPAÑOLA Y AMERICANA* 40 (DECEMBER 8, 1896).

3.3 *Misa de campaña*. Church services for Spanish soldiers preparing for field operations. SOURCE: GILSON WILLETS, *GREATER AMERICA: HEROES, BATTLES, CAMPS* (NEW YORK, 1898).

Thus it was that Baire was Yara all over again. Logistical support and supply capacities faltered. Spanish-held cities in the east were provisioned only with the greatest of effort. Manuel Bueno recalled a supply convoy en route from Nuevitas to Guáimaro, with eleven wagons and sixty-five pack mules, transporting thirteen thousand rations, escorted by a total of six hundred soldiers, and subject to the "attack of an enemy perfectly situated for an ambush and firing from almost invulnerable positions."[34] Slow-moving supply convoys serving Bayamo from Manzanillo often required an armed escort of as many as seven thousand troops.[35] The terrain of the Bayamo-Manzanillo convoy, warned one Spanish officer, offered "the enemy magnificent and multiple positions from which to attack the convoy." Worse yet: "The wagons get bogged down in the mud. Often a yoke of eight or ten oxen is insufficient to extricate the submerged wagons. They are [finally] dislodged, soon to be bogged down again.... Often the rivers rise and flood unexpectedly during the convoy, and soldiers finding themselves isolated are obliged to consume the very foodstuffs being transported in the convoy."[36] Supply convoys into the interior often came to a complete halt during the summer rains. Trees felled by *insurrecto* forces across wretched road systems brought operations to an interminable halt.[37] A well-planned ambush would delay supply convoys for days. An ambush by an *insurrecto* force of 119 men, Virgilio Ferrer Gutiérrez entered into his field journal, sufficed to halt two thousand Spanish soldiers accompanying a convoy from Puerto Príncipe to Guáimaro for three days.[38] General José Lachambre recalled the difficulties associated with maintaining the convoy supply lines in Oriente: "There were no public roads which wagons and their wheeled vehicles could pass, and everything had to be taken on pack-horses and mules. A part of the way was almost impossible, especially during the rainy season, and the remainder of the way was along and between mountains. Thus, the convoy and the column were necessarily strung out in a long line, making it easy to attack at almost any point."[39] "The convoys are our death," General Valeriano Weyler acknowledged.[40]

But the invasion of the west announced a different kind of war. The Ejército Invasor had assumed the form of cavalry units, endowed with mobility, speed, and range.[41] Peralejo, Mal Tiempo, and Coliseo were all open-field battles, mostly Cuban cavalry against Spanish infantry. A vastly superior *peninsular* army engaged in military operations for which it was ill prepared. Cavalry had represented a very small portion of the forces Spain deployed to the island in 1895. The Spanish army command, Arturo Amblard recognized, found itself in "an absolutely impossible situation . . . having to pursue on foot and with a meager cavalry the *insurrectos* who, at the time, were all mounted atop the best horses of the country."[42] Commented one observer with terse sarcasm: "It is not possible that the soldier on foot can overtake the rebel on horseback."[43]

3.4 Armed escort of a convoy from Río Blanco to La Palma, Pinar del Río. SOURCE: *LA ILUSTRACIÓN ESPAÑOLA Y AMERICANA* 40 (NOVEMBER 8, 1896).

The speed with which the Ejército Invasor expanded across the western jurisdictions overwhelmed the Spanish army, prompting the army command to appeal for additional mounted units.[44] "The insurgent bands are able to move five times faster and march five times further than our columns," complained one officer.[45] "The *insurrectos* are all mounted," Gonzalo Reparaz called attention to the reversals befalling the Spanish army in early 1896, adding:

> They form a light cavalry and move with little or no equipment, which enables them to march 70 and 80 kilometers a day without fatigue. The soldiers who pursue them are weighed down with six or often with eight days of rations and necessary ammunition. They are very young, between 19 and 23 years of age, not yet acclimated. Their meals are few and infrequent. Under such circumstances, a march of 80 kilometers reduces them to incapacitating conditions. It is an infantry weighed down with supplies in pursuit of a light mounted infantry. It is a turtle in pursuit of a rabbit.... As a result the enemy has been able to invade the western provinces. Our suffering soldiers cannot be expected to do more than they have done. As a result of the incessant marches and countermarches, the columns lose men and men lose strength.... It is sad to see our troops always lose contact with the enemy and to search for him blindly in wearisome marches. As long as we continue to wage war without cavalry units these conditions will persist and things will go from bad to worse.[46]

"They weigh us down [with supplies] as if we were donkeys," complained Gregorio Castaños.[47] *El Heraldo de Madrid* was succinct: "Our army in Cuba totally lacks what represents the primary and most essential attribute of all armies in a campaign: mobility," adding, "If the war in Cuba had been waged with cavalry, it would not have assumed the dimensions that it has, nor would it have been necessary to deploy so many troops and spend so much money."[48]

The invasion changed everything. It was supposed to. The war had entered a new phase—a war against Spain, of course, but war designed purposely as a politics by another means, a war waged against the very premise of Spanish sovereignty: *la tea incendiaria*, a war of the torch, military operations directed against property. "All production and commerce are expressly prohibited," Máximo Gómez had proclaimed in July 1895—with special attention directed to sugar at the very moment the great estates were preparing for the harvest of 1895–96: "The sugar estates will remain totally inactive and any effort to harvest sugar in violation of this moratorium will result in the burning of the cane fields and the destruction of the mill."[49] The moral was simple: no economy without independence. "Work is a symbol of peace," Gómez insisted, "and those of us who see war as the means of Independence cannot permit it. We cannot allow the sugar harvest.... I remained firm in my orders to my officers to destroy the cane fields and to judge everyone who insists upon working as traitors."[50] The insurrection was now "an economic war," Fermín Valdés Domínguez confided to his diary in March 1896, "against capital and the [various] productions of the country," all of which would "complicate Spanish operations and require them to expend vast sums to sustain an army decimated by both bullets and climate."[51]

Captain General Martínez Campos understood the implications of the invasion. "I am not concerned with a powerful well-armed insurrection in those zones without great wealth," he acknowledged as early as July 1895. "What I fear, what horrifies me, is the breadth [extensión] it possesses, it is the need to protect the wealth which by its peculiarity and its dispersal can never be adequately guarded and reducing us to weakness at all points."[52]

Indeed. The Cubans attacked the economy at every vulnerable point—which was almost everywhere: the farms, fields, and factories; the livestock and the rolling stock; transportation networks and communication systems. The list of bridges destroyed and trains derailed was far too long to itemize, Gonzalo Reparaz wrote from Las Villas.[53] To lay siege to the bounty of the land, in stages, sector by sector moving westward: the coffee estates in Oriente, the cattle ranches in Camagüey, the sugar estates in Las Villas, Matanzas, and Havana, the tobacco fields in Pinar del Río. "Burn and destroy all forms of property in any manner useful to Spain," the insurgent army command enjoined, "as rapidly as possible, everywhere in Cuba."[54] General Eusebio Hernández was explicit:

> Property is the true enemy of the Revolution, on which rests the power of the Spanish government, and on its defense rests all of [Spain's] efforts.... While Cuba is not independent, it is necessary to paralyze the social, political, and economic life of the country; our attacks should be directed principally against property that comforts and supports the Spanish—the essential means of securing that paralysis. Once this is obtained, Spain, its army notwithstanding, will de facto no longer exercise its sovereignty over Cuban territory and will have no recourse but to end a futile war and abandon the island.[55]

How utterly incomprehensible. By 1896, an estimated 35,000 *insurrectos* conducted military operations of one type or another across the full length of the island: 8,000 in Oriente, 3,000 in Camagüey, 6,000 in Las Villas, some 10,000 in Matanzas and

Havana, and 8,000 in Pinar del Río.[56] Vast expanses of the geography in Oriente remained mostly under Cuban control, including the triangle of Manzanillo-Bayamo-Cauto Embarcadero, the expanse of Las Tunas-Holguín-Gibara-Mayarí-Baracoa along the north, and between Guantánamo and Santiago de Cuba on the south. *Insurrecto* commander Rodolfo Bergés recalled Oriente Province in January 1896 as "a free and independent state, given that the enemy was required to turn his attention to the armies of Generals Gómez and Maceo in the West."[57] No one disagreed. "It is with difficulty," Ricardo Donoso Cortés acknowledged in 1896, "that loyal forces today deployed in such a vast province can be effective in repressing such a rebel mass [*tanta masa rebelde*] and at the same time defend and maintain important population centers."[58]

Almost everywhere on the island: Spanish army units routed and in retreat, colonial governance in confusion, leadership in disarray. "From September to the present moment the situation has worsened," Gonzalo Reparaz wrote in forlorn bafflement in late 1895. "The war becomes worse every day. The size of enemy forces increases everywhere."[59] The Madrid daily *El Imparcial* could not make sense of the news it was publishing:

> Insurrectionary forces penetrating the province of Havana, vast kilometers of sugarcane fields set ablaze, insurgent bands asserting their presence in regions never before affected by disorders, threatening the province of Pinar del Río, a terrain so favorable for partisan warfare, columns of the Spanish army disoriented in the persecution of the enemy, Máximo Gómez making a fool of General Martínez Campos: all this and more enters our mind as the most desolate picture for the morale of Spanish patriots.[60]

The war had crossed a frightful threshold. "In this state of affairs the defeat of the country is insufficient," *El Correo Español* enjoined. "It is necessary to conquer it to subject the country to the supreme law of the State and to the sovereign will of the nation."[61] The entire island was up in arms, a Spanish journalist cabled from Havana in December 1895, adding a sober prediction: "From this point on it will be necessary for us to proceed as if this were a war of reconquest" (*una guerra de reconquista*).[62] Mexican consul in Havana Andrés Clemente Vázquez reached a similar conclusion at about the same time: "From Maisí to San Antonio [i.e., from east to west], the entire island is in a state of revolution.... The Spanish control only the ports and large cities. It is clear that Spain will be required to wage a true campaign of reconquest, for this is no longer a small uprising to put down."[63]

War had arrived in the west. "Conditions here are grave," Spanish Colonel Luis Otero y Pimentel summarized a bleak state of affairs in Cuba, "as a result of the difficulties that the terrain presents, the vastness of the topography, the speed with which mounted insurgent forces moved from one place to another, and the aid and intelligence that *insurrectos* received from the pacific population."[64] *La tea incendiaria* moved inexorably westward. "The strong winds that are presently sweeping over this city," Manuel Escobar wrote from Colón, "arrive bearing the ashes of the burning cane fields in the countryside."[65] The "rich cane fields were ablaze coast to coast as if a huge bonfire," *insurrecto* Enrique Loynaz Castillo remembered his march through Matanzas.[66] "Christmas eve in Matanzas was a sad evening," lamented one journalist.[67] At midday on January 3, 1896, Gustavo Pérez Abreu gazed toward the reddish sky of the northeast hinterland of Melena del Sur to see "the burning of the cane fields announcing the presence of the *orientales*."[68]

And for the purposes of the taxonomy in use at the time: *orientales* understood always as a synonym for blacks. Who were the *orientales*, Flora Basulto de Montoya recalled asking the family deliveryman, remembering too that the word *invasión* made her "tremble with terror." And the deliveryman responded, "They are some blacks, more black than me.... They wear rings in their nose and ears and exude fire from their eyes."[69] The peasants of Las Villas provinces described the *orientales* as "Maceo's black rabble" (*las negradas de Maceo*).[70] Manuel Cigés Aparicio recounted the horror with which residents of Batabanó anticipated the arrival of *oriental* commander Quintín Bandera: "That leader was not a man but a tiger with a hunger for killing.... All the hatreds of his race, all the ferocity that the African jungles infuse into beasts and savages, had been aroused in that old slave, who now commanded other slaves of the same type."[71]

The tranquility enjoyed in the west between 1868 and 1878 was no more. Havana descended into panic. White fear ascended, with a sense of immediacy—and proximity—to the insurrection, something of a shock at being overtaken by events, inexplicably and incomprehensibly. The capital filled with trainloads of families fleeing in panic from Matanzas before the dreaded advance of the invading *orientales*. Soon almost all transportation between Havana and the surrounding countryside ended. The capital experienced a scarcity of fruits, vegetables, and milk.[72] On New Year's Day 1896, *habaneros* gazing eastward could see the hinterland sky darken with cinders and ashes carried aloft by plumes of rising smoke announcing the advance of the Ejército Invasor. "Never before has war been seen so close in this part of the Island," a subdued Nicolas Heredia wrote from Havana, "and the experience of the horror of war has caused a profound anxiety within the body social. The torching of the sugar mills has begun.... No one was prepared for such a sight."[73]

Spanish army units withdrew from the countryside to concentrate in the cities, to prepare to defend urban centers as a last recourse. Luis López Allué visited Santa Clara in November, "a city that has assumed the appearance of a large barracks," he

3.5 Depicting insurrection as racial mayhem. SOURCE: *LA CAMPAÑA GRACIA* 26 (NOVEMBER 30, 1895).

wrote. "Everywhere, and in all directions, the streets and the plazas are filled with army chiefs, officers, and soldiers. Santa Clara is a military encampment in which there are twenty soldiers for every citizen."[74] A panic-driven people took refuge in the cities. "In the province of Havana," reported *Ecos de Cuba* in January 1896, "the only sign of life is confined to the capital. A similar situation is found in the provinces of Matanzas, Santa Clara, and Puerto Príncipe, where security from the depredations committed by the arsonists, assassins, and thieves is to be found only in the important cities."[75]

Martínez Campos returned to Havana in December—in retreat. Leadership was in flight. Authority was in question. Policy could not be executed. On January 2, 1896, Martínez Campos proclaimed the provinces of Havana and Pinar del Río under a state of siege.[76] Four days later, the army command instructed *habaneros* to prepare for a street-by-street defense of the capital. "The warning signal [*señal de alarma*] will be five consecutive cannon shots from the Castillo del Príncipe," the communiqué announced, whereupon all military units were to deploy to preselected sites to defend the city.[77] The Voluntarios of Havana were enjoined to prepare for something of a final stand in defense of the capital.[78]

Havana was terror struck. Vice-Captain General (*Segundo Cabo*) José Arderius rallied the defense of Plaza de Armas with the cry of "*Hannibal ad portas.*" In the *municipios* of Guanabacoa, Jesús del Monte, and Vedado, authorities constructed makeshift barricades on the streets designed to impede the advance of *insurrecto* forces. "A horrifying state of morale," Martínez Campos cabled Madrid.[79] "A disquiet seized Havana," wrote Havana attorney Eliseo Giberga. "Shock gave way to panic. For many people in Havana, the insurrection up to that point had been something distant, a figment of the imagination. Suddenly, it became real. Those of us who were attentive to national developments considered ourselves in the presence of a true disaster" (*un verdadero desastre*).[80]

The politics of *la tea incendiaria* were executed with tactical purport, of course, to extend Spanish army lines of defense thinly across the full length of the island and its coasts. To expand into Pinar del Río was to provide the *insurrecto* armies with access to added miles of coastline to receive needed supplies from abroad, a political act executed to obtain military advantage, and vice versa: to oblige Spanish combat troops to defend property and production. Therein lay the deeper strategic purpose of *la tea incendiaria*. To have expanded the reach of the insurgency signified the expansion of the scope of operations, of course. But the expansion of scope implied a difference in kind. "The war in Cuba presents us with characteristics not present in the previous war," *El Correo Militar* understood. "It consists of the fact that the *insurrectos* . . . demonstrate the determination to pursue what is called a strategic objective."[81] The sweep of the invasion into the western jurisdictions brought Cuban armies out from the *manigua* and *monte* onto the open plains of Las Villas, Matanzas, and Havana to wage a different kind of war, to contest the claim of Spanish sovereignty at its source. The logic of the invasion was steeped in the history from which the insurrection originated, to challenge the very raison d'être of the Spanish presence informed with the understanding that the strength of Spanish sovereignty—the protection of property and production—was also its weakness: that a government unable to discharge the purpose upon which it based its moral claim to authority and its political rationale to govern had no justification for continued existence.[82]

To lay waste purposely to the great sugar estates of Las Villas, Matanzas, and Havana on the occasion of the 1895–96 *zafra*. To make a point. "All the cane fields along the route traversed by our army were burned during the Invasion," Miró Argenter recorded in his field diary. "A painful measure to be sure, but necessary. . . . [Spanish] officials had solemnly vowed that the harvest would be fully completed. The Ejército Invasor has demonstrated that it possesses the means to thwart even the certain guarantees offered by the Spanish government."[83] The Cuban purpose, Spanish Captain Ramón Varona understood, was "to employ or use all the means of destruction which exposed the inefficiency of the Spanish Government in Cuba."[84]

3.6 Characterizing the "types" of *insurrectos* in the *manigua*. SOURCE: *LA CAMPAÑA DE GRACIA* 27 (JULY 18, 1896).

A colonialism conditioned by the need to protect sugar as the principal purpose of its authority was necessarily obliged to defend the harvest as a means of its credibility. Spain had been overtaken by the history into which it had inscribed its claim to sovereignty. "The danger to the harvest," Nicolás Heredia wrote in 1895, "the very source of general wealth, and the necessity to protect sugar due to the important interests that it represented, has influenced decisively the organization and distribution of the troops."[85]

The Spanish army command was indeed mindful of the calculus of colonialism, understanding too that the defense of Spanish sovereignty implied the need to defend sugar production. Captain General Martínez Campos could not but act within the parameters of the history from which he learned the way of war in Cuba, almost all derived from the experience of Yara.[86] The first line of defense against the expanding reach of the insurgency, Martínez Campos understood, was the security of sugar and the imperative that determined the deployment of troops. "The experience of the past war [of 1868–78]," Martínez Campos insisted as the insurgency advanced westward toward Las Villas in September 1895, "has demonstrated the necessity to attend to the security of property and the railroads. This has obliged me to divide the forces of the Fifth District [Las Villas] in six great zones . . . within which commanders have a defined responsibility."[87]

Nothing complicated. The task at hand: to defend the great sugar estates in the jurisdictions of Santa Clara, Cienfuegos, Sagua, Remedios, Sancti-Spíritus, and Trinidad. To protect property and production at all costs, even if to concede the east to insurgent control. "The current [insurgent] plan appears to be none other than the destruction of sugar production in Las Villas, Matanzas, and Havana, and perhaps tobacco production in Pinar del Río," *El Correo Militar* understood, and suggested:

> Only the presence of 30,000 troops promises to protect production. . . . To reach this strength it would be necessary to withdraw one-third of the forces that operate in Oriente, Camagüey, and Las Villas. But if this were undertaken, and those zones were to remain with fewer troops, local insurgent bands would be free to burn and occupy population centers and haciendas. But material losses there would be far less than those surely to occur in the provinces of such great wealth. As to the moral effect, obviously the loss of Bayamo or Jiguaní to the *insurrectos* would be of far less importance than the effect of twenty daring men reaching the very door of Havana.[88]

Tens of thousands of soldiers were deployed to protect the 1895–96 harvest, distributed among the more than 1,100 sugar estates spanning 700,000 acres in Las Villas, Matanzas, and Havana, in detachments ranging in size from as few as twenty-five soldiers to as many as one thousand troops.[89] "Every planter demands the protection of one hundred or more soldiers in order to complete the sugar harvest," Mexican consul Andrés Clemente Vázquez reported, "and naturally this vast army contingent is transferred from the field of military operations."[90] The defense of sugar depleted Spanish combat capacities. "The place looks like a military garrison," Edwin Atkins described the deployment of Spanish troops on his estate: "the batey is all barricaded and all approaches are guarded. There is a stone fort behind the sugar house with twenty-seven soldiers in charge of an officer. . . . The Spanish force is always guarding the buildings."[91] On the vast Constancia estate in Cienfuegos, 1,700 troops were deployed to protect the harvest. "The duty of my command," recalled General Tomasco Fernández, "was to guard and protect the mills, machinery, and buildings generally on the *batey* of the Central Teresa":

> These duties were performed to the best of our abilities.... Insurgents operating in the vicinity numbered 300, and those who passed through burned a large amount of cane.... It was therefore impossible for us to prevent destruction, first because the odds of three to one against us were too great; second because it would have been very unwise for us to leave our forts and sally out to fight the insurgents, for aside from the danger of being overwhelmed, there was a very serious danger that while we were out some portion of the insurgents would attack and destroy our forts, carry off our ammunition and supplies, and [set] fire to the mills and buildings; and third, it was wholly useless for a garrison of 100 men to try to prevent 300 insurgents from setting fire to some portions of ... 3,000 to 5,000 acres of cane. Indeed, it is doubtful whether a force of 1,000 soldiers could have done so.[92]

A useless effort indeed, Manuel Escobar understood, for the act of torching a cane field required "only one man and a match."[93]

A mighty effort produced meager results. "The truth is," the British consul in Havana reported tersely in mid-1896, "that never in history has a huge army been employed to so little purpose."[94] Across the expansive landscape of the west, at almost every turn, vast swaths of sugarcane fields were set ablaze. "A perfect roaring hell of fires," P. M. Beals wrote from Cienfuegos; "a sea of fire surrounded Quivicán," was what Spanish Colonel Antonio Vesa remembered.[95] "To travel out into the outskirts of Havana is to witness with shock how a tidal wave of fire has swept over the vast expanse of our fertile countryside," a Spanish journalist cabled Madrid.[96] A bleak landscape to behold indeed. Captain General Martínez Campos was graphic: "We had fire ahead of us, and behind us, and on all sides of us. Even under the very hooves of our horses."[97]

The producing classes could not but contemplate with horror the ruin of the wealth upon which the solvency of their well-being depended.[98] Sugar production collapsed. "Not a single stalk of cane remains standing," Gonzalo Reparaz cabled Madrid.[99] The harvest plummeted from 1 million tons in 1894–95 to 225,000 tons in 1895–96, declining again in 1896–97 to 212,000 tons, decreasing in total value respectively from 45 million pesos, to 13 million pesos, to 10 million pesos. "Many of those who have devoted their lives to this industry of sugar manufacture," reported the British consul in Havana at the end of 1895, "and were men of wealth a few months ago, find themselves on the verge of ruin."[100] José Miró Argenter could contemplate the success of the invasion with a satisfied sense of achievement: "The amount of capital that disappeared in hours is incalculable."[101]

The very outcome that the Spanish presence was supposed to prevent: Spain had failed to fulfill the responsibility upon which it based its claim to sovereignty. "We are obliged to acknowledge in the face of an implacable reality: the failure is enormous" (*el fracaso es enorme*), concluded *El Imparcial*.[102] "More than 100,000 troops were sent to protect the sugar harvest, and failed," wrote longtime resident Tesifonte Gallego. "More than a defeat, it is a disgrace."[103]

As to the question of how 100,000 troops failed to contain the Ejército Invasor of fewer than 10,000 *insurrectos*: in fact, the total number of troops available for combat operations represented less than one-fifth of the full strength of the Spanish army in Cuba. Historian Enrique de Miguel Fernández estimates that 20 percent of the Spanish army was rendered unfit for military operations due to tropical illness and another 40 percent was deployed to garrison the sugar estates.[104] The invasion forced the Spanish army into a defensive posture, to secure population centers, to guard railway stations, but most of all to protect the sugar estates of the west. "The need to protect infinite numbers of strategic points," one Spanish veteran of 1868–78 offered, resulted in "forces that remained inactive in the persecution of the enemy."[105] With predictable results: "Poorly distributed garrisons at the majority of strategic points due to the need to deploy troops to protect agricultural activities and guard the harvest of the great sugar estates," explained Manuel Mariano y Vivo.[106] "The scattered dispersal of small detachments among the sugar estates," wrote Rafael Casset in January, "in addition to their uselessness, for 20 or 25 men cannot prevent fire to a sugar field, acted so utterly to reduce the combat forces available for military operations to the point that the General in Chief of an army of 120,000 men lacked the troops to oppose 10,000–12,000 lightly armed men. This is what allowed Máximo Gómez and Maceo to complete the prodigious march of the Invasion."[107] "The determination to protect the sugar harvest," *El Heraldo de Madrid* surmised, "had the net effect of sequestering or 'imprisoning' all [the soldiers] who are not in the hospitals."[108] *Insurrecto* commander Eusebio Hernández advanced westward from Baracoa to the Júcaro-Morón *trocha*, he wrote, "without seeing a single soldier."[109] The Ejército Invasor appeared to have crossed the island almost without resistance. "We have crossed all of Camagüey without firing a shot," Antonio Maceo wrote to his brother, "and what is more, even crossing the *trocha* without the slightest resistance."[110] General Valeriano Weyler would later describe these conditions as "prevailing anarchy": "The troops were extended over a great many detachments, to protect towns and farms without adequate means of defense. This practice significantly diminished their combat capacity. The towns and farms remained inadequately protected to the point that, when attacked by the enemy, the few troops defending them would watch helplessly as the cane fields were set afire before their eyes."[111]

In ways perhaps still inadequately understood, the invasion reached deeply to disrupt the normative logic upon which Spain based its claim to sovereignty, not as a matter of military reversals—that would come later—but rather by contesting the plausibility of colonial governance. Spain could not govern. That was the point. "It was necessary for the revolution to demonstrate its strength through a thunderous deed," José Miró Argenter recalled preparations for the invasion, the completion of which "would produce panic among the producing classes of the country, reducing to ashes the agricultural wealth associated with the great sugar estates."[112] The invasion released the long-feared forces of revolution into the historically well-protected terrains of prosperity and production. "I am fully persuaded," Salvador Cisneros Betancourt wrote in December 1895, "that it is in Occidente that our war must come to an end soon."[113] A way of life seemed indeed to be coming to an end.

The premise of Spanish sovereignty was no longer sustainable. The internal structures of the colonial system were transacted within a paradigm of common interests and shared benefits: a strategic convergence of multiple and indeed often overlapping reciprocities, always in precarious juxtaposition to one another, to be sure, but held together in common purpose by mutually reinforcing social solidarities sustained with a sense of existential urgency. These were interdependent constituencies bound together through common concerns and by way of collective will in defense of privilege, property, and production, and sharing too—especially—an overriding fear of the social forces released by revolution.

The invasion arrived as a fate foretold, anticipated with a well-rehearsed—and ill-omened—narrative informed with a presentiment of displacement. A fear of an imminent reckoning had long lodged within the collective temperament of a polity formed within the experience of chattel slavery. Slavery had ended in 1886, to be sure, but the brooding fear of race war had not, a fear that was fully revived with the *independentista* purpose: the invasion arrived as the very eventuality that Spanish sovereignty was meant to prevent.

Fear as a source of social solidarity was a powerful means of unanimity of purpose, of course: until the worst fears came to pass, whereupon came the realization that the faith placed in the efficacy of Spanish sovereignty was no longer warranted. Fear reached deeply into the body social, a fear possessed of a proper history, always the dread of *el desbordamiento de los negros* that seemed to have transferred from terror associated with slave rebellion to horror associated with the *independentista* project, a fear that coursed its way through the sensory circuitry of a polity in the grip of fear of extinction. The prominence of commanders of color within the *insurrecto* armies, historian Aline Helg correctly noted, "revived the specter of a Haitian-style black dictatorship."[114] Havana attorney Eliseo Giberga discerned the psychological impact of the invasion, recognizing too the implications of the ensuing crisis of confidence within the privileged classes. Until the invasion, Giberga understood, "no one would have imagined that the Revolution had any likelihood of success." But the "penetration of *separatismo* into the West" had served "to disrupt the moral order," to sow fear

3.7 Depiction of those who wish to make Cuba happy: *insurrectos* as arsonists.
SOURCE: *LA CAMPAÑA DE GRACIA* 26 (AUGUST 24, 1895).

and panic of the "half savage rabble of blacks [*negradas medio salvajes*] given to all types of crimes, the least of which was arson."[115] The Madrid daily *La Epoca* warned of the vast numbers of blacks in the ranks of Maceo's army, "most of whom are naked and commit all types of outrages."[116] The "separatist war of Cuba is *racist*," pronounced *El Heraldo de Madrid* in late 1895, and further insisted that the insurrection was an expression of "the hatred of *mulatos* and the arrogance of the blacks, to whom we should restore their full liberty by shipping them back to the coast of Guinea."[117] A campaign against a "handful of godless men" was how one Spanish officer recounted military operations against Maceo in Pinar del Río, "given to a life of pillage, arson and crime . . . devoted to the worst instincts of an inferior race that wishes to avenge the wrongs of the many years of slavery."[118] The residents of the municipality of El Roque in Matanzas, Bernabé Boza recalled in his memoirs, anticipated the arrival of the *orientales* with a sense of terror: "Slowly they were convinced that we were men of honor and respect. . . . They relaxed upon seeing that we were not hordes of savage black murderers with rings in our noses."[119]

La tea incendiaria was the fulfillment of a prophetic dread, the mayhem long feared by the producing classes: acts of wanton and willful destruction of property, deeds of vandalism and arson, attributed to Cubans of color motivated by the determination to exact racial retribution. "There are very few whites in the *manigua*," Emilio Reverter Delmas commented in 1897. "The majority of the *insurrectos* are black," given to "arson and theft," mostly "hordes of savages that infest the fields of beautiful Cuba," adding:

> It has been said that the current insurrection is a *black stain*, because of the predominance of the descendants of the slaves of yesterday, who in turn were the immediate descendants of the savages of yesterday. . . . It consists of an uprising of the lowest and immoral classes against those hardworking and educated classes. It is African savagery that seeks to impose itself on Spanish civilization. It is similar to a struggle between entities of race and entities of morals: black against white. . . . It is a historic combat . . . a struggle between barbarism and civilization, between people without a nation and people who defend our beloved Spain.[120]

The administrator of the Soledad sugar estate in Cienfuegos witnessed *la tea* from a distance: "A perfect roaring hell of fires all the way to the hills of Trinidad and the sea, one could see nothing but smoke and smouldering ruins," acts committed by insurgents "by far the greater portion of whom are negroes—I should say at least eighty per cent. Amongst these negroes are to be found the most degraded wretches in this country, men who do not recognize any leader and who are willing to seize upon any excuse for rapine and pillage."[121] Journalist Juan de Lasheras was appalled:

3.8 "The Pleasures of Maceo," depicting Antonio Maceo as dining on human body parts. SOURCE: EL IMPARCIAL, MARCH 2, 1896.

One of the most ferocious and devastating wars of the present century. The entire country finds itself invaded by *insurrecto* bands that daily expand in scope and increase in number.... The bands that roam from one end of the island to the other, composed of fanatical people, among whom are prominent for their ferocity and savagery people of color [and] are given to arson, plunder, theft, and assassination, as is the wont of primitive hordes.[122]

The prospects were frightful, physician Martín Salazar warned, calling attention to *mulatos*, who were "precisely the population most distinguished in the war by their cruel and bloodthirsty instincts, reminding us of the cannibalistic character [*el carácter antropofágico*] of their savage black ancestors in Africa."[123]

The *mulato* Antonio Maceo, warned Vicente Torres y González in 1896, with "his bloody instincts and his hatred of whites, is fighting against Spain in preparation to fight against whites."[124] A well-justified white dread, Camilo Polavieja conceded, in the face of Maceo's "known desire to impose a government of his race similar to the government of Haiti."[125] In Spain, Minister of Ultramar Antonio María Fabié warned of a dismal future, with "Cubans passing under the humiliating yoke of the blacks, their former slaves," but pledged that, the "Cubans being who they are, our brothers, we have a sacred duty to protect them from themselves.... They themselves will

3.9
"The Specter of [Cuban] Separatism."
SOURCE: *LOS LUNES DE "EL IMPARCIAL,"* DECEMBER 30, 1895.

thank us."[126] General Juan Salcedo Montillo, the ranking Spanish officer in Santiago de Cuba, could presume to speak with the first-person authority of a field commander in Cuba. "I am fully persuaded," Salcedo assured the Madrid daily *La Epoca* in late 1895, "that the present war is dissimilar from the past insurrection." He continued:

> That war was an uprising of the spirit of the island in pursuit of adventure, as well as a hope for political and economic improvements. The youth took up arms: it was a war of whites against whites. The people of color were of secondary importance in the campaign. Not this time. Today it is a rebellion of a race that foolishly

To Confront Impossible Odds 121

seeks revenge against the whip that the master applied against the slave. And now with the slave finding himself free, with an ingratitude darker than the color of his skin, he no longer seeks to enjoy the benefits of emancipation but aspires to equality, and even superiority over those who liberated him.... It is frightful to contemplate what could happen, but we have distant memories of the race wars in Haiti and Santo Domingo.[127]

To contemplate the demise of Spanish sovereignty was to confront the unbearable possibility of an unthinkable future. "What do we do with the 300,000 blacks who remain in Cuba," asked Rafael Padró,

> who we know do not aspire to liberty as it is commonly understood but rather desire complete libertinage? Does there exist in that ignorant class, humiliated by us and therefore harboring a profound hatred against the white race, the possibility of regeneration? What would happen in Cuba in the absence of the armed forces? ... What comparable force exists in the country capable of confronting the hordes of bandits and malcontents who will remain?[128]

"The worst thing that could happen to Cuba," explained one planter, "would be independence, if that implies the domination of the Gomez band over the civilized inhabitants.... Such a band cannot bring a firm and stable government to the island. Instead of that, devastation, riot, and rebellion might become permanent.... Many of his followers are negros and mongrels"—and to the final point: "We do not want another Hayti."[129] Fernando Yznaga despaired, taking note of the "presence of the large negro element ... many of them come from warlike tribes." Yznaga was persuaded that "suppression of the insurrection by the Spanish is improbable" and insisted that "a return of order and prosperity to Cuba can be secured only by annexation to the United States."[130] Independence implied the distribution of public office to the black leaders, *El Correo Militar* warned, "who would secure not only civil and political rights, but also participation in the government of the island, that is, if they do not seek to keep everything for themselves" (*quedarse con todo*).[131]

Spanish sovereignty collapsed from within, in successive stages, interlocking networks of interests shaken loose from their political moorings, thereupon to reveal an uncertain future and the realization too—most of all—that the pragmatics of shared interests that had served as the source of colonial stability were no longer tenable. The invasion had shattered the premise of daily life: laid bare the limitations of a Spanish sovereignty that could no longer do what it was supposed to do. The invasion set in motion far-reaching realignments of the balance of power upon which the internal equilibrium of colonial governance was calibrated, with once-powerful constituencies unable to arrange outcomes according to their wishes. "The supreme necessity [of the Invasion]," Bernabé Boza explained, "was to make the effect of the insurrection felt, decisively, strong, and bold in all parts of the island. The rest was all a matter of time."[132]

Something of a helplessness insinuated itself into the mood of the producing classes, stranded by a history of their own making. Loyalty was an ephemeral virtue, easily transferable and almost always guided by the logic of interests. The producing classes, always practical and pragmatic, not readily given to chasing the chimera of sentiment—not at least when their interests were involved—took stock of their circumstances, to fear the outcome of a war that Spain could not sustain. Captain General Martínez Campos was lucid about criollo political loyalties. "If there is perhaps a majority of Cubans [*hijos del país*] who as a result of their social position desire a continuation of Spanish rule," Martínez Campos understood, "it is only a minority who *sincerely* wishes [for that continuation]. What the majority fears is Haiti, what terrorizes them is anarchy."[133] In 1896, more than one hundred prominent representatives of the producing classes, including planters, attorneys, industrialists, merchants, and manufacturers, appealed to the United States for protection, imploring President Grover Cleveland for US intervention in their behalf. "We would ask," the petitioners entreated, "that the party responsible to us should be the United States. In them we have confidence, and in them only."[134] The archives of the US State Department are thick with diplomatic dispatches from consular agents across the island transmitting appeals for US intervention by planters, merchants, industrialists, and manufacturers.[135] The transfer of loyalty began early.

On the morning of December 17, Madrid awoke to the headline of "new bad news" on the front page of El Heraldo de Madrid:

> The *insurrectos* are within view of Cienfuegos. The enemy burns the factories and paralyzes the movement of the railroads. He lays waste to the sugar fields and the farms. He sacks and destroys everything in his path. He surprises and overwhelms detachments and columns of the army, or engages in combat such as Mal Tiempo, where our losses made up fully twenty-five percent of the total number of our soldiers. . . . No longer can we say that the rebels flee in the face of army columns, or that they take shelter in the dense *montes* or forests, from which to launch surprise attacks against the sugar mills or small army detachments.

They are now the ones who in fact conduct operations, and who in any given moment concentrate considerable bodies of force and come after us in the important population centers.¹³⁶

Military reversals in Cuba produced political reaction in Spain. Power passed to Conservative Antonio Cánovas del Castillo, signaling the ascendancy of a politics of visceral intransigence swelling into national indignation in defense of *la integridad nacional*. "You can be certain," Cánovas del Castillo as prime minister had vowed in parliament as early as 1891, "that no Spanish political party will ever abandon the island of Cuba; that to defend the island of Cuba we would use, if necessary, the last man and the last *peseta* [*el último hombre y la última peseta*] to defend it with all our forces."¹³⁷ A pledge that Cánovas as president of the Council of Ministers renewed in 1896, vowing to "respond to war with war":

> The Spanish army will never leave Cuba in defeat. The insurrection does not have the material resources or moral and intellectual capacities to force the Spanish army to evacuate the island of Cuba.... That is not the issue. Rather, it has to do with [the *insurrectos*'] determination to test the force and resilience of Spain. They

3.10 Insurgent train derailment between Mata and Cifuentes, Las Villas Province. SOURCE: *EL FÍGARO* 12 (APRIL 5, 1896).

seek to test the Peninsula, to discover if Spain has sufficient faith and sufficient love for the possession of Cuba to continue to spend all its money, [to exert] all its efforts, and [to shed] all the blood of its sons necessary to preserve that piece of land [*aquel pedazo de tierra*] under the Spanish flag.... Spain will send to Cuba all its robust youth continually in the numbers necessary to prevail.... It would be a grave error to believe that Spain will not persist, to believe that Spain, sooner or later, will tire of the sacrifices that the war requires.[138]

Liberal Práxedes Mateo Sagasta could hardly commit to anything less. Spain "is disposed," Sagasta pronounced in April 1895, "to spend the last *peseta* of the national treasury and sacrifice the last of its sons before allowing anyone—absolutely anyone—to seize even one inch of its sacred territory."[139] The crisis in Cuba, Sagasta exhorted, required all *buenos españoles* "to transcend party loyalties and partisan politics to attend exclusively to the sacred interest of the Nation."[140]

A new Conservative ministry in Spain, a new captain general in Cuba. The announcement of the appointment of General Valeriano Weyler signaled the onset of a new ruthlessness to the Spanish war effort. Weyler embodied an unabashed ferocity in defense of national honor—precisely, historian Rafael Núñez Florencio suggested, "what Spanish public opinion demanded."[141] It was not so much that his reputation preceded him. Rather, it was that his reputation followed him, one having been established in the fields of eastern Cuba during the years of Yara. Few failed to understand what was about to follow. "Even the most intransigent conservatives," the weekly *Nuevo Mundo* commented from Madrid, "have trembled contemplating the consequences of the appointment of a general whose reputation for cruelty—true or false—makes for the bloodiest legacy among the Cuban people."[142]

The appointment of Weyler also implied a far-reaching change in the purpose of Spanish arms: no longer to protect Cuban property and production but to defend Spanish *patrimonio* and the dignity of sovereignty, to uphold national honor and preserve national integrity. Weyler arrived in Cuba in February 1896 with a mandate to restore Spanish sovereignty at all costs, without regard to life, without concern for treasure, to wage and win a war of national honor.[143] He made his intentions known immediately: "I will respond to war with war."[144]

The commitment to war with war implied a campaign of an aroused national wrath against wretched subjects who had again dared to threaten *la integridad nacional*, accompanied with a promise of "vigorous military action that public opinion embraced with enthusiasm," commented Pablo Alzola.[145] How utterly implausible. Spain would not be defeated by "men alien to our civilization and to our race," *El Heraldo de Madrid* thundered, and to the point: "The very honor of the nation is at stake."[146] *La Epoca* agreed: "In Cuba we fight for our honor.... There is no going back."[147] No compromise, no concession. "What really matters," Ricardo Donoso Cortés insisted, "is to preserve *la integridad nacional*," adding:

> To impose the authority of sovereignty upon those who fail to recognize it; to annihilate the rebellion; to humiliate the insolent who dares to rise up in arms against *la madre patria*; and to defeat at all costs and establish for all time the indisputable right of the Nation to punish all ... who violate the most sacred duties that correspond to Spanish citizens and to punish all who act against peace and against the right of the State which provides [its citizens] refuge.[148]

"The Metropolis should continue to punish the rebels by way of fire and blood," exhorted Sabas Catá in 1895, "with no other purpose of any type until they have been exterminated. No quarter, no consideration."[149]

A renewed resolve to wage war without distraction, free from political restraint and without moral reservation, with the intransigence of *los buenos españoles* undiminished and the *peninsular* commitment to *la integridad nacional* unwavering. "A war without quarter against the enemies of *la madre patria*," exhorted *El Correo Militar*, "against everyone who directly or indirectly conspires against her."[150] Spain confronted an "implacable separatist movement," Cánovas del Castillo warned, "which Spain must fight against always until it has been literally exterminated."[151] A mood of war. "The insurrection in Cuba," *El Heraldo de Madrid* decried, "is nothing other than a military problem, whose solution corresponds to military practices and methods."[152] Devotion to duty implied unconditional commitment, exhorted V. de Diez Vicario, and "if it were necessary to sacrifice for the Patria as an act of self-immolation, it will be done. Everything to be offered to the integrity of the Patria, that divine symbol which is the soul and most holy and pure incarnation of the ideal."[153]

The war in Cuba would be waged with virulent vindictiveness. "Ever since the *grito de Baire*," *La Correspondencia Militar* exhorted, "we have been saying insistently that *war should waged with war*.... We ask for the extermination of that spurious race that we have created in Cuba, pampered and educated carelessly so that now they assassinate us from behind like traitors." And more:

> If General Weyler remembers what poor Spain has already suffered in this war—the thousands and thousands of beloved sons sacrificed to the machetes, explosives, derailments, and disease ... he should order his columns immediately to shoot every prisoner taken; that the peasant accomplices who have served the *insurrectos* as guides be hung; that the autonomists and reformists also be hung ... and finally for the General-in-Chief to secure an immediate peace

requires the need to cut off many thousands of heads, not leaving in Cuba any inhabitants other than the defenders of *españolismo* and those loyal to Spain, and the army he commands. It is necessary to exterminate that bad race. [Es preciso exterminar a esa mala raza.][154]

"The people who threw off the yoke of the great Napoleon," Emilio Reverter Delmas vowed, "cannot—will not—back down in Cuba in the face of a handful of black and mulatto rebels and another handful of whites who are traitors to their nation and to their blood," and enjoined, "In order to triumph and destroy the criminal *insurrectos*: all the troops necessary, all the efforts and all the sacrifices that the necessities of the campaign requires."[155]

A profound change of mood in 1896, especially among the Spanish soldiery, Manuel Cigés Aparicio remembered. The Cubans had become "mortal enemies," given to "surprises and ambushes, and causing deaths.... Everyone began to feel a profound hatred toward the enemy," adding, "The arrival of Weyler removed all restraints that had held the beast in check. The spirit of revenge sharpened its teeth. [A] spasm of rancor ensued.... Valor succumbed to hatred and lost all its virtue."[156] The war in Cuba entered yet another phase.

Weyler did not fail to appreciate the gravity of conditions in Cuba. He had inherited a demoralized colonial officialdom without the capacity to execute the authority of governance. "It is necessary to combat this state of affairs at all cost," Weyler pronounced solemnly upon his arrival to Havana, "and to revive the morale [*reanimar el espíritu*] of the inhabitants of Cuba, to make everyone understand that I have arrived disposed to lend total support to the loyal and resolved to apply the full rigor of the law to those who in any way aid or glorify the enemy or who choose to disparage the prestige of Spain, or its Army, or the Voluntarios."[157]

The arrival of Weyler announced the onset of a wave of political repression, a time to choose sides. "There is no middle ground in this war," Weyler exhorted: "to the *manigua* to join the black hordes of Maceo or to fight under the flag of the Nation."[158] The jails filled with political prisoners. In April 1896 Weyler imposed censorship on the island press, prohibiting newspapers "from publishing accounts of the war that were not previously approved by the office of the army General Staff."[159]

But it was to the task of waging war that Weyler devoted his energies. He had assumed command of a moribund army, in various conditions of confusion and circumstances of chaos, dispirited and in disarray, under siege and on the defensive almost everywhere in Cuba, with detachments scattered across the island as isolated garrisons on sugar estates. "Absolute disorganization," commented one officer.[160] An army "disoriented," pronounced *Nuevo Mundo*.[161] "The military situation in Cuba is in a true state of chaos," Gonzalo Reparaz reported.[162] The Voluntarios were utterly ineffective, in most instances dispersing without a fight.[163] "It could be readily understood," Weyler recalled of his arrival in Cuba years later, "that the task that awaited me was arduous and overwhelming and that a monumental undertaking was necessary to emerge out from under this chaos."[164] Cavalry units were reinforced with additional recruits from Spain and additional horses from Mexico.[165] The Júcaro-Morón *trocha* was reinforced and a new *trocha* constructed in Pinar del Río, stretching twenty miles between Mariel in the north and Majana in the south.[166] All in all, part of a larger plan to confine the insurgency in self-contained regional zones, thereby isolating *insurrecto* armies from one another: pacification province by province. At full strength, the Júcaro-Morón *trocha* contained a total of sixty forts and twelve military encampments and a vast illumination network with a nighttime reach of some seven hundred meters.[167]

Weyler prepared for war with war methodically, preparations that contemplated a ruthlessness in the conduct of operations—indeed, a ruthlessness in the concept of operations, unencumbered by everything except a determination to wage war singlemindedly with no purpose other than victory and no duty higher than the defense of national honor. The reconcentration policies that Weyler had introduced in the east in 1869 were adopted in 1896 for the entire island. In mid-February 1896, within days of his arrival in Cuba, Weyler ordered the resettlement of all rural residents of Camagüey and Oriente to population centers under Spanish military control.[168] Eight months later, Weyler ordered all inhabitants of rural Pinar del Río "to reconcentrate within eight days in population centers occupied by [Spanish] troops," warning that "all persons found outside the population centers will be considered rebels and dealt with accordingly."[169] And in January 1897 the reconcentration order was extended to the provinces of Havana and Matanzas.[170] By 1897, a total of thirty-four reconcentration centers had been organized, spanning the island from Consolación del Sur in Pinar del Río to Baracoa in Oriente.

The reconcentration policy implied a tactical purpose, of course, to clear the countryside of the rural population suspected of collaborative affinities with the *insurrectos*, what historian Francisco Pérez Guzmán described as the "strategic component" of the war with war.[171] The war-with-war policy had entered another phase. "As long as peasants remained in the countryside," Manuel Corral justified the reconcentration policy, "it was impossible to prevent the rural population from supplying foodstuffs, clothing, medicines and other necessary supplies to the *insur-*

recto forces."[172] Major Florentino Yriondo de la Vara, a member of General Weyler's staff, would later recount the purpose of Spanish policy:

> To carry into effect the reconcentration under the conviction that it was impossible to terminate the war as long as the country people lived in their homes, because these country people gave news and provisions to the Cuban forces, and, besides, their continual visits to the town enabled them to take out all kinds of provisions and medicines and also information and at the same time [take] the livestock which they had, the pigs as well as the cattle, . . . given by them to the insurrection.[173]

"The reconcentration has cleared the countryside of the peasants," Spanish recruit Ricardo Burguete recorded in his field diary in 1896. "The devastation and emptiness are frightful. The countryside offers a desolating view after one year of war. Entire *pueblos* have been incinerated and all the remains are vestiges of their [former] existence among mounds of ashes and burned wood."[174]

But reconcentration implied a larger strategic purpose: to prepare the countryside for war without quarter, thereupon to presume everyone outside the camps to be the enemy, to draw a definitive distinction between friend and foe and wage a war of scorched earth with impunity, to destroy all assets—human and material—of potential value to the enemy, "without which," Captain Antonio Serra Orts understood, "it was impossible [for *insurrectos*] to wage war."[175] That is, to simplify the task of waging total war. Ricardo Donoso Cortés described an ominous consensus:

> On the island of Cuba, all sentiments loyal to *la madre patria* favor the policy of reconcentration, and the Army favors reconcentration completely and without restrictions. We must eliminate all the pretexts for treason outside the population centers and farms. He who is not an *insurrecto*, to be reconcentrated. For those who are not reconcentrated there will be no doubt that they are the enemies of Spain. They should be subject to the very same laws used against those who rebel with weapons in their hands.[176]

After the reconcentration decree, journalist Stephen Bonsal learned, Spanish soldiers had "not only the right but it [was] their duty, to shoot any man, woman, or child found outside the Spanish lines."[177] Entire families, laments the narrator of the Pedro Pablo Martín novel *Adelina* (1901) were "forced to abandon their homes and seek refuge deep in the countryside to avoid becoming victims of Spanish troops."[178] To lay waste to all manner of agricultural production and animal husbandry was a means to starve the *insurrectos* into submission—"so as to leave not a single plant alive atop the soil anywhere on the island," commented Emilio Reverter Delmas.[179] In sum: to destroy the productive capability of the land to deny insurgents subsistence, to produce starvation and induce famine as a method of war. "The principal purpose of the military operations we conducted," recalled Manuel Corral, "was to destroy the farmlands maintained by the enemy and gather up all the livestock, to execute General Weyler's plan to end the insurrection through hunger."[180] Josep Conangla remembered Weyler implementing the reconcentration program, ordering "military columns on operations as well as the cruel guerrillas to destroy the dwellings, the gardens, and the orchards so as to deny liberation forces access to lodging and food."[181] A dismal parallel to the campaign of *la tea incendiaria* waged by the *mambises*. *Insurrecto* commander Serafín Espinosa y Ramos recalled the time of reconcentration in Las Villas Province: "Vast clouds of reddish black smoke darkening the horizon from all directions, obscuring the sun as if it were an eclipse."[182] Correspondent Domingo Blanco accompanied General Weyler during military operations in Pinar del Río in late 1896, to bear witness that "the General in Chief advances with his column through the hills, destroying every peasant hut [*bohío*] he encounters along the way," adding, "All one can see from the distance is the blaze of the immense fires produced by the burning of the *bohíos* and the homes of the country people. Everything will soon be razed to the ground. The *insurrectos* destroy the sugar mills and the large houses to deny revenue to the State; we destroy the *bohíos* of the peasants . . . to deny the *insurrecto* support and shelter."[183]

All with effect. No longer any Spanish pretense to protect property and production. "The country has been obliterated," *El Heraldo de Madrid* reported in mid-1897, "and all its wealth and even the most vital food supplies to sustain life destroyed. The people, obliged to abandon the countryside, have been reconcentrated in the cities and are dying of hunger and misery. They are overwhelmed with famine and fall victim to the diseases endemic to the country. Entire towns have disappeared."[184] Any resource—human and material—of any potential use to *insurrecto* forces was destroyed when it could not be removed. Young Spanish soldiers, many still adolescents, deployed to defend the honor of *la madre patria*, acquitted themselves by burning crops, slaughtering livestock, and razing homes. "The other day we entered into other hills," Spanish recruit Gabriel Alcolea García entered into his diary in mid-1896. "We found many *bohíos* and wooden dwellings as well as farms of tobacco, *boniato*, sugar, and other vegetables. We burned all the dwellings and destroyed the farms."[185] The longer the war continued and the more desperate the Spanish became, the deeper they descended into depravity. Recalled Spanish Captain Enrique Ubieta:

> I remember that the Mayor of Güines presented himself before General Weyler telling him that he had more than 6,000 women and children dying of hunger in his town and that he begged him for resources with which to support them.

Weyler answered him that he had effected the reconcentration precisely with the object that all might die, and the Mayor went back to Güines and there in the streets of Güines I saw women and children die of hunger.[186]

"Army columns enter insurgent-controlled zones," was the December 10, 1896, entry in the field journal of *insurrecto* Major Rodolfo Bergés in Managua, "not for the purpose of pursuing us but with the intent to seize all types of animals that allow us to sustain the war, and along the way they destroy all the fruit and vegetable crops encountered."[187] A lucid understanding of the Spanish purpose. "In this campaign we have orders to kill everything we encounter," Spanish infantryman Lucas Barona wrote home, "even the animals."[188] A *mambí* reconnaissance unit entered what remained of a community that had been recently "cleared" by Spanish forces in mid-1896, Eduardo Rosell recorded in his diary: "They have begun the systematic destruction of everything. We came upon a pile of dead horses, colts, and calves that the Spanish column was unable to take away."[189] A war without quarter indeed. In mid-1897, *insurrecto* Colonel Gustavo Pérez Abreu marched through the Sancti-Spíritus hinterland. "The destruction wrought by the enemy is vast," he wrote in his field notes on June 6. "He razes everything in his path to the ground. Nothing is left standing. The orders must be to destroy everything with the intent of leaving us without provisions. To defeat us through hunger since he cannot exterminate us in the field of battle the way that Weyler had dreamed."[190] A somber stillness settled over the Cuban countryside. "Such is the war that Weyler wages," commented the monthly *Cuba y América* in early 1897. "Even the animals have been converted into the enemy. The Spanish exterminate everything that cannot be reconcentrated. Quarter is offered to nothing, not even dogs and cats.... In one day alone, one officer acknowledged, his soldiers killed more than 300 horses in Guanamón."[191]

The combination of the Cuban *tea incendiaria* and the Spanish reconcentration visited havoc upon the rural populations of Cuba. Cultivated fields were destroyed, stocks of food set ablaze, and herds of livestock seized. *Mambí* Colonel Eduardo Rosell confided his sorrow in a journal entry dated January 3, 1897: "How very sad to see so much of the countryside empty, the fields of cultivation abandoned, so many homes destroyed. It will cost us so much work to reconstruct all this. We pay dearly for our independence and for the obstinacy of our overlords. When will they be convinced this is for them a definitively and irremediably lost cause?"[192]

War with war also implied the need to reconfigure the role of the Spanish army, and especially to relieve soldiers of the responsibility to protect the sugar estates. No longer would the army command deploy troops to protect property and production—"so as not to weaken the armed forces," explained Weyler.[193] The deployment of troops could admit no purpose other than military operations against the *insurrectos*. The Spanish purpose was pacification, not the protection of property. War with war was about Spanish sovereignty as an end, not as means of governance, about the defense of Spanish honor—"*viva España con honra*"—and increasingly about the defense of the honor of the army. Planter Manuel Antonio Recio recalled meeting with General Weyler to request army protection: "He told me that the Spanish Army did not come to Cuba to protect private interests, but only to sustain or defend the Sovereignty of Spain."[194] The Spanish purpose was expressed with stark clarity. "The intent was to wage war, all its consequences notwithstanding," Reverter Delmas remembered, "to wage war to win, to dominate the enemy, without mercy, and with no purpose other than the interests of Spain and national decorum."[195] If Máximo Gómez was disposed to destroy the economy as a way to vindicate *la nación integral*, Valeriano Weyler was equally determined to destroy the economy as a means to defend *la integridad nacional*. During a meeting with members of the municipal council of Sancti-Spíritus, recalled one alderman, Weyler "told us that he had come resolved to put an end to the war, and that if it was necessary for that objective to destroy everything that Máximo Gómez had not destroyed, he would do so. His exact words were the following: 'I shall leave the Island as bare as the palm of a hand.'"[196] Spanish authorities disposed to deplete the national treasury and sacrifice the last man could hardly flinch at the ruination of the Cuban producing classes as the price to pay to preserve *la integridad nacional*.

Responsibility for the protection of property and production was transferred to the planters, who were thereupon authorized to organize private security forces. "It is absolutely necessary to end the posting of detachments on private estates," insisted Ricardo Donoso Cortés. "The *hacendados* must attend to their own needs, and sacrifice accordingly. . . . In this fashion the army will be free to dedicate itself to operate exclusively against the enemy."[197] Costs were transferred to beleaguered planters. Private security forces cost planter Francisco Rosell of Matanzas nearly 100,000 pesos during the war.[198] The administrator of the Soledad estate in Cienfuegos estimated private security to cost between $1,200 and $1,400 monthly.[199] Nor was the redeployment of army detachments without punitive purpose. Critics in Spain bore the Cuban planter class ill will, persuaded that the protection of sugar had imperiled *la integridad nacional*. *El Heraldo de Madrid* denounced the army command for having "sacrificed military objectives in order to save the sugar harvest—which was in the end not saved."[200] Worse yet, the belief took hold that planters had opportunistically availed themselves of army garrisons as a cost-saving measure. "Determined to defend property," Tesifonte Gallego complained in February 1896, "the [army command] scattered army detachments across the entire country. There was not an *hacendado* who failed to ask for troops to guard their estates, a convenient and so inexpensive way to protect their properties."[201] The estrangement between colonial officialdom and the producing classes continued to widen. "We have long believed that Spain's worst enemies are the Spaniards established on the island who form the so-called conservative class," Vicente Blasco Ibáñez warned. "They are the greatest threat to Spanish interests ... wishing that Spain exterminate the entire creole population so as to remain the sole owners of the island."[202]

To the last peso and the last man—hubris and honor combined to summon a renewed intransigence to the Spanish purpose, to defend *aquel pedazo de tierra* even at the cost of *el último hombre y la última peseta*.

But Weyler knew better. He arrived in Cuba lucid about the task at hand, aware too that Spanish resources and resolve were not in fact unlimited—official pronouncements notwithstanding—that the government of Cánovas Castillo could not plausibly sustain political support for and underwrite the cost of an endless war.[203] There would not be another ten years of war in Cuba. "The situation in Cuba is far too serious to delay a solution," Ricardo Donoso Cortés warned as Weyler arrived in Havana in 1896:

> The public mood, based on expectations of an early solution, presently observes expedition after expedition deployed to Cuba, thousands and thousands of soldiers, millions and millions of pesos, consumed and wasted, without results. It believes that each expedition represents the last and definitive effort and will result in the immediate and decisive defeat of the rebels. It now realizes that the insurrection, far from ending, extends across the full length of the island, gathering the capacity to sustain itself indefinitely ... and not a single step taken on the path to peace.... A vast wave of pessimism has formed, suspicion and distrust among mass opinion has reached the highest levels of the high command on the island.[204]

Weyler vowed to end the war within two years of his arrival.[205] "Two years?" the Madrid daily *El Correo Español* reacted with an aghast horror: "What a frightful reality.... What country can sustain two years of war? How many soldiers are yet to die in Cuba? How many empty households in Spain? How many hearts shattered with sorrow? Where will the money come from for these two years of war?"[206] Warned *El Heraldo de Madrid*: "Everyone here understands the gravity of the military and political situation. General Weyler predicted upon his departure he would end the war in two years. Every year represents an expenditure of hundreds of millions of *pesetas*. We know the measure of sacrifice in terms of money. We are also beginning to understand the cost in terms of blood."[207]

Seventeen years after the appalling loss of life between 1868 and 1878, Spanish soldiers returned to Cuba, by the many tens of thousands, endlessly it seemed, shipload after shipload of new recruits. "The men of government in Spain," Damián Isern could not but grieve, "and especially the senior commanders of the army, have learned nothing from the last separatist war in Cuba."[208] By mid-1897, the number of troops deployed to Cuba had surpassed 200,000, an amassing of European soldiery in the tropics with a predictable outcome: staggering mortality.

Perhaps it did not matter. To take political leaders in Madrid at their public pronouncements, the lives of soldiers were expendable. Once again Spanish soldiers succumbed by the many thousands to climate and disease. To contemplate the circumstances of the Spanish soldier in Cuba between 1895 and 1898 with the knowledge of 1868–78 cannot but induce a somber sigh of incredulity. The tropical heat and the humidity, and the torrential rains. And the mosquito. "The number of mosquitos is so great," Domingo Blanco wrote from an army encampment in Ciego de Avila in late 1897, "that officers and soldiers often pass the entire night unable to sleep," adding, "Despairing with horrible suffering, swollen and disfigured as a result of insect bites, they have passed and continue to pass days and days, months and months. Who knows for how much longer."[209] Once asked to name his three best generals, Máximo Gómez responded with clever sarcasm: "*Junio, julio y agosto*"—the peak months of the tropical rains and the season of the mosquito.[210]

Everything seemed to be happening all over again: military operations in the east against an unseen enemy, within an unfamiliar topography. "So strong is the insurrection in the eastern jurisdiction," Santiago Barroeta conceded, "that it could be said to be already Cuba Libre. We control only the important cities on the coast."[211] Ramón Ruiz was overtaken with a presentiment of tragedy as early as 1895: "We will continue to send our valiant soldiers to Cuba, where they are much needed. But we do not expect them to return."[212] Novelist Ubaldo Romero Quiñones arrived at the same conclusion, if with different words: "Cuba is the graveyard of the Spanish army."[213]

Forced marches and countermarches into the dense *manigua*—"which depletes the strength of our troops and spreads fear among recently arrived soldiers," commented one journalist—gained the reputation among Spanish soldiers as "*la jornada de la muerte*."[214] The bleak despair of the Spanish soldiery was recounted by the narrator in Pío Baroja's novel *La lucha por la vida: Mala hierba* (1904): "[The soldier] spoke of life on the island, a horrible life. Always marching and marching, barefoot, with legs sinking deep into the swampy marshland, and air filled with swarming mosquitos that caused blistering sores."[215] Correspondent Domingo Blanco accompanied Spanish soldiers on operations in Pinar del Río in 1896:

> We see day in and day out the file of a procession of misery without the consolation of admiring those young boys [*esos jovencitos*] who defend Spanish sovereignty with their Mausers. We see them always when the weariness and the illnesses relegate them to the hospitals. . . . After many days of marches in the mountains, under downpours of rain, mired in mud up to their waist, without having eaten and sleeping in the open: horrible marches over places that even during times of peace have never seen a human presence, climbing up the hills, holding on to one another so as not to fall off the mountain.[216]

At about the same time, at the other end of the island, from the miasmatic swampland surrounding Bayamo, a fever-ridden Lieutenant Enrique Piqueras Causas scribbled into his field journal: "We departed at dawn . . . traversing the swamp. Soldiers with mud up to their waist. Swarms of mosquitos and my ears are swollen . . . a journey from hell and many enemy ambushes. . . . Today we have many ill soldiers. Of the 290 soldiers in four companies, 23 were hospitalized and another 53 are reduced to inactivity. At this rate, none of us will return."[217] Infantryman José Moure Saco vividly remembered the mosquitos during operations in Caibarién: "swarming and alighting on my face, my being powerless to defend myself, for every time I squashed them off my face my hand was soaked with my blood that oozed from their crushed bodies."[218] Dreaded exercises: "Every day, from sunrise to sunset," wrote one soldier from the field in Puerto Príncipe, "under a blazing sun all day, over trails and roads that are unpassable, barefoot, without rations, drinking mud sludge instead of water and with yellow fever raging all through the ranks."[219] Ricardo Burguete recalled two days of marches between Manzanillo and Bayamo as "debilitating, and to make matters worse the rain downpours in the evening deprived us of much-needed sleep," a convoy "moving slowly, for it was behind oxen carts . . . that would frequently get stalled in the enormous mud quagmires of the trail."[220] One Spanish officer remembered the ordeal of the marches:

> The morning of the tropical day progresses. It is 10 o'clock in morning, the time of a frightful heat in these latitudes. The fields appear to have succumbed to a torpid sleep induced by the scorching temperature. The breeze seems also to have fallen asleep, as if the radiation of the sun has burned its wings. . . . The air suffocates. The branches burn. The land scorches. And the soldier, now mute, advances with his hat draped downward to shield his face, with the rifle resting

on his shoulder, with his body drenched in a sweat that has saturated his clothing.... Poor soldier."²²¹

Insurrecto Lorenzo Despradel could almost feel sorry for Spanish soldiers in his notes of military operations in early 1897 outside Sancti-Spíritus: "Incessantly harassed by our forces, decimated by yellow fever, and punished by the torrential rainfalls that converted the roads into streams, those soldiers offered the most pitiful sights."²²²

The rigor of military operations, including heat prostration, fatigue, and malnutrition, combined with fatal consequences. The "enemy offers little resistance," Manuel Cigés Aparicio wrote of the army marches. "He does well [*hace bien*]. To decimate us there is the sun, the rains, and the quartermaster corps that never comes to our aid."²²³ Manuel Corral attributed thirty thousand deaths directly to fatigue and hunger: "Soldiers on operations died of hunger."²²⁴ Hunger was a chronic condition. "I did not believe I was going to experience so much hunger and such thirst," recruit José Eguiluz confided to his parents, "for I now see that this [war] is not killing soldiers with bullets but through hunger."²²⁵

Very much the Cuban way of war. "General Gómez had a special system of waging war," *insurrecto* commander Juan Masó Parra recalled. "I heard him say on more than one occasion that the Cuban campaign would be won by making the Spanish operate continuous forced marches until they were exhausted."²²⁶ A method of warfare to which General Calixto García also subscribed: "To tire the enemy after which victory will be achieved."²²⁷ The Cubans lacked the capacity to defeat Spain through force of arms, Colonel Juan Lapoulide understood. "Therefore, they direct their efforts above all to prolong the duration of the war for as long as possible in the hope that Spain capitulates as a result of depletion of resources and physical and moral weariness, and that public opinion will rise up to oblige the Government of the Metropolis to end its effort to retain the precious Island."²²⁸

The Cuban way took its toll. Day after day, Spanish army units pursued *insurrecto* forces operating in the west, often relentlessly, deploying vast numbers of soldiers and often with success. But it was not always the success of the day that mattered most, for the night belonged to the *mambises*. A signal facet of the Cuban way of war: "We continued marching all night without stopping and without hearing a single voice," Enrique Collazo recalled.²²⁹ Cubans crossed the *trocha* almost at will "under the cover of night" (*con la obscuridad de la noche*), recalled Miró Argenter.²³⁰ Movement of *insurrecto* forces was undertaken during the nights to avoid detection and escape the heat of the day. "The night was very dark," one *insurrecto* remembered of a nocturnal march. "All the horses had a white handkerchief tied to their tails so as to be visible."²³¹ At times, Manuel Secades Japón wrote, "marching entire nights sleeping on horseback."²³² Never to march by day, recalled Ernesto Usatorres Perdomo, for "the guerrillas were close behind on our trail."²³³ As often as not, the Cubans waged nocturnal campaigns, to beleaguer Spanish encampments at night to deprive *peninsular* soldiers of sleep. "Throughout the entire night, units of cavalry and infantry constantly harassed the enemy," wrote Bernabé Boza of *insurrecto* operations in 1895, to assail the enemy "we do not allow him to sleep," adding:

> This system [of warfare] offers magnificent practical results and constitutes the great advantage we had over the Spanish, who are unable to respond.... Tomorrow this column will be weighed down with wounded and ill soldiers as a result of the fear occasioned by the sniper fire that always surprises them, by the fatigue and weariness, by the interruption of sleep caused by gunfire at irregular intervals ... from all different directions, from an enemy they do not know, in numbers they do not know. The fear of danger heightened by vivid imagination and the darkness of night making it all the more terrifying.²³⁴

Lorenzo Despradel remembered the Cuban way of war during operations in Sancti-Spíritus:

> We continued the march. Us in front, the enemy behind. Fighting all along the way as we retreated and leaving behind visible traces of our trail to encourage him to follow us across those arid lands so fully without water. The pursuit lasted many hours. As late afternoon arrived we penetrated into wetlands, marshy swampland, filled lagoons of brackish water and populated by clouds of mosquitos and sand fleas [*jejenes*]. The enemy column followed us into this terrain as the night descended, obliging him to camp in that location. Meanwhile our light cavalry force rapidly fled in another direction to escape this poisoned environment.

Despradel learned that the next day the Spanish column returned to its base with hundreds of ill soldiers in need of immediate hospitalization.²³⁵ Futile marches and countermarches, complained Juan Bautista Casas, "where the marches are ill-planned and night surprises the soldiers" in unknown and unfamiliar terrain, obliged units "to make exposed camps in open space within easy reach of enemy bullets."²³⁶

Peninsular soldiers succumbed again to disease and tropical illnesses, including yellow fever, malaria, dysentery, cholera, tuberculosis, anemia, enteritis, smallpox, and typhus. Illness wreaked havoc on Spanish ranks, Miguel Macau remembered, especially on troops "newly arrived from Spain, many of whom died within hours of contracting yellow fever."²³⁷ "El Patriota," recalled Vicente de Cortijo, "was the name the *insurrectos* gave to yellow fever, their most reliable ally."²³⁸ Mass hospitalization of soldiers was a chronic condition of the Spanish army in Cuba, and acted to deplete the ranks of the soldiery and diminished the combat capacities of soldiers. Vast numbers of *peninsular* troops—mostly adolescents—conscripted into military service and deployed improperly trained, poorly equipped, and inadequately acclimated, succumbed quickly and easily, often almost immediately upon arrival on the island.[239] A convoy from Puerto Padre to Las Tunas in June 1897 resulted in the death of one soldier and another five wounded due to battle—and the hospitalization of four hundred troops due to disease.[240] Manuel Corral recalled one field operation in which malaria and yellow fever ravaged the encampment almost at the outset of operations, requiring the burial of forty soldiers in a grove of guava trees.[241] "The fevers have ravaged the battalions in the form of a true epidemic," wrote one soldier from field operations in Bayamo, "not only reducing the number of battalions but also resulting in a scarcity of soldiers in the battalions."[242]

At any given moment, an estimated 25,000 troops out of a total deployment of 200,000 soldiers were in varying stages of hospitalization due to illness, disease, fatigue, malnutrition, and battle wounds. Between March and December 1895, nearly 50,000 hospital cases resulted from noncombat sources.[243] Of the 32,000 troops deployed for military operations in Pinar del Río in early 1896, 9,000 required hospitalization for malaria in the first ten days; thereafter more than 1,000 troops entered Havana military hospitals daily. Only one-half of the 14,000 recruits deployed in January 1898 were expected to fill the depleted ranks in Cuba; authorities anticipated the other half to be hospitalized within days of arriving on the island. "It is apparent," commented *El Correo Militar*, "that the reinforcements do not represent a net gain of actual forces."[244] Soldiers "are arriving here in the military hospitals of Havana as an avalanche," Domingo Blanco despaired.[245] From Artemisa in November 1896, a dispatch reported the departure of three trainloads transporting 1,000 sick soldiers to hospitals in Havana.[246] "A horror," Gonzalo Reparaz pronounced from Havana in December 1896. Reparaz enjoyed the confidence of senior army commanders in Cuba and disclosed that "there are some 12,000 sick soldiers in Havana and of these fully one-third of them will continue to die of malaria if not quickly repatriated to Spain." And from Santiago de Cuba, Reparaz received a letter from an army officer: "My battalion should be returned to Spain en masse. I do not have a single soldier fit for duty. They are all wasting away."[247] A battalion of 2,000 officers and men arrived in San Luis in mid-1897, Nicolás Arteagabeita wrote home, adding, "There are not more than 80 soldiers in good condition."[248] A column of 220 men returned from field operations, Manuel Cigés Aparicio wrote: "Not a single casualty caused by the enemy. But 50 soldiers are abandoned to suffer in the hospitals."[249] Of the 3,000 officers and soldiers of the San Fernando battalion in Bahía Honda in October 1896, only 400 were fit for military operations.[250] "The 30,000 ill soldiers who fill the

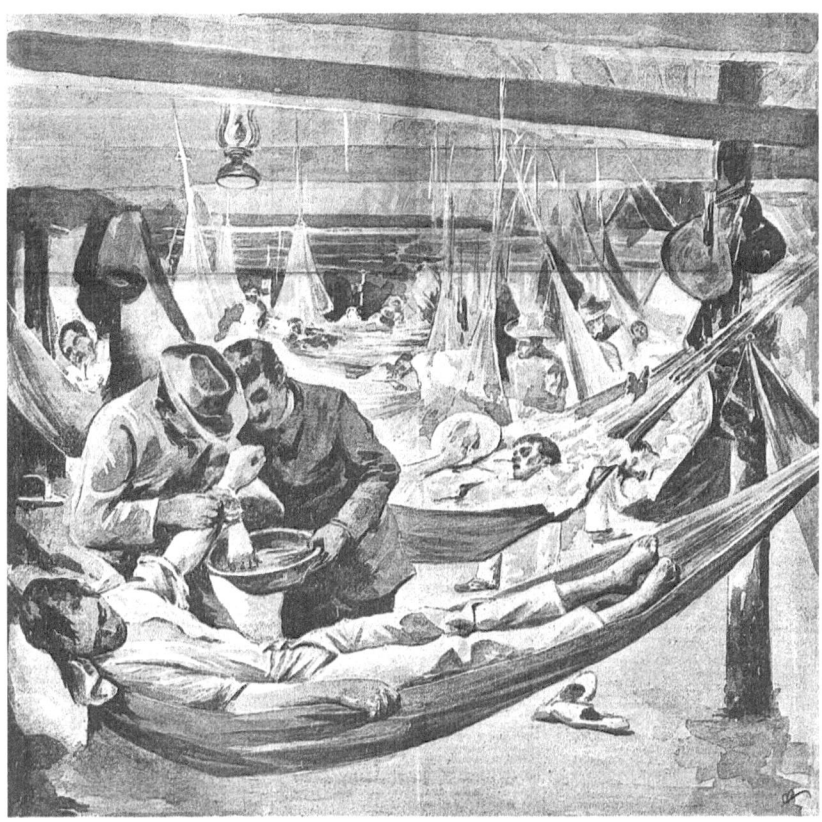

3.11 "Victims of Duty," depicting Spanish military hospital, Havana, ca. 1897.
SOURCE: *LA CAMPAÑA DE GRACIA* 28 (SEPTEMBER 25, 1897).

hospitals of Cuba," *El Imparcial* decried, "the thousands and thousands of cadavers that have transformed the island into an immense Spanish cemetery, and the 20,000 near-death soldiers returning to our shores represent a disgraceful confirmation of our past protests."[251] A relentless rate of mortality rising to the level of official malfeasance, pronounced army physician Felipe Ovilo y Canales in 1899, "resulting in one of the greatest health disasters we have ever suffered."[252]

And almost always: ill-equipped and understaffed military hospitals; Rafael Gasset visited the military hospital in Baracoa in 1895, a facility equipped with fifty beds to serve the needs of 200 ailing soldiers.[253] The ward of the military hospital of Havana, designed to accommodate between 500 and 800 patients filled with more than 2,800 ill soldiers.[254] And a chronic "shortage of doctors," reported one correspondent in Havana, "and the need to improvise new hospitals to provide support for the sick in this wretched climate."²⁵⁵ Spanish infantryman José Moure Saco recalled his hospitalization experience, "assigned to a cot and given a coarse cloth for a sheet infected with lice—in addition to the lice with which I arrived—who devoured me." Moure Saco remembered being discharged from the hospital sicker than when he arrived.²⁵⁶ "Ill soldiers in Cuba," one military medical official reported, "drop to their knees and plead with physicians with tears in their eyes and despair in their hearts to be allowed to return to Spain."²⁵⁷ Manuel Corral recalled the "truly horrific" military hospitals and infirmaries, commonly known as "the slaughterhouses of the soldier" (*mataderos del soldado*), adding:

> It would not surprise the reader to learn that the mortality rates in the hospital reached frightful numbers. Nor was it always the fault of the physicians who often provided selfless services in the hospitals.... The cause of high mortality had to do with the commanders of columns and the physicians on [military] operations who did not separate ill soldiers out from the ranks until they could barely stand on their feet.... Often soldiers were hospitalized en masse, appearing more like cadavers than living beings, and who could not be saved.²⁵⁸

Disease and tropical illness also took a toll on physicians, many of whom shared the fate of their patients.²⁵⁹ Increasingly young physicians were dispatched for military service to Cuba, and increasingly inadequate numbers of health care providers made everything worse. "There are not sufficient numbers of physicians in Cuba to meet the needs of military service," protested one army surgeon in early 1896.²⁶⁰

A war of lost innocence and vanished youth, with nothing to be proud of and no sense of honorable service rendered. Losses in a war due mostly to noncombat causes, "a death without the glory that attends death on the field of battle," army physician Felipe Ovilo y Canales could only lament.²⁶¹ Staggering mortality rates. A total of 100,000 soldiers perished between 1896 and 1898, Emilio Reverter Delmas surmised, approximately 35,000 deaths a year, a frightful loss of "the youth who departed from the Peninsula, robust, healthy, with hearts filled with hopes, [who] were transformed not in combat with the enemy—who they rarely saw—but by a fatal climate, transformed into an army of the walking dead" (*en ejército de espectros*):²⁶²

> The rebel bullets during three years of war barely impaired our ranks if we compare the casualties suffered in combat with those caused by illnesses. Of the 200,000 troops deployed to Cuba, only 114,900 survived. That is, 85,100 soldiers perished in the *manigua* or in the hospitals, or were buried at sea en route

home, or disappeared on the island. Those who had been weakened by anemia and tuberculosis were buried in anonymous grave plots across the towns and villages.... Only in the text of the Holy Scripture does one find examples of a collective disaster on this scale.[263]

"About the war there is little to say," Esteban Uraga wrote to his parents from Sancti-Spíritus in August 1897, "for there are no longer battles. *Insurrectos* are nowhere to be seen. The only thing I can say is that many soldiers are dying from illnesses."[264] Army physician Angel Larra y Cerezo calculated a total of 14,897 deaths among officers and men: 1,708 due to combat, 4,137 to "common illness," including dysentery, typhoid, smallpox, and tuberculosis, and 9,052 to yellow fever.[265] General José Fernández Losada, the inspector general of Sanidad Militar, arrived in Cuba in November 1897 to review conditions in the Spanish army. He was horror-struck. An estimated 32,000 soldiers were confined to hospitals as a result of fatigue and hunger. An "extraordinary number" of soldiers had succumbed to malaria, dysentery, and yellow fever and were consigned to understaffed and ill-equipped hospitals. Army ranks were "filled with large numbers of soldiers in varying conditions of exhaustion, fatigue and malnutrition, all of which reduce[d] the army capacity to conduct vigorous military operations." Entire army units were on the verge of collapse. "Untold numbers of soldiers are unfit for military service and are in conditions of utter prostration. They must promptly be repatriated to Spain in order to save their lives." An entire generation of youth lost, Losada despaired: "¡Es horroroso!"[266]

Soldiers arriving in Cuba were utterly unprepared for combat. New soldiers arriving in Cuba were incorporated directly into the ranks of existing units, Eduardo de la Peña learned, with the expectation that veterans would teach newly arrived recruits "to make camp, to collect water, to prepare hammocks, to march in the *manigua*, to learn the land: in a word, to become accustomed to combat and the unique character of this war, which is unlike all others."[267]

A chilling consensus emerged. "One of the most pitiable conditions existing here," US Consul Fitzhugh Lee reported from Havana in mid-1897, "is the fact that so many of these young men of Spain are transported to this island for soldiers, without drill, without discipline, and un-acclimated, a thin blue uniform is put on their bodies, a straw hat on their heads, a gun in their hands and they are sent out in the interior to get alternatively wet and dry and die of fever. One half of them will never get back to Spain." Concluded Lee: "I do not think the Spaniards can now muster more than 75- or 80,000 soldiers who have strength enough to carry a rifle and a haversack."[268] Observers were uniformly horrified. Most Spanish soldiers were boys, commented one longtime English resident of Cuba:

They are scarcely clothed, and what uniforms they do receive are quite unfit for campaigning work. The average age of the rank and file is from 15 to 18. They are mere boys—raw recruits who, immediately upon their arrival in Havana, are despatched to the interior without drill of any kind. Naturally, they soon fall victim to the climate, for it is not Cuban bullets that have carried off the majority of the Spanish army.... Sickness and bullets will account for the remainder.[269]

Innocent and very young was how Esteban Montejo remembered the Spanish soldiers he engaged in combat, "conscripts that were barely sixteen or eighteen, newly arrived from Spain, having never before been in battle."[270] They "remind one of schoolboys," observed Adelaide Rosalind Kirchner.[271]

Peninsular soldiers were indeed conscripted at ever-younger ages. The number of adolescents levied into military service in Cuba increased all through the last two years of the war. Spanish Major Pedro Cordón in Cruces was horrified to discover that the new recruits arriving from Spain were "children, because there are no other" (*los soldados que vienen son niños, porque no hay otros*).[272] *El Correo Militar* decried the practice of deploying ill-trained young recruits that would "condemn us to look upon our overseas possessions as a vast necropolis in which to bury the flower of Spanish youth."[273] They were young—and they were poor: *niños* conscripted into the army to defend *la integridad nacional*, with neither the resources nor the representation to escape military service. "The soldiers who die in Cuba," Vicente Blasco Ibáñez reminded his readers, "are the poor and always damned: the workers."[274] And increasingly a shortage of officers. In 1897 the phenomenon of the so-called *sietemesinos*: boy cadets (*cadetes casi niños*) with only months of academy training were offered commissions in exchange for voluntary deployment to Cuba. Second lieutenants sixteen years of age were not uncommon.[275] At the end of the war, former Minister of War Marcelo Azcárraga conveyed belatedly official remorse for "deploying of 200,000 soldiers to Cuba, boys without training" (*niños sin instrucción*), explaining the tragedy as the result of a flawed law of compulsory military service that allowed for conscription of youth.[276]

Official mortality rates did not include the many deaths among the estimated 44,000 *repatriados* who returned to Spain in varying stages of life-ending illness, almost all of whom arrived with various physical and psychological afflictions.[277] Ricardo Burguete returned to Spain aboard a ship filled with *repatriados*: "The war returns what is left: malarial victims, men with dysentery, tuberculosis, amputees. Most of them without hope of salvation. Emaciated bodies, hands and feet the color of wax, and faces broken by the horrible pallor of death."[278] Antonio Serra Orts remembered the experience of repatriation, being "ill as a consequence of service in Cuba, with pay in arrears, and returning to the Peninsula more dead than alive, anemic, with fevers, without a penny and lacking winter clothing."[279] Between 1896 and 1897, an estimated 1,300 to 1,500 men were repatriated to Spain every month.[280] Domingo Blanco boarded the *San Agustín* en route to Spain from Cuba in early 1897, which was transporting 480 *repatriados*, soldiers who "only months ago were healthy and in full vigor, and return to us with illness and melancholia." Ninety-one cases of pulmonary tuberculosis, Blanco learned, 146 afflicted with anemia, ninety-five soldiers with malaria, eighty-four wounded in battle, and ten with rheumatic fever. The others were weakened by malnutrition and fatigue. "Death in war without ever seeing war" was Blanco's sardonic comment. He continued:

> It is a small ship for so many people. The entire ship can be said to be an infirmary.... There is no place to sit or corner at which to converse without observing the pitiful sight of anemic soldiers who only wish to live long enough to say goodbye to their mothers.... These are the soldiers with whom I arrived in Cuba nine months ago, the same ones who did not allow us to sleep with their bellowing of patriotic songs, so enthusiastic, so healthy and fat, who wanted the head of Maceo, who boasted of returning home soon, by Christmas eve. Yes—the same ones, although I no longer recognized them, the way their parents will not recognize them when they return to their homes.[281]

Many did not survive the voyage home.[282] Vicente Blasco Ibáñez wrote of 364 *repatriados* aboard the vessel *Isla de Panay* in 1897, fifty of whom were transferred to hospitals in Puerto Rico, too ill to complete the voyage home, and another sixty-four buried at sea en route to La Coruña. "These are good times for the sharks," Blasco Ibáñez commented tersely.[283] "And after all the soldiers endured in Cuba," comments the narrator in Pío Baroja's novel *La lucha por la vida*, "the return to Spain was even sadder still. The entire ship filled with men dressed in striped uniforms [*rayadillos*], a ship filled with a cargo of skeletons and every day five, six or seven died and were buried at sea."[284] Many thousand *repatriados* returned to their respective port cities, to Cádiz, La Coruña, Vigo, or Santander, among others, bearing grim testimony in their persons of the toll of the war in Cuba. Rafael Gasset, editor of *El Imparcial*, traveled to Cádiz to receive a ship returning from Cuba with *repatriados*:

> The onboard infirmary offered a pitiful sight. In the necessarily small space that a ship could allocate to a hospital were found the most gravely ill, one atop another in eighteen bunks. Some were empty. The soldiers who occupied them upon departure from Havana had died en route and were buried at sea. We conversed with the poor soldiers and their discolored lips spoke with weak and labored

effort.... Those gentle boys who not long ago left their homes with confidence and vigor greeted us with weak gestures.... Throughout the ship we saw sick soldiers. Many of them had to be moved clinging to the shoulders of their comrades and in all of them could be seen the terrible effect of tropical sickness that poisoned their blood and destroyed their energy.[285]

"The repatriated," decried Deputy Juan Sol y Ortega in the Spanish parliament, "these poor repatriated, upon arriving in our ports and disembarking did not even appear as cadavers, for a cadaver at least still preserves the body mass approximate to a living being. What appeared to be disembarking on our shores appeared to be fetuses that are preserved in jars used in anatomy laboratories."[286] The war in Cuba laid waste to a generation in Spain. "Many [*repatriados*] return totally incapacitated," *El Imparcial* anguished. "Their injuries have deprived them of the capacity for any type of work. Many return consumed by fevers, destroyed by yellow fever, victims of anemia, exhausted and wasted away. Their skin thinly draped over their bones, their eyes sunken deep into the sockets, without the strength to walk, without appetite, in the worst physiological condition."[287]

The presence of 200,000 soldiers in Cuba belied the Spanish capacity to wage war. A formidable army, to be sure, but almost from the outset, never able to mobilize its superiority of numbers to full advantage. The annual summer rains wreaked havoc on almost all facets of Spanish military operations. Field operations were often suspended for months at a time. "In the moment I write these lines," Rafael Gasset reported from Havana in November 1895, "a torrential downpour is in progress, rain of such magnitude that we Spaniards cannot imagine. The horizon is black, the streets are swollen with water, and we understand the impossibility of any military operations during this rainstorm."[288] The deployment of reinforcements from Spain was almost always deferred and delayed until the end of the rainy season. "In the beginning of June [1896] the rains commenced," General Weyler made note, "thus necessitating the curtailment of operations, and obliging us to struggle against great difficulties, with illnesses preying upon our soldiers, especially with malaria and yellow fever."[289] One month later, Weyler again wrote, "The torrential rains continued, as was to be expected, and malaria and yellow fever caused significant numbers of casualties."[290] And in August: "The rains continued. The number of ill soldiers increased, although in the vast majority of cases they were ordinary fevers and not yellow fever."[291] At about the same time, in July 1896, Bernabé Boza entered in his field journal that Spanish operations had halted, "without any practical results to the Spanish and with great advantage to us, for if they mount operations in this time of heat and rain—*la temporada de mangos y aguacates*—yellow fever and dysentery create daily vast vacancies in their ranks."[292] Domingo Blanco also commented on Spanish military operations in the summer of 1896, describing the "many disasters that occurred in the month of August, a month of rest for nearly all the columns, a month of sadness for the few columns on operations and of much work for the hospitals, given the considerable increase in the number of sick soldiers. We await the month of September with grim resignation."[293]

War with war implied the need for military operations on a scale difficult to sustain. The army command struggled to maintain the combat capacity of 200,000 troops in Cuba, a task complicated by the continuous need to fill vacancies in the ranks created by death, disease, and debilitating tropical illnesses. Hospitalizations and repatriation, due mostly to soldiers succumbing to climate and disease, continued to hamper combat operations. "From the very outset until the end," army physician Felipe Ovilo y Canales insisted in 1899, "our soldiers knew perfectly well that enemy bullets and machetes were the least of their risks. That the true enemy—the climate—stalked them in ambush everywhere, and that a dark and silent death awaited them at all turns."[294] Filling the ranks depleted through illness and disease taxed Spanish recruitment capacities. Minister of War Azcárraga acknowledged in mid-1897 that increasing vacancies in units on military operations due to illness surpassed one thousand a month, and acknowledged too the difficulty in securing replacement recruits.[295]

Weyler lacked the military personnel and material resources to sustain operations across the full length of the island. For the duration of his command, Weyler appealed for additional troops—and always with mixed results. Indeed, Weyler learned early during his command that Spain confronted difficulties in sustaining reinforcements. "Given the difficult conditions in the country," Azcárraga asked Weyler in March 1896, "is there one way or another for you to utilize the services of Cubans [*los hijos del país*], white and black, who on different occasions rendered such valuable service?"[296] Manuel Corral could bear first-person witness to depleting army ranks and described "the lack of adequate numbers of regular troops" as circumstances that "obliged the general in chief to organize local guerrillas."[297]

What sustained a besieged army in the years that followed in the face of catastrophic losses was the expanded role of Cubans in the service of Spanish military operations. If there was a genius to Weyler's preparation for war with war, it lay in his appreciation of the limits of Spanish capacities, more specifically, of the urgency, he understood, to "develop a completely different system of war," and his awareness too of the need to defeat the Cuban armies before disease decimated the Spanish army, and—most of all—that the war could not be long sustained without forces recruited locally.[298] The need to recruit "voluntary forces" (*fuerzas voluntarias*), Weyler explained years later—*hijos del país*—was "to avoid the need for conscripted [Spanish] recruits to engage in combat overseas without being properly acclimated."[299] A way also to reduce staggering mortality rates, losses that were sitting uneasily with a war-weary Spanish public. "Anything that can be done to reinforce the army of Cuba appears well worth the effort," *El Heraldo de Madrid* exhorted. "Through these means Spain can save much blood and much money, and continue the war without exhausting itself in the manner that our enemies expect."[300]

The decision to augment *peninsular* soldiers with Cuban recruits signified more than an improvised response to unanticipated needs. Weyler arrived in Havana in 1896 in the company of a score of experienced senior army commanders. Almost all were veterans of 1868–78 who returned to Cuba with an understanding of the character of the insurgency and informed too with a theory of combat perhaps best described—in twentieth-century vernacular—as methods of counterinsurgency. Most of the thirty-two Spanish generals serving in Cuba in 1896–97, including most prominently generals Arsenio Linares Pombo, Francisco Loño, Juan Salcedo Mantilla, Luis Prats Bergés, Adolfo Jiménez Castellano, Andrés Maroto, Juan Manríquez de Lara, and Enrique Segura, among others, had previously served in Cuba. Spanish commanders understood the importance of auxiliary acclimated forces recruited locally, to augment *peninsular* units, of course, but also—and especially—to enhance the combat capacity of offensive military operations. Spanish Colonel José Ignacio Chacón had served in the Fourth Division in Santa Clara during Yara and was subsequently appointed to the faculty of the Superior War College in Madrid. Chacón prepared one of the earliest primers on methods of counterinsurgency, studying the experience of "irregular wars" in the "modern age," including wars in Afghanistan, China, Mexico, the United States, and of course Cuba during 1868–78. Persuaded that "in military science the study of irregular wars has not received the importance it deserves," Chacón published in 1883 a comprehensive theory of counterinsurgency that was very much in circulation among Spanish military commanders. "When a discontented people of a country initiate a revolution and take to the countryside with the intent of rebellious purpose," Chacón understood, "they can never confront the forces of the regular army":

> For this reason, the creation of mobile forces [*fuerzas ligeras*] is necessary, endowed with the identical conditions of mobility and audacity as the *insurrectos*, to keep pace with them in their rapid marches, to attack with breathtaking speed upon overtaking them or prepare well-planned ambushes that result from

3.12 Militarized unit of Havana firemen. SOURCE: NICOLÁS HEREDIA, *CRÓNICAS DE LA GUERRA DE CUBA* (2 VOLS., HAVANA, 1895–96).

knowledge of the country. *Fuerzas ligeras* are necessary, to be mobile and without the necessities of a regular army, which can be deployed in the vanguard to explore the trails, to surprise small enemy positions.... To achieve these conditions knowledge and familiarity of the country is necessary, without which the guerrilla unit cannot exist.[301]

Weyler returned to Cuba with deep knowledge of colonial insurgency, mindful of the optics of war and attentive to the propaganda of racial solicitude. Almost immediately, the army command militarized units of Havana firefighters (*bomberos*), most of whom were black, from which Weyler selected thirty *bomberos* to serve as a very visible personal security escort: "for me to demonstrate," Weyler acknowledged years later, "my confidence in that race so long committed to Spain."[302] A "bodyguard composed of blacks," observed Adelaide Rosalind Kirchner during her visit to Havana, a way to "offset the prominence the Cuban blacks have attained in the insurrection."[303]

Weyler returned to Cuba also bearing familiarity with the theater of operations, mindful of the challenges posed by topography and terrain, and possessing an understanding of the havoc wreaked by disease and illness. But most of all, he acknowledged, "experience demonstrates that the campaign in Cuba cannot be resolved by way of great military operations that would otherwise present the opportunity of a transcendental battle."[304]

Within weeks of arriving in Cuba, Weyler announced plans to organize three thousand blacks and whites into guerrilla units for military service in Oriente. "Cubans willing to bear arms in defense of Spain," Weyler indicated, recalling "the valuable service that these guerrillas provided in the last war."[305] Weyler expanded the number of *guerrillas locales* "at all points in which military detachments operated to enable [guerrillas] to cooperate in the defense of the perimeter of the town, to acquire intelligence on the enemy, and assist the residents to gather cattle and food supplies." The army command organized additional mounted units of *guerrillas volantes* and *guerrillas montadas* to strengthen cavalry forces.[306] By 1897, a total of nine *tercios* of guerrillas were deployed across the island.[307] "With the coming of General Weyler," US Vice-Consul Walter Barker in Matanzas reported, "came the guerrilla organizations."[308] An estimated twenty thousand guerrillas were deployed in military operations dur-

3.13 *Contra-guerrilla*, Cavalry Regiment de la Reina, ca. 1897. SOURCE: BIBLIOTECA DIGITAL HISPÁNICA/BIBLIOTECA NACIONAL DE ESPAÑA.

3.14 *Guerrilla volante*, Matanzas. SOURCE: NICOLÁS HEREDIA, *CRÓNICAS DE LA GUERRA DE CUBA* (2 VOLS., HAVANA, 1895–96).

ing the first year of Weyler's command. The importance of the guerrilla, historian Octavio Avelino Delgado suggested, "from a strictly military point of view was much higher than their numbers might lead us to believe. . . . They constituted the heart of the whole [army] column."[309] During the 1896–97 campaign, surmised Miguel Varona Guerrero, a staff officer with Máximo Gómez, perhaps as many as 100,000 Cuban guerrillas served the Spanish war effort.[310] At another point, Varona Guerrero estimated that a total of thirty thousand *guerrilleros cubanos* "flourished with an extraordinary vigor" throughout the war. Manuel Piedra Martel—aide-de-camp to Antonio Maceo—similarly estimated thirty thousand Cubans in various guerrilla units. Gil Gelpí y Ferro suggests that "irregular forces" included as many as eighty thousand "*hijos del país*."[311]

Property owners similarly organized paramilitary security forces, also *hijos del país*. The *guerrillas particulares* established small forts (*fortines*) within the estates, designed to protect property and provide security to field laborers engaged in planting and harvesting.[312] Across the western jurisdictions, sugar estates were converted into fortresses garrisoned by *guerrillas particulares*, inevitably to become sites of combat. Bernabé Boza described the España sugar mill in Cárdenas "as an enemy fortress, like all of them, protected by an armed garrison of 200 men, almost all Cubans."[313] Cuban military operations in Cienfuegos, Cuban Colonel Alejandro Rodríguez wrote in mid-1896, encountered numerous sugar estates "defended with *fortines* and each one with a detachment of guerrillas."[314] By mid-1897, most population centers were garrisoned by a combination of guerrillas and Voluntarios.

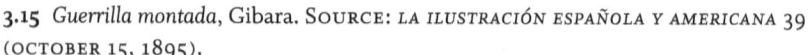

The deployment of guerrilla forces in their multiple operational units—*volantes, locales, montadas,* and *particulares*—transformed the character of the war. The guerrillas served as armed escorts for Spanish supply convoys and protected railway networks. In Las Villas, the Cienfuegos–Sagua–Santa Clara railroad, as well as the Sagua-Placetas-Remedios-Caibarién line—vital lines of supplies and support—were secured principally through the deployment of guerrilla units. Guerrillas rendered important service in the execution of successive reconcentration orders, conducting operations in the rural interior to locate and destroy farms, crops, and livestock and to resettle the *pacífico* population into the reconcentration camps. "The thousands of Cubans who had enrolled in Spanish ranks as *guerrilleros*," Enrique Collazo remembered, "were like bloodhounds, who discovered even the most insignificant traces with which to track the families who had sought refuge in the mountains."[315] Total war. "What I expect of all the columns and guerrillas," Weyler enjoined in January 1897, "is the destruction of all resources of potential use to the enemy as soon as possible."[316]

Guerrillas expanded the scope and increased the efficiency of Spanish military operations.[317] The western regions of Las Villas "no longer required the deployment

3.15 *Guerrilla montada,* Gibara. SOURCE: LA ILUSTRACIÓN ESPAÑOLA Y AMERICANA 39 (OCTOBER 15, 1895).

of a large number of Spanish forces," *La Correspondencia Militar* reported. "A reduced contingent of soldiers is sufficient, which in combination with the mobilized irregular forces [*fuerzas irregulares movilizadas*] is deployed to protect almost all towns and plantations and contribute to weakening the *insurrecto* bands that operate in the region."[318]

The deployment of *guerrillas montadas* enabled the Spanish command to engage the *insurrectos* on their own terms. "The enemy now is engaged at night," Tesifonte Gallego recounted. "He is surprised at dawn. He is harried on the plains and pursued in the *monte* and before battle and during battle, all forces act in coordination. The enemy is denied respite."[319] A formidable fighting force, commented Ricardo Donoso Cortés:

> [*Guerrillas*] possess, in effect, qualities that a regular army obtains only with the passage of much time: acclimation, practical and detailed knowledge of the country, the capacity to understand quickly and fully the plans of the enemy, to anticipate and predict enemy strategy, the capacity to adapt to satisfy their necessities in the same manner as the enemy, to [exercise] influence over the inhabitants of the countryside from whom they obtain with ease information through which to develop exact intelligence concerning the situation and movement of the rebels.[320]

"In the Cuban campaign," Antonio Díaz Benzo understood, "a great many guerrillas are needed." Guerrillas "accustomed to the open life of the countryside" (*á la vida libre del campo*) provided "services of inestimable value." "Major importance must be accorded [to them], for their way of being [*manera de ser*] and their innate conditions confer upon them a special character that fully distinguishes them from the regular armed forces."[321] Captain Severo Gómez Núñez was succinct: "In this war of Cuba, a war of ambush and surprise, a war of great privations, a war in which the astute enemy seeks to make himself invisible: in such a war there is little to analyze and much to execute."[322]

As the war-with-war policy approached the end of the second year, far greater emphasis had been given to expanding guerrilla operations. "Who better than us," asked *El Correo Militar* in mid-1897, alluding to Spanish irregular warfare against Napoleon, "appreciates the advantages of indigenous forces in combat in the mountains, on the plains, in the *manigua* and the desert.... Perhaps the failure to recognize the importance of these circumstances is what has contributed to the prolongation of our colonial wars":

> Many of our colleagues who return from Cuba, when asked about the difficulties attending such a wearying and bloody irregular war, have responded with unanimity that the expansion of the guerrillas would have a salutary effect. It would not only allow for a reduction of the fatigue of the troops and the increase

3.16 Unit of a *guerrilla local*. SOURCE: EL FÍGARO 11 (DECEMBER 1, 1895).

of efficiency of the operation, but it would also create forces having the identical conditions of the enemy in every way that he has advantages. . . . Now more than ever [guerrillas] would deliver excellent results to deliver the final blow to the *insurrectos* and permit the repatriation of a large number of our soldiers.³²³

The war with war developed into something of a war within a war, at times fully assuming the characteristics of civil war. Edwin Atkins recalled learning that during operations in the Trinidad mountains Spanish soldiers seldom encountered *insurrectos*, "although there were skirmishes now and then, chiefly between insurgents and the guerrillas."³²⁴ The correspondence, diaries, field journals, and memoirs of *mambises*, as well as reports of Spanish military operations, including General Valeriano Weyler's five-volume *Mi mando en Cuba*, provide a detailed chronicle of a war that expanded increasingly into a conflict between Cubans.³²⁵

It is difficult to ascertain the politics or determine the motives of the Cubans who enrolled in the ranks of the guerrillas.³²⁶ The voice of the guerrilla is faint indeed. Service as a guerrilla provided gainful employment to many, a way to make do and get by during hard times, including the many thousands of men in need of a means of support and sustenance from among the *reconcentrados* displaced from land and deprived of livelihood. "Thirty, forty thousand *guerrilleros*," *insurrecto* Lieutenant Colonel Segundo Corvisón scorned, "Cuban guides in the countryside, . . . lent their service to the Spanish Government to earn a livelihood through the blood of their brothers."[327] Manuel Corral observed large numbers of peasants joining guerrilla units who, after having "been deprived of their traditional means of subsistence as a result of the reconcentration policy, and rather than dying from hunger, affiliated themselves with the Spanish cause."[328] Spanish soldier Manuel Ciges Aparicio recalled meeting guerrilla recruits and learning that "the reconcentration policy had obliged them to leave the countryside. Hunger had forced them to join a guerrilla unit so that their children would not die in destitution."[329] Years later, in 1949, historian Oswaldo Morales Patiño interviewed former guerrilla Julián García Hernández: "He sought to justify his and his brother's action with the excuse that they had enlisted in the service of Spain in order to guarantee food for their mother."[330] During the last years of the war, *Diario de la Marina* later insisted, "many honorable men of good will," desperate "to provide bread for their children through any type of work," sought employment in the ranks of the guerrillas, "which at that time did not have then a reputation of ignominy."[331]

The matter of loyalty to *la madre patria* is more difficult to ascertain. Bibián Fernández served as a *práctico* for Spanish army units operating in the region between Yaguaremas and Aguada de Pasajeros west of Cienfuegos. Asked how he came "to be opposed to [his] fellow countrymen," Fernández responded, "Because when I obtained [the] use of right and reason, I knew my father [was] with the Spanish arms in hand."[332] Guerrilla officers also often included Cubans of means and standing. Years later, guerrilla officer Isidoro Tomás recalled the "circumstances that obligated me to take up arms in the last civil war": "The circumstances were none other than that I had sworn loyalty and vowed to defend the flag that waved over Cuba long before anyone was speaking anything about revolution. As a man of honor I could hardly sully that condition of being Cuban and a decent person with acts that would bring dishonor and disgrace."[333]

Cubans often enrolled in guerrilla units out of personal grievances, with scores to settle, often having lost livelihood, land, and loved ones as a result of *insurrecto* military operations. Many "people were left destitute," correspondent George Bronson Rea learned during his travel to Cuba in 1897, "and a great many enraged at the treatment they received, went to the town and joined the local guerrillas."[334] Lolo Benítez organized a guerrilla unit to avenge the death of his mother during an insurgent attack.[335] Others perhaps, also like Benítez, volunteered to combat the feared ascendancy of blacks. "I do not understand how any white would rise up against Spain," Lolo Benítez explained. "Here in Cuba there are only two races: the colored race from Africa and ours, which can only be the Spanish race."[336]

Guerrillas took up the Spanish cause with sustained ferocity, "implacable persecutors of the *insurrectos*," recalled Manuel Secades Japón.[337] Miguel Varona Guerrero, an aide to General Máximo Gómez, recalled the guerrillas' "hatred toward the *insurrectos*."[338] Lolo Benítez acquired a reputation for summary execution of *insurrecto* prisoners.[339] Esteban Montejo recalled the guerrillas: "fire blazed from their eyes, men filled with poison, rotten from the inside out. Whenever they came upon insurgents they used to fall on them and those captured were killed automatically."[340]

A number of guerrilla units acquired notoriety among *insurrectos*, including the Guerrilla de Manzanillo under Lolo Benítez; the Guerrilla de Guantánamo under Pedro Garrido; the Guerrilla de Sancti-Spíritus under Rosendo Espina; the Guerrilla de Bahía Honda under Eleuterio Picaza; the Guerrilla de Cruces under Manuel Hernández. The Guerrilla de Niquero under the command of Marcelo O'Ryan was described as "a true Cuban *guerrillero* [*un verdadero guerrillero cubano*], who wages war like the *mambises*, for the unit is composed almost entirely of *prácticos*... whose greatest praises come in the form of denunciation by the *mambises*."[341] The Guerrilla de Yateras, "all Cubans," wrote Manuel de Granda, "all residents of the region who knew the terrain in which they operated inch by inch," and added, "all rabble, more closely resembling a pack of dogs running wild in the *monte*, like bloodthirsty wolves in hot pursuit by way of scent."[342] The Guerrilla de Sabanilla acquired notoriety as having been given license to operate with impunity to wreak havoc with methods of plunder and pillage as the preferred mode of operations.[343]

Guerrillas inflicted grievous casualties upon the ranks of the insurgent leadership. Some of the most prominent *insurrecto* leaders died at the hands of guerrillas. "Many of the young men who responded to the call of duty," reflects the narrator in the short story "Su regalo" by Jesús del Calvario, "had perished by way of the *guerrilleros*' machete. The majority of them."[344] The Guerrilla de Sabanilla was responsible for the death of General Tomás Fernández. Colonel Amador Guerra was killed in combat with *guerrillas locales* of Manzanillo in 1895. Flor Crombet fell mortally wounded in battle in Baracoa in 1895, killed by the Guerrilla de Guantánamo. The Spanish army command deployed an estimated 3,800 guerrillas in Pinar del Río in 1896 in military operations against Antonio Maceo.[345] The death of Maceo at Punta Brava in December 1896, long attributed to Spanish Colonel Francisco Cirujeda, was in fact the result of operations mounted by the combined cavalry unit of eighty-seven *guerrillas montadas* under the command of Doroteo de Peral and twenty-four *guerrillas locales* of Punta Brava.[346] "Everything indicates that Maceo was killed by the guerrilla unit under the command of Peral," General Weyler later wrote.[347] Miró Argenter recalled the guerrillas of Pinar del Río as "zealous and brave defenders of that territory for Spain ... [and] the most aggressive against Maceo."[348] Also killed at Punta Brava was Francisco (Panchito) Gómez Toro, son of Máximo Gómez, whose corpse, it was widely reported, was mutilated by guerrillas.[349] Alejandro del Pozo's chronicle of the *mambises* who perished in the war, *Páginas de sangre* (1898), identifies many hundreds of officers killed by guerrilla units, including Generals Clotilde García, Néstor Aranguren, and Antonio Núñez, and Colonels Rafael Socorro, Alvaro Rodríguez, and Mariano Rivera.[350]

The *mambises* developed an adversarial wariness of the capacities of the guerrillas. *Insurrecto* Israel Consuegra wrote of the "tenacious persecution of the guerrillas."[351] The guerrillas enabled the Spanish army to conduct operations "with great efficiency," recalled Miguel Varona Guerrero, "due to the guides and their local knowledge of the men and ways of towns and the countryside."[352] Guerrilla units "knew how to pursue the *insurrecto*," Orestes Ferrara remembered.[353] "Guerillas [sic] are formidable enough owing to their knowledge of the country and familiarity with Cuban methods," journalist Grover Flint learned during his time among the *insurrectos* in 1896.[354] Guerrilla units organized by *presentados*, former *insurrectos* who often surrendered or otherwise availed themselves of Spanish offers of amnesty, visited a special type of havoc upon *insurrecto* camps. "[They] knew perfectly well where our encampments were hidden," Avelino Sanjenis recalled.[355] Years later Santiago Rey recalled a *presentado* who defected to the Spanish army: "He knew all our secrets, even the most carefully hidden sites of *insurrecto* encampments. He was an enemy to be feared."[356]

Cubans in the ranks of guerrillas were despised as traitors and feared as adversaries. The *guerrilla local* Santa Fe, wrote Waldo Insua, "was the terror of the insurgents" and was "more feared than the regular forces."[357] The *guerrilla local* of Sancti-Spíritus, commented Manuel Martínez-Moles, "were more like wild animals having escaped from the jungle than men in the service of a civilized government, committing all types of disgraces, including the severing of ears of victims as trophies."[358] Comandante Manuel Arbelo recalled the guerrillas in Matanzas, who were "let loose in the countryside like a pack of jackals ... composed of men who knew perfectly well the location of the sites of the most remote places of refuge."[359] Frederick Funston served briefly with the *mambises* and recalled:

> Now and then a band of guerillas [sic], well mounted and thoroughly familiar with the country, would dash by night out of one of the larger garrisons and raid

through the country, cutting up such small bodies of insurgents as they might encounter, and making a speciality of hunting out our hospitals and murdering the helpless wounded found in them. These detestable wretches were more mobile than the insurgents themselves, their horses being better fed, and usually managed to return to their home stations. When they were run down, however, it was a fight to the death, quarter being neither asked nor given.[360]

The *mambises* developed a visceral loathing of guerrillas: uniformly detested as *malos cubanos* and despised as traitors, "our mortal enemy" (*nuestros enemigos mortales*), recalled Manuel Arbelo.[361] "The feeling among these insurgents against these men is implacable," commented journalist N. G. Gonzales.[362] Manuel Piedra Martel was filled with "ire and indignation" toward guerrillas that he scorned as "spurious sons of Cuba."[363] Cubans "did not hate the Spanish as much as they hated the *guerrilleros* for being traitors to their *patria*." Julián Sánchez remembered the adult conversations of his childhood, a hatred that insinuated itself into the very games that children played, often separating into two antagonistic groups: the children of *mambises* and the children of guerrillas.[364]

The *insurrecto* narrative depicted the guerrillas always in the most odious terms. "The Spanish government took special care not to admit honorable men into the ranks of the guerrillas," Bernabé Boza surmised in his diary. "Only assassins, thieves, and criminals, low-lives from the slimy pools of prison."[365] All "bastards and traitors," José Isabel Herrera, bristled, "who for a miserable peso served Spain against their Patria and their brothers."[366] Men "recruited from the flower of [Cuban] criminality," pronounced José Miró Argenter.[367] "Consummate criminals," Angel Rosende recalled hearing during his adolescence, "who for a miserable salary dedicated themselves to the protection of Spanish power, attacking farms, stealing, and commandeering anything possessing any value."[368] "Coming out of social scum" (*procedentes de la escoria social*) was how Manuel Arbelo remembered the guerrillas, adding:

> Upon the creation of guerrilla units as auxiliary forces to columns of the Spanish army, [authorities] recruited into their ranks men of the lowest social condition [*hombres de las más baja condición social*], whites and blacks, all abject human beings, mostly men released from prisons who seized the opportunity to satisfy the basest passions, ferocious instincts, and the inclinations to innate cruelty. The war placed those men ... in circumstances to commit all types of outrages: plunder, assassination, arson and rape.[369]

Spanish soldier Josep Conangla remembered the guerrillas in much the same way, writing of the *guerrillas volantes* of Aguacate as "made up of unscrupulous elements who under orders anticipating the Decree of Reconcentration were engaged in the burning of the humble homes of defenseless families, mostly of impoverished women and children, as well as laying waste to the crops and gardens."[370]

The Cubans waged war within statutory protocols of the Republic-in-Arms. Article 19 of the 1896 Constitution of Jimaguayú enjoined all Cubans "to serve the Revolution in their person or by way of their interests, according to their capacities."[371] Article 48 of the Penal Code of the Republic-in-Arms, enacted in July 1896, defined perpetrators of the "crime of treason" as Cubans who transmitted intelligence and acted as spies and guides, Cubans who defected or encouraged others to defect, Cubans who surrendered military positions, and "Cubans who [took] up arms against the Patria under the Spanish flag." Article 49: "The criminal guilty of the aforementioned crimes will be subject to the death penalty."[372]

The accounts of close-quarters battle between *mambises* and guerrillas acquired their own graphic vernacular. This was a personal violence, intimate, death hand-delivered by way of the machete: *dar machete*, to strike a blow with the machete; the verbs *machetear* and *acuchillar*—to hack with a machete—assumed prominence in first-person accounts of combat. Comandante Miguel del Valle "*dió machete* to the guerrilla unit of San José de las Lajas."[373] Juan Lorente described one battle that ended with the "*macheteo* of 50 *guerrilleros* and *voluntarios*," while Avelino Sanjenis could casually record an entry into his field journal: "Pude dar machete á tres guerrilleros."[374]

A combat norm developed early: captured Spanish soldiers were usually released; captured guerrillas were always executed, by firing squad, or by machete, or hanged preferably from a *guásima* tree for the convenience of low, thick, horizontal branches. A new verb form entered the *insurrecto* vernacular: *guasimar*. Summary executions of guerrillas developed into a commonplace facet of the war. "A number of Spanish soldiers were taken prisoner," Enrique Conill entered in his field journal in 1897. "Cuban *guerrilleros*, on the other hand, were executed by firing squad."[375] Rogelio Castillo recorded in his diary the capture of a guerrilla unit "*la que fué macheteada*."[376] Ricardo Batrell recalled the fate of captured *guerrilleros* at the hands of a comrade: "He dealt one of those *machetazos* known during the war in our lexicon as *balvitarro*, a blow landing at an angle at the right shoulder slicing through from one side, to the other almost cutting the prisoner in half. *Tremendo machetazo!* We all hooted. These dead *guerrillero* prisoners were Cubans. Traitors!"[377] Bernabé Boza similarly recorded in his diary the capture of four prisoners "who were summarily hanged for being Cuban *guerrilleros* in the service of Spain"; and at another point a guerrilla unit "composed of 20 troops was *macheteada* by Captain Arbolay."[378] Manuel Arbelo recalled the Cuban capture of the city of Las Tunas in August 1897: "All the *guerrilleros* in the service of Spain, all Cubans, mostly men of color, were executed." Arbelo was slightly embarrassed by his impulse for mercy, but recognized that "in the face of the ire and the contempt of his comrades in arms toward the *guerrilleros*, an appeal to clemency was out of place."[379] Horacio Ferrer also remembered Las Tunas and the capture of "many Cuban *guerrilleros* in the service of Spain . . . those miserable low-lives who always practiced extreme cruelty so as to demonstrate their loyalty to the Spanish," all of whom were executed the following morning.[380] Ramiro Cabrera was also in Las Tunas in August 1897:

> We seized more than a thousand arms, two cannons, and took an estimated 600 prisoners of soldiers and *guerrilleros*. The Spanish prisoners were very well treated, for we provided them with fresh meat. They themselves told us they were dying of hunger. . . . With regard to the Cubans who waged war against their country, the *guerrilleros* and the guides of the Spanish: all were executed by firing squad. There were about 50 or 60 men, the larger part of whom were black.[381]

Frederick Funston recalled the fate of captured guerrillas: "Cubans seemed to bear no hatred whatever against the Spanish regulars. . . . [For] the hated guerillas [sic], Cuban mercenaries in the Spanish service, it was certain death to fall into the power of the insurgents. It was these wretches who in that war committed many of the horrible atrocities that brought a stain on the Spanish name."[382] "Killing Spaniards does not really matter to us," *insurrecto* Clotilde García explained to the young Julián Sánchez, "unless of course we happen to come upon them in battle. We really wish to save our bullets for the traitors."[383] Not uncommon at all the scene described by Colonel Ricardo Buenamar when he was presented with a prisoner and told: "Ese es un guerrillero, hay que amachetearlo."[384]

The enmities between *insurrectos* and guerrillas deepened into something of a personal visceral animus, not dissimilar to a blood feud sustained with settled hatred and a desire to kill—on both sides—as acts of vengeance. Mario Carrillo recalled an *insurrecto* engagement with a guerrilla unit, with "everyone seeming to pick out his opponent and make the fight a personal affair."[385] Decades later, Miguel Varona Guerrero, on the staff of Máximo Gómez, recalled the guerrillas—"native traitors and mercenaries"—with undiminished antipathy. "The acts of treason and vandalism committed by the Cuban *guerrilleros* in the service of Spain served to heighten passions among the men of the Ejército Libertador and produced a ferocious hatred and rage." Varona recorded the many occasions of summary execution of captured guerrillas: sixty in Las Tunas, two hundred in Arroyo Blanco, one hundred in Pelayo— "and many others that would be far too long to enumerate," Varona Guerrero commented glibly, "*todos acuchillados*," and adding, "Death was meted out immediately to all captured *guerrilleros*. The most enthusiastically sought-after deed of triumph [*el más entusiasta de todos los triunfos*] was *dar machete* to Cubans in a guerrilla unit in the service of Spain."[386] The desire for revenge was palpable. Fermín Valdés Domínguez entered in his field journal in early 1897:

> There is no one among us who does not wish to hear the crack of a machete splitting the skull of the despicable [guerrilla]. This is not a moment of forgiveness; it is a time for struggle without respite, it is a time for punishment. In this struggle there is nothing but victory or death. No one who is convinced of these circumstances can imagine retreat or show consideration to those who both as men and as soldiers are unworthy of respect.... I imagined the pale figure of Panchito [Gómez Toro], who with grace would tell me: my life for the honor of the *patria* and I saw too the deep *machetazo* inflicted by the *guerrillero* and I felt as if the blood of my friend splattered onto my face.... And I remembered my vow, my sole and greatest aspiration of my spirit: revenge.[387]

And Valdés Domínguez at another point in his journal: "I had the good fortune of being able to *machetear* the guerrilla of Villaclara on May 14."[388]

The "valuable service"—per Weyler's judgment—rendered by the guerrillas notwithstanding, in fact, the Spanish war effort had stalled. Military operations continued unabated deep into the year 1897, in fits and starts, occasional Spanish advances and Cuban reversals, and vice versa, but in neither instance did outcomes offer prospects of an imminent end to hostilities. Almost two years of war with war had passed. Two years, Weyler had vowed. The war was supposed to be coming to an end. But it was not. No one was optimistic. The war effort seemed to have settled into strategies simply to hold on. "The battalions are no longer battalions but rather groups of weakened soldiers," journalist Domingo Blanco wrote from Manzanillo in 1897.[389] From the *manigua* in midsummer 1897, General Máximo Gómez observed the grim fate overtaking the Spanish soldiery: "The Spanish are weary, and during these days in which the summer heat acts to suffocate even us I cannot even imagine how these troops move about. The truth is that Weyler is destroying his soldiers. He has them undertaking terrible marches over impassable roads [*por caminos intransitables*] for no purpose other than to seize [rural] families and destroy cultivated fields."[390]

Enmities in Cuba deepened into irreconcilable bitterness. "The hate intensifies," Mexican consul Andrés Clemente Vázquez reported from Havana. "Along the sidewalks, Cubans [*los hijos del país*] speak against the Spanish in a low voice. In the cafés, in the theaters, etc., *peninsulares* keep apart to talk among themselves, even from Cubans who are their own children. Some day soon, when the desperation reaches its peak, there will be true scenes of general extermination in Havana and in all the cities of the island." Vázquez arrived at a somber conclusion at the end of Weyler's first year in Cuba: "The government plan is now clear: by way of death, deportation, and forced migration to exterminate the present Cuban generation infected with revolutionary poison."[391]

In Spain, a disquiet settled into a disaffected public and among disheartened public officials, a national mood gone bad by way of the gap widening between rising popular political expectations and diminishing military results. The war appeared to have settled into a stalemate—the one outcome that was unsustainable. "The urgent need to end the war in Cuba is apparent to everyone," *La Epoca* insisted, "and until this is obtained catastrophe is threatening the Peninsula."[392] "The atmosphere is very heavy and the outlook is certainly dark," US Naval Attaché George Dyer reported from Madrid.[393] Liberal Práxedes Mateo Sagasta anguished at the prospects of war with war without end. "After having deployed 200,000 men to Cuba and having spent one billion *pesetas*," Sagasta worried, "it turns out that, even if conceding that half the island has been pacified—which is to concede a great deal—on the other half our soldiers control nothing more than the terrain upon which they stand" (*no son dueños nuestro soldados más que del terreno que pisan*).[394] Conservative Party President Francisco Silvela sounded a grim warning:

> The war in Cuba represents a conquest of one nationality by another and signifies the subduing of a people entirely hostile to Spain. In this instance . . . it poses an insoluble problem for any nation, however strong it may be. It is necessary to say with clarity and with courage: we must bring this affair to an end. . . . We must organize the war in conditions that we can sustain without the annihilation of our forces and without producing the destruction of our Peninsula.[395]

"How is it possible," *El Imparcial* asked incredulously, "that in the presence of 200,000 Spanish soldiers, the separatists of Camagüey live in perfect security and deliberate in their constituent assemblies with total tranquility?" Weyler had explained his slow progress due to the "refusal of the *insurrectos* to engage in combat." *El Imparcial* could not but respond with mockery: in command of twenty battalions, Weyler's "comment surprised no one, for the rebels have demonstrated a thousand times and in a thousand ways that their plan has always been to avoid combat."[396] *La Epoca* cast a wary eye at the prospects of a prolonged "war of attrition" (*guerra de agotamiento*) and "a perpetual Cuban civil war," while *El Imparcial* questioned the wisdom of "defending the permanence of the present Captain General [Weyler] in the face of the obvious inefficiencies of his methods."[397] An announcement by the Ministry of War in mid-1897 of plans to deploy an additional twenty thousand troops to Cuba aroused the ire of *La Correspondencia de España*: "We are disturbed [by the announcement] for it appears that the government has not abandoned efforts to end the insurrection by military action.... The Cuban conflict cannot be remedied only with *additional soldiers*. Arms cannot achieve anything more than already achieved, other than to convert the island of Cuba into a heap of rubble that will cover the graves of a million and a half Cubans and tens of thousands of Spaniards."[398] *El Heraldo de Madrid* was horrified: "The very idea that it may perhaps be necessary to deploy another 20,000 men to Cuba has scandalized everyone."[399]

The onetime unanimity of national purpose—"the last man and the last peso"—showed signs of fraying. "Nothing is lacking in regard to anything," puzzled *El Imparcial*, "not soldiers, not rifles, not money. Nevertheless, the advances made in the campaign are nowhere visible."[400] Political leaders could no longer be believed; army commanders could no longer be trusted. "We have lost more than 70,000 men and spent more than a billion *pesetas*," decried the weekly *El Nuevo Régimen*. "We are now sending more soldiers and spending more money. It is not clear where our sacrifices will take us if we continue the war."[401] *La Correspondencia de España* identified with the plight of Spanish soldiers: "What a war! We cannot read the most recent telegrams [from Cuba] without experiencing a profound despair for the valiant soldiers who operate within an asphyxiating heat, in a lethal climate, suffering the horrors of torrential rains, in a water-saturated and swampy terrain, to engage a traitorous enemy who almost never shows his face and who hides in the impenetrable mountains or within the dense vegetation that conceals him from view."[402]

The dread of an interminable war settled uneasily over a war-weary people. And in mid-1896, the unthinkable: another colonial insurrection in the Spanish colony of the Philippines. Another forty-six thousand Spanish troops were deployed to the Pacific to fight a war that would continue through the end of 1897.[403] The population of eighteen million Spaniards was paying dearly to defend *la integridad nacional*.

The war in Cuba had settled into a desultory stalemate, laying waste and wreaking havoc everywhere—even as it went nowhere. A war that could not be won waged by a government vowing not to lose. The prospects of a protracted war had become almost as unbearable to contemplate as the idea of a separatist victory had been unthinkable to concede. Spanish military operations seemed to have stalled into a standstill: a stymied war effort in Cuba at a time of depleted army morale, diminished political resolve, and declining public support. The possibility of a Cuban victory shimmered into view. "Our assessment was optimistic," General Carlos García Velez recalled years later. "We were aware of the [disaffected] tenor of Spanish public opinion by way of Madrid newspapers. We read articles denouncing the war, of the enormous costs incurred by the war, of the losses suffered among soldiers never again to return to Spain, of the arrival of the wounded and the ill, of the protests of the mothers, of the clashing opinions of the political leaders."[404] Spain presided over a war in abeyance as if waiting for something to happen, and at great cost. No one had a solution acceptable to everyone. The devastation of the economy, warned *El Imparcial* in mid-1897, "as a result of measures adopted indiscriminately, has increased the suffering of supporters of Spanish sovereignty without weakening the *insurrectos*."[405] The Cuban economy was approaching collapse. "Commerce is found in a state of paralysis," a disconsolate Emilio Reverter wrote from Havana. "The economic crisis is profound, hunger is taking a terrible toll, property has remained destroyed, rents have disappeared. It can be said that in Cuba there are no activities other than the Mauser and the machete, other than fever and hunger."[406] Domingo Blanco visited Manzanillo in late 1897: "The factories are in ruin, the transportation companies are without oxen for draft animals, the cash registers are without money, the hospitals are without the necessary staff."[407]

Los buenos españoles were at a loss and in despair, overtaken by a deepening foreboding of being stranded by history, caught between the receding claim of Spanish sovereignty and the advancing claim of Cuban independence. Disappointment with the slow progress of the war was deeply experienced and widely shared. US Consul Fitzhugh Lee moved freely within colonial officialdom and among representatives of the producing classes. A restless impatience had settled over the supporters and sympathizers of Spanish sovereignty, Lee reported in late 1897: "I find quite a change in the sentiments of most of the Spanish or Peninsular citizens. The last man and last dollar battle cry of [Cánovas] which was so loyally and willingly re-echoed by Weyler has in a great degree subsided and the results following Spain's loss of the Island are being calmly considered by the Spanish merchants and property owners."[408] The "Spanish element," one journalist reported from Havana in early 1897, was "condemning with more and more emphasis the fruitless exhausting policy of General Weyler.... They see that Weyler is making no progress."[409] The very class of Spaniards who originally had supported Weyler, US Vice-Consul William Barker reported from Sagua la Grande in mid-1897, "now silently but bitterly denounce [him]."[410]

The beginning of the end began unexpectedly. On August 8, 1897, while vacationing at the thermal baths of Santa Agueda, Conservative Prime Minister Emilio Cánovas del Castillo was assassinated. The political provenance of war with war was no more. "The continuation of the plan of war as conceived by General Weyler," recalled Spanish Colonel Manuel Mariano y Vivo, "was based on the presence of the Conservative Party in power. The displacement of the latter implied the revocation of the former."[411]

A sequence of bewildering events ensued. The formation of a new ministry elevated Liberals to power in Spain and catapulted Autonomists into government in Cuba.[412] Liberal Prime Minister Práxedes Mateo Sagasta moved quickly to relieve General Weyler of command and to install a home-rule government under a criollo administration—"the exercise of effective sovereignty over the island," a disgruntled Rafael Guerrero complained.[413] All measures designed to end the war by way of political concessions: from waging war with war to making peace through reforms.[414] *El Correo Militar* correctly characterized it as a "radical transformation of the policy of the war."[415] The Sagasta ministry had as a last resort acquiesced to criollo governance, informing the newly appointed Captain General Ramón Blanco that the deployment of new reinforcements from Spain was no longer possible. A new policy: "Ni un hombre ni un peso más."[416] "Let the country [*el país cubano*] know," the Sagasta ministry instructed Blanco, "that the arrival of the new Governor signals a completely different era from all previous ones."[417] A "new politics of empire," observed historian David Sartorius.[418]

"I am charged with the task of inaugurating a new program," General Blanco explained upon arriving in Havana. "To concede *self-government* to Cuba as affirmation of the sovereignty of Spain. To interpret faithfully the intentions of the government that appointed me, I plan to pursue a policy of openness, of generosity, and of forgetting and forgiving as a means to reestablish peace in Cuba by way of liberty."[419] In rapid order, Blanco introduced colonial reforms as gestures of conciliation with insurgent Cubans, offering political concessions and inaugurating a policy of *atracción* through pardons and amnesty and outright cash subsidies to *presentados*.[420] Regimental commanders most closely associated with Weyler were relieved of duty.[421] An estimated six thousand jailed political prisoners were released.[422] Newspapers previously censored were authorized to publish freely. In November 1897, Blanco suspended the reconcentration program, pronouncing, "All who are presently in reconcentration centers, who possess farms, whether as owners or renters, are free to return to their properties with official assistance and protection."[423]

The installation of an Autonomist government shattered what remained of the colonial consensus. *Los buenos españoles* reacted to the new creole government with anguished indignation. Defenders of *la madre patria* viewed home rule as a thinly disguised transition to independence, a concession to Cubans that signaled a breach of faith rising fully to the level of treason. All seemed lost. "Autonomy leads directly to independence," Rafael Pérez Vento feared, "not because Autonomy signifies independence but because it can serve as a bridge to independence" and inevitably weaken "national sentiment in Cuba."[424] Autonomy was "nothing other than the mask that hides separatist aspirations," decried Francisco Moreno.[425] "All classes of Spanish citizens," Consul Fitzhugh Lee cabled from Havana in late 1897, "are violently opposed to real or genuine autonomy because it would throw the control of the island into the hands of the Cubans and rather than that, they would prefer annexation to the United States or some form of an American protectorate."[426] The distinction between *autonomismo* and *independentismo* was lost among *peninsulares*, Richard Weightman reported from Havana in late 1897: autonomy announced the "death knell of civilized society in Cuba."[427]

Worst yet, a deepening despair coursed its way among the loyalist faithful, a brooding presentiment of loss, of autonomy as evidence that *la madre patria* had lost the political will to defend *patrimonio* in Cuba. Not without reason. The disaffected public mood in Spain confirmed the worst fears among *los buenos españoles* in Cuba. "We should resign ourselves to the loss of the island," Francisco Pi y Margall counseled in early 1898. "It is already useless to tell the Cubans that independence may bring them a race war and innumerable conflicts, perhaps even catastrophes. . . . Separated from us by 1,200 leagues of ocean, Cuba is not a province of Spain but a colony. It is madness to pretend that it will live eternally under our domination."[428] A weariness had set in. A palpable weariness. "The problem was political," *Nuevo Mundo* anguished, "and it was turned into a military problem . . . and because critically important factors were not considered, it has resulted in a staggeringly costly failure [*un costosísimo fracaso*]. . . . Weyler has been merely the manifestation of the failure. With his ruthlessness and his maladministration he has revealed in twenty months what perhaps would have taken another general years to discover: the magnitude of the abyss."[429] *La Epoca* was categorical: "In reality, Cuba is lost to Spain," adding, "Autonomy has been the true liquidation of Cuba—more than liquidation, a gamble in which we have given everything in the hope for peace and have received nothing in return."[430]

Nowhere perhaps was the revulsion toward criollo home rule more acutely experienced than within the ranks of the Spanish army in Cuba. A collective indignation swept through the army command. Officers righteous in their wrath: colonial concessions as betrayal and an affront to the honor of the army. If pacification was now a matter of political accommodations, Rafael Guerrero taunted, "the Army no longer has any purpose in Cuba. With what right can the government reasonably ask for continued sacrifice of treasure and lives?"[431] Indeed, how unseemly: to summon soldiers to continue to fight on behalf of a Cuban government considered by many to be the very outcome they had been deployed to prevent. Many were horrified by the suspension of the reconcentration program. "Everyone is convinced that without the aid of the *guajiro* the *insurrectos* could not have sustained the war," José Muñiz de Quevedo bristled. "Everyone knows that every night many *guajiros* among those '*pacíficos*,' armed with machetes and rifles, joined the ranks of the bandits to lay incendiary waste across the entire island."[432] The idea that the *pacífico* population would return to peaceful pursuits was preposterous, scoffed *La Epoca*. "It is more likely that the *guajiros* will return to their roles as allies of the separatist bands, as their spies, as their informers, and as their reserve forces so that the moment a rifle becomes available there will be twenty individuals ready to join the *insurrecto* ranks."[433]

Precisely the reaction that Captain General Blanco had feared most. The captain general, Fitzhugh Lee summarized a meeting with Blanco in late 1897, was worried about charges "by his enemies [of] giving aid and comfort to the rebellion because if these people return to their homes and begin again to plant, the insurgents gain the benefits of their actions."[434] So too with freedom of the press. Suddenly—freedom of expression writ large. What utter folly, critics decried, to extend a liberty that "was incompatible with the state of war in which the Island finds itself."[435] Military authorities denounced the reforms that offered concessions while the Cubans were still under arms, protesting that the "politics of generosity" would be interpreted as a "symptom of weakness," thereupon to encourage the expansion of the insurgency.[436]

Army fears came to pass. Insurgent Cubans did indeed receive autonomy as evidence of Spanish weakness. *Insurrecto* morale soared. "Spain's offer of Autonomy is a sign of her weakening," Provisional President Bartolomé Masó was certain, adding, "We can accept nothing save absolute independence from the hand of Spain."[437] General Calixto García agreed, viewing autonomy "only as a sign of Spain's weakening power and an indication that the end is not far off."[438] Autonomy "is a clear confession that [Spain] is incapable of defeating us through the force of arms," Máximo Gómez exulted.[439] Across the island, *insurrectos* prepared to expand military operations.[440] "The insurgents . . . are everyday more hopeful of forcing Spain to deliver the island to them," Vice-Consul William Barker reported, "and the fact is that they are also more encouraged, seeing Spain demonstrating by offers of reforms and autonomy her tendency of weakness."[441] The prospects for autonomy were bleak.

The bruised sensibilities of the army could not be allayed. The recourse to a political settlement implied a repudiation of a military solution, which suggested too a loss of confidence in the army. "The termination of the campaign of arms," Manuel Mariano y Vivo remembered, "contributed to the loss of enthusiasm, to be replaced with discouragement and distrust, which obliged people to reconcile themselves to the loss of our sovereignty of the Island.... Such a loss was inherent in the installation of the Autonomist regime."[442] An army engaged in war abroad betrayed by the pusillanimity of politicians at home. "Today the country begins to awaken from its lethargy to see with clarity and horror the results of the miserable hoax of Autonomy," decried *La Correspondencia Militar*. "Ever since the installation of Autonomy the rabble of the *manigua* has increased in such numbers as to suggest that Autonomy has served to add kindling to what was a small fire on the verge of being extinguished by the effort of arms."[443]

The two groups upon whose support the success of autonomy depended—loyalists and separatists—spurned home rule and arrived at one common goal, if not a different objective: the separation of Cuba from Spain. To offer home rule while the Cubans were still in rebellion, *La Correspondencia Militar* scoffed, represented a "solution to besmirch the prestige [*desprestigiar*] of Spanish arms," adding:

> The policy of concessions that the government has adopted is truly inconceivable. From one day to the next, for one reason or another, the government provides more evidence of its weakness, or perhaps of its impotence.... And thus we proceed forward. From concession to concession, in a downward decline, in search of an ephemeral peace by any means and at all cost.... On one hand, the Nation, here in the Peninsula, giving all [to the cause]: men, money, strength, and character ... and on the other hand, there, in the very theater of war, the Army, the Nation in arms, firm at its post, dying and fighting with heroism and determination, contemplating passively these political changes, awaiting the moment when this house of cards called Autonomy falls.[444]

But it was not certain that the army was contemplating political changes passively. Developments were tending toward a chaos of another kind. The political solution had failed. Now what? The government that had rejected a military solution confronted a continuing insurgency with an army that had rejected the government. "All this," decried *La Correspondencia Militar*, "is the result of a policy of not wishing the army to prosecute the war with war and for not having allowed the army to complete the task that it had so bravely begun."[445] *El Correo Militar* mocked the premise of home rule, and warned, "If Spain were to see that the principles of Autonomy produced no advantage, and failed to hasten the end of the war, and failed to reduce our sacrifices, a reaction against the policy of concessions is very possible."[446]

Tensions mounted across the island. Newspapers in Havana availed themselves of the newly proclaimed freedom of the press to attack the war-with-war policy and especially to denounce General Weyler's conduct of the war. "One would have thought," a puzzled Domingo Blanco wrote from Havana, "that the generosity of Spain would have been reciprocated by all, beginning with forgetting the past and moving beyond the cursed distrust produced by the conflict between Cubans and *peninsulares*. But no. Instead, all the rancor has been released and has revealed itself in the form of a desire for vengeance for all the suffering."[447] All the while, Andrés Clemente Vázquez observed, "political and personal hatreds intensify and increase."[448]

Anger swelled within military circles. "The failure of the Autonomist regime is complete," *La Correspondencia Militar* pronounced, resulting in an "opera buffa government" that enjoyed "the confidence of neither the public nor the Army. On the contrary, it has incurred the hostility of all good Spaniards [*todo buen español*], for it represents a disgraceful humiliation for the Nation without producing a single practical result." The repudiation of home rule was complete. "We have no confidence in the new policy or diplomacy. . . . We have faith in the skill and valor of the generals that are today deployed in Cuba, in the heroism of the brave Spanish soldiers, and the patriotism of the country, that will not fail to make every effort to preserve that which belongs to [the Nation]: the island of Cuba."[449]

Disgruntled army commanders in Cuba plotted protest. In early 1898, disgruntled officers publicly demanded to be returned to Spain. "Cuba is no longer Spanish," Antonio Serra Orts anguished, and pondered, "No one has understood the reason for continuing the war against the Cubans. From the moment that Autonomy was proclaimed the troops should have retired to the larger population centers . . . and departed leaving the Cubans with their *Cuba libre*."[450] In the weeks that followed, reports of desertions, mutinies, and wholesale surrender to insurgent forces increased. Most of the soldiers in the prestigious Imperial Battalion of Madrid operating in Nuevitas surrendered to local insurgent forces. "Secret information has reached this Consulate," US Vice-Consul Alexander Brice reported from Matanzas, "that volunteers and Spaniards are ready to revolt against General Blanco and the new ministry of Spain."[451] Army units outside Remedios suspended military operations. "Spanish soldiers no longer fight," General Máximo Gómez wrote from the *manigua*, "not for their flag, nor for their King. Now that Cubans have received Autonomy, they do not know what is left for them to defend in Cuba."[452] Consul Fitzhugh Lee arrived at a similar conclusion: "Large number[s] of the officers and men of the Spanish Army . . . cannot be depended upon to obey General Blanco's orders when issued in the interest of Autonomy."[453]

Years earlier, *Diario de la Marina* had warned political leaders in Spain that the hint of independence in Cuba would have grave consequences, "for history would call our honorable resistance [to independence] *the rebellion of the loyal*."[454] So it was. In mid-January 1898, an estimated three hundred officers of the army and Voluntarios, swords in hand, with the exhortation and encouragement of *los buenos españoles* of the *casinos*, *liceos*, and *círculos*, took their fury onto the streets of Havana with cries of "¡Viva España! ¡Viva Weyler! ¡Muera la autonomía!," thereupon to ransack the offices of the pro-government newspapers *La Discusión*, *Diario de la Marina*, and *El Reconcentrado*.[455] A response, commented one observer, against "the excessive freedom given to the press."[456] There was a brooding mood within the army and among *los buenos españoles*, Josep Conangla remembered, a boiling resentment seeking an outlet, to act . . . to do something, to protest the "shameful surrender of Spanish sovereignty."[457] The Parque Central in Havana was "transformed into a military camp," commented the *New York Times*, the site of pitched battles between the mutinous soldiery and loyal troops.[458] Protection of the Plaza de Armas and other principal plazas was secured with a garrison of five thousand soldiers transferred from field operations to maintain order in the capital. In the days that followed the riots, all retail stores in central Havana remained closed. Theaters suspended all programs. The streets of the capital were deserted.[459]

The Havana riot should not be viewed as an isolated act of a small group of disaffected soldiers. On the contrary, the protest gave expression to a deepening military disaffection toward a government denounced as responsible for the "humiliation of Spain," *La Correspondencia Militar* pronounced, endorsing the Havana riots as a "patriotic protest nobly initiated by the Army upon seeing itself offended and disparaged":

> We bear witness to the indifference of the people [*el pueblo*] in the face of the insult, to the imbecility of the politicians, and the general weakness that appears to have destroyed all incentive. . . . We have said on more than one occasion: "The Army will save the Nation!" And fortunately we have not been mistaken. Officers of that Army have been the ones who in Havana . . . have affirmed their energetic and patriotic protest against the Autonomist newspapers that offended them.[460]

Unsettling portents, Consul Lee cabled Washington: a "mob assault" in Havana suggested that colonial authorities lacked the means to "maintain order, preserve life, and keep the peace." Out of concern for the safety of US lives and property, Lee requested an American naval presence in Havana.[461] On January 25, the USS *Maine* anchored in Havana harbor.

NEITHER VICTOR NOR VANQUISHED

4

Reckoning Deferred

We now invite all classes to join us in forgetting that the war ever divided the people of this island. I hope that we will never again speak of victors and vanquished. Spaniards and Cubans to embrace one another . . . to forget past disputes and disagreements and welcome the era of goodwill. Let history take care of the past.
—Máximo Gómez, *La Lucha* (1899)

I do not understand. I will never understand why Máximo Gómez said, in his speech at Quinta de los Molinos at the end of the war, that in Cuba there were neither victors nor vanquished. That was the exact phrase. I heard him say it, because I was there at the time. It irked all the soldiers. . . . There were many who were repulsed by that phrase.
—Esteban Montejo, *Biografía de un cimarrón* (1966)

There are thus neither victors nor vanquished between the Cuban and Spanish forces. Neither one nor the other can claim victory, given the fact that victory, for better or worse, belongs to the American army and which is today the arbiter of Cuban destiny.
—"Ni vencedores ni vencidos," *La Lucha* (1898)

The politics of order, of respect for all, of amity and union, of letting bygones be bygones, were excessive and gave rise to many injustices.
—Manuel Secades Japón, *Episodios de un estudiante en la guerra de independencia de Cuba* (n.d.)

The Americans arrived out of their history—just as they always said they would: that "the whole power of the United States," Secretary of State John Clayton had vowed at midcentury, would be employed to prevent Cuba "from passing into other hands"; that the United States was "resolutely determined that the Island of Cuba shall never be ceded by Spain to any other power than the United States"; that the prospects of Spain ceding Cuba to a "foreign power" would "be the instant signal for war."[1]

The eventuality of Cuba "passing into other hands"—in this instance, into the hands of Cubans themselves—seemed imminent: the "instant signal for war" threshold had been crossed, war to prevent Spain from ceding Cuba to a "foreign power."[2] A "forcible intervention by the United States," President William McKinley explained, "as a neutral," would exercise "hostile constraint on both the parties to the contest."[3] A declaration of war against both Spaniards and Cubans would preempt two competing claims of sovereignty to establish by force of arms a third one. The United States would exercise sovereignty over Cuba on the basis of "the law of belligerent right," McKinley instructed Military Governor John Brooke, that is, Cuba would be administered as "conquered territory."[4] A new sovereign authority would "end disorders," in this instance the Cuban war of independence, deemed a "disorder." "As I view it, we have taken Spain's war upon ourselves," pronounced US General William Shafter at the end of 1898.[5]

Much to the relief of the producing classes, of course: planters, manufacturers, merchants, and industrialists, all who had enjoyed the privilege of colonial patronage, welcomed the American intervention as an act of providential deliverance. They experienced the shifting fortunes of war in brooding contemplation of extinction, overtaken with a deepening sense of foreboding as the fury of a history foretold hurled toward the dreaded denouement. The producing classes had entrusted their well-being—indeed, their survival, they were certain—to the solvency of Spanish sovereignty: a sovereignty floundering in varying degrees of disintegration from within and disarray from without, lacking the political credibility to wage war and bereft of the moral authority to make peace. The fate of the Ever-Faithful Isle was fastened to a distant metropolis lacking the material resources and increasingly losing the national will to defend the sovereignty upon which the well-being of the well-to-do depended.

The producing classes understood well the reciprocities of colonialism and knew also how to deploy the advantage of privilege as a means of access to political favor, after nearly a century of practiced exchange through which to transact the defense of entitlement in ways so self-confirming as to assume the appearance of the proper function of governance. Access to power no longer mattered if power lacked the means and lost the will to discharge the function for which fealty was rendered. Few believed

Spain capable of reviving its sovereignty and restoring its authority—certainly not any time soon; perhaps not ever.

The US intervention in the Cuban war of independence served to rescue a colonial system under siege and—especially—to preserve those arrangements upon which the defense of the prerogative of race served as the premise of governance. A US intelligence report in 1899 summarized the mood prevailing among the producing classes:

> The conservative element of Cuba, composed of property owners, holders of mortgages, etc. required to be assured in the most emphatic manner, that they have due protection from whatever Government that may be established in the island. At present they think of themselves on the verge of a precipice and all their hopes of salvation are fixed on the United States. The direct assurance to them that they shall not be left to the mercy of the revolutionary element will go far towards tranquilizing them as they will know that the United States can make Cuba prosperous.[6]

The collective memory of the producing classes was formed—and fixed—within a history of fear of racial displacement: a body social possessed of an internal logic, riven with contradictions, to be sure, but retaining sufficient coherence to act decisively in defense of its interests during transitions of colonial sovereignties, and most of all acutely attentive to the realities from which it had fixed the trajectory of its political orbit. Remarkable class cohesion, to be sure, with tensions of internal conflicts often mitigated by a shared fear of the social forces released by the legacy of chattel slavery, which implied too—always—the need to accommodate the presence of a sovereign authority possessed of the capacity to defend existing political arrangements and preserve prevailing racial hierarchies. "Every person of the pro-Spanish class," Franklin Matthews learned during his visit to Cuba in 1899, "those who sympathized with Spain and hoped she would defeat the Revolutionists, wanted the United States to retain control of the island. Only in such control did they see any hope of safety for themselves and their property."[7] Planter Julio de Apezteguía, the owner of the vast Constancia sugar estate in Cienfuegos, was direct—and succinct. "You have acquired responsibilities which you are not at liberty to throw away and go back on," Apezteguía admonished the Americans. By ending Spanish sovereignty in Cuba, the United States had assumed a "moral duty which [it was] obliged to fulfill.... The first element of success is the destruction beforehand of all insurgent or insurrectionary element."[8]

These were the reciprocities through which the producing classes sought insulation from the threat of revolution, often opaque and obscure, to be sure, but always the enduring solidarities of common interests through which the premise of privilege was reproduced under a new sovereignty. These were also the reciprocities through which the interests of the producing classes converged with the interests of the United States—and vice versa—to foreclose the ascendancy of the *independentista* polity. Fears well conditioned by a remembered past and uncertainties well grounded in a dreaded future. An intervention to foreclose the sovereignty of Cuba from passing to Cubans, of course: Cuba very much a "foreign power." But it was more complicated. An intervention to foreclose the sovereignty of a people of color, the fear so well deployed by Spanish colonial administration and revived with aplomb by the Americans. Haiti was an enduring and all-encompassing discursive subsidy of Spanish colonialism: a time-tested moral—and metaphor—through which to discredit the proposition of Cuban independence as the prelude of the much-feared and long-foretold tumult of race war.[9]

The United States had claimed authority over a people with a history, not all of whom remembered the same history, of course. But no matter, for the Americans were not interested in the history remembered by all Cubans, only the history of those people whose remembered past possessed instrumental value. The US intervention as a function of that past, to reconstitute the social constituencies and revive the political networks of the colonial status quo as the basis of American authority. There was more than passing wisdom in the observation offered by historian Emilio Roig de Leuchsenring that "one of the great harms the North American military intervention inflicted upon Cuba was rendering it impossible for the Cubans to eradicate the Colony, with all that the Spanish regime had signified . . . resulting in the survival of the men and the institutions as well as the historical, social, and economic conditions, the elimination of which had represented the supreme ideal of the liberating revolution."[10]

The ceremonial transfer of sovereignty from Spain to the United States on January 1, 1899, was completed in a matter of minutes. Spain departed without having made peace with the Cubans, leaving behind the history it had wreaked upon the island. "Upon [Spain] abandoning this enchanted island, whose wealth had been the wonderment of the world," lamented Enrique José Varona, "all that remain of its fertile fields are misery and pestilence. It bequeaths to us in this moment a memory of its long domination over an emaciated people who wander within a vast charnel house, abhorring its past and dreading its future."[11]

Cubans had endured a war of ruinous proportions, of unimaginable suffering and unfathomable losses. Almost everyone: a people displaced and destitute. Almost everywhere: a landscape of desolation and despair. A total war waged against combatants and noncombatants alike, against production, property, and personal possessions, war with the intent to destroy resources and weaken resolve. Total, too, in that the war had involved the populations of nearly all the one thousand towns and villages of the island, by choice or by chance, and where the distinction between soldiers and civilians lost any useful meaning, where neutrality was suspect, and where security was often obtained only behind one battle line or the other, rarely ever outside them, and never between them. "There does not exist a single place on the island of Cuba," Fermín Valdés Domínguez recorded in his field diary, "not even in the most remote recesses of its forests, that does not possess a holy remembrance [*un recuerdo sagrado*] of the long and cruel struggle for independence."[12] There were no noncombatants.

Only a fortunate few could have comprehended that they had survived a population disaster of frightful proportions. The number of Cubans who perished in the course of the nineteenth-century wars of independence is mostly a matter of estimates, but the estimates are staggering. Some 200,000 women, men, and children are believed to have perished between 1868 and 1878. Perhaps as many as another 500,000 women, men, and children—mostly noncombatants—perished in reconcentration camps during 1895–98, largely the result of disease, illness, and malnutrition. Countless thousands of combatants lost their lives in the *manigua* during thirty years of intermittent insurgencies and wars: instant death in battle, slow death of injuries and illness. Many others were executed by firing squads or perished in prisons in Cuba; others perished in penal colonies in Fernando Póo, Ceuta, and the Chafarinas.[13]

Few indeed were the numbers of Cubans who had not suffered in direct and very personal ways. They survived the disarray and disruption of war to succumb to indigence and indignity in peace. The losses were incalculable. Property damage could be assessed and in many instances verified. But material damages were only a part of the losses. What could never be fully known—or imagined—was the suffering, the despair, the heartache. Households had been disrupted. Homes were destroyed. Families were broken. Lives had been shattered. That many survived in sound body did not always mean they were well or whole. Vast numbers bore their pain in their memories, in sadness and sorrow, haunted by the loss of persons and places that had once given their lives purpose and meaning. They carried on with broken hearts and inconsolable grief: widows and orphans, parents who lost children, children who lost parents, the untold numbers who lost entire families, the maimed, the infirmed, the aged, homeless, and jobless—almost all of whom could not even remotely begin to imagine how to put their lives together again.

Nor should it be supposed that the desolation from which Cubans emerged in 1898 was the result of unintended consequences of war. On the contrary, desolation was the Spanish way of war: Cubans as the object of Spanish wrath and rage. Thirty years of war, wrote historian Ismael Sarmiento Ramírez, "during which existing divisions between Spaniards and Cubans deepened and acted to confer on the conflict a frightful character of hatred, vengeance, and extermination, truly a war to the death between the combatants."[14]

Spain had waged total war against the enemies of *la madre patria* in defense of *patrimonio*, to exact reprisal and retribution for the affront to national honor and to uphold at all costs the dignity of sovereignty. Spain disposed to inflict adversity purposely, often indiscriminately, against combatants and noncombatants alike as a means of strategic intent and a mode of tactical advantage, a campaign conducted as if a war of extermination—a purpose that had indeed been contemplated. "Spain has not been able to resolve the problem of Cuba except by force of arms," Captain General Camilo Polavieja acknowledged in 1879, "and the guarantee of Spanish rule in the future may be possible only through the extermination of the majority of the inhabitants of the island."[15] Indeed, *La Correspondencia Militar* had demanded outright "the extermination of that spurious race."[16] A war conducted with such frightful ferocity as to suggest indeed an intent of extermination. "General Weyler's policy has been a war of absolute extermination," an English resident in Cuba commented in mid-1897.[17] Juan Arnao was appalled: How could Spain, "with pretensions as a civilized nation," have "announced in public decrees the intent to exterminate the entire Cuban people" (*la raza cubana*)?[18] Poet Juan Jorge Sobrado remembered Weyler's "violent methods, the executions, the incendiarism, the outrages, the destruction of the countryside, the sinister 'concentration'—all of which made me believe that the intention was to exterminate all Cubans."[19] Mexican consul in Havana Andrés Clemente Vázquez observed the Spanish conduct of war with deepening despair: "The slaughter, the deaths by way of hunger, the *reconcentrados*, the torching of the *bohíos* of the *pacífico* peasantry during the frightful administration of Valeriano Weyler surely must have angered heaven and resulted in the condemnation *Delenda España*."[20] The reconcentration policy, historian John Tone suggests, approximated a program of genocide.[21] For years to come, Cubans would characterize the time of Weyler and the war-with-war campaign as "a war of extermination" (*una guerra exterminadora*).[22]

Something of restive disquiet insinuated itself into the national mood after 1898, a sense of war having ended but a people still living very close to the disruption it had wreaked, continuing to experience the rawness of the many forms of loss: loss of loved ones, loss of community, loss of home, loss of livelihood, a people left to ponder the purpose of sacrifice and suffering, a sense of deeds and misdeeds unacknowledged, of conduct and misconduct unpunished, of aspirations unmet and tasks unfinished. "There is so much natural anger and grief throughout the island," Máximo Gómez confided to his journal in January 1899, "that the people have been unable to celebrate the triumph of the end of their former rulers' power."[23] Many thousands of Cubans asked in the years that followed: "What have we gained by this war?"[24] Serafín Espinosa y Ramos gave voice to the *mambí* lament:

> And when the time came that the vestiges of the disaster began to fade, the tears to dry, and the open wounds to heal over the homeland, which was now free from the tyranny so ferociously resisted, the victors dispersed in all directions. They scattered with timid hopes of finding home, filled with a profound sadness and bitter sorrow. They wondered about the astonishing ease with which in mere days, as an offering to *unity and harmony*, the divisive lines between the patriots and the traitors had vanished. Outraged in their amazement, they were driven to question the point of the tenacity of their purpose in sacrifice and war. As if the freedom and independence of the *patria* had never had enemies, since now all Cubans—absolutely all Cubans—seemed to have defended freedom and independence with the same fierce passion, with the same enthusiasm, and with the same love.[25]

Cuba subject to a foreign occupation, the *mambises* kept at bay and cast aside, to bear witness to positions of public office distributed to persons often having only the most tenuous *independentista* affiliations—or none at all: Washington ordered US military authorities in Cuba to appoint to positions of public office residents "without reference to their connection with the revolution."[26] Political appointments thus included Cubans who had served in the Spanish colonial administration as well as previous Spanish officeholders, former Autonomists and ex-guerrilla officers—"enemies of the Revolution who joined with our tyrants," decried Francisco Silva.[27] Years later, Manuel Secades Japón continued to brood that "large numbers of the liberators, poor, ignorant, but filled with patriotic love, were taken advantage of and exploited by many who had remained indifferent to the cause of the Revolution of liberation or—even worse—who had fought against the Revolution bearing arms. Our generosity and abnegation served to allow the deeds of many enemies of independence to pass unaddressed."[28] Major Manuel Arbelo also remembered the toll of the war. "That after the immense sacrifice of life and treasure," brooded Arbelo, "of indescribable moral and physical suffering, sustained with extraordinary heroism and sublime resignation at the altar of liberty and independence of Cuba, a foreign power, ignorant of the rights which we claimed to our *patria*, denied us all the principles of justice with which we protested Spanish rule."[29] "Something went wrong somewhere," an aging *mambí* would lament to Erna Ferguson many years later.³⁰ "No country in the Americas," Santiago Rey continued to ponder decades later, "none, was obliged to achieve its independence at the cost of the sacrifices made by Cuba. Time and our own special character have erased—or at least diminished—the remembrance of the pain and the suffering we endured."³¹

Cubans enjoined to adapt to conditions of peace without having attained the purpose of war. Spain had departed in January 1899, but the Spaniards remained. An estimated 130,000 Spaniards chose to remain in the nation whose independence so many had opposed.³² *Los buenos españoles* had welcomed war with war: the apologists and *los intransigentes* once disposed to spend the last *peseta* and sacrifice the last son to defend *la integridad nacional*, the planters, merchants, industrialists, and manufacturers who had provided moral support and contributed material assistance to the colonial regime, the Catholic Church and clergy who often dedicated special masses to the success of Spanish military operations—*misa de campaña*, as they were known—and the many thousands of Voluntarios for whom the dictum of *viva España con honra* had served as a moral warrant to harass criollos.³³

Peninsulares in Cuba contemplated the end of Spanish sovereignty with a mixture of fear and foreboding. "What a delicate situation," commented Francisco Cimadevilla, "this intention of the Spanish to remain in Cuba after the end of the sovereignty of Spain."³⁴ The Volunteers, puzzled US General Oliver Howard, "deadly hostile to the Cuban patriots," were "paroled, but unaccountably suffered to remain in the country."³⁵ Spaniards in Havana were prepared for the worst, reported General William Ludlow in 1899: "The large Spanish population of the city, the importers, bankers, shopkeepers, clerks, and business class generally . . . was silent and apprehensive, fearful of what might be in store for them when their flag should finally be lowered, but, with the 20,000 rifles belonging to the disbanded volunteers secreted in their homes, prepared to defend themselves in case of an uprising beyond the control of the Americans."³⁶

Spain had negotiated the right of Spaniards to remain in Cuba as a condition of the peace settlement, the United States to guarantee the security of Spanish property and persons: "All the Spanish forces known as volunteers, mobilizados, and guerrillas who wish to remain in the island of Cuba are permitted to do so under parole during the present war."³⁷ The Spanish who remained resident in Cuba, General Brooke acknowledged, "would hold the United States responsible for all the ills that befell them during their residence there that could be traceable to want of care on the part of the United States Government."³⁸ Indeed, "the military presence of the United

States," historian Aurea Matilde Fernández Muñiz noted, "guaranteed the security of the Spanish residents."[39]

The Spanish presence in Cuba, the Americans were certain, promised to provide a source of stability, a population not without self-interested affinities with the United States, of course, but which could also be relied upon to accommodate US interests.[40] "They would owe allegiance to the United States," journalist Charles Pepper commented tersely in 1899.[41] General James Wilson dedicated effort and energy to befriend Spaniards in Matanzas: "They are thrifty, enterprising, industrious and well off; they control a large portion of the commercial business of the community, and under the influences which I have exerted . . . they will be retained in this country."[42] The Americans were lucid about the future role of Spaniards in Cuba, a community "representing a great deal of wealth," Major John Kennon emphasized, who "would be in a position soon to hold the balance of power, and the faction of Cubans, which would unite with them, would probably be able to control the destinies of the Island."[43] No less important: the fear that the departure of Spaniards would threaten to deplete the strength of the white population. To allow "a sweeping expulsion of all Spanish-speaking residents who did not happen to be born in the island," warned attorney Mayo Hazeltine, would result "in an act of gross barbarity, which, to judge by the Haytian precedent would be the first fatal step toward social convulsion and catastrophe. The white element in Cuba, if it is to remain preponderant, cannot bear any marked depletion. . . . The island, therefore, needs all the white men now sojourning there who are willing to remain as law-abiding citizens under the new order of things."[44]

The census of 1899 seemed to confirm the worst racial fears. People of color accounted for 32 percent of the total population, a statistic that aroused the consternation of *Diario de la Marina*. "If we are honest," *la Marina* acknowledged, "we would have to declare that we did not anticipate that the black race would constitute fully one-third of the native population." And a warning: "The danger to the white race that the interruption of [Spanish] immigration poses is apparent, and hence the need to stimulate this immigration on a far greater scale to prevent definitively this aforementioned danger."[45]

It is difficult to develop a methodologically coherent analysis with which to address the matter of hate, to ascertain the ways that hatred insinuated itself into realms of a national sensibility, thereupon to be transmuted into a semblance of a politics. Perhaps a people to bear hatred as a way of becoming one with themselves, informed with the expectation of a future reckoning, to deploy the memory of harms having been visited upon them in the hope of accountability: to anticipate that at some indeterminate point in the future, the opportunity to right wrongs and redress transgressions would present an occasion for closure—or not.

Few themes run as deep in the first-person chronicles of liberation as the trembling expressions of hatred toward Spain and Spaniards, a hatred burnished deeply into a Cuban way of being (*manera de ser*). "I was born in Cuba when it was ruled despotically by Spain," Manuel Sanguily remembered. "I came of age in a dense atmosphere in which one breathed only hatred of Spain and even of the Spanish people."[46] Fermín Valdés Domínguez was succinct: "As a Cuban, I hate the Spanish."[47] Poet Rafael Merchán recalled his childhood in verse:

¡Qué infancia! ¡Qué recuerdos! Los albores
Allí de mi alma en flor se amancillaron;
Palpitó el hombre en mí, me lo mostraron
No la edad, sino el odio, los rencores!

And Merchán concluded: ¡Ser tan niño y odiar!"[48] Ricardo Buenamar acknowledged a "hatred and desire for vengeance against Spanish cruelty"; Julián Sánchez recalled the experience of the reconcentration camp in San José de Ramos, remembering that "the abuse committed against the Cuban people had incited a hatred that extended even to the children. . . . The hatred was transforming us into heroes."[49] A "cruel and sanguinary people," Tomás Basail remembered, toward whom Cubans would "bear in their hearts an eternal hatred."[50] The protagonist in Tomás Justiz y del Valle's novel *El suicida* (1912), set in the early 1890s, is adamant: "We are preparing ourselves to enter the twentieth century with dignity. . . . Cuba will never be truly civilized as long as one Spaniard remains. It is necessary to kill them! War without quarter!"[51]

Foreign travelers to Cuba rarely failed to comment—like Samuel Hazard in 1871—on "the intense hatred existing between the native Cubans and their Spanish rulers."[52] "There is no hatred in the world," Antonio Gallenga observed two years later, "to be compared with that of the Cuban for Spain and everything Spanish," an intensity James O'Kelly observed the following year: "nearly all the young men of intelligence with whom I have come in contact hate the Spaniards with inconceivable bitterness."[53]

Nor were the Spanish unaware of Cuban hatred. "The hatred and rage with which some Cubans view things Spanish," Francisco Moreno observed in 1887, extended into a hatred "toward everything Spanish."[54] Enrique Donderis described the intensity of Cuban hatred that "produce[d] in them the desire for the extermination of everything Spanish" (*desear el exterminio del españolismo*).[55]

The colonial officialdom lived closely with Cuban hatred. Captain General Domingo Dulce was fully persuaded that "young Cubans learn[ed] to hate the name of Spain at the University of Havana," and indeed actually contemplated closing the university so as to oblige Cubans to study in Spain.[56] Captain General Arsenio Martínez Campos, on the other hand, was certain that Cuban hatreds began in "early primary school." During military operations between Santa Clara and Bayamo in 1895, Martínez Campos concluded that "all the inhabitants hate Spain."[57] A hatred that originated from within the familial intimacy of the Cuban household, Captain General Camilo Polavieja was certain:

> They are motivated by a truly African hatred [*un odio verdaderamente africano*] against us. They do not reason. All means that lead to independence from Spain are deemed proper and even moral. In the press as well as in public meetings, and in private conversations that occur within the intimacy of the family. They wage a war without quarter against us. They educate their children in the loathing of Spain.... They see themselves as enslaved by us and hate us the way that a subjugated people hate their conquerors.[58]

The hatreds of the war survived into the peace. "The Cubans hate the Spaniards with an intensity which we cannot appreciate," General John Brooke reported from Havana early in the US occupation.[59] General Leonard Wood wrote from Santiago de Cuba, "A feeling of bitter hostility existed between the Cubans and Spaniards, and also a very ugly feeling between the Cubans who had acted in harmony with the autonomists in the latter days of the Spanish occupation and those who had been in the Cuban army."[60]

The desire for accountability settled uneasily among Cubans, how to make right in peace the wrongs of war, not knowing what to do with and what to do about the memories of wrongdoings that had accumulated over the many years of war. "The Spanish are the most savage people in the world," decried a letter published in *Patria* in late 1898. "Their crimes have been monstrous. No matter how generous we may be, atonement will be long and difficult.... They wished to kill us in so many ways. They now desire to wish away the hatreds. They want us to be tolerant. We will forgive. But how to forget so much harm? That? Not ever. Never. Never."[61] Manuel Piedra Martel recalled the early months of peace, a time when an "anti-Spanish spirit among the population of Havana appeared to have spread unchecked in the form of insults and threatening attitudes."[62] A time, Charles Pepper observed in 1899, when "the feeling of resentment and revenge was very strong among the Cubans," including "periods of proscriptive agitation against the Spanish classes and of demands for them to leave."[63]

Cubans with irremediable grievances, all made so relentlessly incomprehensible in circumstances associated with the liminal spaces of the neither-victors-nor-vanquished postwar exhortations: enjoined to consent to and concur with the Spanish presence as if nothing had happened. But something had happened: a peace settlement in 1898 to which the Cubans were neither party nor participants but obliged to honor. Cubans denied the opportunity to make peace with Spain but enjoined to make peace with the past, to get over it and carry on, to let bygones be bygones as a way to get on with the future. The past was over and done with, the Americans pronounced. "Both Cubans and Spaniards were notified," General James Wilson reported, "that, as far as the United States were [sic] concerned, the past must be regarded as a sealed book."[64] The peace of Pax Americana.

A long-memoried people, Cubans early developed the capacity to see themselves inside their history, disposed, Ramón Corona observed, to "cultivate the religion of remembrance" (*cultivar la religión del recuerdo*).[65] In fact, Cubans did not relinquish the past to history. They relived it. Hostile confrontations between Cubans and Spaniards erupted often, including assaults against Spanish merchants and shopkeepers, public taunts and insults on the streets, acts of arson against Spanish-owned stores, instances of vandalism against Spanish *casinos*, *círculos*, and *liceos*, anonymous death threats against former Voluntarios.[66] In Santa Clara, in the space of one week in January 1899, eight former Voluntarios were murdered. *Peninsular* clubs and businesses displaying the Spanish flag were attacked, often resulting in street demonstrations and disorder. Protestors in Santiago de Cuba ransacked the municipal Casino Español.[67] The Centro de Dependientes and the Centro Asturiano in Havana were attacked.[68] A Spaniard in Havana raising the Spanish flag outside his home resulted in the house being pelted with rocks by irate Cubans.[69] Mayor of Havana Perfecto Lacoste banned the public display of the Spanish flag on the exterior of any building, in theaters, on *paseos* and streets, and "anywhere else the public assembles."[70] "Is the hatred of Spain of such magnitude," *Diario de la Marina* scorned, "that the mere sight of the Spanish flag provokes conflict and disrupts public order?"[71] In the final weeks of Spanish rule, the *New York Times* reported, crowds of Cubans rushed through the streets of Havana boarding streetcars to compel Spanish passengers to proclaim, "Viva Cuba Libre!"[72] "Life in the capital has been made impossible for every good Spaniard," *La Correspondencia Militar* protested.[73]

Anti-Spanish sentiment waned in time or, perhaps more correctly, gradually ceased to be acted upon, as most Cubans arrived—more or less—at a grudging accommodation of the Spanish presence.[74] "I have been among the first to forgive the Spanish," affirmed *mambí* General Emilio Núñez. "But I will be among the last to forget the barbaric and cruel policies practiced by the Valmasedas and the Weylers, who were always inspired by those Spaniards to whom we must never concede any participation in our affairs.... Nothing remains of Spain except the painful remembrance of its hateful domination.... We must remember always that Spain and the Spanish are the cause of our misfortunes."[75]

Reconciliation with Spaniards was not implausible, of course. Perhaps it was mostly a matter of time until Cubans could envision the possibility of reconciliation between *los cubanos buenos* and *los españoles honrados*, Cubans like Luis de Radillo, who had "solemnly vowed to 'wall off the past' against resentments."[76]

Los cubanos buenos could indeed contemplate reconciliation with *los españoles honrados*. Reconciliation with *los malos cubanos*, however, was another matter. "The rancor of the defeated [Spaniards] is expressed through their passive hostility toward Cuban independence," Alvaro Catá pronounced, and warned, "But if we should dismiss Spanish resentment as the last gasp of [colonial] impotence, the same cannot be done with the collaboration of Cubans in that ignoble effort ... [that] resulted in four centuries of oppression."[77] The Cubans who had acted in the service of the colonial regime would not receive the consideration of reconciliation: not the Autonomists who had served Spain, not the *presentados* who had defected to Spain, and especially not the many tens of thousands of guerrillas who had borne arms against the *mambises*. Artist Frederic Remington had traveled to Cuba to draw the war and mingled with *insurrecto* leaders. He preserved the comment of one *mambí*: "As long as there was a Spanish guerrilla on the island, I would not lay down my arms—never—never—never."[78]

The guerrillas had occupied an anomalous status within the Spanish army. Recruited principally as paramilitary auxiliaries, guerrillas were not among the soldiers repatriated to Spain. The surrender of Santiago de Cuba in July 1898, thus, had included arrangements for the repatriation of Spanish soldiers serving in Oriente, a total of 24,000 troops. In fact, however, General William Shafter reported, "a little less than 3,000 of them [were] guerrillas and volunteers, leaving about ... 21,000 to be shipped."[79] The guerrillas and Voluntarios remained behind. The final armistice settlement included arrangements for the repatriation of all Spanish soldiers in Cuba, a total of nearly 150,000 officers and men. The many thousands of Cubans who had served as guerrillas, however, were not claimed by Spain, thereupon to remain in Cuba, abandoned to their own fate. "With rare exception," Antonio Serra Orts remembered, "the Spanish Government totally forgot about them at the critical moments in which our rule over Cuba ended."[80]

But the Cubans did not forget. The vengeance practiced during war continued as a vendetta pursued in peace. *Insurrecto* commander Manuel Secades Japón recalled the sense of restless anticipation among his soldiers as they prepared to occupy the

LA ESCOBA CUBANA

4.1 "The Cuban Broom," depicting the Cuban desire to sweep away all collaborators of Spanish colonial administration. SOURCE: EL MUNDO, APRIL 14, 1901.

town of Ciego de Avila in the closing days of the war. Conversations turned to the subject of guerrillas:

> The atrocities committed by the enemies of Independence were recounted. The *insurrectos* had scores to settle. The father of one had been murdered. The sister of another had been assaulted. Others told of mothers being beaten or of a brother being attacked. It was painful to listen to the accounts of deeds committed against family members or friends of those who had joined the insurgent forces and at the same time to hear of the accounts of the reprisals they planned to take upon entering Ciego de Avila.[81]

Mambises entering the town of Jíbaro in Las Villas captured a unit of *guerrillas locales* known to have waged war with an "implacable ferocity," and in discharge of Article 48 of the Penal Code of the Republic-in-Arms convoked a war tribunal to prosecute the guerrillas for "acts of high treason against the *Patria*." All were found guilty and executed by firing squad.[82]

Officers and soldiers of guerrilla units were demobilized in haphazard fashion during the final months of Spanish rule, in most instances owed months of uncollected back pay, without resources and without prospects for livelihood.[83] "With the demobilization of the guerrillas," recalled *mambí* officer Avelino Sanjenis, "a vast number of demoralized and corrupted men were abandoned and thrown onto the streets. No one would receive them or attend to them because of the role of traitors and scoundrels they represented. These were the bandits who had threatened us [during the war] and toward whom we must be especially vigilant."[84] Army Captain Richard Wilson wandered the streets of Santiago de Cuba during the early days of the military occupation:

> We met a company of guerrilleros or Spanish irregular troops that had just entered the city. These were Cubans who sympathized with the Spanish government in its administration of the island and aided the Spanish army by acting as scouts or bushwackers in the insurrectionary war. Objects of deepest hatred and scorn by the bulk of the Cuban people, they were called "sin vergüenzas," words which express the most profound detestation and hatred. They had surrendered their arms at the outpost and were seated on the side walk waiting for whatever disposition might be made of them. There were about 50 of them, very worn, tired and dejected looking.[85]

Many thousands of former guerrillas had dispersed into the debris and desolation of postwar Cuba in search of a place to reclaim and a life to resume. Most failed at both. Cubans who had killed Cubans, who had burned crops and destroyed livestock, who had plundered homes and razed communities: there would be no return. Without voice and without representation, guerrillas found peace to be a hostile environment. They were an unwelcome presence, to be shamed and shunned, uniformly scorned and spurned, vilified as mercenaries and loathed as traitors: pariahs among their own people. Members of the guerrilla units of Santa Clara, Major John Logan reported in February 1899, faced an uncertain future:

> Now that the war is over and they have been discharged from the employment of the Spanish crown, they have no protection except that which is given them by our forces, either military or police to be organized. It is hardly likely that

the Cubans will permit them to remain in the towns or seek employment on the plantations. While they might forgive a Spaniard and allow him to remain in their midst, I do not think it probable that they will be so generous toward the Cubans who served in the Spanish "guerrilla" forces.[86]

The guerrillas were marked men in a time of revenge and reprisal writ large. Detested in war, despised in peace. *Guerrillas locales* rarely returned to the communities they once called home. They were known for their deeds and remembered for their misdeeds. Nothing was forgotten. Nothing was forgiven. "This vile being who was born in Cuba!" (¡Este asqueroso ser que nació en Cuba!), poet Juan Jorge Sobrado decried.[87] After the war, historian Octavio Avelino Delgado wrote, "the *guerrillas*, mostly natives of the Island, on trying to resume a normal life in their home towns, only encountered the hostility and hatred of the local population."[88]

Former guerrillas were attacked, assaulted, and assassinated across the island: acts "to avenge some old personal or family grievance," Serafín Espinosa y Ramos surmised.[89] "Everyone knows that the life of a *guerrillero* is not worth the value of a feather quill pen," novelist Carlos Montenegro commented in the short story "El negro Torcuato."[90] Adolfo Jiménez Castellanos, the last Spanish captain general of Cuba, informed his American successor, General John Brooke, of the wave of violence visited upon the former guerrillas: "I received several communications announcing assaults and acts of violence committed in various towns upon the persons of individuals who during the late separatist war served in the Spanish *guerrilla* and irregular forces. It is announced likewise, that during the past week, eight of such individuals have been assassinated in the municipal districts of Ranchuelo and Esperanza in Santa Clara; and like deeds have been committed in Yaguajay."[91]

The *insurrectos* "vowed to kill every *guerrillero* residing in Cuba," reported *El Correo Militar*.[92] No mercy would be extended to "the people who sanctioned the policy of extermination pursued by Weyler," vowed a letter signed anonymously by "Several Veterans" and published in *La Lucha*.[93] In Havana, *Diario de la Marina* reported, Nicolás Salvador González "was attacked by Cuban idlers, who put a rope around his neck from the San Francisco wharf and dragged him nearly a block in quest of a lamp post from which they might hang him. A quick response by custom house inspectors, guards, and clerks prevented the hanging."[94] In another incident, "a squad of Cubans, still in uniform of the late revolution," reported *Diario de la Marina*, attempted to lynch Cresencio Pérez, "a former Spanish *guerrillero*, who narrowly escaped with his life."[95] Ramiro Zaragoza, a former sergeant *práctico* in the *guerrilla local* of Managua, was not so fortunate: he was assassinated by unknown assailants. "He was not well liked [*no gozaba de ninguna simpatía*] among the neighbors of the community," *La Lucha* reported tersely.⁹⁶ Former Lieutenant José Fernández Lobregat of the *guerrilla local* of San Antonio de los Baños was murdered in his home. The return of former *guerrilla local* Bruno Villa to his home in Guantánamo precipitated a street riot: "Having learned that Villa intended to resume his residence in Guantánamo, the people took to the streets in robust protest, obliging the authorities to take him into custody to prevent him from being lynched."⁹⁷ Returning to Santiago de Cuba after the war, former guerrilla Celestino Rodríguez was killed by Antonio Rodríguez, who, upon arrest, Emilio Bacardí Moreau commented, had gained "the approval of popular sentiment."⁹⁸ A *New York Times* dispatch from Santiago de Cuba reported a similar incident:

> Colonel Caravajil, a guerrilla chief, who, it is said, killed men, women, and children by the wholesale during the war and the last three years' insurrection, arrived here this morning on the Spanish steamer Maria Herrera. He was recognized on the street by boys, whose cry was soon taken up by a howling mob. Caravajil had to take refuge in a bank.... He was taken in a cab to the wharf and put on board of a steamer, with order to leave immediately.⁹⁹

In Matanzas, ex-guerrilla Pedro Puerón was assaulted by an angry street crowd. In Pinar del Río, only the intervention of local police saved Lisandro Díaz and Mateo Borrero from being lynched by a mob. Former guerrilla Lieutenant Diego Sánchez in Unión de Reyes was hanged by local residents. *Diario de la Marina* denounced the exercise of "popular justice" and "the growing popularity of *Mob Law*": "We refer to the so-called lynching parties, whose peculiar *sport* would appear to be to persecute, pursue, and seize upon whoever may be pointed out to them as an ex-Spanish Volunteer or *guerrillero*, with the intent and purpose of hanging him to the first lamp-post, telephone or electric light pole they may find in Havana's streets."¹⁰⁰ Long after the war had ended, newspapers across the island continued to report "mysterious" murders of Cubans—mostly former guerrillas—crimes seldom solved and rarely punished.¹⁰¹ Not dissimilar to a desultory blood feud that often persists long after the participants remember why it began. That was how the war of independence ended.

The United States ended the military occupation on May 20, 1902. Much of the content of the politics of the early republic implied dialogue with the past, coming to terms—or not—with the surviving vestiges of colonialism, the anomalies of sharing the national space with people who had opposed the national project: the populations of *peninsulares*, Autonomists, Voluntarios, *presentados*, and guerrillas, many of whom were implicated in the havoc wreaked by the Spanish way of war. "There are some," José Sixto de Sola lamented, "who are not in solidarity with our nationality, or better said, with our *patria*. They do not love it: they detest it. Others, having their souls forged in the crucible of colonialism, cannot enter into the spirit of the new personality of the nation. And others who do not believe in it, who have no faith."[102]

The presence of the guerrillas continued to disturb the national equanimity in the years that followed.[103] That the United States had sanctioned the postwar presence of Voluntarios and guerrillas, General Carlos García Velez decried, "offended me as a Cuban," adding, "Who could conceive of such a diabolical decision to allow those who were at all times our enemies to remain in Cuba, intransigent opponents of reform, defenders of *la integridad nacional* at all costs, defending [Spain] with arms until the last moment.... A ruthless measure at the expense of Cuban dignity."[104] The passage of fifty years did not diminish Esteban Montejo's indignation. "The *guerrilleros* should have been exterminated," Montejo bristled. "When I think about those bastards, while we were fighting against hunger, struggling in the muck and mud, in the stench of war, I feel like hanging them. The sad thing is that the *guerrilleros* were never punished in Cuba.... I would have stood them up against the wall and shot all of them."[105] Horacio Ferrer refused to reconcile himself to the presence of the guerrillas. More than fifty years later, he wrote:

> The evacuation of the Spanish army was completed, and the 40,000 *guerrilleros*—the collaborators of that army—were pardoned for all their horrendous crimes. They remained in residence in the very places of their heinous actions, a presence that served as an incitement for reprisals.... I have never been bitter or vengeful but I have always believed that it was an error to allow those men, the most abhorrent minions in the service of Spain, to remain in Cuba. Given that they fought with such ardor against the independence of their country, they should have been sent to Spain with the rest of their army. They did not have any right to enjoy the independence that they had hated and against which they fought with so much cruelty. They would soon enter national politics and occupy important positions in the Republic.... The poison of the *guerrilleros* remained with us.[106]

Years later, in 1946, on the occasion of the Third National Congress of History, the delegates ratified a resolution decrying "the incalculable harms visited upon Cuba by the decision not to evacuate the Voluntarios and guerrillas from the Island in 1899 who lacking loyalty to their own *patria* were incapable of loving this land."[107]

Memory of the *independentista* purpose became a hallowed remembrance among the *mambí* veterans who had served the cause of Cuba Libre with arms in the *manigua*. Across the island and into all the provinces, in towns large and small, former officers and soldiers of the Ejército Libertador organized into voluntary associations, including the Centro de Veteranos de Sancti-Spíritus, Consejo de Veteranos de la Independencia de Santa Cruz del Sur, Centro de Veteranos de la Independencia de Güines, Veteranos y Sociedades de la Raza de Color, Veteranos de la Independencia de Santiago de Cuba, and Asamblea de Veteranos de Cienfuegos, among many others. Local associations were themselves integrated into the Asociación Nacional de Veteranos de Independencia, an island-wide organization dedicated to "honoring national sentiment and sustaining devotion to the memory of those who gave their lives for the freedom of the *Patria*."[108]

The veterans' associations organized to lobby for pensions and health care, for survivor benefits, to raise funds to construct commemorative statues and monuments, to advocate for observance of patriotic holidays—important birth dates, anniversaries of deaths, occasions of decisive battles—to celebrate the life of heroes and commemorate the death of martyrs.[109] But most of all, the veterans upheld the most exalted representation of patriotic virtue, to claim the role of defenders of the *independentista* faith, "to form and raise the National Conscience" of the republic, a presence, Jorge Mañach commented years later, that represented "the only real moral authority that remains to us in the nation."[110]

The veterans refused to relinquish the past to history, and especially refused also to accommodate themselves to the continued presence of those who, "being Cuban," had aided and abetted the Spanish colonial regime. The former *mambises* took the task of reckoning into their own hands, to demand the expulsion of all who "in past times were representatives of the defamation and the extermination of our people [*el exterminio de nuestro pueblo*] so as to kill their desire for liberty."[111] Political opposition to the appointment of former guerrillas in government persisted into the early years of the republic and provided the veterans' organizations with entrée into the mainstream of national politics as the ever-present voice of the nineteenth-century *independentista* project. It was unseemly, protested the Consejo Nacional de la Asociación de Veteranos, that the "ferocious and intransigent enemies of yesterday" would presume "to participate in the direction of the destinies of Free Cuba":

> Members of the Association of the Veterans of Independence, dedicated to extolling national sentiment and preserving the memory of all who gave their lives to the liberty of the *Patria*, cannot rest in peace in their homes or at work . . . with the knowledge that little by little the enemies of the Revolution are returning. . . . This shocking and monstrous resurgence is slowly returning us to those times of the greatest degradation of the Colony and [restores] the pernicious influence of the sworn enemies of the most precious ideals of patriotic Cubans.[112]

Veterans mobilized to demand the expulsion of all *traidores y guerrilleros* from public office, calling for the modification of the Law of Civil Service—enacted during the US occupation—to enable peremptory dismissal of all government employees with antecedents of service to Spain.[113] To demand that political authorities, exhorted Colonel Cosme de la Torriente, remove "the worst of the *guerrilleros* who fought against Independence."[114] Officials discovered to have had guerrilla affiliations were publicly humiliated and harassed into retirement. Within months of the inauguration of the republic, an official inquiry was launched to investigate the political antecedents of public officeholders with the intentions, reported *Diario de la Marina*, "of discharging all who in some form or other fought against the revolution."[115] The election of a former guerrilla officer in 1906 to the school board of Santiago de Las Vegas provoked citywide demonstrations.[116] Chief of police Felipe Cuza of Santiago de Cuba—a former guerrilla—was dismissed. Rafael Samalea, the subdirector of education in Santiago de las Vegas, a former guerrilla commander, was expelled from office. "That the *guerrilleros* could serve as teachers of our children," thundered General Enrique Loynaz del Castillo, "is precisely what we are determined to avoid. They should be allowed to teach only the students of those parents who wish to have traitors for children and who will assassinate their Patria for a mere ration of food."[117] The Conservative Party candidate for mayor of San Juan y Martínez in 1908 was publicly humiliated, *La Lucha* reported, because "revolutionaries do not forgive anyone who served as a *guerrillero* during the war for independence."[118] *La Lucha* demanded the removal of an alderman in Santa Isabel de Las Lajas who had the "unparalleled effrontery" to sit on the municipal council "when it was well known to all the inhabitants that while serving as a guerrilla corporal during the war he stepped all over Cuban cadavers."[119] "We veterans," affirmed Captain Angel Rosende, "forgive but we do not forget," adding, "And upon recalling those deeds we remember the weak and cowardly actors. We are filled with an immense sadness to see how many of them presently occupy high positions in the government, enjoying the good times offered by the generous Patria, while many who shed precious blood at the altar of a sacrosanct ideal remain in the most reprehensible state of neglect."[120]

Veterans demanded an *independentista* lineage as requisite for all public office. It was necessary, General Emilio Núñez explained, "that all *guerrilleros*, from the highest positions to the most lowly posts, be expelled so as to never allow those who were enemies of our nationality to be favored over a soldier of liberty."[121] As a matter of *sentimiento de la nacionalidad*, Luis Rodolfo Miranda insisted, former *guerrilleros* were not "entitled to aspire to lead a government they had fought against.... I do not consider [them] morally authorized to fill public offices to resolve genuinely Cuban problems when their antecedents failed to sustain the patriotism that should inform the acts of public officials."[122] To arrive at a reckoning in the form of a "campaign of 'Cubanization' and the moralization of our institutions," insisted Colonel Manuel Aranda.[123] The Consejo Nacional de Veteranos was explicit: "We wish only that the Cubans who loved Cuba and did not dishonor its existence replace those disloyal Cubans who presently hold public office.... For positions of public office of the Republic patriots should not be confused with traitors. Those who confuse all Cubans with the vile *guerrillero* have the conscience of a *guerrillero*."[124]

The experience of liberation insinuated itself deeply into the normative framework of nationality, narratives assembled as source of legacy to enact and conduct to emulate: to fashion celebratory chronicles of heroes and heroic deeds, of selfless struggle and sacrifice of a people joining together for noble purpose, the history—in the words of historian Emilio Roig de Leuchsenring—"that constitutes the roots of our national integration."[125] But the master narrative formalized into the consensus of the historical record could not, the weekly *Patria* warned, accommodate those Cubans "who collaborated and aided Weyler to maintain the enslavement of their country."[126] Cubans who had served the Spanish colonial regime hovered as a spectral presence to destabilize the narratives of the heroic nationality, a reminder of the ignominy of traitors and a reminder too of justice denied and wrongs unpunished. Something had gone awry. A people for whom the ideal of *patria* had assumed fully the form of an altar upon which to discharge the duty of self-immolation could not contemplate the presence of the guerrilla with anything less than contempt and shame, a reminder of a "fractured nationality," Aníbal Escalante Beatón anguished, a presence to be purged.[127]

A "fractured nationality" thus implied the need for multiple typologies of "Cuban," that is, who "belonged" to the "family" of Cuban—and who did not: the women and men who had committed to the *independentista* project celebrated as "good Cubans" (*los buenos cubanos*), "the true Cuban people" (*el verdadero pueblo cubano*), "heartfelt Cubans" (*los cubanos de corazón*), and "true sons of Cuba" (*verdaderos hijos de Cuba*). Not to be confused with those Cubans who had supported Spain, variously vilified as *espurios cubanos*, *malos cubanos*, and *falsos cubanos*, what José Martí had scorned as "weak Cubans" (*débiles cubanos*) and Antonio Maceo denounced as "the degenerate son of Cuba" (*el degenerado hijo de Cuba*).[128] *Los buenos cubanos* who had dedicated their lives to *la nación integral* could not—ever—admit *los malos cubanos* into the national community. There was no place for the guerrilla within *el verdadero pueblo cubano*. Not at the time. Not later. Not ever. The guerrillas rendered as despised traitors upon whom to exact the full toll of reckoning, within reach, to settle scores and finish the task of liberation, a presence to be purged from the nationality and expurgated from the foundational narratives of the nation. "We wished to cast the *guerrilleros* and traitors out of the family of Cubans," José Isabel Herrera pronounced, "to destroy [them] with one blow and to stomp them ... so that these bastards could not form part of the Cuban family upon whom they had inflicted so much harm."[129] An imagined community gone bad. Fermín Valdés Domínguez was unequivocal: "Evil traitors who will have to atone for their sins through death, for the man who assassinates his brothers and serves the despot who purchased his services cannot escape punishment.... There is no refuge for the traitor; death is an insufficient fate for the Cuban who served Spain in the ranks of the *guerrilleros*."[130] The task at hand, the weekly *Maceo* exhorted, was "to rid ourselves of all the colonial scum" (*las escorias coloniales*).[131]

The expulsion of *los malos cubanos* from "the family of Cubans"—the "accomplices and abetters of extermination," pronounced General Armando de J. Riva—was a matter of accountability, a reckoning to answer for acts of treason.[132] The misdeeds for which *los malos cubanos* were to be held accountable expanded to take in an ever-larger inventory of transgressions. The designation of *guerrillero y traidor*, pronounced General Armando de la Vega, "contemplates the inclusion of all those persons who BEING CUBAN, whether with arms in their hands, or serving as spies and guides, or through the press, or employed in military hospitals and offices, or dressed in the hated uniform of Voluntario, or in any other form, acted against the Revolution."[133]

The memory of the guerrilla passed on from one generation to the next, not necessarily in the form of history but as something of a representation of the antihero, by word-of-mouth conventions and oral traditions, passing into the popular culture and forming colloquial usage. "My childhood experience," recalled Emilio Laurent (b. 1902), the son of a *mambí* colonel, "developed in a veteran environment [*un ambiente veteranista*] of hatred and contempt for the traitorous guerrillas and always considering the Spanish as the enemies of Cuban freedom."[134] The persona of the guerrilla entered the public imagination as the embodiment of treason and treachery, to serve as an all-purpose discursive category through which to rebuke and repudiate, to heap scorn on and scoff at. "Guerrilla": a Cuban who served in the ranks of the Spanish army, was the definition that lexicologist Argelio Santiesteban offered, "therefore and by extension a synonym for traitor and renegade."[135] José Sánchez-Boudy elaborated: "Traitor ... a bad Cuban [*cubano malo*]. To be a Cuban who is not a patriot ... to be a bad person" (*ser una mala persona*).[136]

The designation of "guerrilla/*guerrillero*" persisted through much of the early twentieth century as the epithet of choice with which to discredit voices of discordant views. The narrator of Carlos Loveira's novel *Los inmorales* (1919) characterizes the angry protagonist Jacinto: "And he thought of the most degrading epithet that one could hurl against a Cuban: '*Guerrillero!*' he screamed."[137] Scorn for the guerrilla flourished in *populista* verse, in the lines of *décimas* and the lyrics of *guarachas*. "They are trash, drunks and perverts," the *décima* "La guerrilla" pronounced, "who for three or four pennies sold their land Cuba, the nation in which they were born."[138] The *décima* "Los guerrilleros cubanos asesinos de mujeres y ancianos" denounced guerrillas as "cowards and assassins, murderers of peasants and machete-wielding killers of the elderly."[139] A taunting verse gained popular currency after the war:

> ¿Dónde están los guerrilleros?
> Están en el río.
> ¿Dónde están los guerrilleros?
> Están "escondío."[140]

In "A guerrillero," poet Juan Jorge Sobrado heaps contempt upon "this vile person who was born in Cuba."[141] The poem "Los guerrilleros del rancho" vows that "the guerrillero tyrants / will never be Cubans."[142] In the *décima* "Respuesta de una cubana pretendida por un guerrillero al servicio de España," a woman courted by a *guerrillero* responds:

> Anda, infame guerrillero,
> ¿cómo te voy a querer
> cuando no te puedo ver
> por canalla y por ratero?
> Asesino, bandolero,
> yo te digo en mi defensa:
> que en mi vida pura, inmensa,
> mis padres nobles han sido,
> y ustedes no han conocido
> ni el honor ni la vergüenza.[143]

The *décima* "A un guerrillero: ¿Dónde tú te meterás?" speaks directly to the guerrilla:

> Me dirijo a mis hermanos
> que están con el español
> porque han perdido el honor
> y también el ser cubanos.[144]

The theme of the guerrilla developed into something of a subgenre of early republic prose fiction. If historians were disinclined to remember the guerrilla, novelists were indisposed to forget. Disquieting truths often revealed themselves in unexpected places among a people often given to knowing how not to know. "You should know," novelist Lesbia Soravilla enjoined through her protagonist Román Porto in *Cuando libertan los esclavos* (1936), "that for each *mambí* who went into the *monte* to defend our liberty, *guerrilleros* multiplied like fleas."[145] The protagonist in the Jesús Castellanos novella *La manigua sentimental* (1910) warns of an approaching guerrilla force, "Machete in hand! These are our brothers but of a bad seed," thereupon to warn of the "band of mercenaries who knew the back roads of the countryside."[146] In the short story "La gallina negra" (1900), novelist Guillermo Schweyer Lamar characterizes members of a guerrilla unit as belonging to "that race of Cain who, for reasons of opportunism, or fear, or to satisfy some old grudge, placed themselves at the service of the tyrant against their brothers who were fighting for the independence of the *patria*"; at the end they are overwhelmed by an "avalanche of *mambí* horsemen who with the heroic weapon [machete] of the Cubans inflicted a horrible carnage upon those degenerates who paid for their treason against the *patria* with their lives."[147] The guerrilla appears often in the novels of Carlos Loveira. In *Los inmorales*, Loveira writes of Saturnino Ramos, "captain of the Spanish guerrilla in the Cuban war for independence, who had emigrated from the *patria* when, at the conclusion of the war, he and the other traitors were threatened with the avenging *guásima* tree."[148] The exchange of battle gunfire ended, the narrator of *Generales y doctores* (1920) comments, "and the machetes completed the bloodcurdling task of finishing off the wounded guerrillas—the inexorable law applied to Cubans who fought in Spanish ranks."[149] The young protagonist Rodolfo in Antonio Penichet's novel *¡Alma rebelde!* (1921) is seized with incomprehension, "for he had heard it said that the war was between Cubans and Spaniards, and therefore he supposed that all Cubans would have to arm themselves to wage war against the Spanish." The narrator continued:

> Thus it was that he viewed with astonishment the formation of guerrilla units of whites, blacks, and mulattos, disposed to go into the field to kill their brothers, the other whites, blacks, and mulattos who were in the *monte*. It seemed so strange to him, for in his young imagination, he calculated there were more Spaniards than Cubans, for Spain was larger than Cuba. Thus, those guerrillas should not be fighting in favor of Spain.... He experienced rage against the guerrillas, whom he considered very bad brothers.[150]

Novelist Arturo Montori in *El tormento de vivir* (1923) writes of a family "gripped in fear thinking that [their loved ones] were surprised by some guerrilla unit and *macheteados* in the middle of the *manigua*."[151] The protagonist in the Jesús Masdeu novel *La raza triste* (1924) recalls stories told by his parents, "when the *guerrilleros* arrived at the homes of Cubans, entered and tied up the patriots and, without even an interrogation, sentenced them to death by hanging from a *guásima* tree."[152] The "*guerrilleros* who sold their conscience to the enemy," laments the narrator in the short story "Su regalo" by Jesús del Calvario, "were the criminal trash elements of the population."[153]

The subject of the guerrilla served as a plot for one of the earliest full-length feature films of the emerging Cuban cinema industry. Subsidized with funds provided by the government of President Mario Menocal, *El capitán mambí ó libertadores y guerrilleros*—celebrated at the time as a "triumph of the Cuban film industry"— debuted in the Payret theater in January 1914 and for weeks thereafter played to sold-out audiences. Each scene of the silent film was designated with a title and included: "brutalities and abuses," "Antonio the traitor," "a savage order against women and children," and "the guerrilla in operation." A "fulsome recapitulation of scenes of the war of independence," one reviewer commented, "an interesting plot chronicling the greatness and suffering of the struggle for liberty, the acts of the *guerrilleros* against the Cubans, the Liberators in the *manigua*, and the Spanish in Cuba." A "sensational debut," pronounced *El Mundo*, "a true cinematographic gem" and "one of the greatest box-office successes of Cuban silent films."[154]

Representations of the past filtered into popular culture through poetry, novels, short stories, music, and film, something of history transacted as narration in the form of prose, lyrics, and scripts. To mediate the past through the interstices of art forms was perhaps easier than to confront history head-on: artistic license as a means of reconciliation with an unsettled history. The memory of the guerrilla faded slowly with the passage of time and the passing of generations. The concept of the guerrilla persisted in the vernacular as an epithet of choice, although it is not certain that any more than a diminishing number of Cubans retained the memory of its nineteenth-century origins. Popular usage persisted, in baseball, for example. Sports writer Rafael Conte dared to predict the victory of the Havana baseball team over Almendares, and in so doing acknowledged, "that in writing these lines, I am absolutely certain that my esteemed *almendarista* coreligionists will consider me a traitor, and even a *guerrillero*."[155] And on that occasion of the Los Industriales–Cienfuegos Elefantes baseball game in the Estadio Latinoamericano in 2002, the home-team fans were reenacting a practice with origins in the nineteenth century: taunting the fans of the visiting "enemy" Cienfuegos team as guerrillas, by definition: traitors in the ballpark of the home team.

Then, too, the history of the guerrilla was overtaken by another history: the guerrilla who emerged from the Sierra Maestra mountains. After 1959, the countenance of the guerrilla assumed iconic attributes of selfless heroism and noble virtue: the guerrilla "who assumes the yearnings of the people for liberation," Ernesto Che Guevara offered, something of a "guardian angel who arrives always to help the poor."[156] The guerrilla was reborn.

The guerrillas of the Sierra Maestra emerged as agents of the history for which they sought redress and a reckoning to complete: a revolution to advance the claim of a moral warrant of historical purpose to complete the deferred *independentista* project. Reckoning writ large as a politics of assault against the counterrevolution: the counterrevolution in this instance meaning those sectors identified with and discredited by their history of association with and defense of the moral order of nineteenth-century colonialism. The paradigm of the revolution as redemption of the sovereign nation expanded into something of a discursive totality. All who remained outside its premises—by definition—were *malos cubanos*. Not since the nineteenth century was the characterization of the *verdadero cubano* as embodiment of moral virtue so explicitly inscribed into a political project. Opponents of the revolution were vilified as traitors, and indeed their very claim to being Cuban disputed. A challenge to the revolution implied a challenge to the nation itself, and by definition subversion and treason. The weekly *Bohemia* drew the historic parallel explicitly in 1960: "Once again, as in all momentous epochs of our past—remember what occurred in 1895—Cubans are divided: between the loyal and the traitors, between the patriots and the renegades, between the free and the sellouts. Annexationists, autonomists, reprobates, and mercenaries have reappeared.... The anti-Cuba, with its roots in the muck of the past, stubbornly refuses to die."[157]

The colonial reckoning presumptively brought to closure within *cien años de lucha*.

Notes

Introduction

1 Santiago C. Rey, *Recuerdos de la guerra, 1895–1898* (Havana: Imprenta P. Fernández, 1931), 42–43.
2 Miguel Barnet, "La historia como identidad," in *Cuba: Cultura e identidad nacional*, ed. Daniel García (Havana: Ediciones Unión, 1995), 213–24.
3 Matías Duque, *El comandante Antonio Duque* (Havana: Imp. Compostela y Chacón, 1928), 11.
4 Lisandro Otero, *Llover sobre mojado: Memorias de un intelectual cubano (1957–1997)* (Mexico City: Planeta, 1999), 12.
5 Jorge Ibarra, "Acerca de las posibilidades de una síntesis histórica en Cuba," in *Aproximaciones a Clío* (Havana: Editorial Ciencias Sociles, 1979), 252.
6 Michel-Rolph Trouillot, *Silencing the Past: Power and the Production of History* (Boston: Beacon Press, 1995), 98.
7 Ramón de la Sagra, *Historia económico-política y estadística de la Isla de Cuba, o sea de sus progresos en la población, la agricultura, el comercio y las rentas* (Havana, 1831), 3–8; Cuba, Capitanía General, *Resumen del censo de población de la Isla de Cuba a fin del año de 1841* (Havana, 1842).
8 By midcentury, the combined population of color—free and enslaved—had expanded into majority status on the island, accounting for almost 60 percent of the total population in 1841. See Cuba, Capitanía General, *Resumen del censo de población.*
9 Félix Varela, "Memoria que demuestra la necesidad de extinguir la esclavitud de los negros en la Isla de Cuba, atendiendo a los intereses de sus propietarios," 1822, in José Antonio Saco, *Historia de la esclavitud desde los tiempos más remotos hasta nuestros días* (2nd ed., 6 vols., Havana: Alfa, 1936–45), 5:165. Varela's reference to the overturning of the old despotism refers to the installation of a brief constitutional monarchy in Spain between 1820 and 1823.

10 José Luis Alfonso to Domingo del Monte, December 1843, in Academia de la Historia de Cuba, *Centón epistolario de Domingo del Monte*, ed. Domingo Figarola-Caneda (7 vols., Havana: Imprenta "El Siglo XX," 1923–28), 5:181.
11 The term *peninsular*, or *peninsulares*, derives from the Iberian Peninsula. As a noun, it refers to Spanish-born residents of Cuba. As an adjective, it likewise refers to the Spanish—for example, *peninsular* officialdom means Spanish officialdom. For a thoughtful examination of the fear of blacks as represented in Spanish novels of the war, see Jorge Camacho, "El racismo y la guerra de Cuba (1895–1898): Un análisis de la representación de las razas, espacios y la herencia en la literatura española colonial," MERIDIONAL: *Revista Chilena de Estudios Latinoamericanos* 10 (April–September 2018): 21–43.
12 Melchor Loret de Mola, *Espisodios de la guerra de Cuba* (Puerto Príncipe, 1893), 23.
13 Pedro Deschamps Chapeaux, *Los batallones de pardos y morenos libres* (Havana: Instituto Cubano del Libro, 1976), 12–13. See also Allan J. Kuethe, *Cuba, 1753–1815: Crown, Military, and Society* (Knoxville, TN: University of Tennessee Press, 1986); Gustavo Placer Cervera, *Ejército y milicias en la Cuba colonial, 1763–1783* (Havana: Editorial de Ciencias Sociales, 2009); Roberto A. Hernández Suárez, *Ejército colonial en Cuba, 1561–1725* (Havana: Casa Editorial Verde Olivo, 2011).
14 Captain T. Syndenham to Henry Wellesley, October 10, 1812, in Arthur Wellesley/Duke of Wellington, *Supplementary Despatches, Correspondence, and Memoranda of Field Marshal Arthur Duke of Wellington* (12 vols., London, 1858–72), 7:450.
15 Félix de Echauz y Guinart, *Lo que se ha hecho y lo que hay que hacer en Cuba* (Havana, 1873), 17.
16 Hortensia Pichardo, "La muerte de Céspedes," in *Sobre la guerra de los 10 años, 1868–1878*, ed. María Cristina Llerena (Havana: Instituto Cubano del Libro, 1971), 216–17.
17 "El cabecilla Armas," *Diario de la Marina*, January 5, 1871, 2.
18 Enrique Collazo, *Desde Yara hasta El Zanjón: Apuntaciones históricas* (2nd ed., Havana, 1893), 193. For the official account, see "Comandancia General del Centro," *Gaceta de La Habana* 268 (November 15, 1871): 41.
19 Vidal Morales y Morales, *Hombres del 68: Rafael Morales y González: Contribución al estudio de la historia de la independencia de Cuba* (Havana: Imprenta y Papelería de Rambla, Bouza y Ca., 1904), 121.
20 Ernest Renan, "What Is a Nation?," in *Nation and Narration*, ed. Homi K. Bhabha (London: Routledge, 1990), 11.
21 Ramiro Guerra y Sánchez, *Guerra de los Diez Años, 1868–1878* (Havana: Cultural, 1950). In 420 pages of text, passing mention of the words *guerrilla* and *guerrillero*, alluding to Cubans in the service of Spain, appears three times on pages 69, 135, and 194.
22 See Herminio Portell Vilá, *Historia de Cuba en sus relaciones con los Estados Unidos y España* (4 vols., Havana: J. Montero, 1938–41); Emilio Roig de Leuch-

senring, *Historia y cubanidad: Discursos pronunciados en la inauguración del Segundo Congreso Nacional de História* (Havana: Sociedad Cubana de Estudios Históricos e Internacionales, 1943); Emilio Roig de Leuchsenring, *1895 y 1898, dos guerras cubanas: Ensayo de revaloración* (Havana: Cultural, 1945); Emilio Roig de Leuchsenring, *13 conclusiones fundamentales sobre la guerra libertadora cubana de 1895* (Mexico City: Colegio de México, 1945); Emilio Roig de Leuchsenring, *Por su propio esfuerzo conquistó el pueblo cubano su independencia* (Havana: Oficina del Historiador de la Ciudad, 1957).

23 Juan Luis Martín, "El combatiente cubano en función de pueblo," *Cuadernos de Historia Habanera* 30 (1945): 53–54.

24 Fernando Portuondo del Prado, *Historia de Cuba* (6th ed., Havana: Editora Universitaria, 1965), 438–39.

25 Jorge G. Juárez y Sedeño, "Organizaciones olvidadas," in Cuba, Congreso Nacional de Historia, *Primer Congreso Nacional de Historia: Trabajos presentados* (2 vols., Havana: Sección de Artes Gráficas del Centro Tecnológico del Instituto Cívico-Militar, 1943), 2:289–93.

26 Miguel Varona Guerrero, "Máximo Gómez: Generalísimo y libertador," *Diario de la Marina*, October 22, 1922, 37. At another point, Varona Guerrero indicates that thirty thousand Cubans served as guerrillas. See Miguel Varona Guerrero, *La guerra de independencia de Cuba, 1895–1896* (3 vols., Havana: Editorial Lex, 1946), 2:1407, 1419; 3:1816.

27 Salvador Massip, *Factores geográficos de la cubanidad* (Havana: Cultural, 1939), 32.

Chapter One. Something to Fear

1 Gaspar Betancourt Cisneros to José Antonio Saco, February 20, 1848, in *Medio siglo de historia colonial: Cartas a José Antonio Saco ordenadas y comentadas (de 1823 a 1879)*, ed. José Antonio Fernández de Castro (Havana: Ricardo Veloso, 1923), 101; Cisneros to Saco, October 19, 1848, in Fernández de Castro, *Medio siglo de historia colonial*, 92.

2 Félix M. Tanco to Domingo del Monte, August 24, 1843, in Academia de la Historia de Cuba, *Centón epistolario de Domingo del Monte*, ed. Domingo Figarola-Caneda (7 vols., Havana: Imprenta "El Siglo XX," 1923–28), 4:231, emphasis in original.

3 Jacinto de Salas y Quiroga, *Viages: Isla de Cuba* (Madrid, 1840), 282.

4 Within the decade of the 1790s, the price of sugar rose from 4 reales per pound to 28 to 30 reales per pound. See Heinrich Friedländer, *Historia económica de Cuba* (Havana: Jesús Montero, 1944), 112.

5 *Estado actual de la Isla de Cuba y medios que deben adoptarse para fomentar su prosperidad con utilidad para la Madre Patria* (Madrid, 1858), 24.

6 See "Ingenios y cafetales," 1832–33, 1834–35, Fondo Miscelánea de Expedientes, Legajo 3772, Número Añ, Archivo Nacional de Cuba, Havana, Cuba (hereinafter

cited as ANC); Jacobo de la Pezuela, *Diccionario geográfico, estadístico, histórico de la Isla de Cuba* (4 vols., Madrid, 1863–66), 1:225; Francisco Pérez de la Riva, *El café: Historia de su cultivo y explotación en Cuba* (Havana: Jesús Montero, 1945); Doria González Fernández, "Acerca del mercado cafetalero cubano durante la primera mitad del siglo XIX," *Revista de la Biblioteca Nacional "José Martí"* 31 (3ra Epoca) (May–August 1989): 151–59.

7   Cuba, Capitanía General, *Cuadro estadístico de la Siempre Fiel Isla de Cuba, correspondiente al año de 1827* (Havana, 1829), n.p.; Cuba, Capitanía General, *Cuadro estadístico de la Siempre Fiel Isla de Cuba, correspondiente al año de 1846* (Havana, 1847), 6; Leví Marrero, *Cuba: Economía y sociedad* (15 vols., Madrid, 1972–88), 10:77.

8   Cuba, Capitanía General, *Cuadro estadístico, año 1827*.

9   Abiel Abbot, *Letters Written in the Interior of Cuba* (Boston, 1829), 206.

10 See Reinaldo Funes Monzote, *De los bosques a los cañaverales: Una historia ambiental de Cuba 1491–1926* (Havana: Editorial Ciencias Sociales, 2008). In the eastern jurisdictions of the island, where sugar expanded more slowly, mixed agricultural farms and diverse land tenure forms persisted deep into the nineteenth century. See "Estado especificado de las fincas y establecimientos rurales y de industria, agrícola existentes en los diversos partidos que comprenden la jurisdicción de esta Capital [Santiago de Cuba]," May 28, 1838, Fondo Gobierno Superior Civil, Legajo 775, Número 26700, ANC; Jurisdicción de Las Tunas, "Padrón general de fincas rústicas," 1866, Fondo Miscelánea de Expedientes, Legajo 30, Número K, ANC; "Relación detallada de los nombres de fincas, sus dueños y caballerías de tierra de la Jurisdicción de Bayamo," 1866, Fondo Gobierno General, Legajo 265, Número 13517; Jurisdicción de Guantánamo, "Padrón de fincas rústicas," 1868, Fondo Miscelánea de Expedientes, Legajo 1565, Número AB, ANC; Jurisdicción de Baracoa, "Resumen estadístico de la población, riqueza urbana, agrícola e industrial, comercio y rentas del expresado año 1861," Fondo Gobierno General, Legajo 403, Número 19148, ANC; Ayuntamiento de Holguín, "Padrón general de fincas," 1860, Fondo Gobierno General, Legal 562, Número 27533, ANC.

11 The total number of sugar mills at midcentury is an unsettled matter. Jacobo de la Pezuela and José García de Arboleya estimated a total of 1,442 mills in 1846. Félix Erenchun offered the number of mills to be 1,560. Carlos Rebello identified a total of 1,365 mills in 1860, while Ramón de la Sagra counted 1,934 mills in the same year. El Centro de Estadísticas identified the existence of 1,531 mills in 1862. See Pezuela, *Diccionario geográfico, estadístico, histórico*, 1:59; José García de Arboleya, *Manual de la Isla de Cuba: Compendio de su historia, geografía, estadística y administración* (2nd ed., Havana, 1859), 137; Félix Erenchun, *Anales de Cuba* (Havana, 1857), 266; Carlos Rebello, *Estados relativos a la producción azucarera de la Isla de Cuba: Formados competentemente y con autorización de la Intendencia de Ejército y Hacienda* (Havana,

1860), 108; Ramón de la Sagra, *Cuba en 1860, o sea cuadro de sus adelantos en la población, la agricultura, el comercio y las rentas públicas* (2nd ed., Paris, 1863), 105; Cuba, Centro de Estadísticas, *Noticias estadísticas de la Isla de Cuba, en 1862* (Havana, 1864), n.p.

12 Franklin W. Knight, *Slave Society in Cuba during the Nineteenth Century* (Madison: University of Wisconsin Press, 1970), xviii.

13 Ramón de la Sagra, *Historia económico-política y estadística de la Isla de Cuba, o sea de sus progresos en la población, la agricultura, el comercio y las rentas* (Havana, 1831), 103.

14 Salas y Quiroga, *Viages*, 198.

15 Manuel Moreno Fraginals, *El ingenio: Complejo económico social cubano del azúcar* (Havana: Editorial de Ciencias Sociales, 1978), 1:96.

16 Enslaved women and men accounted for 436,000 of the total population of 1 million inhabitants. See Kenneth F. Kiple, *Blacks in Colonial Cuba, 1774–1899* (Gainesville: University of Florida Press, 1976). See also Sagra, *Historia económico-política y estadística*, 4–6; Cuba, Capitanía General, *Resumen del censo de población de la Isla de Cuba a fin del año de 1841* (Havana, 1842), 56.

17 José Ferrer de Couto, *Los negros en sus diversos estados y condiciones* (New York, 1864), 144.

18 "La Isla de Cuba," *Revista Bimestre Cubana* 2 (April 1832): 219. See also Domingo del Monte, "Datos y consideraciones sobre el estado de la Iglesia, de la esclavitud y de la población blanca y de color de la Isla de Cuba, en 1838–1839," in *Escritos de Domingo del Monte*, ed. José A. Fernández de Castro (2 vols., Havana, 1929), 1:152–53.

19 Lucas Alamán, *Historia de México* (5 vols., México: Impr. de Victoriano Aguero, 1883–85), 1:335.

20 *La Concordia Cubana* 31 (November 23, 1823): 3.

21 Domingo del Monte, "Proyecto de Memorial a S.M. la Reina, en nombre del Ayuntamiento de la Habana, pidiendo leyes especiales para la Isla de Cuba," 1838, in del Monte, *Escritos de Domingo del Monte*, 1:86–87.

22 José Antonio Saco, "Ideas sobre la incorporación de Cuba en los Estados Unidos," in *Contra la anexión*, ed. Fernando Ortiz (2 vols., Havana: Cultural, 1928), 1:46–47.

23 Domingo del Monte to editor, *El Globo*, August 1844, in del Monte, *Escritos de Domingo del Monte*, 1:200.

24 Anastasio de Arango, "Informe sobre el plan de defensa de Cuba," March 15, 1825, *Boletín del Archivo Nacional* 28 (January–February 1929): 130.

25 José Antonio Saco to José Valdés Fauli, September 6, 1878, in José Antonio Saco, *José Antonio Saco: Documentos para su vida*, ed. Domingo Figarola-Caneda (Havana: Imprenta "El Siglo XX," 1921), 303.

26 Richard R. Madden, *The Island of Cuba: Its Resources, Progress, and Prospects* (London, 1853), 85.

27 Domingo del Monte, "Peligros de los planes anexionistas y conducta que deben observar los patriotas cubanos," October 1844, in del Monte, *Escritos de Domingo del Monte*, 1:230–31.
28 Dionisio Alcalá Galiano, *Cuba en 1858* (Madrid, 1859), 36–37.
29 Fredrika Bremer, *The Homes of the New World: Impressions of America*, trans. Mary Howitt (2 vols., New York, 1858), 2:364.
30 José Ahumada y Centurión, *Memoria histórico política de la Isla de Cuba, redactada de orden del Señor Ministro de Ultramar* (Havana, 1874), 256.
31 José Antonio Saco, *La supresión del tráfico de esclavos africanos en la isla de Cuba* (Paris, 1845), 50.
32 Domingo del Monte, "Estado de la población blanca y de color de la Isla de Cuba en 1839," in del Monte, *Escritos de Domingo del Monte*, 1:157–58.
33 José Antonio Saco, *Historia de la esclavitud de la raza africana en el Nuevo Mundo y en especial en los países Américo-Hispanos* (4 vols., 1879–83; repubd., Havana: Cultural, 1938), 3:29.
34 Roland T. Ely, *Cuando reinaba su majestad el azúcar* (Buenos Aires: Editorial Sudamérica, 1963), 496.
35 Salas y Quiroga, *Viages*, 96, 149.
36 Madden, *The Island of Cuba*, 71.
37 Gertrudis Gómez de Avellaneda, *La Avellaneda (autobiografía y cartas)*, ed. Lorenzo Cruz de Fuentes (2nd ed., Madrid: Imprenta Helénica, 1914), 41; Gertrudis Gómez de Avellaneda, *Sab, novela original* (Madrid, 1841), 136.
38 Francisco Dionisio Vives, "Un interrogatorio absuelto por el Capitán General Don Francisco Dionisio Vives," October 9, 1832, *Revista Cubana: Periódico Mensual de Ciencias, Filosofía, Literatura, y Bellas Artes* 11 (1899): 449.
39 Arango, "Informe sobre el plan de defensa de Cuba," 129.
40 José del Castillo to Andrés de Arango, May 1838, in Academia de la Historia de Cuba, *Centón epistolario de Domingo del Monte*, 3:150.
41 *La Concordia Cubana* 6 (August 28, 1823): 3–4.
42 Félix Varela, "Tranquilidad de la Isla de Cuba," 1824, in *Obras*, ed. Eduardo Torres Cuevas et al. (3 vols., Havana: Editorial Cultura Popular, 2001), 2:171.
43 Miguel de Aldama to Domingo del Monte, November 9, 1844, in Academia de la Historia de Cuba, *Centón epistolario de Domingo del Monte*, 6:120.
44 "Isla de Cuba," *Revista Bimestre Cubana* 1 (August 1831): 225–29. The article is a commentary on the publication of Francisco Dionisio Vives, *Carta geográfica y topográfica de la Isla de Cuba, dedicada al Rey N.S.* (Havana, 1831).
45 Sagra, *Historia económico-política y estadística*, 319.
46 Sagra, *Historia económico-política y estadística*.
47 See D. E. Pichardo, "Carta topográfica de Matanzas y su jurisdicción real ordinaria con la vencidad de su circunferencia," *Memorias de la Sociedad Patriótica de La Habana* 7 (1838): 247–54; José Ildefonso Sánchez, "Topográficos estadísticos del Mariel," *Memorias de la Sociedad Patriótica de La Habana* 8

(1839): 154–60; Fernando G. Campoamor, "Cartografía cubana," *Bohemia* 63 (October 15, 1971): 4–5; Carlos Venegas Fornias, *Cuba y sus pueblos: Censos y mapas del los siglos XVIII y XIX* (Havana: Centro de Investigación y Desarrollo de la Cultura Cubana Juan Marinello, 2002), 79–125.

48 See "Expediente relacionado con el estado de la población y los caminos," 1826–28, Fondo Asuntos Políticos, Legajo 129, Número 11, ANC; "Padrón de los ingenios, tejares, hatos, estancias, puertos y embarcaderos que comprende en su territorio, con el nombre de sus dueños, del cuartón Parada, partido de Caimán Jorro," 1826, Fondo Gobierno General, Legajo 490, Número 25136, ANC; Gobierno y Capitanía de General, *Año de 1828: Censo de la Siempre Fidelísima ciudad de la Habana, capital de la Siempre Fidelísima Isla de Cuba* (Havana, 1829); Vives, *Carta geográfica y topográfica de la Isla de Cuba*; Miguel Moreno and Tomás González, *Carta de la Isla de Cuba con las islas, cayos, bancos y canales adyacentes*... (Madrid, 1832); "Censo de población de la Isla de Cuba á fin del año de 1841," *Memorias de la Sociedad Patriótica de La Habana* 18 (1844): 285–92; Felipe Poey, *Compendio de la geografía de Cuba* (Havana, 1851); Juan Bautista Sagarra, *Compendio de la geografía física y política de la Isla de Cuba* (Havana, 1854); Esteban Pichardo, *Geografía de la Isla de Cuba* (Havana, 1854). On geography: Arboleya, *Manual de la isla de Cuba*; Pichardo, *Geografía de la Isla de Cuba*; Pezuela, *Diccionario geográfico, estadístico, histórico*; Miguel Rodríguez Ferrer, *Naturaleza y civilización de la grandiosa Isla de Cuba* (Madrid, 1876); Esteban Pichardo, *Isla de Cuba: Carta geotopográfica de la Isla de Cuba* (Havana, 1875); Felipe Poey, *Compendio de la geografía de la Isla de Cuba* (Havana, 1836). On cartography: Francisco Javier Báez, *Plano de la Habana y su bahía* (Havana, 1823); Rafael Rodríguez, *Atlas cubano* (Havana, 1841); José María de la Torre, *Mapa de la Isla de Cuba y tierra circunvecinas según las divisiones de los naturales* (Havana, 1837); Esteban Pichardo, *Mapa físico-político e itinerario de la Isla de Cuba* (Havana, 1863). And gazetteers: Erénchun, *Anales de la Isla de Cuba: Diccionario administrativo, económico, estadístico y legislativo del año 1855*.

49 Censuses of the *dotaciones* received careful official scrutiny. See, for example, "Resumen general de partidos, número de esclavos de la dotación de los ingenios nuevos y viejos que molieron antes del año 1804, y de los cafetales que se hallan en el Obispado de La Habana," 1804–35, Fondo Miscelánea de Expedientes, Legajo 3772, Número Añ, ANC; "Relacion de los negros que existen en el partido de la Sabanilla, sus dueños y nombre de las haciendas donde habitan," 1830, Fondo Gobierno Superior Civil, Legajo 1065, Número 38004, ANC; "Padrón de los esclavos de ambos sexos que se hallan empleados en el servicio doméstico en el barrio de Barrancones, jurisdicción de Santiago," 1844–49, Fondo Gobierno General, Legajo 393, Número 18671, ANC.

50 See Cuba, Comisión de Estadísticas de La Habana, *Estado general de la población de la isla de Cuba, dispuesto por el excmo. Sr. D. José Cienfuegos* (Havana,

1821); Francisco Dionisio Vives, *Cuadro estadístico de la siempre fiel isla de Cuba, correspondiente al año de 1827* (Havana, 1829); Manuel Pastor, *Año de 1828: Censo de la Siempre Fidelísima ciudad de la Habana, capital de la Siempre Fiel Isla de Cuba* (Havana, 1829); Cuba, Capitanía General, *Resumen del censo de población de la Isla de Cuba a fin del año de 1841*; Vicente Vázquez Queipo, *Informe fiscal sobre fomento de la población blanca en la Isla de Cuba y emancipación progresiva de la esclava* (Madrid, 1845); Cuba, *Cuadro estadístico de la siempre fiel isla de Cuba, correspondiente al año de 1846* (Havana, 1847); España, Junta General de Estadística, *Censo de la población de España, según el recuento verificado en 25 de diciembre de 1860* (Madrid, 1863); Conde Armíldez de Toledo, *Noticias estadísticas de la Isla de Cuba en 1862* (Havana, 1864).

51 On *padrones*, see, for example, "Padrón general de habitantes blancos de los ocho partidos de campo de la ciudad de Santiago de Cuba, con expresión de sus nombres, haciendas donde habitan, si están alistados en los cuerpos de Milicia y si poseen o no caballos," 1812, Fondo Gobierno General, Legajo 392, Número 18623, ANC; "Padrón general de la villa de San Juan de los Remedios y sus partidos, con expresión de sexo, edad, calidad y oficio, así como del número y clases de establecimientos urbanos y fincas," 1820, Fondo Gobierno Superior Civil, Legajo 864, Número 29229, ANC; "Cuadro sinóptico de las estadísticas general del distrito de Sagua la Grande, con expresión de población por raza, edad, estado y ejercicio, así como establecimientos, número y clase de fincas, ganadería, productos anuales y administración," 1840, Fondo Gobierno General, Legajo 512, Número 26446, ANC; "Padrón general de habitantes y fincas de todas clases de la jurisdicción de Cárdenas," 1846, Fondo Gobierno General, Legajo 423, Número 20318, ANC. On demographic transformations, see, for example, Mariano Torrente, *Bosquejo econónmico político de la Isla de Cuba* (Madrid, 1852); "Estadísticas de ingenios y cafetales de La Habana, Matanzas y Las Villas, con expresión de su número, dueño, parroquias y partidos donde se encuentran," 1834–35, Fondo Miscelánea de Expedientes, Legajo 3772, Número Añ, ANC; "Estadística: Censo general de la industria agrícola de la Isla de Cuba," *Memorias de la Sociedad Patriótica de La Habana* 7 (1838): 63–80.

52 Robert L. Paquette, *Sugar Is Made with Blood: The Conspiracy of La Escalera and the Conflict between Empires over Slavery in Cuba* (Middletown, CT: Wesleyan University Press, 1988), 84.

53 See Alonso Benigo Muñoz, "Memoria sobre construcción caminos, formada por D. Alonso Benigo Muñoz, por encargo de la clase de industria popular, y presentada á la Sociedad Patriótica, en junta de 3 de diciembre de 1795," in *Memorias de la Real Sociedad Económica de La Habana* 6 (June 30, 1817): 181–95; José Antonio Saco, *Memoria sobre los caminos de la Isla de Cuba* (New York, 1830).

54 Oscar Zanetti Lecuona and Alejandro García Alvarez, *Caminos para el azúcar* (Havana: Editorial de Ciencias Sociales, 1987), 6.

55 Sagra, *Historia económico-política y estadística*, 320; Ramón de la Sagra, *Historia física, política y natural de la Isla de Cuba* (7 vols., Paris, 1842–55), 1:131, 133.
56 Sagra, *Historia económico-política y estadística*, 321; D. M. Estorch, *Apuntes para la historia sobre la administración de Marqués de la Pezuela en la Isla de Cuba* (Madrid, 1856), 33–34.
57 José G. de la Concha, *Memorias sobre el estado político, gobierno y administración de la Isla de Cuba* (Madrid, 1853), 45; José G. de la Concha to Presidente del Consejo de Ministro, March 31, 1851, in *Boletín del Archivo Nacional* 4 (July–August 1905): 64.
58 See Francisco Castillo Meléndez, *La defensa de la isla de Cuba en la segunda mitad del siglo XVII* (Seville: Diputación Provincial de Sevilla, 1986); César García del Pino, *El corso en Cuba. Siglo XVII: Causas y consecuencias* (Havana: Editorial de Ciencias Sociales, 2001); John Robert McNeill, *Atlantic Empires of France and Spain: Louisbourg and Havana, 1700–1763* (Chapel Hill: University of North Carolina Press, 1985).
59 Félix Varela, "Memoria que demuestra la necesidad de extinguir la esclavitud de los negros en la Isla de Cuba, atendiendo a los intereses de sus propietarios," 1822, in José Antonio Saco, *Historia de la esclavitud desde los tiempos más remotos hasta nuestros días* (2nd ed., 6 vols., Havana: Alfa, 1936–45), 5:163.
60 Fernando Redondo Díaz, "La Guerra de los Diez Años (1868–1878)," in Centro Superior de Estudios de la Defensa Nacional, *La presencia militar española en Cuba (1868–1895)* (Madrid: Ministerio de Defensa, 1995), 35–36. The organization of the *milicias* in Cuba drew upon traditions with deep colonial antecedents, a practice with origins in Spanish colonial administration of the New World. See Christon I. Archer, *The Army in Bourbon Mexico, 1760–1810* (Albuquerque: University of New Mexico Press, 1977); Leon G. Campbell, *The Military and Society in Colonial Peru, 1750–1810* (Philadelphia: American Philosophical Society, 1978); Allan J. Kuethe, *Military Reform and Society in New Granada, 1773–1808* (Gainesville: University of Florida Press, 1978); Lyle N. McAlister, *The "Fuero Militar" in New Spain, 1764–1800* (Gainesville: University of Florida Press, 1957); Juan Marchena Fernández, *La institución militar en Cartagena de Indias, 1700–1810* (Seville: Escuela de Estudios Hispano-Americanos, 1982); Juan Marchena Fernández, *Ejércitos y milicias en el mundo colonial americano* (Madrid: Mapfre, 1992); Lucio Mijares Pérez, "La organización de las milicias venezolanas en la segunda mitad del siglo XVIII," in *Memorias del III Congreso Venezolano de Historia* (Caracas: Academia Nacional de la Historia, 1979), 261–82; Santiago Gerardo Suárez, *Las milicias: Instituciones militares hispanoamericanas* (Caracas: Academia Nacional de la Historia 1984); Santiago Gerardo Suárez, ed., *Las fuerzas armadas venezolanas en la colonia* (Caracas: Academia Nacional de la Historia, 1979); Ben Vinson, *Bearing Arms for His Majesty: The Free-Colored Militia in Colonial Mexico* (Stanford, CA: Stanford University Press, 2001); Anthony McFarlane and Marianela

Santoveña Rodríguez, "Los ejércitos coloniales y la crisis del imperio español, 1808–1810," *Historia Mexicana* 58 (July–September 2008): 229–85.

61 Ramón Just, *Las aspiraciones de Cuba* (Paris, 1859), 133.
62 Vázquez Queipo, *Informe fiscal sobre fomento de la población blanca*, 12.
63 Justo Zaragoza, *Las insurrecciones en Cuba: Apuntes para la historia política de esta Isla en el presente siglo* (Madrid, 1872), 657.
64 Pezuela, *Diccionario geográfico, estadístico, histórico*, 2:267.
65 Antonio L. de Letona, *Isla de Cuba, reflexiones sobre su estado social, político y económico; su administración y gobierno* (Madrid, 1865), 89.
66 Un Miliciano, "Las milicias de Cuba: Recuerdos de un veterano," *El Correo Militar*, July 28, 1887, 1. "The flower of Havana society," wrote historian Allan Kuethe in *Cuba, 1753–1815: Crown, Military, and Society* (Knoxville: University of Tennessee Press, 1986), 58–60.
67 Pezuela, *Diccionario geográfico, estadístico, histórico*, 2:266.
68 Alacalá Galiano, *Cuba en 1858*, 133.
69 José Antonio Saco, "Memoria sobre la vagancia en la Isla de Cuba," *Revista Bimestre Cubana* 2 (April 1832): 41.
70 Leopoldo Barrios y Carrión, *Sobre la historia de la guerra de Cuba: Algunas consideraciones* (Barcelona, 1888), 213. Recruits that Maturin Ballou characterized as the "yeomanry of Cuba" in *History of Cuba; or, Notes of a Traveler in the Tropics* (Boston, 1854), 141.
71 Kuethe, *Cuba, 1753–1815*, 176–77.
72 Rafael Duharte Jiménez, *Nacionalidad e historia* (Havana: Editorial Oriente, 1991), 89. Service in the *milicia de color*, historian Herbert Klein suggested, implied "enormous prestige and power," adding, "Not only were militia officers granted pensions and other honors by the state, but they were also accorded general respect for their rank in the community at large, and this enabled them to break through the social and economic barriers, either for themselves, or more usually for their children. . . . The creation of the colored militia of Cuba provided the free colored the basic right as citizens to defend *their* state." See Herbert S. Klein, "The Colored Militia of Cuba, 1568–1868," *Caribbean Studies* 6 (July 1966): 26–27, emphasis in original. "By law excluded from all civil offices," James Rawson commented during a midcentury visit to Cuba, the free people of color nevertheless "compose a large part of the militia." See James Rawson, *Cuba* (New York, 1847), 12. See also María del Carmen Barcia, *Los ilustres apellidos: Negros en La Habana colonial* (Havana: Editorial de Ciencias Sociales, 2007), 232–307; David Sartorius, *Ever Faithful: Race Loyalty, and the Ends of Empire in Spanish Cuba* (Durham, NC: Duke University Press, 2013), 82–93.
73 Rebello, *Estados relativos a la producción azucarera*, 3–82.
74 Sagra, *Cuba en 1860*, 12.
75 "Ejército de la Isla de Cuba: Cuadro que manifiesta la fuerza y situación que tenían los cuerpos de todas armas de este ejército en 1º de Octubre de 1854,"

in José G. de la Concha, *Memoria dirigida al Escmo. Sr. Don Francisco Serrano y Domínguez, Capitán General de la Isla de Cuba* (Madrid, 1867), 13; Pezuela, *Diccionario geográfico, estadístico, histórico*, 2:248–54; Cuba, Gobierno y Capitanía, *Estado militar de la Isla de Cuba en el año de 1864* (Havana, 1864).

76 Cuba, Gobierno y Capitanía General, *Reglamento para la organización y régimen de siete escuadrones de caballería milicias urbanas rurales de Fernando VII, formado en el año de 1825, de orden del Excmo. Sr. Capitán General de la Isla Don Francisco Dionisio Vives* (Havana, 1847), 9.

77 José Antonio Saco, *Réplica de D. José Antonio Saco a la contestación del Señor Fiscal de la Real Hacienda de La Habana D. Vicente Vázquez Queipo* (Madrid, 1847), 34. See also Octavio Avelino Delgado, "The Spanish Army in Cuba, 1868–1898: An Institutional Study" (PhD diss., Columbia University, 1980), 262–63.

78 Sagra, *Historia económico-política y estadística*, 319–25.

79 Pezuela, *Diccionario geográfico, estadístico, histórico*, 2:265, 267.

80 John G. Wurdemann, *Notes on Cuba* (Boston, 1844), 85.

81 Abbot, *Letters Written in the Interior of Cuba*, 160–61.

82 Arango, "Informe sobre el plan de defensa de Cuba," 127.

83 Vázquez Queipo, *Informe fiscal sobre fomento de la población blanca*, 11–12.

84 Joseph J. Dimock, *Impressions of Cuba in the Nineteenth Century*, ed. Louis A. Pérez Jr. (Wilmington, DE: Scholarly Resources, 1998), 108.

85 See Leyda Oquendo, "Las rebeldías de los esclavos en Cuba, 1790–1830," in Departamento de Historia, Academia de Ciencias, *Temas acerca de la esclavitud* (Havana: Editorial de Ciencias Sociales, 1988), 49–70; Gloria García Rodríguez, *Conspiraciones y revueltas: La actividad política de los negros en Cuba (1790–1845)* (Santiago de Cuba: Editorial Oriente, 2003); Manuel Barcia Paz, *Seeds of Insurrection: Domination and Resistance on Western Cuban Plantations, 1808–1848* (Baton Rouge: Louisiana State University Press, 2008); Pedro Deschamps Chapeaux, *Sublevación de esclavos en Cuba, 1533–1880* (San Juan, PR: Ediciones Puerto, 2013); Aisha K. Finch, *Rethinking Slave Rebellion in Cuba: La Escalera and the Insurgencies of 1841–1844* (Chapel Hill: University of North Carolina Press, 2015), 48.

86 Vives, "Un interrogatorio absuelto por el Capitán-General don Francisco Dionisio Vives," 453–54.

87 Miguel Tacón, "Informe acerca de la denuncia hecha de que los emancipados se entregan por cierto estipendio para las labores del campo," August 31, 1836, in *Correspondencia reservada del Capitán General Don Miguel Tacón*, ed. Juan Pérez de la Riva (Havana: Consejo Nacional de Cultura, Biblioteca Nacional José Martí, 1963), 264. See also Miguel Tacón, "Estado de la isla de Cuba, temores que dan los negros y medidas tomadas," February 5, 1836, Biblioteca Virtual de Defensa, https://bibliotecavirtual.defensa.gob.es/BVMDefensa/es/catalogo_imagenes/grupo.do?presentacion=pagina&posicion=7&path=94845&texto_busqueda&registrardownload=0.

88 Miguel de Aldama to Domingo del Monte, November 9, 1843, in Academia de la Historia de Cuba, *Centón epistolario de Domingo del Monte*, 5:148. On the slave uprising during these years, see Fernando Ortiz, *Los negros esclavos* (1916; repubd., Havana: Editorial de Ciencias Sociales, 359–91; Oquendo, "Las rebeldías de los esclavos de Cuba," 49–70.

89 "Memorial dirigido al Gobierno de España sobre el estado de Cuba en 1844," 1844, in del Monte, *Escritos de Domingo del Monte*, 1:161–62, 169.

90 Domingo de Aldama, "Informe: Excmo. Sr. Gobernador Político y Capitán-General de la Isla de Cuba," *Revista Cubana: Periódico Mensual de Ciencias, Filosofía, Literatura y Bellas Artes* 7 (March 2, 1844): 251.

91 "Exposición al Excelentísimo Sr. Gobernador General de la Isla de Cuba," December 23, 1843, in Saco, *Historia de la esclavitud desde los tiempos*, 5:285. Saco adds an editorial note indicating that the petition, originally to be signed by "50 or 60 principal hacendados," was in the end forwarded by only three planters.

92 Ahumada y Centurión, *Memoria histórico política de la Isla de Cuba*, 217.

93 See Francisco González del Valle y Ramírez, *La conspiración de la Escalera* (Havana: Imprenta "El Siglo XX," 1925); Ortiz, *Los negros esclavos*, 385–94; Rita Llanes Miqueli, *Víctimas del año del cuero* (Havana: Editorial de Ciencias Sociales, 1984); Paquette, *Sugar Is Made with Blood*; Barcia Paz, *Seeds of Insurrection*, 25–48; García Rodríguez, *Conspiraciones y revueltas*; Finch, *Rethinking Slave Rebellion in Cuba*.

94 Pedro Antonio Alfonso, *Memorias de un matancero: Apuntes para la historia de la Isla de Cuba* (Matanzas, 1854), 224.

95 Miguel del Aldama to Domingo del Monte, February 9, 1844, in Academia de la Historia de Cuba, *Centón epistolario de Domingo del Monte*, 6:6.

96 Wurdemann, *Notes on Cuba*, 357.

97 Leopoldo O'Donnell to Minister of State, November 28, 1844, *Boletín del Archivo Nacional* 5 (March–April 1906): 27.

98 Gaspar Betancourt Cisneros to Domingo del Monte, February 6, 1844, in Academia de la Historia de Cuba, *Centón epistolario de Domingo del Monte*, 6:5.

99 Colonial authorities agreed to expand outposts of the *milicias rurales* with the condition that planters underwrite the cost of the permanent posts. Planters denounced the levy. In Matanzas, planters organized and prepared a formal protest against the levy, calculating that the subsidy would total more than 2 million pesos annually to maintain additional troops. See Miguel de Aldama to Domingo del Monte, November 10, 1843, in Academia de la Historia de Cuba, *Centón epistolario de Domingo del Monte*, 5:181–82; José Luis Alfonso to Domingo del Monte, December 1843, in Academia de la Historia de Cuba, *Centón epistolario de Domingo del Monte*, 5:181.

100 "Importante exposición de los hacendados de Matanzas al Gobernador General, pidiendo la supresión de la trata," November 29, 1843, in Saco, *Historia de la esclavitud de la raza africana*, 4:195–200.

101 Saco, *La supresión del tráfico de esclavos africanos*, 51.
102 For the published proceedings in the weeks following the claims of conspiracy, see "Sentencia pronunciada por la Sección de la Comisión Militar establecida en la ciudad de Matanzas para conocer de la causa de la conspiración de la gente de color," *Diario de la Marina*, September 29, 1844, 3–4; *Diario de la Marina*, October 28, 1844, 3; *Diario de la Marina*, December 4, 1844, 3; *Diario de la Marina*, December 15, 1844, 3; *Diario de la Marina*, December 25, 1844, 3; "Sentencia pronunciada por la Sección de la Comisión Militar establecida en la ciudad de Matanzas para conocer de la causa de conspiración de gente de color," in Joaquín Llaverías, *La Comisión Militar Ejecutiva y Permanente de la Isla de Cuba* (Havana: Imprenta "El Siglo XX," 1929), 147–57.
103 Francisco Arango y Parreño, "Discurso sobre la agricultura en La Habana," January 8, 1793, in Francisco Arango y Parreño, *Obras del Excmo. Señor D. Francisco de Arango y Parreño* (2 vols., Havana, 1888), 1:96–97.
104 Varela, "Memoria que demuestra la necesidad de extinguir la esclavitud," 5:162.
105 See Cuba, Gobierno y Capitanía General, *Reglamento para la organización y régimen de siete escuadrones de caballería*.
106 *Estado actual de la Isla de Cuba*, 16.
107 Vázquez Queipo, *Informe fiscal sobre fomento de la población blanca*, 13.
108 Fernando J. Padilla Angulo, "Volunteers of the Spanish Empire (1855–1898)" (PhD diss., University of Bristol, 2018), 48. See Justo Zaragoza, *Reglamento para los cuerpos de Voluntarios* (Havana, 1869); Evaristo Martín Contreras, *Los Voluntarios de la Isla de Cuba* (2nd ed., Valladolid, 1876); Simón Pascual y González, *Reglamento de los Voluntarios de la Isla de Cuba* (2nd ed., Havana, 1883), 9; José Joaquín Ribó, *Historia de los Voluntarios cubanos* (2 vols., Madrid, 1872–76); "Los Voluntarios de Cuba," *El Eco de la Patria* 1 (April 5, 1896): 2; Marilú Uralde Cancio, *Voluntarios de Cuba española (1850–1868)* (Havana: Editorial de Ciencias Sociales, 2011); Padilla Angulo, "Volunteers of the Spanish Empire"; Pezuela, *Diccionario geográfico, estadístico, histórico*, 2:270, 276.
109 Quoted in Zaragoza, *Las insurrecciones en Cuba*, 591. Padilla Angulo indicates that the ranks of the Voluntarios expanded to 80,000 during the Ten Years' War and to 85,000 during the Cuban war for independence, 1895–98. See Padilla Angulo, "Volunteers of the Spanish Empire," 19.
110 Leopoldo Barrios y Carrión, *Sobre la historia de la guerra de Cuba: Algunas consideraciones* (Barcelona, 1888), 213–14.
111 Domingo del Monte, "Proyecto de Memorial a S.M. la Reina, en nombre del Ayuntamiento de la Habana, pidiendo leyes especiales para la Isla de Cuba," 1838, in del Monte, *Escritos de Domingo del Monte*, 1:74.
112 Gaspar Betancourt Cisneros to José Antonio Saco, February 20, 1848, in Fernández de Castro, *Medio siglo de historia colonial*, 94.
113 For the full text of the Ostend Manifesto, see US Congress, House of Representatives, House Executive Document, No. 93, 33rd Congress, 2nd Session, 127–32.

114 On Narciso López, see Herminio Portell-Vilá, *Narciso López y su época* (3 vols., Havana: Cultural, 1930–58); Tom Chafin, *Fatal Glory: Narciso López and the First Clandestine U.S. War against Cuba* (Charlottesville: University of Virginia Press, 1996); "Historia de las insurrecciones de Cuba: La expedición pirática de López, en 1851," *Revista Técnica de Infantería y Caballería* 7 (February 1, 1896): 119–28.

115 José G. de la Concha to Ministro de Estado, July 21, 1854, in Carlos de Sedano y Cruzat, ed., *Cuba desde 1850 á 1873: Colección de informes, memorias, proyectos y antecedentes sobre el gobierno de la Isla de Cuba* (Madrid, 1873), 121.

116 José G. de la Concha to Minister of Justice, January 9, 1851, *Boletín del Archivo Nacional* 4 (May–June 1905): 46–47. De la Concha used the data that appeared in Gobierno y Capitanía General de Cuba, *Cuadro estadístico de la Siempre Fiel Isla de Cuba correspondiente al año de 1846*. The data on the Centro Department is found on pp. 145–211. A point of clarification: in the published version of de la Concha's communication in the *Boletin del Archivo Nacional*, there appears to be a typographical error. The number of *peninsulares* that appears in print is 15,305. In fact, it is 5,305. See also de la Concha, *Memorias sobre el estado político, gobierno y administración*, 202–3.

117 As recounted by US Minister to Spain Cornelius P. Van Ness to John Forsyth, December 10, 1836, in *Diplomatic Correspondence of the United States: Inter-American Affairs*, ed. William R. Manning (12 vols., Washington, DC: Carnegie Endowment For International Peace, 1932–39), 11:303.

118 Federico de Roncali [Conde de Alcoy] to Ministerio de la Gobernación, "Manifiesta el estado de tranquilidad y los auxilios que se nececitan para asegurar la Isla contra todo evento," September 9, 1849, *Boletín del Archivo Nacional* 16 (July–August 1917): 280–81.

119 See Mariano Torrente, *Política ultramarina, que abraza todos los puntos referentes a las relaciones de España con los Estados Unidos, con la Inglaterra y las Antillas* (Madrid, 1854), 112–14.

120 De la Concha, *Memorias sobre el estado político, gobierno y administración*, 355. See also Antonio de las Barras y Prado, *La Habana al mediados del siglo XIX: Memorias* (Madrid: Imprenta de la Ciudad Lineal, 1926), 29–30.

121 "Comunicación del Capitán-General de la Isla José G. de la Concha al Excmo. Ministro de Guerra," December 10, 1854, Manuscrito Número 20282/134, Milicias de Color, Biblioteca Nacional de Madrid; de la Concha, *Memoria dirigida al Escmo. Sr. Don Francisco Serrano y Domínguez*, 15–16.

122 Estorch, *Apuntes para la historia sobre la administración*, 160.

123 "De oficio," *Diario de la Marina*, August 9, 1855, 1; Erénchun, *Anales de la Isla de Cuba*, 3:2200–2206; Pezuela, *Diccionario geográfico, estadístico, histórico*, 2:266.

124 Zaragoza, *Las insurrecciones en Cuba*, 657–58. See also Depósito de la Guerra, *Organización y estado militar de España y Ultramar en 1º de enero de 1869* (Madrid, 1869), 290–91.

125 De la Concha, *Memoria dirigida al Escmo. Sr. Don Francisco Serrano y Domínguez*, 33–34; Cuba, Gobierno y Capitanía General, *Estado militar de la Isla de Cuba en el año 1864* (Havana, 1864), 9–14. See also de la Concha, *Memorias sobre el estado político, gobierno y administración*, 143–44.
126 Alexander Jones, *Cuba in 1851, Containing Authentic Statistics of the Population, Agriculture and Commerce for a Series of Years* (New York, 1851), 49.
127 William H. Robertson to William L. Marcy, May 7, 1854, in Manning, *Diplomatic Correspondence of the United States*, 11:773, emphasis in original. See also C. Stanley Urban, "The Africanization of Cuba Scare, 1853–1855," *Hispanic American Historical Review* 37 (February 1957): 29–45.
128 Horatio J. Perry to Franklin Pierce, January 10, 1853, in Manning, *Diplomatic Correspondence of the United States*, 11:690, emphasis in original.
129 Ballou, *History of Cuba*, 96.
130 Charles W. Davis to William L. Marcy, May 22, 1854, in Manning, *Diplomatic Correspondence of the United States*, 11:789, 794.
131 David Turnbull, *Travels in the West. Cuba; and with Notices of Porto Rico, and the Slave Trade* (London, 1840), 171.
132 Gaspar Betancourt Cisneros to Domingo del Monte, June 20, 1841, in Academia de la Historia de Cuba, *Centón espistolario de Domingo del Monte*, 5:32.
133 Dionisio Vives to Secretary of State, June 23, 1825, *Boletín del Archivo Nacional* 8 (November–December 1909): 200. See also Cuba, Gobierno y Capitanía General, *Reglamento para la organización y régimen de siete escuadrones de caballería, milicias urbanas rurales de Fernando VII: Formado el año de 1825 de orden del Excmo. Sr. Capitán General de la isla don Francisco Dionisio Vives* (Havana, 1847).
134 As recounted by US Minister to Spain Cornelius P. Van Ness to John Forsyth, December 10, 1836, in Manning, *Diplomatic Correspondence of the United States*, 11:303.
135 Federico de Roncali [Conde de Alcoy] to Ministerio de la Gobernación, "Manifesta el estado de tranquilidad y los auxilios que se necesitan para asegurar la Isla contra todo evento," September 9, 1849, *Boletín del Archivo Nacional* 16 (July–August 1917): 281–82.
136 Alcalá Galiano, *Cuba en 1858*, 13–14.
137 Gaspar Betancourt Cisneros to José Antonio Saco, April 13, 1849, in Fernández de Castro, *Medio siglo de historia colonial*, 104. See also Estorch, *Apuntes para la historia sobre la administración*, 33.
138 José G. de la Concha to Ministro de la Guerra, July 2, 1854, in Sedano y Cruzat, *Cuba desde 1850 á 1873*, 136.
139 Horatio J. Perry to Franklin Pierce, January 10, 1853, in Manning, *Diplomatic Correspondence of the United States*, 11:690, 693, emphasis in original.
140 Charles W. Davis to William L. Marcy, May 22, 1854, in Manning, *Diplomatic Correspondence of the United States*, 11:792–93.

141 William H. Robertson to William L. Marcy, April 21, 1854, in Manning, *Diplomatic Correspondence of the United States*, 11:765–66.
142 Bremer, *The Homes of the New World*, 2:437.

Chapter Two. Half Defeated upon Arrival

1 Hugh Thomas, *Cuba, the Pursuit of Freedom* (New York: Harper & Row, 1971), 241. See also María Dolores Domingo Acebrón, "Los hacendados cubanos ante la guerra de los diez años," *Revista de Indias* 172 (1983): 101–21.
2 Suggestive demographic profiles of rural Oriente are found in Jurisdicción de Guantánamo, "Padrón de fincas rústicas," 1868, Fondo Miscelánea de Expedientes, Legajo 1565, Número Ab, Archivo Nacional de Cuba, Havana, Cuba (hereinafter cited as ANC); "Padrones nominales de la población blanca y de color de la jurisdicción de Jiguaní, partido de Baire," March 15, 1861, Fondo Miscelánea de Expedientes, Legajo 3782, Número Az, ANC; Jurisdicción de Las Tunas, "Padrón general de fincas rústicas," 1866, Fondo Miscelánea de Expedientes, Legajo 30, Número K, ANC; "Relación detallada de los nombres de las fincas, dueños y caballerías de tierra de la jurisdicción de Baracoa," 1866, Fondo Gobierno General, Legajo 265, Número 13503, ANC; Ayuntamiento de Holguín, "Copia literal y detallada del último padrón municipal de fincas rústicas con separación por partidos y clases de finca," 1866, Fondo Gobierno General, Legajo 266, Número 13538, ANC.
3 Cuba, Capitanía General, *Resumen del censo de población de la Isla de Cuba a fin del año de 1841* (Havana, 1842), 19–23.
4 For an exposition of grievances of the producing classes of Oriente, see Louis Despaign et al. [Santiago de Cuba] to Captain General, June 21, 1859, Fondo Gobierno Superior Civil, Legajo 1184, Número 46392, ANC. As early as 1811, *orientales* registered complaints over inadequate assistance from Havana. See Ignacio Zarragotia [Bayamo], "Memoria," March 5, 1811, Fondo Real Consulado y Junta de Fomento, Legajo 93, Número 3953, ANC.
5 See "Papel oficial del Gobierno de Santiago de Cuba," April 29, 1825, Fondo Gobierno Superior Civil, Legajo 630, Número 19886, ANC.
6 Camilo Polavieja, *Relación documentada de mi política en Cuba: Lo que vi, lo que hice, lo que anuncié* (Madrid, 1896), 178–80.
7 Eduardo Machado Gómez, *Autobiografía de Eduardo Machado Gómez* (1908; repubd., Havana: Universidad de La Habana, Comisión de Extensión Universitaria, 1969), 11; Carlos Manuel de Céspedes, "Proclama de Barrancas," October 18, 1868, in *Escritos*, ed. Fernando Portuondo and Hortensia Pichardo (2 vols., Havana: Editorial de Ciencias Sociales, 1982), 1:109–10; Carlos Manuel de Céspedes y Quesada, *Carlos Manuel de Céspedes* (Paris, 1895), 261; José María Izaguirre, "La acción de Río Abajo," 1870, in *Asuntos cubanos: Colección de artículos y poesías*, ed. José María Izaguirre (New York, 1896), 63–64. The

actual number of Cubans who enrolled in the ranks of the insurgency by the end of 1868 is uncertain. Gabriel Cardona and Juan Carlos Losada estimate 15,000. Fernando Redondo Díaz suggests that the insurgency had increased to as many as 10,000 by 1874–75. Spanish Lieutenant Colonel Francisco J. de Moya indicates that the forces that assaulted Bayamo numbered 5,000 *insurrectos*, reaching a high of 40,000 by the 1870s. See Gabriel Cardona and Juan Carlos Losada, *Weyler, nuestro hombre en La Habana* (Barcelona: Planeta, 1997), 49; Fernando Redondo Díaz, "La Guerra de los Diez Años (1868–1878)," in Centro Superior de Estudios de la Defensa Nacional, *La presencia militar española en Cuba (1868–1895)* (Madrid: Ministerio de Defensa, 1995), 44; Francisco J. de Moya, *Consideraciones militares sobre la campaña de Cuba* (Madrid: Imprenta del Cuerpo de Artillería, 1901), 92, 155.

8 Antonio Miguel Alcover, *Bayamo (su toma, posesión y incendio), 1868–1869* (Havana: Imprenta La Australia, 1902). Spanish officer Dionisio Novel é Ibáñez recalled the "complete isolation of Bayamo" and learning that "relief and reinforcements were unavailable." See Dionisio Novel é Ibáñez, *Memoria de los sucesos ocurridos en la insurrección que estalló en la ciudad de Bayamo en octubre de 1868 y observaciones sobre el estado en que la poblacion se encontraba . . . hasta fin de enero de 1869* (Granada, 1872), 26–37. See also Luis Otero y Pimentel, *Política militar y civil* (Cádiz: Imprenta de la Revista Médica, 1903), 161, 163.

9 Moya, *Consideraciones sobre la campaña de Cuba*, 87–88; Cuba, Capitanía General, *Infantería del ejército de la Isla de Cuba: Escalafón general* (Havana, 1880). A review of the Spanish army in Cuba in 1854 indicated the presence of 16,180 troops, most of whom were deployed in the western jurisdictions, with fully one-third (5,331 soldiers) stationed in Havana. See Ejército de la Isla de Cuba, "Cuadro que manifiesta la fuerza y situación que tenían los cuerpos de todas armas de este ejército en 1 de octubre de 1854," in Emilio A. Soulère, *Historia de la insurrección de Cuba (1869–1879)* (2 vols., Barcelona, 1879–80), 1:687; José de la Concha, *Memoria dirigida al Escmo. Sr. Don Francisco Serrano y Domínguez, Capitán General de la Isla de Cuba* (Madrid, 1867), 18–19.

10 "La guerra de Cuba, 1868–78: Datos estadísticos," *Revista Técnica de Infantería y Caballería* 7 (October 15, 1896): 359–61; Leopoldo Barrios y Carrión, *Sobre la historia de la guerra de Cuba: Algunas consideraciones* (Barcelona, 1888), 26; Adolfo Jiménez Castellanos, *De las insurrecciones en Cuba y sistema para combatirlas, según lo que aconseja la experiencia* (Madrid, 1883), 13–14; Tesifonte Gallego, *La insurrección cubana: Crónicas de la campaña* (Madrid, 1897), 21–22; Ramiro Guerra y Sánchez, *Guerra de los Diez Años, 1868–1878* (Havana: Cultural, 1950), 183–87.

11 Antonio López de Letona, *Isla de Cuba: Reflexiones sobre su administración y gobierno* (Madrid, 1865), 98.

12 Moya, *Consideraciones militares sobre la campaña de Cuba*, 87.

13 Jacobo de la Pezuela, *Diccionario geográfico, estadístico, histórico de la Isla de Cuba* (4 vols., Madrid, 1863–78), 1:155. Major Leopoldo Barrios y Carrión estimated the total military force on the island to number approximately 20,000 officers and men, of which only 8,000–10,000 were combat ready. See Barrios y Carrión, *Sobre la historia de la guerra de Cuba*, 26. For a complete profile of the Spanish army in Cuba at the outbreak of the insurrection, see Spain, Ministro de la Guerra, El Depósito de la Guerra, *Organización y estado militar de España y ultramar en 1º de enero de 1869* (Madrid, 1869), 275–304.

14 Daniel E. Sickles to Hamilton Fish, September 25, 1868, in *Correspondence between the Department of State and the United States Minister at Madrid and Consular Representative of the United States in the Island of Cuba*, US Congress, House of Representatives, 41st Congress, 2nd Session, Ex. Doc. No. 160 (Washington, DC, 1870), 52. See also Susan J. Fernández, *Encumbered Cuba: Capital Markets and Revolt, 1878–1895* (Gainesville: University of Florida Press, 2002), 37–81.

15 Barrios y Carrión, *Sobre la historia de la guerra de Cuba*, 35–36. See also José María Velasco, *Guerra de Cuba: Causas de su duración y medios de terminarla* (Madrid, 1872), 32–53.

16 Luis Fernández Golfin, *Breves apuntes sobre las cuestiones mas importantes de la Isla de Cuba* (Barcelona, 1866), 146–47, 156–57.

17 Francisco de Acosta y Albear, *Compendio histórico del pasado y presente de Cuba y de su guerra insurreccional* (Madrid, 1875), 9; Eugenio Antonio Flores, *La guerra de Cuba (Apuntes para la historia)* (Madrid, 1895), 10.

18 Moya, *Consideraciones sobre la campaña de Cuba*, 93.

19 Soulère, *Historia de la insurrección de Cuba*, 1:23. See also José de Granda, *Reflexiones sobre la insurrección de Cuba* (Madrid, 1870), 17–18, 93–94.

20 Francisco Acosta y Albear, *Apreciaciones sobre la insurrección de Cuba* (Havana, 1872), 8.

21 See "La integridad nacional," *La Voz de Cuba*, March 31, 1870, 2.

22 "Al Excmo. Sr. General Don Cándido Pieltan," *La Voz de Cuba*, August 15, 1873, 2.

23 The distinctions among the designations of settlements are not always clearly defined or consistently used. *Caseríos* were rural communities between five and twenty households; an *aldea* designated a community of twenty to fifty households; *pueblo* signified more than fifty to one hundred households. *Villas* and *ciudades* were often used interchangeably to designate settlements larger than one hundred households. See Esteban Pichardo, *Geografía de la Isla de Cuba* (Havana, 1854), vii–viii.

24 The population of color—free and enslaved—in Santiago de Cuba accounted for 68,285 inhabitants out of a total population of 96,028. In Guantánamo the population of color was 14,285 out of a total of 19,619. See Capitanía General de Cuba, Centro de Estadísticas, *Noticias estadística de la Isla de Cuba en 1862* (Havana, 1864).

25 See Ada Ferrer, *Insurgent Cuba: Race, Nation, and Revolution, 1868–1898* (Chapel Hill: University of North Carolina Press, 1999), 22–28.
26 Franklin Knight, *Slave Society in Cuba during the Nineteenth Century* (Madison: University of Wisconsin Press, 1970), 168.
27 Rebecca J. Scott, *Slave Emancipation in Cuba: The Transition to Free Labor, 1860–1899* (Princeton, NJ: Princeton University Press, 1985), 63.
28 See José M. Abreu Cardet, "Esclavos y reclutamiento insurrecto: Cuba 1868–1878," in *De la libertad y la abolición: Africanos y afrodescendientes in Iberoamérica*, ed. Juan Manuel de la Serna (Mexico City: Instituto Nacional de Antropología e Historia, 2013), 219–40, https://books.openedition.org/cemca/1635?lang=en.
29 María del Carmen Barcia Zequeira, *Elites y grupos de presión: Cuba, 1868–1898* (Havana: Editorial de Ciencias Sociales, 1998), 7.
30 Dionisio Alcalá Galiano, *Cuba en 1858* (Madrid, 1859), 48–49.
31 Vicente García Verdugo, *Cuba contra España: Apuntes de un año para la historia de la rebelión de la Isla de Cuba, que principió el 10 de octubre de 1868* (Madrid, 1869), 22, 24.
32 Nicolás Azcárate, *Votos de un cubano* (Madrid, 1869), 9, 11.
33 "Las revoluciónes," *El Voluntario de Cuba* 1 (October 11, 1870): 1.
34 Juan Güell y Ferrer, *Rebelión cubana* (Barcelona, 1871), 12–13.
35 Federico Ordas Avecilla, *El pasado, el presente y el porvenir de la Isla de Cuba* (Havana, 1893), 29–30.
36 Nicolás Pardo Pimentel, *La isla de Cuba: Su prosperidad ó su ruina. Breves observaciones sobre su cuestión social y política* (Madrid, 1870), 12, 14.
37 José Ahumada y Centurión, *Memoria histórico-político de Cuba, redactada de orden del Señor Ministro de Ultramar* (Havana, 1874), 153.
38 Consuelo Naranjo Orovio, "La amenaza haitiana, un miedo interesado: Poder y fomento de la población blanca en Cuba," in *El rumor de Haití en Cuba: Temor, raza y rebeldía, 1789–1844*, ed. Maria Dolores González-Ripoll et al. (Madrid: Consejo Superior de Investigaciones Científicas, 2004), 93.
39 "En Cuba y fuera de Cuba," *Diario de la Marina*, September 7, 1872, 2.
40 See Joan Casanovas Codina, "Los peninsulares y la sociedad colonial en el ámbito urbano cubano (1833–1898)" (December 2000): 208–12, https://www.vr-elibrary.de/doi/pdf/10.7767/jbla.2000.37.1.201.
41 Julio Le Riverend, "Perspectivas y significación de la revolución de 1868," in *Sobre la guerra de los 10 años 1868–1878*, ed. María Cristina Llerena (Havana: Instituto Cubano del Libro, 1973), 80.
42 José Antonio Saco to José Valdés Fauli, September 6, 1878, in José Antonio Saco, *José Antonio Saco: Documentos para su vida*, ed. Domingo Figarola-Caneda (Havana: Imprenta "El Siglo XX," 1921), 303.
43 Guerra y Sánchez, *Guerra de los Diez Años*, 2:341–42.
44 Ferrer, *Insurgent Cuba*, 126.

45 Tomás Fernández Robaina, "El negro espacio del negro. Raza y nación en Cuba: Entrevista con Tomás Fernández Robaina," in *La imaginación contra la norma: Ocho enfoques sobre la república de 1902*, ed. Julio César Guanche (Havana: Ediciones La Memoria, 2004), 110.
46 "Para el porvenir," *La Voz de Cuba*, August 24, 1877, 2.
47 *Diario de la Marina*, December 26, 1869, 2. The Cubans had embarked upon a "war against our nationality," Nicolás Pardo Pimentel decried. See Pardo Pimentel, *La isla de Cuba*, 10.
48 *Diario de la Marina*, January 26, 1869, 2.
49 "Cuba no se pierde," *El Voluntario de Cuba* 1 (October 23, 1870): 1.
50 "La insurrección en Cuba," *El Imparcial*, January 20, 1869, 1.
51 Soulère, *Historia de la insurrección de Cuba*, 1:137.
52 "Esfuerzos vanos," *La Voz de Cuba*, August 31, 1873, 2. In Madrid, US Minister Daniel E. Sickles reported learning from Spanish Minister of State Manuel Silvela that the call "Death to Spain" had "alienated the sympathies of the nation and obliged the government to accept the impolitic contest to which it was provoked." See Daniel E. Sickles to Hamilton Fish, August 14, 1868, in *Correspondence between the Department of State and the United States Minister at Madrid*, 24.
53 Vicente García Verdugo, *Cuba contra España*, 16–17.
54 Antonio Porrua y Fernández de Castro, *Cuba española: Apuntes para un estudio de política antillana* (Cienfuegos, 1895), 28, italics in original.
55 See "Nomenclaturas políticas," *Diario de la Marina*, April 30, 1873, 3.
56 Soulère, *Historia de la insurrección de Cuba*, 1:740; Juan Güell y Ferrer, *Rebelión cubana* (Barcelona, 1871), 8–11; Gil Gelpi y Ferro, *Situación de España y de sus posesiones de ultramar al principo del año 1875* (Madrid, 1875), 79–82.
57 "A los Voluntarios," *La Voz de Cuba*, July 13, 1873, 2.
58 See Guerra y Sánchez, *Guerra de los Diez Años*, 188–93. For the *peninsular* population of Cuba, see Capitanía General de Cuba, *Noticias estadísticas*.
59 Juan de Almansa y Tavira, *La revolución de Cuba y el elemento español* (Havana, 1870), 21.
60 José Ramón Betancourt, *Las dos banderas: Apuntes históricos sobre la insurrección de Cuba* (Sevilla, 1870), 24. The Banco Español in Havana pledged 15,000 pesos monthly for three months to support a unit of five hundred Voluntarios. See *Gaceta de La Habana*, November 20, 1868, 1. See also "Exposición," *Gaceta de La Habana*, November 28, 1868, 1; "Gobierno Superior de la Siempre Fidelísima Isla de Cuba: Secretaría," *Gaceta de La Habana*, December 1, 1868, 1.
61 See "Voluntarios de la Isla de Cuba," *Boletín Oficial de los Voluntarios* 5 (January 4, 1880): 8; "Voluntarios de Cuba," *Boletín Oficial del los Voluntarios* 5 (January 11, 1880): 6–7; Justo Zaragoza, *Reglamento para los cuerpos de Voluntarios de la Isla de Cuba* (Havana, 1869); José Joaquín Ribó, *Historia de los Voluntarios cubanos* (2 vols., Madrid, 1872); Evaristo Martín Contreras, *Los Voluntarios de la Isla de Cuba: Reconocimiento de su heroísmo y vindicación a su honor* (Val-

ladolid, 1876); Luis Otero Pimentel, *Memoria sobre los Voluntarios de la Isla de Cuba: Consideraciones relativas a su pasado, su presente y su porvenir* (Havana, 1876); Simón Pascual y González, *Reglamento de los Voluntarios de la Isla de Cuba* (Havana, 1883).

62 Eusebio Sáenz y Sáenz, *La siboneya, o episodios de la guerra de Cuba* (Cienfuegos, 1881), 307.
63 Gil Gelpi y Ferro, *Album histórico de la guerra de Cuba* (Havana, 1870), 50–53, 65.
64 Martín Contreras, *Los voluntarios de la isla de Cuba*, 11.
65 Jiménez Castellanos, *De las insurrecciones en Cuba*, 19.
66 Guerra y Sánchez, *Guerra de los Diez Años*, 193, 395–96; Barrios y Carrión, *Sobre la historia de la guerra de Cuba*, 260.
67 Edward Plumb to J. C. B. Davis, October 21, 1869, in US Congress, *In Compliance with a Resolution of the Senate of the 8th Instant, Information in Regard to the Progress of the Revolution in Cuba, and the Political and Civil Condition of the island*, 41st Congress, 2nd Session, Ex. Doc. No. 7 (Washington, DC, 1870), 84.
68 Nicolás Estévanez, *Fragmentos de mis memorias* (Madrid: Hijos de R. Álvarez, 1903), 362.
69 Dolores María de Ximeno y Cruz, *Memorias de Lola María*, ed. Ambrosio Fornet (Havana: Editorial Letras Cubanas, 1983), 166.
70 Richard Gibbs to H. R. de La Reintrie, December 11, 1868, in *Correspondence between the Department of State and the United States Minister at Madrid*, 184.
71 Edward Plumb to Hamilton Fish, June 4, 1869, in *Correspondence between the Department of State and the United States Minister at Madrid*, 92.
72 Antonio Reyes Zamora, *Episodios en la vida de un estudiante del 68 hasta 30 años después* (Santiago de Cuba: Imprenta Arroyo Hnos, 1920), 8, 19.
73 Barrios y Carrión, *Sobre la historia de la guerra de Cuba*, 214. The Voluntarios acted to "arm the *peninsulares* and marginalize the criollos from the military system," historian Fernando Padilla Angulo noted. See Fernando J. Padilla Angulo, "Volunteers of the Spanish Empire (1855–1898)" (PhD diss., University of Bristol, 2018), 22.
74 See *Diario de la Marina*, January 27, 1869, 2.
75 See Fermín Valdés Domínguez, *Los voluntarios de La Habana en el acontecimiento de los estudiantes de medicina* (Madrid, 1873).
76 F. A. Conte, *La lucha política en Cuba: Los unos y los otros* (Havana, 1889), 29–42.
77 See Inés Roldán de Montaud, *La Unión Constitucional y la política de España en Cuba (1868–1898)* (Madrid Editorial de la Universidad, 1991); Rafael Montoro, *Ideario autonomista* (Havana: Casa Montalvo Cárdenas, 1936); Mildred de la Torre, *El autonomismo en Cuba, 1878–1898* (Havana: Editorial de Ciencias Sociales, 1997).
78 Gil Gelpi y Ferro, *Historia de la revolución y guerra de Cuba* (Havana, 1887), 136.
79 Gonzalo Fernández, *Estrategia militar en la Guerra de los Diez Años* (Santiago de Cuba: Editorial Oriente, 1983), 12–14. For a detailed first-person account of

the Valmaseda campaign, see Teodorico Feijóo y de Mendoza, *Diario de un testigo de las operaciones sobre los insurrectos de la Isla de Cuba llevadas a cabo por la columna a las órdenes del Excmo. Sr. General Conde de Valmaseda* (Madrid, 1869).

80 Conde de Valmaseda to Captain General, January 21, 1870, *La Bandera Española* (Santiago de Cuba), January 23, 1870, 2.

81 See Francisco Lersundi, "Parte oficial. Estado Mayor: Order General del Ejército 3 de enero de 1869," in *La guerra desde La Gaceta de La Habana (10 de octubre de 1868–23 de abril de 1869)*, ed. Roberto Antonio Hernández Suárez (Havana: Casa Editorial Verde Olivo, 2011), 143–45.

82 *Diario de la Marina*, January 22, 1869, 2; *Diario de la Marina*, January 28, 1869, 2. See also "Publicando el glorioso hecho de armas ocurrido el 23 del pasado en la villa del Cobre," *Boletín Oficial de la Capitanía General de la Isla de Cuba* 7 (December 5, 1868), 43.

83 "Parte Oficial," *Gaceta de La Habana*, June 7, 1870, 1.

84 Justo Zaragoza, *Las insurrecciones de Cuba: Apuntes para la historia política de esta isla en el presente siglo* (2 vols., Madrid, 1872–73), 2:301.

85 In Soulère, *Historia de la insurrección de Cuba*, 1:51.

86 Luis Lagomasino, *Reminiscencias patrias* (Manzanillo: Tipografía El Repórter, 1902), 14.

87 Knight, *Slave Society in Cuba*, 156.

88 Soulère, *Historia de la insurrección de Cuba*, 1:25, 285.

89 Ramón Domingo de Ibarra, *Cuentos históricos: Recuerdos de la primera campaña de Cuba, 1868–78* (Santa Cruz de Tenerife: Tipografía de A. J. Benitez, 1905), 93–94.

90 On the Guáimaro Constituent Assembly, see Jorge Ibarra, "La Asamblea de Guáimaro," in *Sobre la Guerra de los 10 Años, 1868–1878*, ed. María Cristina Llerena (Havana: Instituto Cubano del Libro, 1971), 241–50.

91 Barrios y Carrión, *Sobre la historia de la guerra de Cuba*, 21–22.

92 José de la Concha, *Memoria sobre la guerra de la Isla de Cuba y sobre su estado político y económico desde abril de 1874 hasta marzo de 1875* (Madrid, 1875), 17.

93 Francisco J. Ponte Domínguez, *La idea invasora y su desarrollo histórico* (Havana: Cultural, 1930), 20–28.

94 José Manuel Mestre to José Antonio Saco, September 7, 1869, in *Medio siglo de historia colonial: cartas a José Antonio Saco ordenadas y comentadas (de 1823 a 1879)*, ed. José Antonio Fernández de Castro (Havana: R. Veloso, 1923), 394.

95 Eduardo Machado Gómez, *Autobiografía de Eduardo Machado Gómez* (1908; repubd., Havana, 1969), 12. See also Pedro Pablo Rodríguez, *La primera invasión* (Havana: Unión de Escritores y Artistas de Cuba, 1986).

96 Estévanez, *Fragmentos de mis memorias*, 357.

97 All through the war, insurgent Cubans targeted telegraph communication within the provinces and between the provinces and Havana. At one point in 1870, the interruption of telegraph service between Havana and Puerto Príncipe hampered military operations for weeks.

98 Máximo Gómez to Miguel Aldama, 1875, in Antonio Pirala, *Anales de la guerra de Cuba* (3 vols., Madrid, 1895–98), 3:218.

99 "Arrival of Gen. Sickles," *New York Times*, December 23, 1871, 7.

100 For a complete list of the army detachments deployed to garrison coffee estates and sugar plantations in the eastern jurisdictions, see "Estado de los destacamentos establecidos en el territorio de los Departamentos Central y Oriental," in José L. Riquelme, *Contestación a la memoria publicada por el Senor Marqués de La Habana en su último mando en Cuba* (Madrid, 1876), 358–73.

101 T. Ochando, *El General Martínez Campos en Cuba: Reseña político-militar de la última campaña (Noviembre de 1876 á Junio de 1878)* (Madrid, 1878), 15.

102 Luis Eugenio Togores Sánchez, "Guerra cubana de los diez años," in *Aproximación a la historia militar de España* (3 vols., Madrid: Ministerio de Defensa—Secretaría General Técnica, 2006), 546.

103 James J. O'Kelly, *The Mambi-Land, or Adventures of a Herald Correspondent in Cuba* (Philadelphia, 1874), 119–20.

104 Cándido Pieltain, "Contrate de trabajadores para la trocha del este por cuenta de los hacendados," July 5, 1873, in Cándido Pieltain, *La Isla de Cuba, desde mediados de abril a fines de octubre de 1873* (Madrid, 1879), 237–40.

105 Leopoldo Barrios y Carrión, *Bosquejo geográfico militar de la provincia de Puerto Príncipe* (Barcelona, 1881), 62.

106 Cándido Pieltain, "Habitantes de la Siempre Fiel Isla de Cuba," June 4, 1873, Archivo Militar de Madrid, Ultramar Cuba, Subcarpeta No. 22.9.1, https://www.latinamericanstudies.org/archive/Partes-Oficiales-junio-septiembre-1873.pdf.

107 Ochando, *El General Martínez Campos en Cuba*, 27.

108 Tesifonte Gallego, *Cuba por fuera* (2nd ed., Havana, 1892), 98. See also "Sobre la guerra en Cuba: La trocha," *Revista Técnica de Infantería y Caballería* 7 (February 15, 1896): 177–85.

109 "Estimate of the Spanish Forces Composing the 'Army of Cuba,' Compiled from the Statement Published in *La Iberia* of December 26, 1869, and from Semi-official Sources of Information," enclosure, Daniel E. Sickles to Hamilton Fish, December 29, 1869, in *Correspondence between the Department of State and the United States Minister at Madrid*, 67–68; Redondo Díaz, "La Guerra de los Diez Años," 39. Octavio Avelino Delgado indicates a total of 186,489 soldiers were deployed to Cuba between November 1868 and May 1878. See Octavio Avelino Delgado, "The Spanish Army in Cuba, 1868–1898: An Institutional Study" (2 vols., PhD diss., Columbia University, 1980), 2:338–54.

110 José de Chessa, "Parte oficial: Estado Mayor," *Gaceta de La Habana*, October 22, 1868, 1.

111 Soulère, *Historia de la insurrección de Cuba*, 2:235.

112 Antonio Ortiz, "Parte oficial: Estado Mayor," *Gaceta de La Habana*, October 18, 1868, 1.

113 Daniel Sickles to Hamilton Fish, August 21, 1869, in *Correspondence between the Department of State and the United States Minister at Madrid*, 29–30.
114 Valmaseda to Captain General, January 21, 1870, in *La Bandera Española* (Santiago de Cuba), January 23, 1870, 2.
115 Gonzalo Reparaz, *La guerra de Cuba: Estudio militar* (Madrid, 1896), 84.
116 Ochando, *El General Martínez Campos en Cuba*, 13.
117 Alexander Humboldt, *The Island of Cuba*, ed. J. S. Thrasher (New York, 1856), 316.
118 Pieltain, *La Isla de Cuba*, 48–49.
119 Barrios y Carrión, *Sobre la historia de la guerra de Cuba*, 26, 36. Barrios y Carrión provides a detailed commentary on the execrable conditions of the road networks in the Central Department in Barrios y Carrión, *Bosquejo geográfico militar de la provincia de Puerto Príncipe*.
120 Un Testigo Presencial [Fabián Navarro], *La cuestión de Cuba: Orígen, caracter, vicisitudes y causas de la prolongación de aquella guerra. Memoria político-militar* (Madrid, 1878), 24.
121 Adolfo J. Castellanos, "La guerra en Cuba: Dificultades que presentan los campos de Cuba para los movimientos de las tropas," *Revista Técnica de Infantería y Caballería* 6 (March 15, 1895): 266–67; Otero y Pimentel, *Política militar y civil*, 223.
122 Reparaz, *La guerra de Cuba*, 135–36; Leopoldo Barrios y Carrión, *Importancia de la historia de las campañas irregulares y en especial la guerra de Cuba* (Madrid, 1893), 20–22.
123 Ochando, *El General Martínez Campos en Cuba*, 16–17.
124 See Gelpi y Ferro, *Historia de la revolución y guerra de Cuba*, 1:195–96.
125 Antonio López de Letona to Juan Prim, August 20, 1869, in Ildefonso Antonio Bermejo, *Historia de la interinidad y guerra civil ed España desde 1868* (3 vols., Madrid, 1876–77), 2:931–32.
126 Valmaseda to Adelardo López de Ayala, March 15, 1875, in Pirala, *Anales de la guerra de Cuba*, 3:211.
127 Reparaz, *La guerra de Cuba*, 122; Francisco de Arredondo y Miranda, *Recuerdos de las guerras de Cuba: Diario de campaña (1868–1871)*, ed. Aleida Plasencia Moro (Havana: Biblioteca Nacional José Martí, 1962), 26. See also Oscar Zanetti and Alejandro García, *Caminos para el azúcar* (Havana: Editorial De Ciencias Sociales, 1987), 133–34.
128 "Convoyes de Manzanillo a Bayamo," *Revista Técnica de Infanteria y Caballería* 8 (September 15, 1897): 817–23. Santiago Barroeta Scheidnagel indicated that convoys resulted in an average of twenty-five to thirty Spanish casualties. See Un Español Incondicional [Santiago Barroeta Scheidnagel], *Los sucesos de Cienfuegos y la situación actual de la Isla de Cuba* (New York, 1897), 105.
129 Francisco Estrada y Céspedes to Adolfina Céspedes, March 22, 1875, in *Cartas familiares: Francisco Estrada y Céspedes*, ed. Ricardo Repilado (Santiago de Cuba: Imprenta Universitaria—Universidad de Oriente, 1980), 86.

130 Luis Navarro García, *Las guerras de España en Cuba* (Madrid: Ediciones Encuentro, 1998), 65.
131 Feijóo y de Mendoza, *Diario de un testigo de las operaciones sobre los insurrectos*, 19.
132 Jiménez Castellanos, *De las insurrecciones en Cuba*, 24.
133 Ramón Hernández Poggio, "Remembranzas médicas de la guerra separatista de Cuba: Alimentación," *La Gaceta de Sanidad Militar* 5 (January 10, 1879): 7–8.
134 Barrios y Carrión, *Sobre la historia de la guerra de Cuba*, 27. See also Hernández Poggio, "Remembranzas médicas de la guerra separatista de Cuba," 5–16.
135 Barrios y Carrión, *Sobre la historia de la guerra de Cuba*, 26.
136 In Cándido Pieltain, *La isla de Cuba desde mediados de abril á fines de octubre de 1873* (Madrid, 1879), 52.
137 Soulère, *Historia de la insurrección de Cuba*, 2:260.
138 Adolfo Jiménez Castellanos, "La guerra en Cuba: Dificultades que presentan los campos de Cuba para los movimientos de las tropas," *Revista Técnica de Infantería y Caballería* 6 (March 15, 1895): 265–66.
139 Gelpi y Ferro, *Album histórico de la guerra de Cuba*, 2:317.
140 Flores, *La guerra de Cuba*, 26.
141 Barrios y Carrión, *Sobre la historia de la guerra de Cuba*, 13.
142 Barrios y Carrión, *Sobre la historia de la guerra de Cuba*, 54–55.
143 Luis Martínez Casado, *El gorrión* (Havana, 1869), 29.
144 Moya, *Consideraciones militares sobre la campaña de Cuba*, 91.
145 Antonio del Rosal y Vázquez Mondragón, *En la manigua: Diario de mi cuativerio* (Madrid, 1879), 283–84. This memoir appeared previously as *Los mambises: Memoria de un prisionero* (Madrid, 1874).
146 Acosta y Albear, *Apreciaciones sobre la insurrección de Cuba*, 60.
147 Antonio López de Letona to Juan Prim, August 20, 1869, in Bermejo, *Historia de la interinidad y guerra civil ed España desde 1868*, 2:932.
148 Juan V. Escalera, *Campaña de Cuba (1869 á 1875): Recuerdos de un soldado* (Madrid, 1876), 14–15, 17.
149 "Convoyes de Manzanillo a Bayamo," *Revista Técnica de Infantería y Caballería* 8 (September 15, 1897): 821.
150 Granda, *Reflexiones sobre la insurrección de Cuba*, 5.
151 José Alvarez Pérez, *Aventuras de tres voluntarios: Episodios de la guerra en la isla de Cuba* (2nd ed., Madrid, 1870), 283; Pedro de Zea, "Alocución," *Diario de la Marina*, September 19, 1874, 2.
152 Angel R. Chaves, "En la manigua: Recuerdos de la otra guerra," *Blanco y Negro* 6 (March 7, 1896): n.p.
153 Rosal y Vázquez Mondragón, *En la manigua*, 15, 36.
154 Francisco de Camps y Feliú, *Españoles é insurrectos: Recuerdos de la guerra de Cuba* (Havana, 1890), 293.
155 Walter Goodman, *The Pearl of the Antilles, or An Artist in Cuba* (London, 1873), 246–47.

156 Ochando, *El General Martínez Campos en Cuba*, 16.
157 Cuba, Gobierno y Capitanía General, *Cuadro estadístico de la Siempre Fiel Isla de Cuba, correspondiente al año de 1846* (Havana, 1847), 217.
158 Un Testigo Presencial [Fabián Navarro], *La cuestión de Cuba*, 23.
159 López de Letona, *Isla de Cuba*, 106–7.
160 Barrios y Carrión, *Sobre la historia de la guerra de Cuba*, 26, 36.
161 Jiménez Castellanos, *De las insurrecciones en Cuba*, 172.
162 Pirala, *Anales de la guerra de Cuba*, 1:567–68; 3:14.
163 Barrios y Carrión, *Sobre la historia de la guerra de Cuba*, 26.
164 Pirala, *Anales de la guerra de Cuba*, 1:604.
165 Reparaz, *La guerra de Cuba*, 158–59.
166 Juan Luis Martín, *Papeles cubanos: El combatiente cubano de la revolución* (Havana: Editorial Atalaya, 1943), 10.
167 See Barrios y Carrión, *Sobre la historia de la guerra de Cuba*, 82.
168 Camps y Feliú, *Españoles é insurrectos*, 108, 294.
169 Acosta y Albear, *Compendio histórico del pasado y presente de Cuba*, 30–31, 100.
170 Barrios y Carrión, *Sobre la historia de la guerra de Cuba*, 26. See also Jiménez Castellanos, *De las insurrecciones en Cuba*, 34.
171 In early 1874, General Manuel Armiñan led six battalions (four thousand soldiers) and six hundred *guerrilleros* into three days of battle at Guásimas. See Acosta y Albear, *Compendio histórico del pasado y presente de Cuba*, 30–31.
172 Reparaz, *La guerra de Cuba*, 86; de la Concha, *Memoria sobre la guerra de la Isla de Cuba*, 42. Lieutenant Colonel Francisco J. de Moya later wrote that the Spanish column at Palo Seco was slaughtered: "Fueron acuchillados por completo los 550 hombres que componían la columna." See Moya, *Consideraciones militares sobre la campaña de Cuba*, 130.
173 Soulère, *Historia de la insurrección de Cuba*, 2:86.
174 Barrios y Carrión, *Sobre la historia de la guerra de Cuba*, 85–86.
175 In Navarro García, *Las guerras de España en Cuba*, 65. Infantry General Adolfo Jiménez Castellanos used very similar language: "Since we had very little knowledge of the terrain and of enemy forces and their situation, it could well be said that our troops moved about blindly." See Jiménez Castellanos, *De las insurrecciones en Cuba*, 23.
176 Cuba, Centro de Estadística, Capitanía General, *Noticias estadísticas de la Isla de Cuba, en 1862* (Havana, 1864); Cuba, Capitanía General, *Resumen del censo de población de la Isla de Cuba a fin del año de 1841*, 18.
177 Antonio López de Letona to Juan Prim, August 20, 1869, in Bermejo, *Historia de la interinidad y guerra civil ed España desde 1868*, 2:931–32.
178 Acosta y Albear, *Compendio histórico del pasado y presente de Cuba*, 113–14.
179 José L. Riquelme to Captain General, December 30, 1872, in Riquelme, *Contestación a la memoria publicada por el Senor Marqués de La Habana*, 334–35.
180 De la Concha, *Memoria sobre la guerra de la Isla de Cuba*, 43, 158.

181 Reparaz, *La guerra de Cuba*, 119.
182 Escalera, *Campaña de Cuba*, 151, 154.
183 Antonio Serra Orts, *Recuerdos de las guerras de Cuba: 1868 á 1898* (Santa Cruz de Tenerife: A. J. Benítez, 1908), 4.
184 Máximo Gómez to Julio Sanguily, October 1, 1877, in Pi y Margall, *Historia de Espana en el Siglo XIX* (7 vols., Barcelona: Seguí, 1902–3), 4:1027.
185 Anselmo Suárez y Romero, *Francisco* (1875; repubd., Havana: Instituto del Libro, 1970), 51.
186 "Disposición conveniente," *La Voz de Cuba*, January 26, 1877, 2.
187 José Clairac y Blasco, *La fiebre amarilla* (Madrid, 1893), 18.
188 Estévanez, *Fragmentos de mis memorias*, 185.
189 Flores, *La guerra de Cuba*, 199–200.
190 Reparaz, *La guerra de Cuba*, 195.
191 Acosta y Albear, *Compendio histórico del pasado y presente de Cuba*, 94.
192 José de Argumosa, "Todavía más sobre fiebre amarilla," *El Siglo Médico: Boletín de Medicina y Gaceta Médica* 18 (January 1, 1871): 6–7.
193 Pirala, *Anales de la guerra de Cuba*, 1:566–67.
194 Navarro García, *Las guerras de España en Cuba*, 69.
195 Acosta y Albear, *Compendio histórico del pasado y presente de Cuba*, 18.
196 Ramón Hernández Poggio, "Remembranzas médicas de la guerra separatista de Cuba," *La Gaceta de Sanidad Militar* 4 (June 25, 1878): 277–78; Ramón Hernández Poggio, "La pacificación de Cuba y la higiene pública," *La Gaceta de Sanidad Militar* 4 (June 10, 1878): 276. On weather and climate, see Ramón Hernández Poggio, "Remembranzas médicas de la guerra separatista de Cuba," *La Gaceta de Sanidad Militar* 4 (August 25, 1878): 394–400.
197 Ramón Hernández Poggio, "Remembranzas médicas de la guerra separatista de Cuba: Marchas," *La Gaceta de Sanidad Militar* 5 (November 20, 1879): 524–36. Ramón Hernández Poggio prepared a comprehensive treatise on climate and the tropics in *Aclimatación e higiene de los europeos en Cuba* (Cádiz, 1874).
198 C. H. Bithorn to Edward Plumb, August 28, 1869, US Congress, House of Representatives, *Struggle for Independence on the Island of Cuba*, 41st Congress, 2nd Session, Ex. Doc. No. 160 (Washington, DC, 1870), 130. Juan Escalera remembered his military service in Cuba during the summer months, when operations were impossible due to the "condition of the roads and as well as the illnesses that assailed the soldiers, weakening the columns in a horrendous manner." See Escalera, *Campaña de Cuba*, 81–82.
199 Federico Parreño Ballesteros, "Recuerdos de Cuba: En marcha," *Revista Técnica de Infantería y Caballería* 8 (January 15, 1897): 62–63.
200 Cándido Pieltain to Ministro de la Guerra, August 30, 1873, in Pieltain, *La Isla de Cuba*, 201–3.
201 Pieltain, *La Isla de Cuba*, 70.

202 A. E. Phillips to Hamilton Fish, January 3, 1870, in *Correspondence between the Department of State and the United States Minister at Madrid*, 188.
203 See Stanford E. Chaillé, "Report to the United States National Board of Health on Yellow Fever in Havana and Cuba," in US Congress, House of Representatives, Annual Report of the National Board of Health, 1880, 46th Congress, 3rd Session, Ex. Doc. No. 8 (Washington, DC, 1882), 239–45. See also Spain, Ministro de la Guerra, *El Depósito de la Guerra, Organización y estado militar de España y ultramar en 1º de enero de 1869* (Madrid, 1869), 302–4.
204 "Ejército de Ultramar en Cuba," *La Gaceta de Sanidad Militar* 1 (June 25, 1875): 346.
205 Otero y Pimentel, *Política militar y civil*, 84.
206 Antonio López de Letona to Juan Prim, August 20, 1869, in Bermejo, *Historia de la interinidad y guerra civil ed España desde 1868*, 2:931–32. "Cholera is thinning the ranks of [the Spanish] brigade faster than the bullets of the insurgents," US Consul Leopold Price reported from Nuevitas in mid-1869. See Leopold Price to Edward Plumb, June 26, 1869, in *Correspondence between the Department of State and the United States Minister at Madrid*, 113.
207 Escalera, *Campaña de Cuba*, 39.
208 Camps y Feliú, *Españoles é insurrectos*, 393.
209 Caleb Cushing to Hamilton Fish, July 2, 1874, in *Papers Relating to the Foreign Relations of the United States* (Washington, DC, 1874), 892.
210 Ramón Hernández Poggio, "Remembranzas médicas de la guerra separatista de Cuba: Campamentos," *La Gaceta de Sanidad Militar* 6 (July 25, 1880): 367–68. See also Ramón Hernández Poggio, "Remembranzas médicas de la guerra separatista de Cuba: Campamentos," *La Gaceta de Sanidad Militar* 6 (August 25, 1880): 431–37.
211 See "Libros de difunciones de militares en el Hospital Militar de Holguín," Libro Hospital Militar Holguín, 1866–77; "Libro 2º de difunciones del Hospital Militar de Holguín," Libro Hospital Militar Holguin, 1877–78; "Libro de difunciones del Hospital Militar de la Plaza y Villa de Gibara," Libro Hospital Militar de Gibara, 1875–98; Archivo Histórico Provincial, Holguín, Cuba. Scanned copies of these volumes have been donated to and are available for consultation at Wilson Library, University of North Carolina at Chapel Hill.
212 Pieltain, *La Isla de Cuba*, 48.
213 See Santiago Ramón y Cajal, *Mi infancia y juventud* (2nd ed., Buenos Aires: Espasa Calpe Argentina, 1942), 211–34. Like many other Spanish physicians and health care providers, Ramón y Cajal would himself fall victim to malaria and tuberculosis. In 1906 he would receive the Nobel Prize for medicine. On alcoholism among Spanish officers and soldiers, see also Ramón Hernández Poggio, "Remembranzas médicas de la guerra separatista de Cuba: Alimentación," *La Gaceta de Sanidad Militar* 5 (January 25, 1879): 29–44; Francisco Barado, *Nuestros soldados: Narraciones y episodios de la vida militar en España* (Barcelona: Imprenta de Henrich y Cía, 1909), 9.

214 Emilio Mola Vidal, *Obras completas* (Valladolid: Libreria Santaren, 1940), 933–34.
215 José Clairac, "Estadística general de enfermos asistidos en los hospitales y enferemerías militares de la Isla de Cuba durante la campaña, ó sea desde 1º de noviembre de 1868 á fin de junio de 1878," in *Transactions of the First Pan-American Medical Congress held in the City of Washington DC* (2 parts, Washington, DC, 1895), 1:767–69; Miguel Slocker, "Fiebre amarilla," *Revista de Sanidad Militar* 9 (October 15, 1895): 319–20.
216 Pirala, *Anales de la guerra de Cuba*, 3:683–84.
217 Moya, *Consideraciones militares sobre la campaña de Cuba*, 200.
218 Joaquín Jovellar, "Soldados, marinos y voluntarios," *La Voz de Cuba*, June 16, 1878, 2.
219 Daniel E. Sickles to Hamilton Fish, August 16, 1872, in *Correspondence between the Department of State and the United States Minister at Madrid*, 563.
220 Camps y Feliú, *Españoles é insurrectos*, 105; Otero y Pimentel, *Política militar y civil*, 283; Barrios y Carrión, *Importancia de la historia de las campañas irregulares*, 15.
221 Togores Sánchez, "Guerra cubana de los diez años," 550; Enrique de Miguel Fernández, "Azcàrraga, Weyler y la conducción de la guerra de Cuba" (unpublished manuscript, 2011), 80, http://www.racv.es/files/Guerra_Cuba_0.pdf.
222 Eladio Baldovín Ruiz, *Cuba: El desastre español del siglo XIX* (León: Editorial. Editorial Akron S.L., 2010), 235–36.
223 Andreas Stucki, *Las guerras de Cuba: Violencia y campos de concentración (1868–1898)*, trans. Lareano Xoaquín Araujo Cardalda (Madrid: La Esfera de los Libros, 2013), 163.
224 Luis Otero y Pimentel, *Reflejos de la vida militar* (Havana, 1894), 206.
225 Ramon O. Williams to John L. Cadwalader, November 15, 1875, in *Correspondence between the United States Government and Spain in Relation to the Island of Cuba*, US Congress, House of Representatives, 44th Congress, 1st Session, Ex. Doc. 90 (Washington, DC, 1876), 34.
226 Pieltain, *La Isla de Cuba*, 25.
227 Jiménez Castellanos, *De las insurrecciones en Cuba*, 96.
228 The *trocha* developed annually into a site of infectious diseases, physician Santiago Ramón y Cajal wrote years later. Between April and October, during the summer rains, the fortifications flooded and the terrain was transformed into marsh, an ideal incubator for mosquitos. See Ramón y Cajal, *Mi infancia y juventud*, 226–27.
229 The decree was signed on April 4, 1869. See *Diario de la Marina*, April 29, 1869, 2.
230 [M. L. M.] Melchor L. Mola y Mora, *Espisodios de la guerra de Cuba* (Puerto Príncipe, 1893), 8; Juan Jerez Villarreal, *Gesta de bravos* (Havana: Talleres Tipográficos de Cuba Intelectual, 1926), 65–94; Eva Adán de Rodríguez, *Hojas de recuerdos* (Havana: Imprenta Molina y Cía, 1935), 33–35.

231 A. E. Phillips to Hamilton Fish, January 3, 1870, in *Correspondence between the Department of State and the United States Minister at Madrid*, 188.
232 "Los cazadores del Balmaseda," January 6, 1871; "Los cazadores del Balmaseda," February 28, 1871, "Los cazadores del Balmaseda," December 25, 1872, all in Valeriano Weyler Papers, Archives and Special Collections, University of Connecticut, https://archives.lib.uconn.edu/islandora/object/20002:19700006.
233 "Comandancia General del Centro," *Gaceta de La Habana*, July 30, 1871, 2.
234 Navarro García, *Las guerras de España en Cuba*, 52.
235 Serafín Espinosa y Ramos, *Al trote y sin estribos (Recuerdos de la Guerra de Independencia* (Havana: J. Montero, 1946), 219.
236 Pirala, *Anales de la guerra de Cuba*, 2:791.
237 Pirala, *Anales de la guerra de Cuba*, 2:320.
238 Barrios y Carrión, *Sobre la historia de la guerra de Cuba*, 37. See also Capitanía General de la Siempre Fiel Isla de Cuba, Estado Mayor, "Sobre modificación en el reglamento de táctica de guerrilla," April 15, 1871, *Boletín Oficial de la Capitanía General de la Isla de Cuba* 10 (April 20, 1871), 384.
239 "Aviso," *Diario de la Marina*, August 12, 1870, 3.
240 Rosal y Vázquez Mondragón, *En la manigua*, 29.
241 Un Testigo Presencial [Fabián Navarro], *La cuestión de Cuba*, 97.
242 Pieltain, *La Isla de Cuba*, 63.
243 "La contra-guerrilla de Ferrazón," *Diario de la Marina*, December 27, 1870, 2.
244 Granda, *Reflexiones sobre la insurrección de Cuba*, 142.
245 Barrios y Carrión, *Sobre la historia de la guerra de Cuba*, 35–37, 62.
246 General José L. Riquelme to Captain General, December 30, 1872, in Riquelme, *Contestación a la memoria publicada por el Senor Marqués de La Habana*, 291–92.
247 Cuba, Ejército, Estado Mayor, *Reglamento de contra-guerrillas* (Havana, 1872), 3.
248 Jiménez Castellanos, *De las insurrecciones en Cuba*, 62; José Ignacio Chacón, *Guerras irregulares* (2 vols., Madrid, 1883), 1:260–61.
249 Jiménez Castellanos, *De las insurrecciones en Cuba*, 44; Eleuterio Llofriu y Sagrera, *Historia de la insurrección y guerra de la Isla de Cuba* (4 vols., Madrid, 1870–72), 3:336, 370.
250 Acosta y Albear, *Apreciaciones sobre la insurrección de Cuba*, 47.
251 Ochando, *El General Martínez Campos en Cuba*, 157–58. See also Llofriu y Sagrera, *Historia de la insurrección y guerra de la Isla de Cuba*, 2:100.
252 "Orden General del 27 de mayo de 1873," in Pieltain, *La Isla de Cuba*, 169–70.
253 General José L. Riquelme to Captain General, December 30, 1872, in Riquelme, *Contestación a la memoria publicada por el Senor Marqués de La Habana*, 291–92; Pirala, *Anales de la guerra de Cuba*, 2:510.
254 Barrios y Carrión, *Sobre la historia de la guerra de Cuba*, 37, 62; Chacón, *Guerras irregulares*, 1:256–57. The relationship between service and pay was sharply

drawn. The former was contingent on the latter, military authorities understood, and indeed the matter of adequate pay was superseded in importance only by the need for punctual pay. "It is hardly reasonable," General Acosta y Albear warned, "to expect that they remain loyal without pay, without rations, and their families perishing of hunger, as well as being subject to abusive and arbitrary treatment by some of their chiefs." Barrios similarly underscored the importance of the punctuality of pay. "Almost all the *guerrilleros* del pais," Barrios understood, "have families to maintain, and as a result of these circumstances and for political considerations ... they should be paid punctually, for otherwise their families will be deprived of the means of livelihood and sustenance, and they [*guerrilleros*] restless and disgruntled" (*disgustado*). Captain General Cándido Pieltain was categorical. "Given that the guerrillas are indispensable to the three divisions [of operations]," he enjoined the director of the island treasury in mid-1873, "it is indispensable that they be paid with total punctuality." See Acosta y Albear, *Compendio histórico del pasado y presente de Cuba*, 12–14; Barrios y Carrión, *Sobre la historia de la guerra de Cuba*, 49; Candido Pieltain to the Intendente-General de Hacienda, July 3, 1873, in Pieltain, *La Isla de Cuba*, 181–82.

255 Barrios y Carrión, *Sobre la historia de la guerra de Cuba*, 86.
256 Soulère, *Historia de la insurrección de Cuba*, 1:183.
257 Barrios y Carrión, *Sobre la historia de la guerra de Cuba*, 37.
258 Sáenz y Sáenz, *La siboneya, o episodios de la guerra de Cuba*, 173.
259 Acosta y Albear, *Apreciaciones sobre la insurrección de Cuba*, 49; José Ferrer de Couto, *Cuba puede ser independiente: Folleto político de actualidad* (New York, 1872), 84.
260 Eusebio Hernández, "Resumen del discurso pronunciado por el doctor Eusebio Hernández, Nueva York," October 10, 1895, in Eusebio Hernández, *Ciencia y patria*, ed. Rafael Cepeda (Havana: Editorial de Ciencias Sociales, 1991), 98; José Luciano Franco, *Antonio Maceo: Apuntes para una historia de su vida* (3 vols., Havana: Editorial de Ciencias Sociales, 1975), 1:134.
261 Santiago Perinat, *La guerras mambisas* (Barcelona: Ediciones Carena Acidalia, 2002), 137.
262 O'Kelly, *The Mambi-Land*, 221.
263 Franco, *Antonio Maceo*, 1:134.
264 Ignacio Mora, "Diario de campaña de Ignacio Mora," in Nydia Sarabia, *Ana Betancourt Agramonte* (Havana: Editorial de Ciencias Sociales, 1970), 181, 209.
265 Rosal y Vázquez Mondragón, *En la manigua*, 250.
266 Acosta y Albear, *Compendio histórico del pasado y presente de Cuba*, 101.
267 Alvarez Pérez, *Aventuras de tres voluntarios*, 36.
268 De la Concha, *Memoria sobre la guerra de la Isla de Cuba*, 100.
269 "Carta de Madrid al 'Herald' de Nueva York," *La Epoca*, January 26, 1878, 1.
270 Scott, *Slave Emancipation in Cuba*, 65.

271 Pirala, *Anales de la guerra de Cuba*, 3:72.
272 José de la Concha, "Parte oficial," *Gaceta de La Habana*, May 5, 1874, 1; Acosta y Albear, *Compendio histórico del pasado y presente de Cuba*, 101.
273 Escalera, *Campaña de Cuba*, 163.
274 Ochando, *El General Martínez Campos en Cuba*, 157–58.
275 Ochando, *El General Martínez Campos en Cuba*, 66.
276 Francisco Ortiz, *Misterios de Cuba* (2 vols., Santiago de Cuba, 1892–93), 2:242–43.
277 De la Concha, *Memoria sobre la guerra de la Isla de Cuba*, 34.
278 De la Concha, *Memoria sobre la guerra de la Isla de Cuba*, 160.
279 Mora, "Diario de campaña de Ignacio Mora," 214.
280 Francisco Estrada y Céspedes to Adolfina Céspedes, September 27, 1873, and Francisco Estrada y Céspedes to Adolfina Céspedes, October 5, 1875, in Repilado, *Cartas familiares*, 78, 88.
281 Enrique Collazo, *Desde Yara hasta Zanjón: Apuntaciones históricas* (2nd ed., Havana, 1893), 131.
282 Mola y Mora, *Episodios de la guerra de Cuba*, 107.
283 See Flores, *La guerra de Cuba*, 243–41.
284 Mora, "Diario de campaña de Ignacio Mora," 215. For conditions within the Cuban forces, see Vanessa Michelle Ziegler, "The Revolt of 'the Ever-Faithful Isle': The Ten Years War in Cuba, 1868–1878" (PhD diss., University of California, Santa Barbara, 2007), 38–90.
285 Domingo Méndez Capote, "El Pacto de Zanjón," April 1929, in Domingo Méndez Capote, *Trabajos* (2 vols., Havana: Molina y compañia, 1929), 212.
286 Redondo Díaz, "La Guerra de los Diez Años," 49.
287 Guerra y Sánchez, "La guerra durante los mandos de Rodas y del Conde Valmaseda," in Ramiro Guerra y Sánchez et al., *Historia de la nación cubana* (10 vols., Havana: Editorial Historia de la Nación Cubana, 1952), 5:129.
288 Tomás Estrada Palma to Félix Figueredo, September 19, 1875, in Félix Figueredo Díaz, *La guerra de Cuba (la protesta de Baraguá)* (Havana: Ministerio de Salud Pública, 1973), 232.
289 See Ejército Español, Estado Mayor General, "De oficio," *Diario de la Marina*, October 17, 1873, 1; Ejército Español, Estado Mayor General, "De oficio," *Diario de la Marina*, November 18, 1873, 1; Ejército Español, Estado Mayor General, "De oficio," *Diario de la Marina*, February 18, 1874, 1; "Operaciones militares," *La Voz de Cuba*, April 7, 1877, 2; Jiménez Castellanos, *De las insurrecciones en Cuba*, 103–15.
290 Serra Orts, *Recuerdos de las guerras de Cuba*, 12.
291 "Noticias de Cuba," *La Epoca*, January 3, 1878, 1.
292 Barrios y Carrión, *Sobre la historia de la guerra de Cuba*, 48.
293 Barrios y Carrión, *Sobre la historia de la guerra de Cuba*, 47–48.
294 Pieltain, *La Isla de Cuba*, 53.

295 Pirala, *Anales de la guerra de Cuba*, 3:394. For press accounts of guerrilla operations in the final months of the war, see "Crónica general," *Diario de la Marina*, May 6, 1877, 2; "Crónica general," *Diario de la Marina*, July 15, 1877, 2; "Noticias de la guerra," *Diario de la Marina*, August 14, 1877, 2; "Crónica general," *Diario de la Marina*, December 21, 1877, 2; "Crónica general," *Diario de la Marina*, January 13, 1878, 2.

296 Jiménez Castellanos, *De las insurrecciones en Cuba*, 61; Adolfo Jiménez Castellanos, "La guerra en Cuba: Guerrillas," *Revista Técnica de Infantería y Caballería* 6 (April 1, 1895): 331.

297 Chacón, *Guerras irregulares*, 1:257.

298 Calixto García, "Manifiesto del Comité Revolucionario Cubano," New York, October 1878, in Cuba, Archivo Nacional, *Documentos para servir a la historia de la Guerra Chiquita* (3 vols., Havana: Archivo Nacional de Cuba, 1949–50), 1:43.

299 In Pirala, *Anales de la guerra de Cuba*, 2:123.

300 "Fallecimiento," *La Lucha*, September 2, 1898, 3.

301 Llofriu y Sagrera, *Historia de la insurrección y guerra de la Isla de Cuba*, 5:651.

302 Escalera, *Campaña de Cuba*, 86.

303 Pieltain, *La Isla de Cuba*, 63. See also Gelpi y Ferro, *Historia de la revolución y guerra de Cuba*, 2:13.

304 Arredondo y Miranda, *Recuerdos de las guerras de Cuba*, 98–99; Gelpi y Ferro, *Historia de la revolución y guerra de Cuba*, 2:13.

305 O'Kelly, *The Mambi-Land*, 116–17.

306 Camps y Feliú, *Españoles é insurrectos*, 66, 76.

307 Ramón Roa, *Con la pluma y el machete* (3 vols., Havana: Imprenta "El Siglo XX," 1950), 1:67.

308 Togores Sánchez, "Guerra cubana de los diez años," 549.

309 "Cartas de Cuba," *La Epoca*, December 18, 1877, 4.

310 Soulère, *Historia de la insurrección de Cuba*, 2:268–69.

311 Arsenio Martínez Campos to Antonio Cánovas del Castillo, March 19, 1878, in Antonio Cánovas del Castillo, *Obras completas de Antonio Cánovas del Castillo*, CD-ROM ed., Fundación Cánovas del Castillo, Madrid: Agencia Estatal, 2001.

312 Togores Sánchez, "Guerra cubana de los diez años," 550; Miguel Fernández, *Azcàrraga, Weyler y la conducción de la guerra de Cuba*, 79.

Chapter Three. To Confront Impossible Odds

1 Eusebio Hernández Pérez, *El período revolucionario de 1879 a 1895* (Havana: Imprenta "El Siglo XX," 1914); Diana Abad et al., *La guerra de los diez años: La tregua fecunda* (Havana: Ministerio de Educación Superior, 1989); Raúl Rodríguez La O, *Cruenta tregua* (Havana: Ediciones Verde Olivo, 1999); María del Carmen Barcia, *La turbulencia del reposo: Cuba, 1878–1895* (Havana: Editorial de Ciencias Sociales, 1998); Jorge Aurelio Hernández Ibáñez, "Tregua fecunda y cubanía: Examinar

desde la enseñanza de la historia patria," *Boletín Virtual* 7 (January 16, 2018): 109–15; Manuel Fernández Carcassés, "La revolución en la tregua fecunda: 1879–1895," *Bohemia* (Edición Extraordinaria) 110 (October 2018): 26–29.

2 The little war has produced a large body of scholarship. See Francisco Pérez Guzmán and Rodolfo Sarracino, *La Guerra Chiquita, una experiencia necesaria* (Havana: Editorial Letras Cubanas, 1982); Oscar Loyala Vega, "La dirección revolucionaria en la Guerra Chiquita," *Universidad de La Habana* 223 (September–December 1984): 162–84. For a guide to this literature, see Mirian Hernández Soler, ed., *Bibliografía de la Guerra Chiquita, 1879–1880* (Havana: Biblioteca Nacional José Martí, 1975).

3 Emilio Reverter Delmas, *Cuba española: Reseña histórica de la insurrección cubana en 1895* (6 vols., Barcelona: A. Martín, 1897–99), 1:27, 35. For a similar disregard of the importance of the outbreak of the insurrection, see "Buenas señales," *El País* (Havana), March 2, 1895, 2.

4 Edwin Atkins, *Sixty Years in Cuba: Reminiscences of Edwin F. Atkins* (Cambridge, MA: Riverside Press, 1926), 145.

5 "Deposition of General Jose Lachambre," Central Teresa vs. the United States, Claim No. 97, Entry 352, Records of the Boundary and Claims Commission and Arbitration, Record Group 76, National Archives, Washington, DC (hereinafter cited as RBCC/RG 76).

6 Luis Lagomasino Alvarez, *Reminiscencias patriotas* (Manzanillo: Tipografía "El Reporter," 1902), 104–44.

7 Nicolás Heredia, *Crónicas de la guerra de Cuba: Relación detallada de las operaciones de la campaña* (2 vols., Havana, 1895–96), 1:68; Rafael Gutiérrez, *Oriente heroico* (Santiago de Cuba: Tipografía El Nuevo Mundo, 1915), 15–16; Regino E. Boti, "El 24 de febrero de 1895," *Anales de la Academia de la Historia* 4 (January–June 1922): 69–143.

8 See Zoe Sosa Borjas and Pedro Manuel Castro Monterrey, eds., *La oficialidad negra y mulata en el ejército mambí* (Santiago de Cuba: Ediciones Caserón, 2018).

9 Antonio Maceo, "Exposición a los delegados a la Asamblea Constituyente," September 30, 1895, in *El pensamiento vivo de Maceo*, ed. José A. Portuondo (3rd ed., Havana: Editorial de Ciencias Sociales, 1971), 112.

10 Máximo Gómez, "Carta al presidente del Club 'Obreros de Independencia,'" n.d., *Casa de las Américas* 9 (September–October 1968): 123.

11 Un Español [Antonio Díaz Benzo], *Pequeñeces de la guerra de Cuba* (Madrid, 1897), 60.

12 Alexander Gollan to Foreign Office, June 14, 1895, Foreign Office Records, Group 277, Item No. 57, National Archives, Kew, Richmond, England.

13 Antonio Maceo to María Cabrales, August 20, 1895, in Gonzalo Cabrales Nicolarde, ed., *Epistolario de héroes: Documentos históricos* (1922; repubd., Havana: Editorial de Ciencias Sociales, 1996), 62.

14 Octavio Avelino Delgado, "The Spanish Army in Cuba, 1868–1898: An Institutional Study" (2 vols., PhD diss., Columbia University, 1980), 1:100.
15 "Al fin," *El Globo* (Madrid), July 25, 1895, 1. "After Peralejo," Máximo Gómez entered in his campaign diary, "the Revolution attained additional vitality." See Máximo Gómez, *Diario de campaña* (Havana: Centro Superior Technológico, 1941), 436. See also "La acción de Peralejo," *El Fígaro* 11 (August 25, 1895): 383–84.
16 See Gómez, *Diario de campaña*, 347.
17 Fernando Gómez, "Desde Santa Clara," *El Imparcial*, January 7, 1896, 1. The dispatch was dated December 18, 1895.
18 Reverter Delmas, *Cuba española*, 4:242.
19 José Miró Argenter, "Extracto de las operaciones militares realizadas por el Ejercito Invasor al mando del Lugarteniente General Antonio Maceo, desde su salida de Oriente hasta su llegada a Mantua, provincia de Pinar del Río," *Boletín del Archivo Nacional* 44 (1945): 179; José Miró Argenter, *Cuba: Crónicas de la guerra (La campaña de Invasión)* (3 vols., Havana: Editorial Lex, 1909), 1:205.
20 For a chronicle of the invasion, see José Miró Argenter, "Extracto de las operaciones militares realizadas por el Ejéricito Invasor al mando del lugarteniente general Antonio Maceo, desde su salida de Oriente hasta su llegada a Mantua, provincia del Pinar del Río," January 23, 1896, *Boletín del Archivo Nacional* 45 (1946): 173–94. On the invasion, see René E. Reyna Cossío, *Estudios histórico-militares sobre la guerra de independencia de Cuba* (Havana: Oficina del Historiador de la Ciudad, 1954), 9–68.
21 Ministerio de la Guerra, *Anuario Militar de España 1895* (Madrid, 1896), 224–25; Avelino Delgado, "The Spanish Army in Cuba," 1:130. Donoso Cortés quoted in Drocir de Osorno, *Cuba española: El problema de la guerra* (Madrid, 1896), 41; Reverter Delmas, *Cuba española*, 1:169–71.
22 Gonzalo Reparaz, "La guerra de Cuba," *El Heraldo de Madrid*, September 22, 1895, 1. "At the start of 1895," an incredulous *El Heraldo de Madrid* decried, "there were fewer troops in Cuba than in 1868." See Gonzalo Reparaz, "Política de guerra," *El Heraldo de Madrid*, December 16, 1895, 1.
23 See "Estado de fuerza del Ejército de la Isla de Cuba en diciembre de 1896," Ministerio de la Guerra, *Anuario Militar de España 1896* (Madrid, 1897), 782–83; Ministerio de la Guerra, *Anuario Militar de España 1897* (Madrid, 1897), 778–89; "Tropas a Cuba," *El Correo Militar*, January 21, 1896, 1; Heredia, *Crónicas de la guerra de Cuba*, 2:18–20.
24 "La semana militar," *La Correpondencia de España*, January 28, 1897, 1.
25 "Matanzas invadida," *El Heraldo de Madrid*, December 20, 1895, 1. Observers in Spain were indeed baffled at the performance of the army. "We are at loss to explain the apparent inaction of the majority of our forces in such a critical moment," affirmed *La Correpondencia de España*. "What are 113,000

men doing?" See "La situación de los insurrectos," *Correspondencia de España*, December 27, 1895, 3.

26 "Comentarios de la redacción, *La Correspondencia de España*, January 7, 1896, 3.

27 Reverter Delmas, *Cuba española*, 3:418.

28 Cristóbal Reina y Massa, *Reflexiones militares de Don Ramiro sobre la guerra de Cuba* (Cádiz, 1896), 5.

29 "La manifestación subsiste," *La Epoca*, January 4, 1896, 1.

30 Reverter Delmas, *Cuba española*, 3:197.

31 Manuel Corral, *¡El desastre! Memorias de un voluntario en la campaña de Cuba* (Barcelona, 1899), 61–63.

32 Enrique Piqueras Causas, "Diario de operaciones en Cuba: Por el teniente de infantería Don Enrique Piqueras Causas," *Revista de Historia Militar* 83 (1997): 208, https://publicaciones.defensa.gob.es/media/downloadable/files/links/r/h/rhm_083.pdf.

33 Manuel Arbelo, *Recuerdos de la última guerra por la independencia de Cuba: 1896 a 1898* (Havana: Imprenta Tipografía Moderna, 1918), 209.

34 Manuel Bueno y Javaloyes, *El 1er Batallón de María Cristina en el Camagüey* (Matanzas: La Propaganda, 1897), 19–21.

35 Calixto García to Tomás Estrada Palma, February 7, 1897, *Boletín del Archivo Nacional* 33 (1934): 64; Calixto García to Tomás Estrada Palma, May 11, 1897, *Boletín del Archivo Nacional* 33 (1934): 73.

36 "Convoyes de Manzanillo á Bayamo," *Revista Técnica de Infantería y Caballería* 8 (September 15, 1897): 818.

37 See José Moure Saco, *1102 días en el ejército español: Recuerdos de un soldado en la guerra de Cuba*, ed. Ramón Dacal Moure (Havana: Ediciones Boloña, 2001), 53, 120.

38 Virgilio Ferrer Gutiérrez, *Diario de campaña de un estudiante mambí* (Havana: Ediciones de la Revista "Indice," 1945), 39.

39 "Deposition of General Jose Lachambre," RBCC/RG 76. See also Drocir de Osorno, *Cuba española*, 48.

40 Valeriano Weyler, *Mi mando en Cuba (10 de febrero 1896 á 31 de octubre 1897: Historia militar y política de la última guerra separatista durante dicho mando* (5 vols., Madrid: Imprenta, Litografía y Casa Editorial de Felipe González Rojas, 1910–11), 1:32.

41 Miguel Varona Guerrero, "Operaciones militares cubanas," *Revista Bimestre Cubana* 55 (1945): 250–51.

42 Arturo Amblard, *Notas coloniales* (Madrid: Imprenta Ambrosio Pérez y Cía, 1904), 139–40. "The enemy does not dare pursue us," Máximo Gómez entered in his field diary on December 3, "no doubt lacking the strength. In the meantime, we continue to march westward." See Gómez, *Diario de campaña*, 348.

43 Un Amante de la Nación, *Estudio de la guerra de Cuba: Sus errores y medios de vencer, de acuerdo con las últimas disposiciones* (n.p., 1896), 6. See also J.

Guzmán, "La caballería en guerras irregulares," *Revista Técnica de Infantería y Caballería* 8 (December 15, 1897): 1105–6.

44 "Más refuerzos," *El Correo Militar*, January 11, 1896, 1; "Más caballería," *El Correo Militar*, January 11, 1896, 2; "Nuevos refuerzos de caballería," *El Imparcial*, January 11, 1896, 3; "Caballería a Cuba," *El Imparcial*, January 12, 1896, 1.

45 Reina y Massa, *Reflexiones militares de Don Ramiro*, 8.

46 Gonzalo Reparaz, "La guerra en Cuba," *El Heraldo de Madrid*, January 4, 1896, 1. "The majority of the rebels are mounted," Ricardo Donoso Cortés commented in 1896, "which is in the first instance the principal difficulty in trying to overtake them when they are pursued.... Notwithstanding that the insurrectionary force is mounted, they do not engage in combat as a cavalry force, but as a mounted infantry, which explains the ease and speed with which they extend beyond the range of our firearms and especially beyond our bayonets." See Drocir de Osorno, *Cuba española*, 141–42.

47 Gregorio Castaños to brother, September 22, 1896, in Manuel Montero, ed., *Las guerras de Cuba y Filipinas contadas por soldados del pueblo* (Madrid: Ediciones Beta, 2015), 384.

48 "No basta," *El Heraldo de Madrid*, September 16, 1895, 2; "La guerra de Cuba: Caballería," *El Heraldo de Madrid*, October 1, 1896, 1.

49 Máximo Gómez, "A los Sres. hacendados y dueños de fincas ganaderas," July 1, 1895, Fondo Archivo Máximo Gómez, Legajo 243, Número 6, Archivo Nacional de Cuba, Havana, Cuba (hereinafter cited as ANC); Máximo Gómez, "A los hombres honrados víctimas de la tea," November 11, 1895, Fondo Archivo Máximo Gómez, Legajo 7, Número 212, ANC. The moratorium extended into the following year. See "Manuscrito del acuerdo del Consejo de Gobierno en sesión 13 de julio de 1896 en relación a la prohibición de la zafra de 1896 a 1897," July 30, 1896, Fondo Donativos y Remisiones, Legajo 624, Número 34, ANC; "Documento manuscrito que contiene acuerdo tomado por el Consejo de Gobierno donde quedan prohibidas todas las operaciones de zafra de 1896 a 1897," November 6, 1896, Legajo 553, Número 19, Fondo Donativos y Remisiones, ANC; Máximo Gómez, "Orden General del día 21 de enero de 1897," Fondo Donativos y Remisiones, Legajo 547, Número 44, ANC.

50 Máximo Gómez to Tomás Estrada Palma, December 8, 1895, *Boletín del Archivo Nacional* 12 (1923): 223; Máximo Gómez to Tomás Estrada Palma, August 11, 1897, *Boletín del Archivo Nacional* 30 (1931): 75; Carlos M. Trelles, "El azúcar y la independencia," *Patria*, March 20, 1897, 2.

51 Fermín Valdés Domínguez, *Diario de soldado*, ed. Hiram Dupotey Fideaux (4 vols., Havana: Universidad de La Habana, 1972–74), 1:197.

52 Arsenio Martínez Campos to Tomás Castellanos, July 8, 1895, in Weyler, *Mi mando en Cuba*, 1:26.

53 Gonzalo Reparaz, "Campaña de las Villas," *El Heraldo de Madrid*, November 8, 1895, 1.

54 "'Proclamation,' Headquarters of the Army of Liberation," July 4, 1896, in *Correspondencia diplomática de la delegación cubana en Nueva York durante la guerra de 1895 a 1898*, ed. Joaquín Llaverías y Martínez (5 vols., Havana: Imprenta "El Siglo XX," 1943–46), 5:176–77.

55 Eusebio Hernández y Pérez, *Dos conferencias históricas* (Havana: Cultural, 1935), 72–73.

56 Drocir de Osorno, *Cuba española*, 139. Estimates of the size of the Ejército Libertador vary. General Arsenio Martínez Campos estimated in January 1896 a total of forty thousand insurgents. See Arsenio Martínez Campos to Ministry of War, January 14, 1896, in Weyler, *Mi mando en Cuba*, 1:58–59.

57 Rodolfo Bergés, *Cuba y Santo Domingo: Apuntes de la guerra de Cuba de mi diario en campaña 1895-96-97-98* (Havana: El Score, 1905), 49.

58 Drocir de Osorno, *Cuba española*, 164.

59 Gonzalo Reparaz, "Política de la guerra," *El Heraldo de Madrid*, December 19, 1895, 1.

60 "El avance de los insurrectos," *El Imparcial*, January 4, 1896, 1.

61 "Pesimismo," *El Correo Español*, February 4, 1896, 1.

62 "Lo del día," *El Correo Militar*, December 18, 1895, 2.

63 Andrés Clemente Vázquez to Ignacio Mariscal, January 28, 1896, and Andrés Clemente Vázquez to Ignacio Mariscal, March 4, 1896, in Salvador E. Morales, ed., *Espacios en disputa: México y la independencia de Cuba* (Mexico City: Centro de Investigación Científica "Ing. Jorge L. Tamayo," 1998), 268, 311.

64 Luis Otero y Pimentel, *Política militar y civil* (Madrid: Imprenta de la Revista Médica, 1903), 299.

65 Manuel Escobar, "Desde Colón: Nuestro redactor corresponsal," *La Correspondencia de España*, January 23, 1896, 3.

66 Enrique Loynaz Castillo, *Memorias de la guerra* (Havana: Editorial de Ciencias Sociales, 1989), 252.

67 G. Esteban, "Los insurrectos en Matanzas," *La Correspondencia de España*, January 14, 1896, 2.

68 Gustavo Pérez Abreu, *En la guerra con Máximo Gómez* (Havana: Editorial Carbonell, 1952), 17.

69 Flora Basulto de Montoya, *Una niña bajo tres banderas (Memorias)* (Havana: Cía. Edit de Libros y Folletos, 1954), 59–60, 62.

70 "La insurrección en Cuba," *La Epoca*, December 14, 1895, 1.

71 Manuel Cigés Aparicio, *El libro de la crueldad: Del cuartel y de la guerra* (Madrid: B. Rodríguez, 1906), 311–12.

72 "Revista Decenal del *Avisador Comercial*," *Ecos de Cuba*, January 20, 1896, 1.

73 Heredia, *Crónicas de la guerra de Cuba*, 2:58.

74 Luis López Allué, "La insurrección de Cuba: Desde Santa Clara," *El Imparcial*, November 21, 1895, 3.

75 "Revista Decenal del *Avisador Comercial*," *Ecos de Cuba*, January 30, 1896, 1.

76 Gobierno General de la Isla de Cuba, "Bando," *La Gaceta de La Habana* 58 (January 3, 1896): 17; "Estado de guerra," *La Lucha*, January 3, 1896, 2.
77 Ejército de Operaciones de Cuba, Segunda Comandancia General, Estado Mayor, "Orden General de 6 de enero de 1896, en la Habana," in Weyler, *Mi mando en Cuba*, 1:45–46.
78 Arsenio Martínez Campos, "Alocución: Voluntarios de La Habana," *La Lucha*, January 4, 1896, 4.
79 Arsenio Martínez Campos to Tomás Castellano y Villarroya, January 10, 1896, in "El lúcido pesimismo del Gobernador General de la isla de Cuba: La correspondencia de Martínez Campos con el Ministerio de Ultramar (Junio de 1895–Enero de 1896)," ed. Carlos Forcadell Alvarez, *Universidad de La Habana* 250 (1999): 112.
80 Eliseo Giberga, "Apuntes sobre la cuestión de Cuba," 1897, in *Obras de Eliseo Giberga* (4 vols., Havana: Imprenta y Papelería de Rambla, Bouza y Ca., 1930–31), 3:228–29.
81 "Cosas de la guerra," *El Correo Militar*, December 16, 1895, 1.
82 Lorenzo G. del Portillo, *La guerra de Cuba (el primer año)* (Key West, FL, 1896), 43–44; Miriam González and Aloima Ravelo, "La guerra del 95: La Invasión," in *La Invasión: Estrategia fundamental en nuestras guerras revolucionarias* (Havana Instituto Cubano del Libro, 1972), 150–261.
83 Miró Argenter, "Extracto de las operaciones militares realizadas por el Ejéricito Invasor al mando del lugarteniente general Antonio Maceo, desde su salida de Oriente hasta su llegada a Mantua, provincia del Pinar del Río," *Boletín del Archivo Nacional* 44 (1945), 185. See also Rafael M. Cañizares y Quierós, "Diario de operaciones del teniente coronel Rafael M. Cañizares y Quierós," *Boletín del Archivo Nacional* 48 (1949): 104–51.
84 "Deposition of Captain Ramón Varona," Central Teresa vs. the United States, Claim No. 196, Entry 352, RBCC/RG 76.
85 Heredia, *Crónicas de la guerra de Cuba*, 1:123.
86 Antonio Fernández Martínez, *La cuestión antillana: Orígines del relevo del General Martínez Campos* (2nd ed., Zaragoza, 1897), 19–32.
87 Arsenio Martínez Campos, "Instrucciones para las fuerzas que ha de operar en Las Villas," August 24, 1895, *La Correspondencia de España*, September 25, 1895, 1.
88 "Táctica contra táctica," *El Correo Militar*, January 4, 1896, 1.
89 "¿150.000 hombres?," *El Correo Militar*, December 18, 1895, 1.
90 Andrés Clemente Vázquez to Ignacio Mariscal, January 17, 1896, in Morales, *Espacios en disputa*, 252.
91 Atkins, *Sixty Years in Cuba*, 227.
92 "Deposition of General Tomasco Fernández," Central Teresa vs. the United States, Claim No. 97, Entry 352, RBCC/RG 76.
93 Manuel Escobar, "Desde Colón: Nuestro redactor corresponsal," *La Correspondencia de España*, January 23, 1896, 3.

94 Alexander Gollan to Foreign Office, June 4, 1896, Foreign Office Records, Group 277, Item No. 57, National Archives, Kew, Richmond, England.
95 P. M. Beals to Edwin Atkins, in Atkins, *Sixty Years in Cuba*, 186; Antonio Vesa y Fillart, *Historial del Regimiento Caballería de Jaruco y de su estandarte* (Barcelona: Vda. de José Cunill, 1908), 245.
96 "A las puertas del hambre," *El Heraldo de Madrid*, February 3, 1896, 2.
97 In Sanitago Perinat, *Las guerras mambisas* (Barcelona: Ediciones Carena, 2002), 229.
98 See José Menéndez Caravia, *La guerra en Cuba: Su origen y desarrollo* (Madrid, 1896), 19–21.
99 Gonzalo Reparaz, "La guerra en Cuba," *El Heraldo de Madrid*, January 26, 1896, 1.
100 Alexander Gollan to Foreign Office, December 13, 1895, Foreign Office Records, Group 277, Item No. 57, National Archives, Kew, Richmond, England.
101 Miró Argenter, *Cuba*, 1:168.
102 "El fracaso," *El Imparcial*, January 7, 1896, 1.
103 Tesifonte Gallego, "La guerra y los corresponsales," *El Heraldo de Madrid*, February 10, 1895, 3.
104 Enrique de Miguel Fernández, "Azcárraga, Weyler y la conducción de la guerra de Cuba" (PhD diss., Universitat Jaume I, 2008), 113. See also Yolanda Díaz Martínez, "Dos ejércitos en lucha: Táctica y estructuras militares en la guerra de Cuba, 1895–1898," *Revista Complutense de Historia de América* 20 (1994): 257–74.
105 "Operaciones en Cuba," *La Epoca*, January 14, 1896, 1; "Opiniones de un veterano," *La Epoca*, January 14, 1896, 2–3; "La guerra en la manigua," *El Correo Militar*, November 9, 1895, 1.
106 A + B [Manuel Mariano y Vivo], *Apuntes en defensa del honor del ejército* (Madrid, 1898), 21–23, 37–38. More than half of Spanish forces of operation were distributed as detachments to protect the estates. See Drocir de Osorno, *Cuba española*, 83.
107 Rafael Casset, "Cuba: De la guerra," *El Imparcial*, January 13, 1896, 1.
108 "Matanzas invadida," *El Heraldo de Madrid*, December 20, 1895, 1. *El Heraldo de Madrid* denounced the army commands for having "sacrificed military objectives in order to save the sugar harvest—which was not, in the end, saved." See "Con toda claridad," *El Heraldo de Madrid*, January 15, 1896, 1.
109 Eusebio Hernández to Manuel Sanguily, July 3, 1896, in Eusebio Hernández, *Eusebio Hernández: Ciencia y patria*, ed. Rafael Cepeda (Havana: Editorial de Ciencias Sociales, 1991), 102.
110 Antonio Maceo to José Maceo, November 30, 1895, in Antonio Maceo, *Antonio Maceo, ideología política: Cartas y otros documentos* (2 vols., Havana: Editorial de Ciencias Sociales, 1998), 2:173. See also Antonio Maceo to María Cabrales de Maceo, November 20, 1895, in Gonzalo Cabrales, ed., *Epistolario de héroes: Cartas y documentos históricos* (Havana: Imprenta "Siglo XX," 1922), 84–85; Valeriano Weyler to Minister of War, September 20, 1897, in Weyler, *Mi mando*

en Cuba, 5:113; Mariano Corona Ferrer, *De la manigua (eco de la epopeya)* (Santiago de Cuba: Imprenta de "El Cubano Libre," 1900), 42–43.

111 Weyler, *Mi mando en Cuba,* 1:130–31. See also J. J. de Murviedro, *Bosquejo de un plan de campaña en la Isla de Cuba* (Madrid, 1896), 4–12.

112 Miró Argenter, *Cuba,* 10. See also Juan J. E. Casasús, *La Invasión: Sus antecedentes, sus factores, su finalidad. Estudio crítico-militar* (Havana: Imprenta Habana, 1960).

113 Salvador Cisneros Betancourt to Tomás Estrada Palma, December 6, 1895, in Elda Cento Muñoz and Ricardo Muñoz Gutiérrez, eds., *Salvador Cisneros Betancourt: Entre la controversia y la fe* (Havana: Editorial de Ciencias Sociales, 2009), 264–65.

114 Aline Helg, *Our Rightful Share: The Afro-Cuban Struggle for Equality, 1886–1912* (Chapel Hill: University of North Carolina Press, 1995), 54.

115 Giberga, "Apuntes sobre la cuestión de Cuba," 3:233–35.

116 "La insurrección en Cuba," *La Epoca,* December 12, 1895, 1.

117 "Donde está la causa," *El Heraldo de Madrid*, September 2, 1895, 1, emphasis in original; "El voto de la nación," *El Heraldo de Madrid*, September 3, 1895, 1.

118 Un Testigo, *Cuadros de la guerra: Acción de Cacarajícara* (Havana, 1896), 19.

119 Bernabé Boza, *Mi diario de la guerra: Desde Baire hasta la intervención americana* (2 vols., Havana: Imprenta La Propagandista, 1900–1904), 1:79.

120 Reverter Delmas, *Cuba española,* 1:602, 2:137, 2:525, 586, emphasis in original.

121 J. N. S. Williams to Edwin Atkins, November 25, 1895, in Atkins, *Sixty Years in Cuba,* 179; P. M. Beal to J. N. S. Williams to Edwin Atkins, December 27, 1895, in Atkins, *Sixty Years in Cuba,* 186.

122 Juan de Lasheras, "Escenas de la guerra," *Blanco y Negro* 6 (January 18, 1896): n.p.

123 M. Martín Salazar, "Esbozos antropológicos sobre la isla de Cuba," *Revista de Sanidad Militar* 10 (January 1, 1896): 8.

124 Vicente Torres y González, *La insurrección de Cuba* (Madrid, 1896), 9, 14.

125 Camilo Polavieja, *Relación documentada de mi política en Cuba: Lo que vi, lo que hice, lo que anuncié* (Madrid, 1896), 180–81.

126 Antonio María Fabié to Camilo Polavieja, December 28, 1890, in Antonio María Fabié, *Mi gestión ministerial respecto a la isla de Cuba* (Madrid, 1897), 341.

127 "Lo que dice el general Salcedo," *La Epoca,* September 1, 1895, 1.

128 Un Cubano Práctico [Rafael Padró], *El porvenir de Cuba* (New York, 1898), 8–9.

129 A Planter in Cuba, "The Argument for Autonomy," *Outlook* 58 (April 23, 1898): 1012–13.

130 Fernando A. Yznaga, "The Wanton Destruction of American Property in Cuba," *Forum* 22 (January 1897): 572–73.

131 "En el campo insurrecto," *El Correo Militar,* February 23, 1897, 1.

132 Boza, *Mi diario de la guerra,* 2:vii.

133 Arsenio Martínez Campos to Tomás Castellanos, June 29, 1895, in "Cartas y telegramas remitidos por el Capitán General de Cuba, Arsenio Martínez Campos

al Ministro de Ultramar, Tomás Castellanos (junio 1895–enero 1896)," in Cayuela Fernández, ed., *España en Cuba: Final del siglo* (Zaragoza: Institución Fernando el Católico, 2000), 42.

134 "To the President of the Republic of the United States of America," enclosure in Fitzhugh Lee to Richard Olney, June 24, 1896, Richard Olney Papers, Manuscript Division, Library of Congress, Washington, DC.

135 See William J. Calhoun to William McKinley, June 25, 1897, Special Agents, Department of State, Volume 48, General Records of the Department of State, Record Group 59, National Archives, Washington, DC (hereinafter cited as DS/RG 59); Alexander C. Brice to William R. Day, November 17, 1897, Despatches from United States Consuls in Matanzas, 1820–1899, DS/RG 59; Fitzhugh Lee to William R. Day, November 23, 1897, Despatches from United States Consuls in Havana, 1783–1906, DS/RG 59 (hereinafter cited as Despatches/Havana); Fitzhugh Lee to William R. Day, February 15, 1898, Despatches/Havana.

136 "Las malas nuevas," *El Heraldo de Madrid*, December 17, 1895, 1.

137 Congreso de los Diputados, *Diario de las Sesiones de Cortes*, Legislatura de 1891 (July 3, 1891): 2797. See Leonor Meléndez, *Cánovas y la política exterior de España* (Madrid: Instituto de Estudios Políticos, 1944), 345–46; Antonio María Fabié, *Cánovas del Castillo (Su juventud–su edad madura–su vejez)* (Barcelona: Gustavo Gili, 1928), 329–30.

138 Congreso de los Diputados, *Diario de las Sesiones de Cortes*, Legislatura de 1896 (August 7, 1896): 2134–35.

139 Congreso de los Diputados, *Diario de las Sesiones de Cortes*, Legislaturas de 1894–1895, 7 (April 2, 1895): 2521.

140 "Cuba, el gobierno y los partidos políticos," *La Correspondencia de España*, January 8, 1896, 1.

141 Rafael Núñez Florencio, *El ejército español en el desastre de 1898* (Madrid: Arco Libros, 1997), 40.

142 M. Troyano, "Crónica política," *Nuevo Mundo* 3 (February 6, 1896): 4.

143 In Juan Ortega Rubio, *Historia de la regencia de María Cristina Habsbourg Lorena* (5 vols., Madrid: Felipe González Rojas, 1905–6), 3:11; Luis de Armiñan, *Weyler* (Madrid: Gran Capitán, 1946), 163–65.

144 "El general Weyler en la Habana: Alocuciones," *La Epoca*, February 12, 1897, 1.

145 Pablo de Alzola y Minondo, *El problema cubano* (Bilbao, 1898), 20.

146 "A sangre y fuego," *El Heraldo de Madrid*, December 26, 1895, 1; "El fracaso," *El Heraldo de Madrid*, January 7, 1896, 1.

147 "Tristezas y esperanzas," *La Epoca*, January 6, 1896, 1.

148 Drocir de Osorno, *Cuba española*, 16.

149 Sabas B. Catá, *Verdades amargas: Exposición de los males que afligen a Cuba, causas que lo determinan y remedios que se aconsejan para su salvación* (Havana, 1895), 20.

150 "Las reformas de Cuba," *El Correo Militar*, November 6, 1895, 1.
151 Congreso de Diputados, *Diario de Sesiones de Cortes*, Legislatura de 1896 (August 19, 1896), 2861.
152 "Fusiles, no reformas," *El Heraldo de Madrid*, March 19, 1896, 1.
153 V. de Diez Vicario, "Impresiones cubanas," *El Globo*, November 23, 1897, 2.
154 *La Correspondencia Militar*'s editorial appeared in "Conformes," *El Motín*, March 28, 1896, 3, emphasis in original.
155 Reverter Delmas, *Cuba española*, 1:602, 2:137, 2:588.
156 Cigés Aparicio, *El libro de la crueldad*, 347–48.
157 Valeriano Weyler, "Habitantes de Cuba," *La Gaceta de La Habana* 58 (February 11, 1896): 281; Tesifonte Gallego, "Una entrevista con Weyler," *El Heraldo de Madrid*, February 13, 1896, 1.
158 *La Correspondencia Militar*'s editorial appeared in "Conformes," *El Motín*, March 28, 1896, 3.
159 Gobierno General de la Isla de Cuba, "Bando," *La Gaceta de La Habana* 58 (April 29, 1896): 801.
160 Testifonte Gallego, "La nueva situación," *El Heraldo de Madrid*, March 9, 1896, 1.
161 M. Troyano, "Crónica política," *Nuevo Mundo* 3 (January 16, 1896): 3.
162 Gonzalo Reparaz, "La guerra en Cuba," *El Heraldo de Madrid*, January 26, 1896, 1.
163 Weyler, *Mi mando en Cuba*, 1:63.
164 Weyler, *Mi mando en Cuba*, 1:127–28; Valeriano Weyler to Ministro de Guerra, September 20, 1897, in Weyler, *Mi mando en Cuba*, 5:114.
165 See Tesifonte Gallego, "La caballería en Cuba," *El Heraldo de Madrid*, February 16, 1896, 1; "Caballería para Cuba," *El Heraldo de Madrid*, January 16, 1896, 2; "Reorganización de la caballería: Sus jefes," *El Heraldo de Madrid*, February 13, 1896, 2.
166 Luis de Urzáiz, "Guerra de Cuba: Apuntes sobre la línea militar de Mariel á Majana," *Memorial de Ingenieros del Ejército* 52 (March 1897): 68–71.
167 Valeriano Weyler, *Memorias de un general: De caballero cadete a general en jefe*, ed. María Teresa Weyler (Barcelona: Ediciones Destino, 2004), 204–5; Weyler, *Mi mando en Cuba*, 1:127–28; Valeriano Weyler y López de Pugna, *En el archivo de mi abuelo: Biografía del Capitán General Weyler* (Madrid: Ediciones Verdad, 1946), 100–105; Emilio Roig de Leuchsenring, *Weyler en Cuba* (Havana: Habana, 1947), 71–72; "La trocha de Júcaro," *El Imparcial*, June 22, 1897, 2.
168 Gobierno General de la Isla de Cuba, "Bando," *La Gaceta de La Habana* 58 (February 16, 1896): 321.
169 See Gobierno General de la Isla de Cuba, "Bando," *La Gaceta de La Habana* 58 (October 23, 1896): 785.
170 See Gobierno General de la Isla de Cuba, "Bando," *La Gaceta de La Habana* 59 (January 6, 1897): 33.
171 Francisco Pérez Guzmán, *Herida profunda* (Havana: Ediciones Unión, 1998), 29. Estimates of the number of Cubans who perished in reconcentration camps

vary widely. Most commentators agree, however, that several hundred thousand Cubans lost their lives in the camps. See Miguel Varona Guerrero, *La guerra de independencia de Cuba, 1895–1896* (3 vols., Havana: Editorial Lex, 1946), 2:780; Raimundo Cabrera, *Episodios de la guerra: Mi vida en la manigua: (Relato del coronel Ricardo Buenamar)* (Philadelphia, 1898), 265–70; Roig de Leuchsenring, *Weyler en Cuba*, 90–102; Francisco de P. Machado, *¡Piedad! Recuerdos de la reconcentracion* (Havana: Imprenta y Papelería de Rambla, Bouza y Ca., 1927), 20–22.

172 Corral, *¡El desastre!*, 69.
173 "Deposition of Major Florentino Yriondo de la Vara," Hormiguero Central Company vs. the United States, Entry 352, Claim No. 293, RBCC/RG 76.
174 Ricardo Burguete, *¡La guerra! Cuba (Diario de un testigo)* (Barcelona: Maucci, 1902), 167.
175 Antonio Serra Orts, *Recuerdos de las guerras de Cuba: 1868 á 1898* (Santa Cruz de Tenerife: A. J. Benítez, 1908), 60.
176 Drocir de Osorno, *Cuba española*, 223.
177 "Testimony of Stephen Bonsal," in US Congress, Senate, *Report of the Committee on Foreign Relations: Affairs in Cuba*, 55th Congress, 2nd Session, Report No. 885 (Washington, DC, 1898), 405.
178 Pedro Pablo Martín, *Adelina, ó, la huérfana de La Habana: Novela histórica basada en hechos ocurridos durante la guerra civil de Cuba del año 1895 al 98* (Havana: Imprenta "El Arte," 1901), 152.
179 Reverter Delmas, *Cuba española*, 5:559–60.
180 Corral, *¡El desastre!*, 97. Nor were these measures without effect. Across extensive swaths of the *manigua*, *insurrecto* forces experienced conditions of hunger. See Enrique J. Conill, *Enrique J. Conill, soldado de la patria*, ed. Gaspar Carbonell Rivero (Havana: Editorial Carbonell, 1956), 18–19; Serafín Espinosa y Ramos, *Al trote y sin estribos (Recuerdos de la guerra de independencia)* (Havana: Jesús. Montero, 1946), 172; Israel Consuegra y Guzmán, *Mambiserías: Episodios de la guerra de independencia, 1895–1898* (Havana: Imprenta del Ejército, 1930), 61–62.
181 Josep Conangla I. Fontanilles, *Memorias de mi juventud en Cuba: Un soldado del ejército español en la guerra separatista (1895–1898)*, ed. Joaquín Roy (Barcelona: Ediciones Península, 1998), 174.
182 Espinosa y Ramos, *Al trote y sin estribos*, 76.
183 Domingo Blanco, "En campaña," *El Imparcial*, December 6, 1896, 2.
184 "La situación de Cuba," *El Heraldo de Madrid*, June 8, 1897, 2.
185 Gabriel Alcolea García, "Diario inédito de un soldado en la Guerra de Cuba, 1896–1899," ed. Eloy Recio Ferreras, *Revista de Historia de América* 112 (1991): 39.
186 "Deposition of Enrique Ubieta," Claim 196, Case No. 293, Hormiguero Central Company vs. the United States, RBCC/RG 76.
187 Bergés, *Cuba y Santo Domingo*, 98.

188 Lucas Barona to parents, March 1, 1897, in Montero, *Las guerras de Cuba y Filipinas*, 446.
189 Eduardo Rosell y Malpica, *Diario del teniente coronel Eduardo Rosell y Malpica (1895–1897)*, ed. Benigno Souza (2 vols., Havana: Academia de la Historia de Cuba, 1950), 2:57.
190 Pérez Abreu, *En la guerra con Máximo Gómez*, 152.
191 "Página negra," *Cuba y América* 1 (April 15, 1897): 14.
192 Rosell y Malpica, *Diario del teniente coronel Eduardo Rosell y Malpica*, 153.
193 Weyler, *Memorias de un general*, 205.
194 "Deposition of Manuel Antonio Receio de Morales," Constancia Sugar Company vs. the United States, Entry 352, Claim No. 196, RBCC/RG 76. See also Severo Pina to Lieutenant Colonel Rafael Castillo, April 20, 1896, Fondo Donativos y Remisiones, Legajo 302, Número 13, ANC.
195 Reverter Delmas, *Cuba española*, 3:59.
196 "Deposition of Lauriano Llorente," The Mapos Sugar Company vs. the United States, Entry 352, Claim No. 121, RBCC/RG 76.
197 Drocir de Osorno, *Cuba española*, 202.
198 Laird Bergad, *Cuban Rural Society in the Nineteenth Century: The Social and Economic History of Monoculture in Matanzas* (Princeton, NJ: Princeton University Press, 1990), 313.
199 Atkins, *Sixty Years in Cuba*, 178. Atkins was indignant upon learning "that all Government assistance was to be withdrawn and detachments replaced by private guards," and promptly protested to the US consul in Havana (256).
200 "Con toda claridad," *El Heraldo de Madrid*, January 15, 1896, 1.
201 Tesifonte Gallego, "La guerra y los corresponsales," *El Heraldo de Madrid*, February 10, 1895, 3.
202 Vicente Blasco Ibáñez, "Los patriotas de Cuba," October 28, 1896, in Vicente Blasco Ibáñez, *Artículos contra la guerra en Cuba*, ed. J. L. León Roca (Valencia: León Roca, 1978), 231–33.
203 Fabié, *Cánovas del Castillo*, 353–54; Antonio Elorza and Elena Hernández Sandoica, *La guerra de Cuba (1895–1898): Historia política de una derrota colonial* (Madrid: Alianza Editorial, 1998), 234–56.
204 Drocir de Osorno, *Cuba española*, 187–88.
205 Weyler, *Mi mando en Cuba*, 1:116.
206 "¡Guerra para dos años!," *El Correo Español*, January 28, 1896, 1.
207 "Acerca a Cuba," *El Heraldo de Madrid*, March 18, 1896, 1.
208 Damián Isern, *Del desastre nacional y sus causas* (Madrid, 1899), 254.
209 Domingo Blanco, "Hacia Oriente," *El Imparcial*, December 12, 1897, 1.
210 Benigno Souza y Rodríguez, *Máximo Gómez, el generalísimo* (Havana: Editorial Trópico 1936), 228–29. See also José Rolando la Rosa Cabrera, "Ya Gómez lo dijo: ¿Mis tres mejores generales? Junio, julio y agosto. Los generales de

Gómez en Colón, 1895–1898. Costo humano," *Anales de la Real Academia de Cultura Valenciana* 93 (2018): 731–48.

211 Un Español Incondicional [Santiago Barroeta Scheidnagel], *Los sucesos de Cienfuegos y la situación actual de la Isla de Cuba* (New York, 1897), 104.
212 Ramón Ruiz, "Día desastroso," *El País*, December 16, 1895, 1.
213 Ubaldo Romero Quiñones, *La cariátide: Novela por la guerra de Cuba* (Madrid, 1897), 134.
214 "De nuestro redactor corresponsal," *La Correspondencia de España*, December 18, 1895, 3; Corral, *¡El desastre!*, 97–112. For a denunciation of the practice of forced marches and countermarches, see the report by army physician José González Granda, *Higiene de las marchas en el ejército de la isla de Cuba* (Madrid, 1897).
215 Pío Baroja, *La lucha por la vida: Mala hierba. Novela* (Madrid: Fernando Fé, 1904), 237.
216 Domingo Blanco, "En campaña," *El Imparcial*, December 7, 1896, 2.
217 Piqueras Causas, "Diario de operaciones en Cuba," 218–19.
218 Moure Saco, *1102 días en el ejército español*, 81–82.
219 "Cómo se hace la guerra," *El Correo Militar*, December 24, 1895, 2.
220 Burguete, *¡La guerra! Cuba*, 74, 86.
221 Federico Parreño Ballesteros, "Recuerdos de Cuba: En marcha," *Revista Técnica de Infantería y Caballería* 8 (January 15, 1897): 65.
222 Lorenzo Despradel, "Máximo Gómez y la campaña del 97," appendix in Orestes Ferrara, *Mis relaciones con Máximo Gómez* (2nd ed., Havana: Molina, 1942), 298.
223 Cigés Aparicio, *El libro de la crueldad*, 378.
224 Corral, *¡El desastre!*, 102, 124; "La alimentación de las tropas," *El Correo Militar*, December 31, 1895, 1; "La alimentación del soldado en Cuba," *La Epoca*, December 30, 1895, 2.
225 José Eguiluz to parents, February 5, 1896, in Montero, *Las guerras de Cuba y Filipinas*, 336.
226 Juan Masó Parra, *Primera parte de un libro para la historia: Cuba* (Curaçao: Bethencourt, 1904), 24. Masó Parra surrendered in early 1898, thereupon to organize a guerrilla unit in defense of the Autonomist government against the United States.
227 Rodolfo Miranda, *Calixto García Iñiguez, estratega* (Havana: Academia de la Historia de Cuba, 1951), 11.
228 Juan Lapoulide, "La guerra de Cuba," *La Epoca*, March 16, 1896, 1. See also Juan Lapoulide, *¡Pobre España! (Memorias de un coronel jefe de zona)* (Madrid, 1889).
229 Enriquez Collazo, *Cuba heroíca* (Havana: Imprenta La Mercantil, de Suárez, Solana y Cía., 1912), 279.
230 Miró Argenter, *Cuba*, 1:151–52. See also Rosell y Malpica, *Diario del teniente coronel Eduardo Rosell y Malpica*, 2:29, 41, 75; Santiago C. Rey, *Recuerdos de la guerra, 1895–1898* (Havana: Imprenta "Tipografía Moderna," 1931), 21.

231 In Sanitago Perinat, *Las guerras mambisas*, 142.
232 Manuel Secades Japón, *Episodios de un estudiante en la guerra de independencia de Cuba* (1958; Miami: n.a., 1997), 14.
233 Ernesto L. Usatorres Perdomo, *Impresiones de la guerra: Campaña de Pinar del Río* (Guanajay, 1899), 10.
234 Boza, *Mi diario de la guerra*, 1: 62–63.
235 Despradel, "Máximo Gómez y la campaña del 97," 292. See also Avelino Sanjenis, *Mis cartas: Memorias de la revolución de 1895 por la independencia de Cuba* (Sagua la Grande: Imprenta "El Comercio," 1900), 188, 247.
236 Juan Bautista Casas, *La guerra separatista de Cuba: Sus causas. Medios de terminarla y de evitar otras* (Madrid, 1896), 138.
237 Miguel A. Macau, *Mi vía crucis (Relato autobiográfico)* (Havana: Taller Gráficos de Albino Rodríguez, 1947), 33.
238 Un Testigo Presencial [Vicente de Cortijo], *Apuntes para la historia de la pérdida de nuestras colonias* (Madrid, 1899), 21.
239 See "El uniforme y el equipo en Cuba," *El Correo Militar*, June 11, 1897, 1; "Soldados de quince días," *El Imparcial*, November 19, 1895, 2.
240 Francisco Arroyo Alday to mother, June 29, 1897, in Montero, *Las guerras de Cuba y Filipinas*, 496.
241 Corral, *¡El desastre!*, 109–10; "Diario de un soldado," *El Correo Militar*, December 28, 1895, 2.
242 "Carta de un soldado," *El Correo Militar*, February 11, 1897, 2.
243 Felipe Ovilo Canales, *La decadencia del ejército: Estudio de higiene militar* (Madrid, 1899), 30.
244 "Refuerzos para Cuba," *El Correo Militar*, January 3, 1898, 2.
245 Domingo Blanco, "En el hospital," *El Imparcial*, November 9, 1896, 7. On military hospitals in Cuba, see "Los hospitales militares en Cuba," *La Medicina Militar y la Revista Clínica, Terapéutica y Farmacia* 2 (September 1896): 273–76.
246 "Desde Artemisa," *El Imparcial*, November 22, 1896, 3.
247 Gonzalo Reparaz, "La guerra en Cuba," *El Heraldo de Madrid*, December 30, 1896, 1.
248 Nicolás Arteagabeita to parents, June 22, 1897, in Montero, *Las guerras de Cuba y Filipinas*, 486.
249 Cigés Aparicio, *El libro de la crueldad*, 357.
250 Piqueras Causas, "Diario de operaciones en Cuba," 208.
251 "El soldado de Cuba," *El Imparcial*, December 5, 1897, 1.
252 Ovilo y Canales, *La decadencia del ejército*, 24.
253 Rafael Gasset, "Excursión por el Departamento Oriental," *El Imparcial*, November 22, 1895, 3.
254 Domingo Blanco, "En el hospital," *El Imparcial*, November 9, 1896, 7.
255 "Carta de Cuba," *El Correo Militar*, June 6, 1897, 1.
256 Moure Saco, *1102 días en el ejército español*, 57, 66.

257 "El problema de la repatriación en la campaña de Cuba," *La Medicina Militar y la Revista Clínica, Terapéutica y Farmacia* 3 (April 1897): 163.
258 Corral, *¡El desastre!*, 124–34. On the condition of military hospitals, see Miguel Fernández, "Azcárraga, Weyler y la conducción de la guerra de Cuba," 270–79; Yolanda Díaz Martínez, "La sanidad militar del ejército español en la guerra de 1895 en Cuba," *Asclepio: Revista de Historia de la Medicina y de la Ciencia* 50 (1898): 159–73; Bonifacio Esteban Martfil, "Los hospitales militares en la isla de Cuba durante la guerra de 1895–1898," *Asclepio: Revista de Historia de la Medicina y de la Ciencia* 53 (2001): 173–99.
259 Enrique de Miguel Fernández indicates that of the seven hundred physicians who served in Cuba, one hundred died on the island. See Miguel Fernández, "Azcárraga, Weyler y la conducción de la guerra de Cuba," 346.
260 C. Lázaro Adradas, "Los médicos militares y el ejército," *El País*, January 6, 1898, 2.
261 Ovilo Canales, *La decadencia del ejército*, 25.
262 Reverter Delmas, *Cuba española*, 6:192. General Weyler acknowledged the death of 21,000 officers and men between February 1896 and September 1897. See Weyler, *Mi mando en Cuba*, 5:148.
263 Reverter Delmas, *Cuba española*, 6:138–62; "Las bajas del ejército español," *Patria*, August 6, 1898, 2.
264 Esteban Uraga to parents, August 5, 1897, in Montero, *Las guerras de Cuba y Filipinas*, 520.
265 Angel Larra y Cerezo, *Datos para la historia de la campaña sanitaria en la guerra de Cuba (Apuntes estadísticos relativos al año de 1896)* (Madrid: Imprenta de Ricardo Rojas, 1901), 5–7.
266 José Fernández Losada, "El informe del Inspector General de Sanidad del Ejército de Cuba," *El Imparcial*, December 6, 1897, 1; "José Fernández Losada, Inspector General de Sanidad Militar, explicando el estado en que había quedado el Ejército de Cuba al dejar el mando el General Weyler," December 5, 1897, in Amblard, *Notas coloniales*, 148–52; Domingo Blanco, "El estado del ejército," *El Imparcial*, December 1, 1897, 2; Reverter Delmas, *Cuba española*, 6:190–202.
267 Eduardo de la Peña, "El país de la guerra," *El Heraldo de Madrid*, November 1, 1896, 2.
268 Fitzhugh Lee to William R. Day, July 14, 1897, Despatches/Havana; Fitzhugh Lee to William R. Day, August 25, 1897, Personal Correspondence, General Fitzhugh Lee to the Secretary of State, 1897–1898, John Bassett Moore Papers, Manuscript Division, Library of Congress, Washington, DC.
269 "The Situation in Cuba," *London Times*, October 15, 1897, 4.
270 Esteban Montejo, *Biografía de un cimarrón*, ed. Miguel Barnet (Havana: Instituto de Etnología y Folklore, 1966), 169.
271 Adelaide Rosalind Kirchner, *A Flag for Cuba* (New York, 1897), 35–36.

272 Luis de Altamira, "Los comandantes Capdevila y Cordón," *Diario de la Marina*, September 5, 1921, 8. See also Damián Isern, *Del desastre nacional y sus causas* (Madrid, 1899), 245–63.
273 "Refuerzos para Cuba," *El Correo Militar*, January 3, 1898, 2.
274 Vicente Blasco Ibáñez, "Resultados del empréstito," November 23, 1896, in Blasco Ibáñez, *Artículos contra la guerra en Cuba*, 261.
275 Gabriel Cardona and Juan Carlos Losada, *Weyler, nuestro hombre en La Habana* (Barcelona: Planeta, 1997), 195; Stanley G. Payne, *Politics and the Military in Modern Spain* (Stanford, CA: Stanford University Press, 1967), 76.
276 "Opiniones de Azcárraga," *El Día*, September 28, 1898, 1; "Habla el general Azcárraga," *El Correo Militar*, September 28, 1898, 2. See also "Patogenia de los medios militares en la actual campaña de Cuba," *La Medicina Militar y la Revista Clínica, Terapéutica y Farmacia* 4 (February 1898): 145–53.
277 W. F. Brunner, "Morbidity and Mortality in the Spanish Army in Cuba during the Calendar Year 1897," *Public Health Report* 13 (April 29, 1898): 411–12. Arturo Amblard estimated that between March 1895 and June 1898, forty-four thousand soldiers were repatriated to Spain, "most of whom were most assuredly returned to Spain in order to save their lives." See Amblard, *Notas coloniales*, 165–66.
278 Ricardo Burguete, *¡La guerra! Cuba*, 194.
279 Serra Orts, *Recuerdos de las guerras de Cuba*, 17.
280 Larra y Cerezo, *Datos para la historia de la campaña sanitaria*, 13; Reverter Delmas, *Cuba española*, 6:808. In 1897, nearly seventeen thousand officers and men were repatriated due to poor health. See Avelino Delgado, "The Spanish Army in Cuba," 1:233. The Spanish press provided weekly news accounts of soldiers returning from Cuba. See, for example, "Los que regresan de Cuba," *El Correo Militar*, December 3, 1897, 2; and January 17, 1898, 2. On the fate of repatriated soldiers, see "Heridos y enfermos de Cuba," *Nuevo Mundo* 4 (January 28, 1897): 5; and Silvia Sánchez Abadía, "Olvidos de una guerra: El cost humano y económico de la independencia (Cuba-España, 1895–1898)," *Revista de Indias* 61 (2001): 114–40.
281 Domingo Blanco, "A bordo del 'San Agustín,'" *El Imparcial*, January 31, 1897, 1.
282 See "Los que mueren al regreso," *El Correo Militar*, September 3, 1897, 2. See also Antonio García Ramos and José Luis Fuentes Perea, "Los enfermos: La otra cara de la Guerra de Cuba," *Yanasta: Revista de Historia*, April 2014, https://studylib.es/doc/6939616/los-enfermos.-la-otra-cara-de-la-guerra-de-cuba.
283 Vicente Blasco Ibáñez, "Carne para tiburones," September 21, 1897, in Blasco Ibáñez, *Artículos contra la guerra en Cuba*, 295–98.
284 Baroja, *La lucha por la vida*, 238.
285 Rafael Gasset, "Para los soldados de Cuba," *El Imparcial*, September 28, 1896, 1.
286 Spain, *Diario de Sesiones de Cortes, Congreso de los Deputados*, Legislatura de 1898, 8 (Madrid, 1899), 1939.

287 "Para los heridos de Cuba," *El Imparcial*, October 23, 1896, 1.
288 "Desde La Habana de nuestro director: Primeras impresiones," *El Imparcial*, November 7, 1897, 1.
289 Weyler, *Mi mando en Cuba*, 2:5.
290 Weyler, *Mi mando en Cuba*, 2:55.
291 Weyler, *Mi mando en Cuba*, 2:157.
292 Boza, *Mi diario de la guerra*, 2:206.
293 Domingo Blanco, "De la guerra," *El Imparcial*, September 19, 1896, 1. The report was filed on September 2.
294 Ovilo Canales, *La decadencia del ejército*, 25.
295 "Lo que dice el Sr. Azcárraga," *El Imparcial*, June 29, 1897, 2.
296 In Miguel Fernández, "Azcárraga, Weyler y la conducción de la guerra de Cuba," 350.
297 Corral, *¡El desastre!*, 42. Guerrilla units organized during the Ten Years' War had been demobilized after 1878 to reduce the colonial budget. See Adolfo Jiménez Castellanos, *De las insurrecciones en Cuba y sistema para combatirlas, según lo que aconseja la experiencia* (Madrid, 1883), 222.
298 Weyler, *Mi mando en Cuba*, 1:130.
299 Weyler, *Memorias de un general*, 80–81.
300 "Refuerzos de Cuba," *El Heraldo de Madrid*, November 24, 1897, 1.
301 José Ignacio Chacón, *Guerras irregulares* (Madrid, 1883), 9, 157–59. The subject of irregular war increasingly occupied the attention of the Spanish army. See Virgilio Cabanellas, *La táctica en Cuba, Africa y las Filipinas y en todo país cubierto y accidentado (sorpresas, emboscadas é impedimentas)* (Madrid, 1896); Adrián Carrera, "La grande y pequeña guerra," *Revista Técnica de Infantería y Caballería* 8 (May 1, 1897): 385–93; Guzmán, "La caballería en la guerras irregulares," 1105–6.
302 Weyler, *Mi mando en Cuba*, 3:6.
303 Kirchner, *A Flag for Cuba*, 126.
304 "La guerra: Las operaciones del día," *La Correspondencia Militar*, March 10, 1897, 1.
305 "Trabajos de Weyler—guerrillas," *La Epoca*, February 14, 1896, 2; "Mundo militar: Cuba," *El Correo Militar*, February 14, 1896, 1; "Tercios de guerrillas," *El Correo Militar*, May 9, 1896, 2.
306 Gobierno General de la Isla de Cuba, "Bando," *Gaceta de La Habana* 58 (March 8, 1896): 465; Weyler, *Memorias de un general*, 205, 210; Weyler, *Mi mando en Cuba*, 1:128–29, 152; Gonzalo Reparaz, "La interinidad," *El Heraldo de Madrid*, February 19, 1896, 1.
307 Ejército de la Isla de Cuba, Capitanía General, Estado Mayor, Sección de Campaña, "Orden General del día 26 de febrero de 1896, en La Habana," in Weyler, *Mi mando en Cuba*, 1:180–82; Eduardo Guardado y Corrás, *Manual de detal y contabilidad para el Ejército de Cuba* (Havana, 1896), 32–34.
308 Walter H. Barker to Fitzhugh Lee, July 14, 1898, Despatches/Havana.

309 Avelino Delgado, "The Spanish Army in Cuba," 1:275.
310 Miguel Varona Guerrero, "Máximo Gómez: Generalísimo y libertador," *Diario de la Marina*, October 22, 1922, 37. See also Ejército Libertador de Cuba, 4º cuerpo, 1ª División, 2ª Brigada, "Guerrillas locales y su personal," 1897, Fondo Donativos y Remisiones, Legajo 135, Número 36-A, ANC.
311 These figures assume salience, for Miguel Varona Guerrero also reported a total of 29,730 Cubans had enrolled in the Ejército Libertador. See Varona Guerrero, *La guerra de independencia de Cuba*, 2:1407, 1419; 3:1814–16; Manuel Piedra Martel, *Campañas de Maceo en la última Guerra de Independencia* (Havana: Editorial Lex, 1946), 93; Gil Gelpí y Ferro, *Historia de la revolución y guerra de Cuba* (2 vols., Havana, 1887–89), 2:154. Local data is found in "Estado de fuerza del Ejército de la Isla de Cuba en diciembre de 1896," in Ministerio de la Guerra, *Anuario Militar de España 1897* (Madrid, 1897), 782–83; "Consulta en el expediente iniciado por el Ayuntamiento de Santa Ysabel de las Lajas para el sostenimiento de una guerrilla local en dicho término," December 30, 1895, Fondo Consejo General de Administración, Legajo 114, Número 9970, ANC; "Expediente promovido por el ayuntamiento de Sagua la Grande, solicitando autorización para crear recurso con los que atender al sostenimiento de cuatro guerrillas locales en aquella jurisdicción," n.d., Fondo Consejo General de Administración, Legajo 39, Número 4252, ANC. The total number of officers and men in the Ejército Libertador remains uncertain. Inspector General O. Ernst, who supervised the demobilization of the Cuban army at the end of the war, registered a total of 48,083 officers and men. See General O. Ernst to Adjutant General, April 23, 1899, File 1665, Letters Received, Records of the Bureau of Insular Affairs, Record Group 350, National Archives, Washington, DC.
312 Planter Carreño organized a *guerrilla particular* of some 150 recruits to protect the 1895–96 sugar harvest. See Menéndez Caravia, *La guerra en Cuba*, 15–16; Drocir de Osorno, *Cuba española*, 160–62; Enrique Rodríguez-Solís, *¡Viva España! Historia popular de la guerra de Cuba* (2 vols., Barcelona, 1897), 1:487; "Alquizar," *El Eco de la Patria* 16 (July 14, 1896): 10; Tesifonte Gallego, "Desde La Habana," *El Imparcial*, February 23, 1896, 1.
313 Boza, *Mi diario de la guerra*, 2:118.
314 Alejandro Rodríguez to Tomás Estrada Palma, June 16, 1896, in *Boletín del Archivo Nacional* 45 (1946): 208–11. See also Espinosa y Ramos, *Al trote y sin estribos*, 172.
315 Collazo, *Cuba heroica*, 283.
316 Weyler, *Mi mando en Cuba*, 3:296.
317 For accounts of encounters between *mambises* and guerrillas, see Carlos Roloff to Tomás Estrada Palma, November 14, 1895, *Boletín del Archivo Nacional* 45 (1946): 165–73; "Sorpresa de una guerrilla," *La Epoca*, June 28, 1897, 1.
318 "La guerra: Las operaciones del día," *La Correspondencia Militar*, March 29, 1897, 1.
319 Tesifonte Gallego, "Aspecto de la guerra," *El Heraldo de Madrid*, March 17, 1896, 1.

320 Drocir de Osorno, *Cuba española*, 66, 216–17.
321 Un Español [Antonio Díaz Benzo], *Pequeñeces de la guerra de Cuba*, 101–4.
322 Severo Gómez Núñez, *La acción de Peralejo* (Havana, 1895), 24.
323 "Aumentan las guerrillas," *El Correo Militar*, June 7, 1897, 1.
324 Atkins, *Sixty Years in Cuba*, 230.
325 See "Apuntes históricos, geográficos y varias anécdotas históricas sobre acciones de las guerrillas españoles en la guerra del 95," Fondo Donativo y Remisiones, Legajo 217, Número 50, ANC; "Operaciones realizadas en la comarca de Cienfuegos por las fuerzas a las órdenes del Jefe de Operaciones de dicha comarca Coronel Alejandro Rodríguez," August 8, 1896, *Boletín del Archivo Nacional* 45 (1946): 211–14; Carlos Roloff to Delegado, Partido Revolucionario Cubano, September 30, 1895, *Boletín del Archivo Nacional* 44 (1945): 161–65; Carlos Roloff to Tomás Estrada Palma, November 15, 1895, *Boletín del Archivo Nacional* 44 (1945): 165–73; Lino Dóu, "Extracto de las operaciones militares realizadas por el Ejéricito Invasor al mando del lugarteniente general Antonio Maceo, desde el día 9 de febrero hasta el 19 de marzo de 1896," *Boletín del Archivo Nacional* 44 (1945): 195–208; Alejandro Rodríguez to Tomás Estrada Palma, June 16, 1896, *Boletín del Archivo Nacional* 44 (1945): 208–11. Among first-person accounts of engagements between *insurrectos* and guerrillas see José Isabel Herrera, *Impresiones de la guerra de independencia: Narrado por el soldado del Ejército Libertador* (Havana: Editorial de Ciencias Sociales, 2005); Weyler, *Mi mando en Cuba*.
326 Drocir de Osorno, *Cuba española*, 172.
327 Segundo Corvisón, *En la guerra y en la paz* (Havana: Cultural, S.A., 1939), 175–76. George Rea Bronson arrived at a similar conclusion: "They are mercenaries; they enlist for pay." See "Statement of George Bronson Rea on the 11th Day of June 1898," in US Congress, Senate, *Report of the Committee on Foreign Relations: Relative to Affairs in Cuba*, 55th Congress, 2nd Session, Senate Report 885 (Washington, DC, 1898), 382, 406.
328 Corral, *¡El desastre!*, 44–45.
329 Manuel Ciges Aparicio, *Del cautiverio* (Madrid: La Editorial Moderna, 1903), 164–65.
330 The interview was completed in 1949. See Oswaldo Morales Patiño, *El capitán Chino, teniente coronel Quirino Zamora: Historia de un mambí en la provincia de La Habana* (Havana: Oficina del Historiador de la Ciudad, 1953), 93–94.
331 "La prensa," *Diario de la Marina*, September 10, 1899, 2.
332 "Deposition of Bibián Fernández," Constancia Sugar Company vs. the United States, PI Claim No. 196, Entry 352, RBCC/RG 76.
333 "La renuncia del Sr. Tomás," *El Mundo*, November 24, 1911, 16.
334 "Testimony of George Bronson Rea," in US Congress, Senate, *Report of the Committee on Foreign Relations: Affairs in Cuba*, 55th Congress, 2nd Session, Report No. 885 (Washington, DC, 1898), 388.

335 Juan de Lasheras, "La muerte de Lolo Benítez," *Blanco y Negro* 6 (March 28, 1896): 4.
336 F. Ovilo, "Lolo Benítez," *El Correo Militar*, February 28, 1896, 1.
337 Secades Japón, *Episodios de un estudiante en la guerra*, 204.
338 Varona Guerrero, *La guerra de independencia de Cuba*, 2:1006.
339 F. Ovilo, "Lolo Benítez," *El Correo Militar*, February 28, 1896, 1.
340 Montejo, *Biografía de un cimarrón*, 198–99.
341 "Carta de un soldado," *El Correo Militar*, June 14, 1897, 3; "A los guerrilleros del distrito," *El Heraldo Militar*, October 30, 1900, 1–2.
342 Manuel J. de Granda, *Memoria revolucionaria* (Santiago de Cuba: Tipografía Arroyo Hermanos, 1926), 84, 98–99.
343 María Josefa Granados retained vivid childhood memories of the Guerrilla de Sabanilla. See María Josefa Granados, *La otra María, o la niña de Artemisa*, ed. Ana Núñez Machín (Havana: Arte y Literatura, 1975), 59–60, 61, 81.
344 Jesús del Calvario, "Su regalo," *Bohemia* 27 (June 9, 1935): 8–9, 65.
345 Pablo Llaguno y de Cárdenas, "Campaña del Mayor General Antonio Maceo en la provincia de Pinar del Río, enero 8 de 1896 a diciembre 4 del mismo año," *Boletín del Archivo Nacional* 48 (1949): 82–83.
346 Fernando Gómez, *La insurrección por dentro; apuntes para la historia; datos recogidos de documentos originales insurrectos* (2nd ed., Madrid: M. Ruiz y Cía., 1900), 437, 463.
347 Weyler, *Mi mando en Cuba*, 3:37.
348 Miró Argenter, *Cuba*, 3:77.
349 Miró Argenter, *Cuba*, 3:180, 207.
350 Alejandro del Pozo y Arjona, *Páginas de sangre: El libro del cubano. Relación de los caudillos cubanos muertos en la actual campaña, 1895 a 1898* (Havana, 1898).
351 Consuegra y Guzmán, *Mambiserías*, 131. "We sustained a tenacious persecution of these reptiles," Rodolfo Bergés explained, "the worst of the worse." See Bergés, *Cuba y Santo Domingo*, 130.
352 Miguel Varona Guerrero, "Máximo Gómez: Generalísimo y libertador," *Diario de la Marina*, October 22, 1922, 37.
353 Orestes Ferrara, *Mis relaciones con Máximo Gómez* (2nd ed., Havana: Molina y Cía., 1942), 39.
354 Grover Flint, *Marching with Gomez: A War Correspondents Field Notebook Kept during Four Months with the Cuban Army* (Boston: Lamson, Wolffe & Company, 1898), 33. See also "Carta del Capitán José Francisco Lamas, de la escolta del General Alejandro Rodríguez," *Revista de Cayo Hueso* 1 (November 28, 1897): 16–18.
355 Sanjenis, *Mis cartas*, 240.
356 Rey, *Recuerdos de la guerra*, 72.
357 Waldo A. Insua, *Finis: Ultimos días de España en Cuba* (Madrid: Romero, 1901), 21.
358 Manuel Martínez-Moles, *Tradiciones, leyendas y anécdotas espirituanas* (7 vols., Havana, 1926–28), 3:78.

359 Arbelo, *Recuerdos de la última guerra*, 58–59.
360 Frederick Funston, *Memories of Two Wars: Cuba and Philippine Experiences* (Philadelphia: C. Scribner's Sons, 1911), 98.
361 Arbelo, *Recuerdos de la última guerra*, 63.
362 N. G. Gonzales, *In Darkest Cuba* (Columbia, SC: The State Company, 1922), 174.
363 Manuel Piedra Martel, *Mis primeros treinta años: Memorias* (Havana: Minerva, 1945), 296.
364 Julián Sánchez, *Julián Sánchez cuenta su vida*, ed. Erasmo Dumpierre (Havana: Instituto del Libro, 1979), 28, 48.
365 Boza, *Mi diario de la guerra*, 1:114.
366 Herrera, *Impresiones de la guerra de independencia*, 70.
367 Miró Argenter, *Cuba*, 2:65.
368 Angel E. Rosende y de Zayas, *De nuestras memorias de la guerra, 1895–1898: Conspirador y de soldado a capitán* (Havana: NA, 1928), 21.
369 Arbelo, *Recuerdos de la última guerra*, 43–44, 59.
370 Conangla I. Fontanilles, *Memorias de mi juventud en Cuba*, 100.
371 Joaquín Llaverías and Emeterio S. Santovenia, eds., *Actas de las Asamblea de Representantes y del Consejo de Gobierno durante la Guerra de Independencia* (6 vols., Havana: Imprenta "El Siglo XX," 1932–33), 1:35. See *Constitución del Gobierno Provisional de la República de Cuba proclamada solemnemente en Jimaguayú el 16 de septiembre de 1895* (New York, 1896).
372 República de Cuba, Secretaría de Gobernación, "Ley Penal," in *Documentos históricos* (Havana: Imprenta de Rambla y Bouza, 1912), 107–8; Domingo Méndez Capote, "Legislación penal de la República en armas," in *Trabajos* (2 vols., Havana: Molina y Compañia, 1929), 1:37–89.
373 R. de Cárdenas to Alejandro Rodriguez, June 24, 1898, *Boletín del Archivo Nacional* 45 (1946): 514.
374 Juan Lorente, "Operaciones practicadas por las fuerzas de la 3ra División del 6º Cuerpo," September 26, 1897, *Boletín del Archivo Nacional* 45 (1946): 375; Avelino Sanjenis, *Memorias de la revolución de 1895 por la independencia de Cuba* (Havana: Imprenta "El Comercio," 1913), 221.
375 Conill, *Enrique J. Conill, soldado de la patria*, 19. See also Sanjenis, *Memorias de la revolución de 1895*, 213.
376 José Rogelio Castillo y Zúñiga, *Para la historia de Cuba: Autobiografía* (Havana: Imprenta y Papelería de Rambla, Bouza y Ca., 1910), 108.
377 Ricardo Batrell, *Para la historia: Guerra de independencia en la provincia de Matanzas. Apuntes autobiográficos* (Havana: Seone y Alvarez, 1912), 115. Emilio Rodríguez similarly recorded summary executions of captured guerrillas by way of *machetazos*. See Emilio Rodríguez, *En la manigua* (Valparaíso: Imprenta del Universo de G. Helfmann, 1900), 75–76, 143–46.
378 Boza, *Mi diario de la guerra*, 1:67, 2:118.
379 Arbelo, *Recuerdos de la última guerra*, 265–66.

380 Horacio Ferrer, *Con el rifle al hombro* (1950; repubd., Havana: Editorial de Ciencias Sociales, 2002), 88.
381 Ramiro Cabrera, *¡A sitio Herrera!* (Havana: Imprenta y Papelería de Rambla, Bouza y Ca., 1922), 254–55. It happened too that George Musgrave was also present at the capture of Las Tunas: "The bloody guerillas [sic] taken in Las Tunas were tried by court-martial and sixty of them executed. All conscripted Spaniards were spared. The guerilla fiends received no mercy from the Cubans. . . . I think greater clemency might have been exercised. Men avenging the honor and death of wives and sisters at the hands of such brutes may be excused severity, but despite their crime, an execution of sixty at once was demoralizing to the victorious force." See George Clarke Musgrave, *Under Three Flags in Cuba: A Personal Account of the Cuban Insurrection and the Spanish-American War* (Boston, 1899), 198. For a contemporary account of Las Tunas, see Manuel Sanguily, *Victoria de Las Tunas: Bosquejo del asalto y toma de Las Tunas de Bayamo en agosto de 1897 por fuerzas cubanas al mando del mayor-general Calixto García Iñiguez* (New York, 1897).
382 Funston, *Memories of Two Wars*, 92–93. Grover Flint recounted a similar experience: "Regular Spanish soldiers are invariably released as a matter of policy; but *guerrilleros* are usually regarded as traitors, and fair game for the machete." See Flint, *Marching with Gomez*, 60.
383 Sánchez, *Julián Sánchez cuenta su vida*, 33.
384 Cabrera, *Episodios de la guerra*, 174. Francisco Estrada y Céspedes recounted the capture of twenty guerrillas in 1876: "They were all killed by way of the machete" (Todos fueron muertos al machete). See Francisco Estrada y Céspedes to Adolfina Céspedes, May 6, 1876, in Ricardo Repilado, ed., *Cartas familiares: Francisco Estrada y Céspedes* (Santiago de Cuba: Imprenta Universitaria/Universidad de Oriente, 1980), 91.
385 Mario Carrillo, *In the Saddle with Gomez* (New York, 1898), 136.
386 Miguel Varona Guerrero, "Máximo Gómez: Generalísimo y libertador," *Diario de la Marina*, October 22, 1922, 37.
387 Valdés Domínguez, *Diario de soldado*, 3:260, 4:177.
388 Valdés Domínguez, *Diario de soldado*, 4:177.
389 Domingo Blanco, "La guerra por dentro," *El Imparcial*, December 29, 1897, 1.
390 Máximo Gómez to Tomás Estrada Palma, July 20, 1897, *Boletín del Archivo Nacional* 30 (1930): 74.
391 Andrés Clemente Vázquez to Ignacio Mariscal, April 25, 1896, in Morales, *Espacios en disputa*, 305–6, 422–23.
392 "Un paso avanzado hacia la unión," *La Epoca*, January 8, 1898, 1.
393 George Leland Dyer to Susan Dyer, September 15, 1897, George Leland Dyer Papers, East Carolina Manuscript Collection, J. Y. Joyner Library, East Carolina University, Greenville, NC.
394 "Respuesta del Sr. Sagasta," *El Imparcial*, May 24, 1897, 1.

395 "Discurso del Sr. Silvela," *El Heraldo de Madrid*, June 13, 1897, 3.
396 "La opinión despertará," *El Imparcial*, June 22, 1897, 1. Reference to constituent assemblies was to the convocation of insurgent congresses in Jimaguayú and La Yaya, both in Camagüey Province.
397 "Los que perserverán," *La Epoca*, June 15, 1897, 1; "La contrarrevolución en Cuba y las Filipinas," *La Epoca*, January 2, 1898, 1; "El único remedio," *El Imparcial*, June 7, 1897, 1.
398 "Comentarios de la redacción: Cuba," *La Correspondencia de España*, June 30, 1897, 1, emphasis in the original.
399 "La guerra de Cuba," *El Heraldo de Madrid*, June 29, 1897, 1.
400 "La elocuencia de los hechos," *El Imparcial*, February 21, 1897, 1.
401 "Elecciones," *El Nuevo Régimen*, January 15, 1898, 1.
402 "Comentarios de la redacción: Cuba," *La Correspondencia de España*, July 7, 1897, 1.
403 See Carlos Ría-Baja, *El desastre filipino: Memorias de un prisionero* (Barcelona, 1899).
404 Carlos García Velez, "Cuaderno manuscrito contenido diarios del General Carlos García Velez, 1950–1960," Fondo Donativos y Remisiones, Número 123 (fuera de caja), ANC.
405 "El dolor más agudo," *El Imparcial*, June 10, 1897, 1.
406 Reverter Delmas, *Cuba española*, 4:430.
407 Domingo Blanco, "La guerra por dentro," *El Imparcial*, December 29, 1897, 1.
408 Fitzhugh Lee to William R. Day, November 17, 1897, Personal Correspondence, General Lee to the Secretary of State, 1897–1898, Moore Papers.
409 *New York World*, March 22, 1897, 7.
410 William B. Barker to William R. Day, June 19, 1897, Despatches from United States Consuls in Sagua la Grande, 1878–1900, DS/RG 59 (hereinafter cited as Despatches/Sagua la Grande).
411 A + B [Manuel Mariano y Vivo], *Apuntes en defensa del honor del ejército*, 95.
412 See *Real decreto de 25 de noviembre de 1897 estableciendo en la Isla de Cuba el régimen autonómico* (Havana, 1898).
413 Rafael Guerrero, *Crónica de la guerra de Cuba y de la rebelión de Filipinas (1895–96–97)* (5 vols., Barcelona, 1895–97), 5:600.
414 On the Autonomist Party, see Rafael Montoro, *El ideal autonomista* (3 vols., Havana, 1936); and Ramón Infiesta, *El autonomismo cubano: Su razón y manera* (Havana: Jesús Montero, 1939).
415 "¿Como va la guerra?," *El Correo Militar*, January 25, 1898, 1.
416 Ortega Rubio, *Historia de la regencia*, 3:186.
417 "Instrucciones al General Blanco," *La Correspondencia Militar*, October 25, 1897, 1.
418 David Sartorius, *Ever Faithful: Race, Loyalty, and the Ends of Empire in Spanish Cuba* (Durham, NC: Duke University Press, 2003), 208.

419 "Alucución del general Blanco," *El Imparcial*, November 1, 1897, 1. *Self-government* appeared in English.
420 See Ramón Blanco, "Al tomar posesión del mando: Habitantes de la Isla de Cuba," *La Correspondencia Militar*, December 1, 1897, 2; Gobierno General de la Isla de Cuba, "Circular," *Gaceta de La Habana* 59 (November 13, 1897): 931.
421 See "Movimiento militar en Cuba: Cambio de destinos," and "Mandos en Cuba," *La Correspondencia Militar*, November 2, 1897, 2.
422 Gobierno General de la Isla de Cuba, "Bando," *Gaceta de La Habana* 59 (November 13, 1897): 931.
423 Gobierno General de la Isla de Cuba, "Bando," *Gaceta de La Habana* 59 (November 14, 1897): 939.
424 Rafael Pérez Vento, *Antes y después de la guerra* (Havana, 1896), 3, 55.
425 Francisco Moreno, *Cuba y su gente* (Madrid, 1887), 139.
426 Fitzhugh Lee to William R. Day, November 17, 1897, Despatches/Havana.
427 Richard Weightman, "Past Abuses in Cuba," *Washington Post*, December 8, 1897, 1, 3.
428 Francisco Pi y Margall, "Cuba," *El Nuevo Régimen*, January 8, 1898, 1.
429 "Crónica política," *Nuevo Mundo* 4 (November 10, 1897): 4.
430 "Venga la paz," *La Epoca*, January 8, 1898, 1; "Regreso a la realidad" *La Epoca*, January 12, 1898, 1; "Más sobre la autonomía," *La Epoca*, January 9, 1898, 1.
431 Guerrero, *Crónica de la guerra de Cuba*, 5:619.
432 José Muñiz de Quevedo, "Clara-Luz: Cuento de la guerra," *La Correspondencia Militar*, December 23, 1897, 1; "Una entrevista con Weyler," *Nuevo Mundo* 4 (December 22, 1897): 13–14.
433 "La nueva era para Cuba," *La Epoca*, October 24, 1897, 1.
434 Fitzhugh Lee to William R. Day, November 17, 1897, Despatches/Havana.
435 "Desordenes en La Habana," *La Epoca*, January 14, 1898, 1.
436 See "El deber del Ejército," *La Correspondencia Militar*, October 27, 1897, 1.
437 *New York Journal*, February 24, 1898, 12.
438 Calixto García to Editor, *New York Journal*, January 5, 1898, 7; Calixto García, "Al Departamento de Oriente," November 1897, in Calixto García, *Palabras de tres guerras* (Havana, 1942), 79–80.
439 Máximo Gómez to Francisco Gregorio Billini, February 6, 1898, in Máximo Gómez, *Papeles dominicanos de Máximo Gómez* (Ciudad Trujillo [Santo Domingo]: Editora Montalvo, 1954), 428–30.
440 "Copia manuscrita y mecanografiada de un diario de campaña, incluye circulares y órdenes emitidas por el General en Jefe Máximo Gómez y José Miguel Gómez," March 16–August 29, 1898, Fondo Donativos y Remisiones, Legajo 602, Número 62, ANC.
441 William B. Barker to William R. Day, October 18, 1897, Despatches/Sagua la Grande.
442 A + B [Manuel Mariano y Vivo], *Apuntes en defensa del honor del ejército*, 96.

443 "El ejército y la autonomía," *La Correspondencia Militar*, March 2, 1898, 1.
444 "Protesta necesaria," *La Correspondencia Militar*, December 8, 1897, 1; "La política del gobierno en Cuba," *La Correspondencia Militar*, December 8, 1897, 3. To criticize "the valiant officers of the Army," *La Correspondencia Militar* warned, "is not only to lie but to insult; it is to stain the dignity of the bravery of the officer corps of the Spanish Army." See "El honor de la Patria y el honor nacional," *La Correspondencia Militar*, January 31, 1898, 2.
445 "Callejón sin salida," *La Correspondencia Militar*, February 7, 1898, 1.
446 "Milicias de Cuba," *El Correo Militar*, December 4, 1897, 1.
447 Domingo Blanco, "Los sucesos de La Habana," January 31, 1898, *El Imparcial*, 1.
448 Andrés Clemente Vázquez to Ignacio Mariscal, December 2, 1897, in Morales, *Espacios en disputa*, 488.
449 "Problemas de la guerra: Caballería a Cuba," *La Correspondencia Militar*, January 5, 1898, 1; "El problema cubano," *La Correspondencia Militar*, November 15, 1897, 3.
450 Serra Orts, *Recuerdos de las guerras de Cuba*, 75, emphasis in original.
451 Alexander C. Brice to William R. Day, November 17, 1897, Despatches from United States Consuls in Matanzas, 1820–1899, DS/RG 59.
452 Máximo Gómez to Tomás Estrada Palma, February 12, 1898, *Boletín del Archivo Nacional* 31 (January–December 1932): 96. Three weeks later, Gómez entered in his field diary: "We fight an enemy that has very little in common with that other enemy under the bloody Weyler." See Gómez, *Diario de campaña*, 402.
453 Fitzhugh Lee to William R. Day, January 8, 1898, Personal Correspondence, General Lee to the Secretary of State, 1897–1898, Moore Papers.
454 "En Cuba y fuera de Cuba," *Diario de la Marina*, September 7, 1872, 2, emphasis in original.
455 "Motín militar en La Habana," *El Heraldo de Cuba*, January 13, 1898, 1; "Lo de La Habana: Responsabilidad," *La Correspondencia Militar*, January 15, 1898, 3; Enrique Piñeyro, *Como acabó la dominación de España en América* (Paris: Garnier Hermanos, 1908), 163–64.
456 "Sedición militar en la Habana," *El País*, January 14, 1898, 1.
457 Conangla I. Fontanilles, *Memorias de mi juventud en Cuba*, 181.
458 "Officers Riot in Havana," *New York Times*, January 13, 1898, 7.
459 See Domingo Blanco, "El motín de La Habana," *El Imparcial*, January 14, 1898, 1; Andrés Clemente Vázquez to Ignacio Mariscal, January 13, 1898, and Andrés Clemente to Ignacio Mariscal, January 17, 1898, in Morales, *Espacios en disputa*, 494–97; María del Carmen Barcia Zequeira, *Una sociedad en crisis: La Habana a final del siglo XIX* (Havana: Editorial de Ciencias Sociales, 2009), 55–77.
460 "Rechazando vergüenza," *La Correspondencia Militar*, January 14, 1898, 1; "La conducta del ejército," *La Correspondencia Militar*, January 17, 1898, 1. *La Correspondencia Militar* attacked autonomy relentlessly as a "humiliation of the nation," an "act of treason," and a "shameful blunder." See "Para Cuba: 50,000

hombres y 200 millones," *La Correspondencia Militar*, November 4, 1897, 1; "Balas y no notas," *La Correspondencia Militar*, November 5, 1897, 1; "La autonomía: Respuesta de los traidores," *La Correspondencia Militar*, November 6, 1897, 1. See also Insua, *Finis*, 33–35.

461 Fitzhugh Lee to William R. Day, January 13, 1898, in *Papers Relating to the Foreign Relations of the United States* (Washington, DC: Government Printing Office, 1901), 1025.

Chapter Four. Neither Victor nor Vanquished

1 John M. Clayton to Daniel M. Barringer, August 2, 1849, in *Diplomatic Correspondence of the United States: Inter-American Affairs*, ed. William R. Manning (12 vols., Washington, DC: Carnegie Endowment for International Peace, 1932–39), 11:69–70. Few US foreign policies in the nineteenth century were sustained with greater continuity than the American position on Cuba. Thomas Jefferson was unequivocal, as early as 1823: "We will oppose, with all our means, the forcible interposition of any other power, as auxiliary, stipendiary, or under any other form or pretext, and most especially, [Cuba's] transfer to any power by conquest, cession, or acquisition in any other way." US Minister to Spain Washington Irving emphasized the "determination" of the United States "to maintain Spain in the possession of Cuba by force of arms, if necessary, and to consider it a cause of war for any other power to attempt to possess itself of the Island." Fearing in 1840 that a new cabinet in Spain had "lost sight of" US interests, Secretary of State John Forsyth instructed the American chargé d'affaires in Madrid to communicate a warning to the new Spanish government: "Should you have reason to suspect any design on the part of Spain to transfer voluntarily her title to the island, whether of ownership or possession, and whether permanent or temporary, to ... any other power, you will distinctly state that the U[nited] States will prevent it, at all hazard." Another warning was issued ten years later. "[The US] government," the US minister in Madrid assured Spanish authorities, "is resolutely determined that the Island of Cuba should never be in the possession of any other power than that of Spain or the United States." See Thomas Jefferson to James Monroe, October 24, 1823, in *The Works of Thomas Jefferson*, ed. H. A. Washington (9 vols., New York, 1884), 7:37; and in Manning, *Diplomatic Correspondence of the United States*: Washington Irving to Abel P. Upshur, March 2, 1854, 11:335; John Forsyth to Aaron Vail, July 15, 1840, 11:23–24; Daniel M. Barringer to John M. Clayton, June 19, 1850, 11:506.

2 US consular agents across the island informed Washington that autonomy had failed. See Pulaski F. Hyatt to William R. Day, February 1, 1898, Despatches from United States Consuls in Santiago de Cuba, 1799–1906, Record Group 59, General Records of the Department of State, National Archives, Washington,

DC (hereinafter cited as DS/RG 59); Walter B. Barker to William R. Day, November 11, 1897, Despatches from United States Consuls in Sagua la Grande, 1878–1900, DS/RG 59; Fitzhugh Lee to William R. Day, March 14, 1898, Despatches from United States Consuls in Havana, 1783–1906, DS/RG 59. The Department of State had arrived at this conclusion in early 1898: "There are no active operations by the Spaniards," Secretary of State William Day reported. "It is now evident that Spain's struggle in Cuba has become absolutely hopeless.... Spain is exhausted financially and physically, while the Cubans are stronger." See "Recognition of Independence," n.d., William Day Papers, Manuscript Division, Library of Congress, Washington, DC.

3 31 *Congressional Record* 3699, 3701 (1898). Different modes of intervention in Cuba had been under discussion as early as August 1897. See Alvey A. Adee to John Sherman, August 19, 1897, William McKinley Papers, Manuscript Collection, Library of Congress, Washington, DC.

4 William McKinley to John R. Brooke, December 22, 1898, John R. Brooke Papers, Pennsylvania Historical Society, Philadelphia, Pennsylvania.

5 "Shafter's Opinion of Cubans," *New York Times*, December 19, 1898, 2.

6 "Cosas de Cuba," 1899, File 294/24, Records of the Bureau of Insular Affairs, Record Group 350, National Archives, Washington, DC (hereinafter cited as BIA/RG 350).

7 Franklin Matthews, *The New-Born Cuba* (New York, 1899), 42.

8 "Statement of Marquis de Apezteguia," September 9, 1898, in US Department of Treasury, *Appendix to the Report on the Commercial and Industrial Condition of the Island of Cuba* (Washington, DC, 1899), 232.

9 The specter of Haiti was very much in the official US imagination. Cuban independence was unthinkable, US Minister in Spain Stewart Woodford warned President McKinley as Spanish sovereignty waned in early 1898, and could "only result in a continuous war of races, and ... this means that independent Cuba must be a second Santo Domingo," leading to a government "supported by the great majority of the blacks" and inevitably resulting in "disorder, insecurity of persons and destruction of property." General Leonard Wood feared that independence would result in "the establishment of another Haitian Republic in the West Indies." The "agitators in Cuba," scorned General Daniel Sickles, "who are clamoring for what they call independence, if allowed to have their own way, will make Cuba another Haiti." See Stewart L. Woodford to William McKinley, March 9, 1898, Despatches from United States Consuls to Spain, 1792–1906, DS/RG 59; Stewart L. Woodford to William McKinley, March 17, 1898, Private Correspondence, and General Woodford to the President, August 1897 to May 1898, John Bassett Moore Papers, Manuscript Division, Library of Congress, Washington, DC; "Gen. Wood on the Cubans," *New York Times*, June 24, 1899, 1; "Gen. Sickles's Views of Cuban Conditions," *New York Times*, May 5, 1901, 12.

10 Emilio Roig de Leuchsenring, *Los Estados Unidos contra Cuba Libre* (2 vols., Havana Editorial Oriente, 1959), 2:34.
11 Enrique José Varona, "1868–1898," *Patria*, October 10, 1898, 1.
12 Fermín Valdés Domínguez, *Diario de soldado*, ed. Hiram Dupotey Fideaux (4 vols., Havana: Universidad de La Habana, 1973), 2:49.
13 For accounts of Cuban executions, see "Fusilados en La Habana: Fortaleza de la Cabaña," and "Fusilados en Matanzas," *Cuba y América* 3 (September 5, 1899): 18–19. On deportations, see Francisco Javier Balmaseda, *Los confinados a Fernando Póo, e impresiones de un viaje a Guinea* (New York, 1869); F. Tarrida del Marmol, "Los cubanos en el presidio de Ceuta," *Revista de Cayo Hueso* 1 (July 18, 1897): 3–4; Emilio Valdés Infante, *Cubanos en Fernando Póo; horrores de la dominación española* (Havana, 1898); Rafael Caso y Vidal, *Tres años en manos de españoles* (Matanzas, 1899); Ambrosio Valentín López Hidalgo, *De la Habana a Chafarinas; los cubanos deportados en el vapor Santiago* (Matanzas: Imprenta y Librería Galería Literaria, 1900); Manuel María Miranda, *Memorias de un deportado* (Havana: Imprenta La Luz, 1903); Pablo de la Concepción, *Prisioneros y deportados cubanos 1895–1898 en la Guerra de Independencia* (Havana: Imprenta P. Fernández y Cia., 1932); María del Carmen Barcia, "Los deportados de la guerra: Cuba 1895–1898," in Consuelo Naranjo Orovio et al., *La nación soñada: Cuba, Puerto Rico y Filipinas ante el 98* (Madrid: Doce Calles, 1996), 635–46; Juan Luis Bachero, "La deportación en la guerra cubana de los diez años (1868–1878)," *Cuban Studies* 50 (2021): 207–29.
14 Ismael Sarmiento Ramírez, "Visión en la sociedad antillana de la separación de España: La actitud de españoles y cubanos durante la guerra de Cuba," *Anales del Museo de América* 8 (1998): 31.
15 Camilo G. Polavieja to Ramón Blanco, June 4, 1879, in Camilo G. Polavieja, *Relación documentada de mi política en Cuba: Lo que ví, lo que hice, lo que anuncié* (Madrid, 1898), 32–34.
16 *La Correspondencia Militar*'s editorial appeared in "Conformes," *El Motín*, March 28, 1896, 3.
17 "Situation in Cuba," *London Times*, October 15, 1897, 4.
18 Juan Arnao, *Páginas para la historia de la Isla de Cuba* (Havana: Imprenta "La Nueva," 1900), 265.
19 Juan Jorge Sobrado y Martínez, *Recuerdos de la guerra*, ed. Alfredo Pérez Portal (Remedios, 1898), 11.
20 Andrés Clemente Vázquez to Ministry of Foreign Affairs, August 17, 1898, in *Espacios en disputa: México y la independencia de Cuba*, ed. Salvador E. Morales (Mexico City: Centro de Investigación Científica "Ing. Jorge L. Tamayo," 1998), 512.
21 See John Lawrence Tone, *War and Genocide in Cuba, 1895–1898* (Chapel Hill: University of North Carolina Press, 2006).
22 See Pablo L. Rousseau, *Cuestiones generales; colección de artículos sobre asuntos sociales, económicos y de educación* (Cienfuegos: Imprenta Mestre, Sta.

Cruz y S. Luis, 1902), 45; J. Just Lloret, *Criminalogía de los gobiernos españoles: Estudio político-social* (Barcelona: Ramón Pujol, 1906), 127–33. General Carlos Velez would recall the "ferocious war yells of the Spaniards: 'Exterminio de los cubanos!'" See Carlos García Velez, "Cuba against Spain, 1895–1898," in *The American-Spanish War: A History Told by the War Leaders* (Norwich, CT, 1899), 47.

23 Máximo Gómez, *Diario de campaña del Mayor General Máximo Gómez* (Havana: Comisión del Archivo de Máximo Gómez 1941), 424.

24 "Confidential Report: Province of Santiago de Cuba," n.d., Records of the Post Office Department, Record Group 28, National Archives, Washington, DC; *La Lucha*, April 11, 1899, 2; *La Discusión*, September 23, 1900, 1.

25 Serafín Espinosa y Ramos, *Al trote y sin estribos.(Recuerdos de la guerra de independencia)* (Havana: Jesús Montero, 1946), 282, emphasis in original.

26 Henry Corbin to Francis V. Greene, December 5, 1898, File 243553, Records of the Adjutant General's Office, 1780s–1917, Record Group 94, National Archives, Washington, DC.

27 Francisco E. Silva, *Al pueblo de Cuba. Grito de alerta: Folleto político contra los autonomistas* (Havana: Imprenta "La Independencia," 1900), 3. In Las Villas, General José de J. Monteagudo complained that the Americans were acting "on the advice of the intransigent Spaniards and American planters in Cienfuegos" and appointed former guerrillas to local government positions. See José de J. Monteagudo to Gonzalo de Quesada, February 17, 1899, in *Archivo de Gonzalo de Quesada: Epistolario*, ed. Gonzalo de Quesada y Miranda (2 vols., Havana: Imprenta "El Siglo XX," 1948–51), 2:90–92.

28 Manuel Secades Japón, *Episodios de un estudiante en la guerra de independencia de Cuba* (1958; Miami: San Lázaro Printing, 1997), 8.

29 Manuel Arbelo, *Recuerdos de la última guerra por la independencia de Cuba, 1896–1898* (Havana: Imp. "Tipografía Moderna," , 1918), 304.

30 Erna Ferguson, *Cuba* (New York: Alfred A. Knopf, 1946), 148.

31 Santiago C. Rey, *Recuerdos de la guerra: 1895–1898* (Havana: Imprenta P. Fernández, 1931), 54.

32 US War Department, *Informe sobre el censo de Cuba, 1899* (Washington, DC: Government Printing Office, 1900), 104; José Antonio Vidal Rodríguez, "La inmigración española en Cuba durante la primera ocupación militar norteamericana (1899–1902): El control del mercado laboral," *Migraciones y Exilios* 4 (2004): 31–49; Jordi Maluquer de Motes, *Nación e inmigración: Los españoles en Cuba (ss. XIX y XX)* (Oviedo: Ediciones Jucar, 1992), 108–10; Manuel Villanova, "Españoles y cubanos," *Revista Cubana* 10 (1889): 83–86.

33 In fact, the Spanish presence in Cuba continued to expand. Many tens of thousands of Spaniards immigrated to Cuba, including an estimated 55,000 Spaniards between 1899 and 1902 and a total of 550,000 Spaniards between 1902 and 1920. Vast swaths of the economy remained in the possession of Spaniards, including commerce, retail trade, import-export, industry, and

manufacturing. "In many respects," A. Hyatt Verrill wrote as late as 1931, "the Spaniards control Cuba more completely today than when the island was a colony of Spain." See Cuba, Secretaría de Hacienda, Sección de Estadística, *Inmigración y movimiento de pasajeros*... (Havana: Ministerio de Hacienda, 1902–21); A. Hyatt Verrill, *Cuba of Today* (New York: Dodd, Mead and Company, 1931), 33. See also Maluquer de Motes, *Nación e inmigración*, 108–23.

34 Francisco Cimadevilla, *Labor de los españoles en Cuba* (Madrid: Imprenta de Juan Pueyo, 1921), 58.

35 Oliver Otis Howard, *Fighting for Humanity* (New York, 1898), 198.

36 William Ludlow, "Report of Brigadier General William Ludlow, Commanding Department of Havana and Military Governor of the City of Havana, Cuba," August 1, 1899, in United States War Department, *Annual Reports of the War Department: Report of the Major-General Commanding the Army*, House of Representatives, 56th Congress, 1st Session, House Document No. 2, Ser. 3901 (Washington, DC, 1899), 217.

37 "Terms of Military Convention," July 16, 1898, in *Correspondence Relating to the War with Spain and Conditions Growing Out of the Same* (2 vols., Washington, DC: Government Printing Office, 1902), 1:152, 154; Emilio Bacardí Moreau, *Crónicas de Santiago de Cuba* (10 vols., 2nd ed., Madrid: Graf. Breogán, 1972–73), 10:99–100. See also Maluquer de Motes, *Nación e inmigración*, 97–99.

38 *Hearing before the Committee on Relations with Cuba: Statement of Maj. Gen. John R. Brooke, January 29, 1900* (Washington, DC: Government Printing Office, 1900), 9.

39 Aurea Matilde Fernández Muñiz, "La presencia española en Cuba después de 1898: Su reflejo en el *Diario de la Marina*," in Naranjo Orovio et al., *La nación soñada*, 509, 511.

40 See Edwin F. Atkins, "The Spaniards of the Island of Cuba," *Economic Bulletin of Cuba* 1 (March 1922): 133–34.

41 Charles M. Pepper, *Tomorrow in Cuba* (New York, 1899), 169.

42 James Harrison Wilson to Goldwin Smith, March 3, 1899, General Correspondence, James Harrison Wilson Papers, Manuscript Division, Library of Congress, Washington, DC. To concede independence without security for Spaniards, US planter Walter Beal cautioned in late 1898, would see *peninsulares* "retire en masse to Spain, not having any faith in the Cubans as a governing power"—and with disastrous results: "The whole backbone of Cuba is centered in the Spaniards, and if they leave the island the backbone of Cuba is gone." "Statement of Walter G. Beal, of Boston, Mass.," in Robert P. Porter, *Report on the Industrial and Commercial Condition of the Island of Cuba* (Washington, DC, 1898), 262, 264.

43 "Notes of Conversation between General Maximo Gomez and March John Kennon," March 5, 1899, Brooke Papers.

44 Mayo W. Hazeltine, "What Is to Be Done with Cuba," *North American Review* 167 (September 1898): 322.

45 See US Department of War, Office of the Census, *Informe sobre el censo de Cuba, 1899* (Washington, DC: Government Printing Office, 1900), 210–27; "El censo de Cuba," *Diario de la Marina*, April 21, 1900, 4; "El censo," *Diario de la Marina*, April 22, 1900, 2.

46 Manuel Sanguily, "Un insurrecto cubano en la corte," *Revista Cubana* 8 (1885): 390. See also Manuel Sanguily, "Diario de Manuel Sanguily, desde agosto 19 de 1896 al 29 de diciembre de 1897," Fondo Donativos, Caja 86, Número 152, Archivo Nacional de Cuba.

47 Valdés Domínguez, *Diario de soldado*, 1:47.

48 Rafael M. Merchán, "A la abolición de la esclavitud en la isla de Cuba," *El Repertorio Colombiano* 13 (February 1887): 495.

49 Raimundo Cabrera, *Episodios de la guerra: Mi vida en la manigua (Relato del Coronel Ricardo Buenamar)* (3rd ed., Philadelphia, 1898), 142; Julián Sánchez, *Julián Sánchez cuenta su vida*, ed. Erasmo Dumpierre (Havana: Instituto del Libro, 1970), 48, 50. See also Julio Rosas, *Mi odio a España* (Key West, FL, 1897).

50 Tomás Basail, *En poder de los españoles* (Sagua la Grande, 1898), 7, 9.

51 Tomás Justiz y del Valle, *El suicida* (Havana: Imprenta de "Cuba Intelectual," 1912), 198.

52 Samuel Hazard, *Cuba with Pen and Pencil* (Hartford, 1871), 553.

53 Antonio C. Gallenga, *The Pearl of the Antilles* (London, 1873), 39; James J. O'Kelly, *The Mambi-Land, or Adventures of a Herald Correspondent in Cuba* (Philadelphia, 1874), 94. "Hatred to Spain seems to be imbibed in the air of Cuba," George Musgrave recalled of his time among the *mambises*. See George Clarke Musgrave, *Under Three Flags in Cuba: A Personal Account of the Cuban Insurrection and the Spanish-American War* (Boston, 1899), 76.

54 Francisco Moreno, *Cuba y su gente* (Madrid, 1887), 139, 188.

55 Enrique Donderis, *La cuestión de Cuba por un español* (New York, 1876), 25.

56 Justo Zaragoza, *Las insurrecciones de Cuba: Apuntes para la historia política de esta isla en el presente siglo* (2 vols., Madrid, 1872–73), 2:340.

57 Arsenio Martínez Campos to Antonio Cánovas de Castillo, July 25, 1895, in Carlos O'Donnell y Abreu, *Apuntes del ex-Ministro de Estado Duque de Tetuán para la defensa de la política internacional y gestión diplomática del gobierno Liberal-Conservador* (2 vols., Madrid: Tipografía de R. Péant, 1902), 2:115–17. See Arsenio Martínez Campos to Tomás Castellanos, June 29, 1895, in "Cartas y telegramas remitidos por el Capitán General de Cuba, Arsenio Martínez Campos al Ministro de Ultramar, Tomás Castellanos (junio 1895–enero 1896)," in *España en Cuba: Final del siglo*, ed. José Cayuela Fernández (Zaragoza: Institución Fernando el Católico, 2000), 42.

58 Polavieja, *Relación documentada de mi política en Cuba*, 115.

59 US Congress, Senate, Committee on Relations with Cuba, *Affairs in Cuba*, 56th Congress, 2nd Session, Document No. 224, Ser. 3425 (Washington, DC: Government Printing Office, 1900), 10–11.

60 Leonard Wood, "Special Report of Brig. Gen. Leonard Wood, U.S.V., Commanding the Department of Santiago and Puerto Principe," September 20, 1899, in John R. Brooke, *Civil Report of Major-General John R. Brooke, U.S. Army, Military Governor, Island of Cuba* (Washington, DC: Government Printing Office, 1900), 367.
61 "Carta de La Habana," *Patria*, October 22, 1898, 2, 3.
62 Manuel Piedra Martel, *Mis primeros treinta años: Memorias* (Havana: Minerva, 1945), 357.
63 Pepper, *Tomorrow in Cuba*, 170.
64 "Special Report of Brig. Gen. James H. Wilson, U.S.V., Commanding the Department of Matanzas and Santa Clara, on the Industrial, Economic, and Social Conditions Existing in the Department at the Date of the American Occupation and at the Present Time," September 7, 1899, in Brooke, *Civil Report of Major-General John R. Brooke*, 330.
65 Ramón Corona, "Saludos a los congresistas," in Congreso Nacional de Historia, *Historia y americanidad: Cuarto Congreso Nacional de Historia* (Havana: Municipio de La Habana, 1946), 17.
66 Among the final deeds of Spanish sovereignty was a general amnesty extended to all members of the Voluntarios "for any and all charges of crime resulting from military operations. See "Bando de indulto," *El Correo Militar*, January 5, 1899, 2.
67 "Conflicto en Santiago," *La Epoca*, December 20, 1898, 2.
68 "Contra ira, prudencia," *Diario de la Marina*, September 26, 1899, 4; "La bandera," *Diario de la Marina*, October 5, 1899, 3.
69 "Un motín," *La Epoca*, January 31, 1899, 2.
70 "La bandera española prohibida," *Diario de la Marina*, October 6, 1899, 1.
71 "La bandera y el cónsul," *Diario de la Marina*, October 8, 1899, 2.
72 "Spaniards Leaving Cuba," *New York Times*, December 19, 1898, 7; "La situación en la Habana," *La Correspondencia de España*, December 24, 1898, 2.
73 "Los españoles en Cuba," *La Correspondencia Militar*, September 29, 1898, 2; "Carta de Cuba," *La Correspondencia Militar*, December 17, 1898, 2. "Life was being made unsafe for Spanish residents in Cuba," *Diario de la Marina* similarly warned on September 8, 1898, 2.
74 Alejandro García Alvarez and Consuelo Naranjo Orovio, "Cubanos y españoles después del 98: De la confrontación a la convivencia pacífica," *Revista de Indias* 58 (1998): 102–29.
75 Emilio Núñez, "Los españoles en Cuba Libre," *Patria*, September 28, 1898, 3.
76 Luis de Radillo y Rodríguez, *Autobiografía del cubano Luis de Radillo y Rodríguez, o episodios de su vida histórico-político revolucionario* (Havana, 1899), 2. See Avelino Sanjenis, *Memorias de la revolución de 1895 por la independencia de Cuba* (Havana: Imprenta y Papelería de Rambla, Bouza y Ca., 1913), 319.
77 Alvaro Catá, *Cuba y la intervención: Folleto político* (Havana, 1899), 10–11.

78 Frederic Remington, "Under Which King," in *The Collected Writings of Frederic Remington*, ed. Peggy Samuels and Harold Samuels (Garden City, NY: Doubleday, 1979), 358.

79 William R. Shafter to Henry C. Corbin, August 22, 1898, in *Correspondence Relating to the War with Spain*, 1:248.

80 Antonio Serra Orts, *Recuerdos de las guerras de Cuba: 1868 á 1898* (Santa Cruz de Tenerife: A. J. Benítez, 1908), 87. Among the few Cuban guerrillas who returned to Spain were Gregorio Cárdenas Urrutia, José Esnal Gutiérrez, and Andrés Valdés, who were properly celebrated as heroes of *la madre patria*. See "Tres valientes," *Nuevo Mundo* 5 (October 12, 1898): 13. A number of guerrilla officers emigrated to Spain, thereupon to appeal for compensation and pensions. See "Los oficiales de las *guerrillas*," *El Correo Militar*, November 22, 1898, 2; and "Voluntarios y guerrilleros," *El Correo Militar*, February 2, 1899, 2.

81 Secades Japón, *Episodios de un estudiante en la guerra*, 265–66.

82 Matías Duque, *El comandante Antonio Duque* (Havana: Imprenta y Papelería de Rambla, Bouza y Ca., 1928), 33–34.

83 "Remisión de armamentos de las guerrillas de distintos localidad de la provincia de La Habana durante el mes de noviembre de 1898"; and Colonel Luis Fontana to Captain General, November 5, 1898; and Comandante Martín Fostola to Captain General, November 12, 1898; and José Valle to Captain General, November 11, 1898; and Comandante Alfredo Martínez to Captain General, November 11, 1898, all in Fondo Asuntos Políticos, Legajo 238, Número 23, Archivo Nacional de Cuba, Havana, Cuba; "Los movilizados," *La Lucha*, October 8, 1898, 2. The *tercio* unit of guerrillas of Cienfuegos demobilized without payment of back wages that had accrued during the final months of the war. In many instances, former guerrillas refused to disarm, fearful of finding themselves unarmed and at the mercy of former *insurrectos*, and sought refuge in the *manigua* and *monte*, to live life outside the law. The former guerrillas, Major John Logan wrote from Santa Clara as early as February 1899, have "no recourse but to turn to brigandage in order that their very existence be secured, as well as for subsistence." See Major John A. Logan to Adjutant General, Department of Santa Clara, February 3, 1899, File 294/11, BIA/RG 350. See also Serra Orts, *Recuerdos de las guerras de Cuba*, 86–87.

84 Avelino Sanjenis, *Mis cartas: Memorias de la revolución de 1895 por la independencia de Cuba* (Havana: Imprenta "El Comercio," 1900), 351.

85 Richard H. Wilson, "Richard H. Wilson's Part in the Spanish American War," unpublished ms., Richard H. Wilson Papers, American Heritage Collection, University of Wyoming, Laramie.

86 Major John A. Logan to Adjutant General, Department of Santa Clara, February 3, 1899, File 294/11, BIA/RG 350.

87 Juan Jorge Sobrado y Martínez, "A guerrillero," in *Recuerdos de la guerra*, 11.

88 Octavio Avelino Delgado, "The Spanish Army in Cuba, 1868–1898: An Institutional Study" (2 vols., PhD diss., Columbia University, 1980), 1:275.
89 Espinosa y Ramos, *Al trote y sin estribos*, 276.
90 Carlos Montenegro, "El negro Torcuato," in Carlos Montenegro, *Dos barcos* (Havana: Ediciones Sábado, 1934), 164.
91 Adolfo J. Castellanos to John Brooke, January 16, 1899, File 58, Records of the Military Government of Cuba, Record Group 140, National Archives, Washington, DC.
92 "El capitán Carvajal," *El Correo Militar*, January 11, 1899, 2.
93 "Sic nos non vobis," *La Lucha*, May 18, 1901, 5.
94 *Diario de la Marina*, September 8, 1899, 2.
95 "Spanish Life Unsafe in the Capital," *Diario de la Marina*, September 8, 1899, 2.
96 "Reyerta en Managua: Un muerto," *La Lucha*, July 20, 1903, 2.
97 "El guerrillero Villa," *La Lucha*, November 3, 1905, 2.
98 Bacardí Moreau, *Crónicas de Santiago de Cuba*, 10:203.
99 "Mob Pursues a Guerrilla," *New York Times*, November 10, 1898, 7.
100 "Impasibles," *Diario de la Marina*, September 9, 1899, 2; "Cuba Lynch Law Menaces Foreign Life," *Diario de la Marina*, September 8, 1899, 4. See also "De Alquizar: Asesinato frustrado," *La Lucha*, February 19, 1906, 2. English language used in original.
101 See "Editorial," *Diario de la Marina*, September 12, 1899, 1; "Via-Crucis," *Diario de la Marina*, September 15, 1899, 4; "Get Out of Town or You'll Be Lynched!," *Diario de la Marina*, September 29, 1899, 3; "De Caibarién," *Diario de la Marina*, May 30, 1901, 2; "Impresiones de la isla," *La Lucha*, October 3, 1902, 2; "De provincia," *Diario de la Marina*, November 4, 1904, 3; "Los crímenes de Cruces," *La Lucha*, July 4, 1904, 3; "El asesinato de Sagua," *La Lucha*, February 16, 1905, 1; "Baturrillo: La cuestión palpitante," *Diario de la Marina*, October 31, 1911, 1–2.
102 José Sixto de Sola, "El pesimismo cubano," *Cuba Contemporánea* 3 (December 1913): 275.
103 Opponents of the US military occupation often threatened to return to the *manigua* to fight the United States. "In case of a conflict," warned one Cuban officer, "we would not only have to fight Americans, who number eighty millions. Our own countrymen, thousands of them, unhesitatingly fought with Spain for the sake of mere rations, and they would certainly offer themselves today, when sure of receiving sound dollars, to the American government, which would not hesitate to utilize the former guerrillas." See "The Questions of the Day," *La Lucha*, January 9, 1901, 7.
104 Carlos García Velez, "Prólogo a la 1ra Edición," in Aníbal Escalante, *Calixto García: Su campaña en el 95* (3rd ed., Havana: Editorial de Ciencias Sociales, 2001), xxiii–xxiv.
105 Esteban Montejo, *Biografía de un cimarrón*, ed. Miguel Barnet (Havana: Instituto de Ethnología y Folklore, 1966), 199–200, 201.

106 Ferrer, *Con el rifle al hombro* (Havana: Imprenta "El Siglo XX," 1950), 136, 140.
107 Cuba, Congreso Nacional de Historia, "Acta Final: Declaración de Principios," in *Tercer Congreso Nacional de Historia: La colonia hacia la nación* (Havana: Municipio de La Habana, 1946), 66.
108 Consejo Nacional de la Asociación de Veteranos de la Independencia, "Los Veteranos de la Independencia, al pueblo de Cuba," January 29, 1910, in *La justicia en Cuba: Patriotas y traidores*, ed. Manuel Secades Japón and Horacio Díaz Pardo (2 vols., Havana: P. Fernández, 1912), 1:49.
109 See Consejo Territorial de Matanzas, *Institución Asociación de Veteranos de la Independencia de Cuba: Reglamento interior del Consejo Territorial de Matanzas* (Matanzas, 1899).
110 Salvador Cisneros Betancourt et al., "Ni desunidos, ni dispersos," *El Veterano* 2 (January 16, 1910): 8. "Los Veteranos de la Independencia, al pueblo de Cuba," October 28, 1911, in Secades Japón and Díaz Pardo, *La justicia en Cuba*, 1:60; Jorge Mañach, "Respuesta a los veteranos," *Bohemia* 44 (April 6, 1952): 51.
111 "Los Veteranos de la Independencia, al pueblo de Cuba," January 29, 1910, in Secades Japón and Díaz Pardo, *La justicia en Cuba*, 1:49–50.
112 "Los Veteranos de la Independencia al Pueblo de Cuba," January 29, 1910, in Secades Japón and Díaz Pardo, *La justicia en Cuba*, 1:46–49.
113 See "Los guerrilleros y el senado: Modificación de la Ley del Servicio Civil," November 10, 1911, in Secades Japón and Díaz Pardo, *La justicia en Cuba*, 1:66–67.
114 Cosme de la Torriente, *La campaña de los veteranos: El problema de actualidad* (Havana: Imprenta y Papelería de Rambla, Bouza y Ca., 1911), 7.
115 "Excesos y peligros," *Diario de la Marina*, August 16, 1902, 2.
116 "De Santiago de Las Vegas," *La Lucha*, April 30, 1906, 2.
117 "El General Loinaz se separa del Dr. Eusebio Hernández," *La Lucha*, November 17, 1911, 3.
118 See "De Santiago de las Vegas," *La Lucha*, May 1, 1906, 4; "El candidato conservador fue guerrillero," *La Lucha*, July 21, 1908, 5.
119 "De Sta. Isabel de Las Lajas," *La Lucha*, June 28, 1906, 5.
120 Angel E. Rosende y de Zayas, *De nuestras memorias de la guerra, 1895–1898: Conspirador y de soldado a capitán* (Havana: n.p., 1928), 22–23.
121 Emilio Núñez, "Consejo Nacional de Veteranos de la Independencia," November 21, 1911, in Secades Japón and Díaz Pardo, *La justicia en Cuba*, 1:90; "Consejo Nacional de Veteranos de la Independencia," *El Mundo*, November 22, 1911, 1.
122 Luis Rodolfo Miranda, *Reminiscencias cubanas de la guerra y de la paz* (Havana: Fernández y Cía, 1941), 283–84.
123 "Colonel Aranda Talks," *La Lucha*, February 19, 1912, 7; "Del coronel Aranda," *El Mundo*, November 16, 1913, 12.

124 "Los veteranos de la independencia, al pueblo cubano," 1911, in Secades Japón and Díaz Pardo, *La justicia en Cuba*, 2:115. All through the 1910s, the Veteranos continued to identify public officeholders with guerrilla antecedents and demanding—and obtaining—their expulsion. See "La campaña de los veteranos," *La Lucha*, October 21, 1911, 1.

125 Emilio Roig de Leuchsenring, "Función social del historiador," in Congreso Nacional de Historia, *Historia y americanidad: Cuarto Congreso Nacional de Historia* (Havana: Municipio de La Habana, 1946), 43.

126 "Los anticubanos," *Patria*, September 24, 1898, 2.

127 Escalante Beatón, *Calixto García: Su campaña en el 95* (Havana: Editorial de Ciencias Sociales, 1978), 680.

128 See Calixto García, "Manifiesto del Comité Revolucionario Cubano," October 1878, in Archivo Nacional de Cuba, *Documentos para servir a la historia de la Guerra Chiquita* (3 vols., Havana: Archivo Nacional de Cuba, 1949), 1:43; Carlos Manuel de Céspedes to Ana de Quesada, February 10, 1874, in Carlos Manuel de Céspedes, *Cartas de Carlos M. de Céspedes a su esposa Ana de Quesada* (Havana: Comisión Nacional de la Academia de Ciencias de la República de Cuba, 1964), 205; Luis Quintero, "Unión—Patriotismo," *El Pueblo*, October 13, 1875, 2; José A. López, "Nuestro deber," *La Nueva República* 1 (July 3, 1897): 10; Valdés Domínguez, *Diario de soldado*, 1:470; "A la memoria de los mártires cubanos," *El Republicano*, October 17, 1874, 3; "Discurso pronunciado por José Martí en el Steck Hall de la Ciudad de New York," January 24, 1880, in Archivo Nacional de Cuba, *Documentos para servir a la historia de la Guerra Chiquita*, 3:96; Antonio Maceo to Camilo Polavieja, May 16, 1891, in Antonio Maceo, *Antonio Maceo, ideología política: Cartas y otros documentos* (2 vols., Havana: Editorial de Ciencias Sociales, 1998), 1:155; Diego Vicente Tejera, "Anexionistas y autonomistas," November 14, 1897, in Diego Vicente Tejera, *Textos escogidos*, ed. Carlos del Toro (Havana: Editorial de Ciencias Sociales, 1981), 150, 154, 157.

129 José Isabel Herrera, *Impresiones de la guerra de independencia* (Havana: Editorial de Ciencias Sociales, 2005), 234.

130 Valdés Domínguez, *Diario de soldado*, 1:237.

131 "La concordia," *Maceo: Semanario Político Independiente* 1 (October 27, 1898): 7.

132 "Los veteranos: Carta del General Riva," *Diario de la Marina*, November 14, 1911, 3-4.

133 "Que se entiende por guerrillero," *Diario de la Marina*, December 5, 1911, 1, emphasis in original.

134 Emilio Laurent, *De oficial a revolucionario* (Havana: Ucar Garcia y Cía., 1941), 37.

135 Argelio Santiesteban, *El habla popular cubana de hoy* (Havana: Editorial de Ciencias Sociales, 1997), 18.

136 José Sánchez-Boudy, *Diccionario mayor de cubanismos* (Miami: Ediciones Universal, 1999), 343.

137 Carlos Loveira, *Los inmorales* (Havana: Sociedad Editorial Cuba Contemporánae, 1919), 210.
138 "La guerrilla," in *La nueva lira criolla* (Havana: La Moderna Poesía, 1918), 23.
139 "Los guerrilleros cubanos asesinos de mujeres y ancianos," in *La nueva lira criolla*, 51–52.
140 Angel Rosende y de Zayas, *Con sombrero de yagua* (Havana: Molina, 1932), 53.
141 Sobrado y Martínez, "A guerrillero," 44.
142 "Los guerrilleros del rancho," in *Poetas guajiros: Colección de poesías recopiladas por un vueltabajero* (Havana: Imprenta y Librería "Canelo," 1904), 66.
143 "Respuesta de una cubana pretendida por un guerrillero al servicio de España," in Samuel Feijóo, ed., *Cuarteta y décima* (Havana: Editorial Letras Cubanas, 1980), 111.
144 "A un guerrillero: ¿Dónde tú te meterás?," in Feijóo, *Cuarteta y décima*, 126.
145 Lesbia Soravilla, *Cuando libertan los esclavos* (Havana: Editorial Cultura, 1936), 88.
146 Jesús Castellanos, *La manigua sentimental* (Havana: Imprenta de A. Miranda, 1910), 18–19.
147 Guillermo Schweyer Lamar, "La gallina negra," *El Fígaro* 16 (May 20, 1900): 234.
148 Loveira, *Los inmorales*, 190.
149 Carlos Loveira, *Generales y doctores* (Havana: Sociedad Editorial Cuba Contemporánea, 1920), 286.
150 Antonio Penichet, *¡Alma rebelde!* (Havana: Imprenta "El Deal" de la Federación de Torcedores, 1921), 10, 17.
151 Arturo Montori, *El tormento de vivir* (Havana: Imprenta y Papelería "La Propagandista," 1923), 92.
152 Jesús Masdeu, *La raza triste* (Havana: Imprenta y Papelería de Rambla, Bouza y Ca., 1924), 135.
153 Jesús del Calvario, "Su regalo," *Bohemia* 27 (June 9, 1935): 8–9, 65.
154 "El capitán mambí ó libertadores y guerrilleros," *El Mundo*, January 24, 1914, 5; "Vida teatral," *El Mundo*, February 9, 1914, 5; Enrique Díaz Quesada, dir., *El capitán mambí o Libertadores y guerrilleros*, EcuRed, accessed February 20, 2023, https://www.ecured.cu/El_capit%C3%A1n_mamb%C3%AD_o_Libertadores_y_guerrilleros.
155 Rafael Conte, "Mi último artículo de sport," *El Mundo*, February 28, 1912, 12.
156 Ernesto Che Guevara, "La guerra de guerrillas," in *Ernesto Che Guevara: Obra revolucionario*, ed. Roberto Fernández Retamar (2nd ed., Mexico City: Ediciones Era, 1968), 47.
157 "A los 52 años: La posición de *Bohemia*," *Bohemia* 52 (May 22, 1960): 52.

Index

Abbot, Abiel, 14, 25–26
abolition of slavery, 4, 16, 27, 37–38, 45, 90
accountability, 177–79, 190
Acosta y Albear, Francisco de, 43–44, 65, 69–71, 89, 224n254; on guerrillas, 85, 88, 95
Agramonte, Ignacio, 2
agriculture, 11, 19, 22, 50, 81, 85, 131; coffee, 13–14, 21, 89, 108, 217n100; tobacco, 14, 108, 114, 130. *See also* plantations; sugar/sugar estates
Agüero, Joaquín de, 32
Ahumada y Centurión, José, 11, 18, 28
Alamán, Lucas, 15
Alcalá Galiano, Dionisio, 17, 24, 38, 45–46
Alcolea García, Gabriel, 130
Aldama, Domingo de, 28
Aldama, Miguel de, 20, 27–29, 53
aldea, 44, 70, 212n23
Alfonso, José Luis, 4, 31
Alfonso, Pedro Antonio, 28
Almansa, Juan de, 51
Alvarez Pérez, José, 65–66, 89
Alzola, Pablo, 125
Amblard, Arturo, 106, 243n277
ammunition, 22–23, 33, 43–44, 61–62, 74, 81–82, 107, 115
amnesty, 91–92, 96, 155, 163, 186, 259n66
Angulo, Padilla, 207n109

annexation to the United States/annexationism, 3, 5, 31–34, 38, 122, 194
Antomarchi, Baron J., 97
Apezteguía, Julio de, 171
Aranda, Manuel, 189
Arango, Anastasio de, 17, 19, 26
Arango, Augusto, 8
Arango y Parreño, Francisco, 30
Arbelo, Manuel, 104, 155–58, 175
Arboleya, José García de, 198n11
Arderius, José, 111
Armas, Antonio de, 8
Armenteros, Isidro, 32
Armiñan, Manuel, 220n171
Arnao, Juan, 174
Arredondo y Miranda, Francisco de, 95
Arteagabeita, Nicolás, 138
artillery units, 25, 42, 53, 58, 68–69, 101
Asociación Nacional de Veteranos de Independencia, 186–89
assassinations, 95, 162, 184–85
Atkins, Edwin, 99, 114, 152, 239n199
authority/authorities, 6, 46, 126, 170, 172, 187; colonial, 21–22, 26, 28–29, 33, 44, 55–57; military, 54, 59, 71, 87–88, 92, 165, 175, 224n254; Spanish, 7, 36, 39, 59, 89, 91, 101, 132, 253n1
Autonomist Party, 5, 163–67, 175, 179, 181, 240n226
autonomy, 164–66, 252n460, 253n2

Avelino Delgado, Octavio, 100, 149, 184
Azcárate, Nicolás, 46
Azcárraga, Marcelo, 142, 145

Bacardí Moreau, Emilio, 185
Baire, Oriente, 98–100, 105, 126
Ballou, Maturin, 35–36
Bandera, Quintín, 110
Barcia Zequeira, María del Carmen, 45
Barker, Walter, 148
Barker, William, 162, 165
Barnet, Miguel, 1
Baroja, Pío, 134–35, 143
Barona, Lucas, 131
Barrios y Carrión, Leopoldo, 24, 55, 58–59, 62, 69, 212n13, 224n254; on cavalry, 87–88; on Cuban topography, 70; on irregular struggle, 83–84; on lack of supplies, 43; on the *monte*, 64; on Spanish army, 68; on Ten Years' War, 40
Barroeta Scheidnagel, Santiago, 134, 218n128
Basail, Tomás, 178
Basulto de Montoya, Flora, 110
batallones (battalions), 6, 10, 24–25, 30, 85
Batrell, Ricardo, 157
Bayamo, Cuba, 53–54, 61
bayonets, 36, 68–69, 231n46
Beal, Walter, 257n42
Benítez, Lolo, 153–54
Bergés, Rodolfo, 109, 131, 247n351
Betancourt, José Ramón, 51
Betancourt Cisneros, Gaspar, 29, 36, 38, 51, 117; on annexation, 31; on rights, 12
Black Cubans/Cubans of African descent, 10–11, 16–17, 35, 89–92, 99; enslaved, 2–4, 15, 20–22, 32; in *milicias de color*, 24–25, 29–30, 204n72
Blanco, Domingo, 134–35, 143, 145, 159, 162–67; on military hospitals, 138; Weyler and, 130
Blasco Ibáñez, Vicente, 133, 142–43
bohíos, 81–82, 130, 174
Boitel, José, 95
Bolívar, Simón, 15–16

Bonachea, Ramón Leocadio, 93
Bonsal, Stephen, 129
Borrero, Mateo, 185
Boza, Bernabé, 123, 137, 144–45, 149, 156–58
Bremer, Fredrika, 17, 39
Brice, Alexander, 167
bridges, 21, 57, 60–61, 91, 104, 108
Bronson Rea, George, 153
Brooke, John, 170, 179, 184
budget, colonial, 43, 244n297
Buenamar, Ricardo, 158, 178
Bueno, Manuel, 105
Burguete, Ricardo, 129, 135, 142

Cabrera, Ramiro, 158
cafetales (coffee estates), 13–14, 21, 89, 108, 217n100
Calatrava, José María, 11, 33, 36–37
Calvario, Jesús del, 154, 193
Camagüey, Cuba, 42, 54–55, 57–58, 78, 95, 108–9
Camps, Francisco de, 66, 68–69, 95
Cánovas del Castillo, Antonio, 124–26, 133, 162–63
Cárdenas, Cuba, 27–28, 56, 149
Cárdenas Urrutia, Gregorio, 260n80
Cardona, Gabriel, 210n7
carretas (oxen-pulled wagons), 59–61, 105
Carrillo, Mario, 158
caseríos, 44, 70, 212n23
casinos, Spanish, 51, 167–68, 180
Casset, Rafael, 116
Castañón, Gonzalo, 53
Castaños, Gregorio, 107
Castellanos, Adolfo, 51
Castellanos, Jesús, 192
Castillo, José del, 19–20
Castillo, Rogelio, 157
casualties, 93, 133–34, 173, 185, 242n259, 242n262; from guerrillas, 8, 154–57; Spanish, 7, 57, 65, 70, 138–44, 218n128, 220n172
Catá, Alvaro, 181
Catá, Sabas, 126
Catholic Church, 20, 51, 102, 105, 176

266   Index

cavalry units, 25–26, 69–70, 87–88, 100, 128; in Ejército Invasor, 106; *mambises* and, 8; pacification campaign and, 53
Ceballos, Francisco de, 84
censorship, 127, 163
censuses, Cuban, 3, 22, 44, 177
central jurisdictions, Cuban, 13–14, 32–33
Céspedes, Carlos Manuel de, 2, 8, 41, 55
Chacón, José Ignacio, 94, 146–47
chattel slavery, 3–4, 16, 20, 31, 36, 117, 171
Chaves, Angel, 66
Chessa, José de, 59
children, 90, 130–31, 155–56, 178, 188, 190; as casualties, 7, 93, 173; orphaned, 16, 173
Cholera, 74–75, 77–79, 222n206
Ciego de Avila, Cuba, 181–82
Cienfuegos, Cuba, 27, 33, 35, 171
Cigés Aparicio, Manuel, 110, 127, 136, 138, 153
Cimadevilla, Francisco, 176
cimarrones (runaway/fugitive slaves), 34, 59, 70
Cirujeda, Francisco, 154
civilians, 7, 81, 93, 172–74, 185
civil wars, 8–9, 16, 48, 54, 152–53, 160–61
class, social, 11–12, 91, 119, 176. *See also* planters; producing classes
Clayton, John, 170
clemency, 91–92, 96, 163, 186, 249nn381–82
Cleveland, Grover, 123
climate/weather, 7, 59–61, 71, 96, 97, 104–5, 142–44; infectious diseases and, 76, 137–41, 223n228; tropical, 43, 62, 74, 83, 134–36
coffee/coffee estates (*cafetales*), 13–14, 21, 89, 108, 217n100
Collazo, Enrique, 40, 92, 136, 150
colonial administration, Spanish, 3–6, 8–10, 14–15, 175, 181–83, 189; abuses under, 12, 20, 178, 193; authority, 7, 36, 39, 59, 89, 91, 101, 132, 253n1; extermination campaign of, 173–74; internal security under, 20–27, 29–30, 41; producing classes and, 19–20,

41–43, 123, 133, 176; racial fears stoked by, 89–90, 172
colonialism. *See specific subjects*
commerce, 11, 13, 20, 46, 52, 56–57, 162
communication/communication systems, 23–24, 57, 70, 85, 94, 108; telegraph, 67, 84, 216n97; transportation and, 41, 59
Conangla, Josep, 156–57, 168
Concha, José G. de la, 22–23, 32–34, 38, 55, 69, 71, 90, 208n116; on *insurrectos*, 89, 91–92
Conill, Enrique, 157
Consejo Nacional de Veteranos, 186–89
constituent assemblies, 160, 250n396
Constitution of Jimaguayú (1896), 100, 157
Consuegra, Israel, 155
Conte, Rafael, 193
contra-guerrillas, 6, 83–85, 93–94, 148
Contreras, Evaristo Martín, 51
convoys, military, 6, 59–61, 65–66, 95, 104–6, 135, 218n128; diseases and, 75; guerrillas escorting, 150
Cordón, Pedro, 142
Corona, Ramón, 180
Corral, Manuel, 104, 130, 136–38, 145, 153
Cortijo, Vicente de, 137
Corvisón, Segundo, 153
cost/s, 23; of war, 16, 94–96, 107–8, 124–25, 132–34, 161–62, 206n99
counterinsurgency, 7, 146
countermarches, 71, 74, 107, 134, 240n214
counterrevolution, 6, 10, 194
Crane, Stephen, 98
crimes/criminals, 1, 86, 118–19, 156–57, 179
criollos/criollidad (creoles), 4–5, 12–13, 32, 163–64, 176, 215n73; in *milicias*, 6, 24–25, 30–31; *peninsulares* and, 16–20, 45–46, 52–53; Spanish sovereignty defended by, 23, 36–37, 123
Crombet, Flor, 154
cruelty, 154–57, 180–81, 182–83, 192–93
Cuatro-Villas, Cuba, 26
Cuba Libre (Free Cuba), 2, 5, 10, 56, 67, 134, 167, 180, 186

Index 267

Cuba y América (publication), 131
Cuerpo de Voluntarios, 30–31, 51–52
Cuza, Felipe, 188

Davis, Charles, 36, 38–39
death/s, 2, 15, 130–31, 138, 187, 237n171, 242n259, 242n262; by assassination, 95, 162, 184–85; caused by *guerrilla*, 8, 154–55; of civilians, 7, 173–74; of Maceo, 154–55; of patriots, 192–93. *See also* casualties; executions
defectors (*presentados*), 8, 92, 94–95, 155, 163, 181
demobilization, 183, 245n311, 260n83
demographics, 25–27, 32, 44–45, 99, 210n2, 212nn23–24, 257n33; in censuses, 3, 22, 44, 177; enslaved Africans in, 2–4, 15
demoralization, 43, 60, 82, 92
Despradel, Lorenzo, 136–37
Diario de la Marina (newspaper), 48–49, 53–54, 83, 153, 180, 188; on Cuban independence, 167–68; on race, 177; on violence against *guerrilleros*, 184–85
Díaz, Lisandro, 185
Díaz Benzo, Antonio, 100, 151
Diego de Villate, Blas, 53
Diez Vicario, V. de, 126
Dimock, Joseph, 26–27
diseases, infectious, 7, 43, 60, 75, 135–46, 222n206, 223n228. *See also specific diseases*
displacement, 3, 153, 171–73
Domingo de Ibarra, Ramón, 55
Donderis, Enrique, 178
Donoso Cortés, Ricardo, 98, 125–26, 129, 132–33, 151, 231n46; on insurgent forces, 101, 109
dotaciones (enslaved plantation labor forces), 22, 25, 27, 41–43, 58, 90–92, 201n49
Duharte Jiménez, Rafael, 24
Dulce, Domingo, 179
Duque, Matías, 2
Dyer, George, 160
dysentery, 74–78, 137, 141–42, 144–45

eastern jurisdictions, Cuban, 42, 57–58, 87, 134, 198n10; de la Concha on, 71; insurgents in, 44; military hospitals in, 78, 80
Echauz, Félix de, 7
economy, Cuban, 3, 13–15, 108, 132, 162, 257n33; of colonialism, 17, 41, 56–58; rural, 42, 81
Ecos de Cuba (newspaper), 111
education, 5, 53, 68, 119, 126, 179, 188
Ejército Invasor, 100–101, 106–7, 110, 112, 116
Ejército Libertador, 186–87, 245n311
El Correo Español (newspaper), 109, 133
El Correo Militar (newspaper), 97, 122, 126, 142, 166, 184; on *insurrectos*, 112; on military reinforcements, 138; on sugar production, 114
"el desbordamiento de los negros," 46, 89, 117–18
El Heraldo de Madrid (newspaper), 102, 107, 116, 119, 123–26, 146, 234n108; on Weyler, 133–34, 161
El Imparcial (newspaper), 109, 116, 138–39, 143–44, 160–62
El Mundo (newspaper), 193
El Nuevo Régimen (publication), 161
Ely, Roland, 18
emancipation of enslaved people, 4, 19, 28, 34–35, 37–39, 122
employment, 24, 87, 152–53, 183–84, 187–88. *See also* wages/payment
Ernst, O., 245n311
Escalante Beatón, Aníbal, 189
Escalera, Juan, 65, 71, 91, 95, 221n198
Escobar, Manuel, 109, 115
Esnal Gutiérrez, José, 260n80
españolismo, 51, 57, 126–27, 178
Espinosa y Ramos, Serafín, 130, 175, 184
Estévanez, Nicolás, 52, 56, 74
Estrada Palma, Tomás, 93
Estrada y Céspedes, Francisco, 61, 92
Estrampes, Francisco, 32
Europe, 23, 40, 64, 68–70
evacuation/withdrawal of Spanish army, 100, 109–11, 186
Ever-Faithful Isle, Cuba as, 3, 20, 170

executions, 8, 29, 53, 173–74; of guerrillas, 157–59, 183–84, 248n377, 249n384, 249nn381–82
expansionism, US, 32, 38
exports, 13, 15, 22, 257n33
extermination, war of, 53, 126–33, 173–74, 184, 187

Fabié, Antonio María, 120–21
famine, 129–30
farms (*fincas*), 14, 81
fatigue, 65, 70–71, 74–75, 80, 83–84, 136–38, 151–52
fear/s, 45, 57, 123; of "*el desbordamiento de los negros*," 46, 89, 117–18; of *manigua*, 62–63, 117–18; racial, 32–39, 89–90, 117–22, 172; of slaves rebellions, 16–19, 27–29
Feijóo, Teodorico, 61–62
Félix, Juan Enrique, 32
Ferguson, Erna, 175–76
Fernández, Bibián, 153
Fernández, Enrique de Miguel, 116, 242n259
Fernández, Tomaso, 115, 154
Fernández Golfin, Luis, 43
Fernández Lobregat, José, 184–85
Fernández Losada, José, 141
Fernández Muñiz, Aurea Matilde, 176–77
Ferrara, Orestes, 155
Ferrer, Horacio, 158, 186
Ferrer de Couto, José, 15, 88
Ferrer Gutiérrez, Virgilio, 105
field diaries, 9, 101, 112, 129, 173, 230n42, 252n452
Figueredo, Félix, 40–41
fincas (farms), 14, 81
Finch, Aisha, 27
fires/burning, 114, 118–20, 123–24, 129–30, 157–58, 183; of sugar estates, 107–8, 110, 112, 115–16
firing squad, 53, 157–58, 173, 183
Flint, Grover, 155, 249n382
floods, 60–61, 74, 105, 223n228
Flores, Eugenio Antonio, 43–44, 64, 74
forced marches, 134, 136, 240n214

Forsyth, John, 208n117, 209n134, 253n1
France/French colonies, 6, 13, 32
Franco, José Luciano, 88–89
Free Cuba (*Cuba Libre*), 2, 5, 10, 56, 67, 134, 167, 180, 186
freedom of the press, 165–67
free people of color/African descent, 3–4, 30, 32, 35–36, 91–92, 204n72; growing population of, 24; La Escalera revolt and, 28; Moret Law on, 90
fuerzas ligeras (mobile forces), 146–47
fugitive/runaway slaves (*cimarrones*), 34, 59, 70
Funston, Frederick, 155–56, 158

Gallego, Tesifonte, 58, 116, 132–33, 151
Gallenga, Antonio, 178
García, Alejandro, 22
García, Calixto, 88, 94, 136, 165
García, Clotilde, 155, 158
García, Vicente, 55
García Hernández, Julián, 153
García Velez, Carlos, 161–62, 186
García Verdugo, Vicente, 46, 50, 55
Gasset, Rafael, 139, 143–44
Gelpi y Ferro, Gil, 51, 54, 64, 149
geography, 21–22, 54–55, 60–61, 70, 83–84
Gibbs, Richard, 52
Giberga, Eliseo, 111–12, 118
Gómez, Fernando, 100
Gómez, Máximo, 10, 57, 71–72, 100, 167, 169, 175, 230n42, 231n49, 252n451; on autonomy, 165; *la tea incendiaria* and, 107–9; on mosquitos, 134; on race wars, 89; Weyler compared to, 132
Gómez de Avellaneda, Gertrudis, 19
Gómez Núñez, Severo, 151
Gómez Toro, Francisco (Panchito), 154
Gonzales, N. G., 156
González, Nicolás Salvador, 184
González Granda, José, 240n214
Goodman, Walter, 67
governance, colonial, 15, 20, 30, 45, 109, 117, 122–23; producing classes and, 36; sugar production and, 42

Grajales, Mariana, 2
Granados, María Josefa, 247n343
Granda, José de, 65, 83
Granda, Manuel de, 154
Grito de Baire, 98–100, 105, 126
Grito de Yara, 42–44, 52–54, 92, 114
Guantánamo, 34, 185, 212n24
Guerra, Amador, 154
Guerra y Sánchez, Ramiro, 9–10, 51–52, 93
Guerrero, Rafael, 164–65
guerrillas/guerrilleros (Spanish irregular troops), 98, 196n21, 220n171, 225n154, 256n27, 260n27, 260n80, 260n83; casualties from, 8, 154–57; *contraguerrillas*, 6, 83–85, 93–94, 148; cruelty of, 154–57, 182–83, 192–93; employment of, 87, 152–53, 183–84, 187–88; executions of, 157–59, 183–84, 248n377, 249n384, 249nn381–82; Guerrilla de Sabanilla, 154, 247n343; Guevara recouping, 193–94; *insurrectos* and, 6, 10, 93–95, 154–58, 260n83; *mambises* and, 8, 93–95, 154–57, 175–76, 181–83; in novels, 191–93; in public office, 175, 186–89; sugar harvest protected by, 245n312; as traitors, 157–58, 183–93, 263n124; types of, 84–88, 148–51; in war-with-war policy, 151–55. See also insurgent Cuban forces (*insurrectos*)
Guevara, Ernesto Che, 194

Haiti, 29, 120, 122–23, 172, 177, 254n9
harvests, sugar, 57, 108, 114, 116, 132, 234n108, 245n312
hatred, 3, 52–53, 110, 119, 120, 127, 177–80; of *guerrilleros*, 156, 183–91
Havana, 25–27, 108–12, 147, 168, 211n9, 214n60, 216n97; anti-Spanish sentiment in, 179; coffee estates in, 14; de la Concha in, 90; racial fear in, 33–35; Spanish population in, 51, 176–77, 180
Hazard, Samuel, 178
Hazeltine, Mayo, 177
Helg, Aline, 118
Heredia, Nicolás, 110, 113

Hernández, Eusebio, 88, 108, 116
Hernández Poggio, Ramón, 62
heroism/heroes, 40, 166–67, 175, 193–94
Herrera, José Isabel, 156, 190
hierarchies, racial, 3–4, 16–20, 45, 89, 99, 171
highway, 22–23, 60
historiography, 2–3, 6, 8–10, 98
home-rule/self-government, 1, 7, 5, 12, 17, 19, 48, 163, 167
honor, national, 31, 125–26, 128, 174
horses/horseback, 64, 69–71, 128, 131, 136–37, 150, 156, 192; in convoys, 61, 104–6. See also cavalry units
hospitals, 145, 155–56, 162; military, 22, 62, 71, 74–79, 91, 116, 137–41, 190
Howard, Oliver, 176
Humboldt, Alexander, 59
hunger, 130–31, 136, 174, 186, 238n180

Ibarra, Jorge, 2, 10
independence, Cuban, 40, 122, 162–63, 165–67, 172, 175, 254n9, 257n42; *criollos* on, 12–13; race war and, 89, 164; slavery and, 16–18
independentista project, 5, 45–46, 117–18, 172, 186–89, 194; nationhood and, 49; public office and, 175; rebellions and, 98
infantry units (*milicias de infantería*), 25–27, 69, 106–7
infrastructure, 21–22, 57–60, 91, 105–6, 218n119, 221n198
Insua, Waldo, 155
insurgent Cuban forces (*insurrectos*), 52–56, 126–28, 210n7, 216n97, 232n56, 238n180, 261n83; Ejército Invasor by, 100–101, 106–7, 110, 112, 116; guerrillas and, 6, 10, 93–95, 154–58, 260n83; hatred of *guerrilleros* by, 156, 184; *manigua* navigating proficiency of, 62–71, 104, 113–14; property destruction by, 27, 57–59, 107–17, 119–20, 123–24, 172–75; race and, 45, 88–92, 110–11, 117–20; Spanish army overwhelmed by, 98–116. See also fires/burning
intervention, US, 170–72, 254n3

"irregular forces/wars," 83–84, 146, 151
Irving, Washington, 253n1
Isern, Damián, 134

Jacás, Ramón, 8
Jamaica, 26, 27
Jefferson, Thomas, 253n1
Jiménez Castellanos, Adolfo, 51, 60, 63, 85, 94, 184, 220n175
Jones, Alexander, 34
Juárez y Sedeño, Jorge, 10
jurisdictions, Cuban, 13–14, 22, 26, 28–29, 34, 94, 114; central, 13–14, 32–33; eastern, 42, 44, 57–58, 71, 78, 80, 87, 134, 198n10; western, 25, 56, 107, 112, 149, 221n9
Just, Ramón, 23
Justiz y del Valle, Tomás, 178

Kennon, John, 177
Kirchner, Adelaide Rosalind, 142, 147
Klein, Herbert, 204n72
Knight, Franklin, 14, 45, 54–55
Kuethe, Allan, 24

labor, slave, 15, 56; *dotaciones* (enslaved plantation labor forces) as, 22, 25, 27, 41–43, 58, 90–91, 201n49
Lachambre, José, 99, 105–6
La Concordia Cubana (publication), 16, 20
La Correspondencia de España (newspaper), 102, 161
La Correspondencia Militar (newspaper), 150–51, 166–67, 174, 180, 252n444, 252n460
Lacoste, Perfecto, 180
La Epoca (newspaper), 89–99, 104, 114, 121–22, 126, 160, 165
La Escalera, (revolt), 28–29
Lagomasino, Luis, 54
La Guerra Chiquita (Little War), 3, 98
la integridad nacional (national integrity), 30–31, 44, 49, 51, 125–26, 161, 176; former guerrillas impacting, 186; Gómez, M., and, 132; *los buenos cubanos* and, 189; Spanish army defending, 58, 124, 142

La Lucha (newspaper), 169, 184, 188
la madre patria (Spain), 5, 33, 58–59, 129–30, 153, 163–64, 174, 260n80; budgets and, 43; Catholic Church and, 51; *la integridad nacional*, 126; property owners and, 36
la nación integral, 42, 49, 132, 189
land surveys, 21, 42
Lapoulide, Juan, 136
Larra y Cerezo, Angel, 141
Lasheras, Juan de, 119–20
Las Villas, Cuba, 25, 58, 108–9, 130, 150–51
la tea incendiaria (a war of the torch), 107–17, 119–20, 130–31
Laurent, Emilio, 190
La Voz de Cuba (newspaper), 44, 50, 74
Law of Civil Service, Cuba, 188
Lee, Fitzhugh, 141, 162, 164–65, 167–68
Lersundi, Francisco, 53–54
Letona, Antonio de, 24, 43, 61, 65, 67, 70
liberation, Cuba, 4–5, 56, 99–100, 189–90; narratives, 1–3, 8, 10, 178
liberto (slave) companies, 90–92
Little War (*La Guerra Chiquita*), 3, 98
livestock, 13–14, 84–85, 94, 108, 129–31, 150, 183
Logan, John, 183–84, 260n83
López, Narciso, 32
López Allué, Luis, 110–11
Lorente, Juan, 157
Loret de Mola, Melchor, 5
Losada, Juan Carlos, 210n7
los buenos españoles, 50–53, 125–26, 162–64, 167–68, 176–77
los malos cubanos, 8, 181, 189–90, 194
Loveira, Carlos, 5, 190–91, 192
loyalists, 30–31, 48, 50
Loynaz del Castillo, Enrique, 110, 188
Ludlow, William, 176
lynchings, 126–27, 184–85

Macau, Miguel, 137
Maceo, Antonio, 2, 8, 93, 99–100, 154–55, 189; inspired by Haiti, 120; march by, 116
Machado Gómez, Eduardo, 56

Index   271

machetes, 56–57, 63, 69–70, 191–92, 248n377, 249n382, 249n384; death by, 154, 157–59
Madden, Richard, 17, 19
Maine, USS, 168
malaria, 65, 138, 141, 143–44, 222n213
malfeasance, official, 17, 139
malnutrition, 75–76, 136, 138, 141, 143, 173
mambí/mambises, 8–9, 92, 98, 186–87, 190, 192; guerrillas and, 8, 93–95, 154–57, 175–76, 181–83
Mañach, Jorge, 187
manigua (rural interior), 54–55, 92, 117–18, 173, 192–93, 238n180, 260n83; guerrillas in, 85, 93–95; impacting Spanish army, 59–60, 62–71, 96–97, 104, 113–14; *insurrectos* in the, 62–71, 104, 113–14
Manzanillo, Cuba, 61, 162
marches, 65–66, 70–71, 76, 79, 82–83, 137, 159; Burguete on, 135; counter, 71, 74, 107, 134, 240n214; forced, 134, 136, 240n214; de Letona on, 61
Mariano y Vivo, Manuel, 116, 162–63, 165–66
Marín, Sabas, 70
Martí, José, 2, 99, 189
Martín, Juan Luis, 10, 68
Martín, Pedro Pablo, 129
Martínez Campos, Arsenio, 95, 100–101, 108–9, 114–15, 179, 232n56; on *criollos*, 123; in Havana, 111–12
Martínez Casado, Luis, 64
Martínez-Moles, Manuel, 155
Masdeu, Jesús, 192–93
Masó, Bartolomé, 165
Masó Parra, Juan, 136, 240n226
Massip, Salvador, 10
Matanzas, Cuba, 14, 25, 27–29, 101, 108–10, 185; *pardo* and *moreno* troops in, 35; Puerón assaulted in, 185; Spaniards in, 177
Matthews, Franklin, 171
McKinley, William, 170, 254n9
memory, 9, 16, 172–73, 176–81, 186–88, 190–93; collective, 171

Méndez Capote, Domingo, 93
Menocal, Mario, 193
Merchán, Rafael, 178
Mestre, José Manuel, 56
Mexico, 15, 32–33, 50
milicias, 7, 203n61, 206n99; creole, 6, 24–25, 30–31; *de color*, 24–25, 29–30, 34, 91–92, 204n72; *de infantería*, 25, 27, 69; *disciplinadas*, 23, 25, 26, 53
military guides, Spanish (*prácticos*), 8, 70, 83, 85, 95, 97, 153–54
military occupation, US, 175–77, 179–80, 183–86, 188, 261n103
mills, sugar, 14, 33, 57, 89, 110, 123–24, 130, 198n11. *See also* plantations
Miranda, Luis Rodolfo, 188
Miró Argenter, José, 101, 112, 116–17, 136, 156
mobile forces (*fuerzas ligeras*), 146–47
Mola, Melchor, 92
Monte, Domingo del, 16–18, 27–28, 31
monte (woodlands), 54–55, 64–65, 68, 95, 260n83
Monteagudo, José de J., 256n27
Montejo, Esteban, 142, 169, 186
Montenegro, Carlos, 184
Montero Gabuti, Juan, 62
Montori, Arturo, 192
Mora, Ignacio, 89, 92
morale, 8, 58, 74, 93, 109, 165; Martínez Campos on, 111–12; Spanish army, 70, 80, 127–28, 134–35, 161
Morales Patiño, Oswaldo, 153
Morales y Morales, Vidal, 8
moral/s, 1–2, 20, 35, 56–57, 99, 114, 189, 194; authority, 170, 187
Moreno, Francisco, 164, 178
Moreno de la Tejera, Vicente, 97
Moreno Fraginals, Manuel, 15
Moret Law, 90
mortality rates, 74, 140, 142, 146
mosquitos, 7, 134–35, 223n228
Moure Saco, José, 135, 140
Moya, Francisco J. de, 43–44, 64–65, 210n7, 220n172
Muñiz de Quevedo, José, 165

272   Index

murder, 27, 93, 180, 182, 184–85
Musgrave, George, 249n381

Napoleon, 6, 127, 151
narratives, liberation, 1–3, 8, 10, 178
National Congress of History, 10, 186
nationality, 2–3, 37, 49, 67, 189
nation/nationhood, sovereign, 2, 12, 14, 49
Navarro, Fabián, 60, 67
Navarro García, Luis, 61, 75, 82
"neutral"/"neutrality," 52, 170, 173
newspapers, 20, 127, 163, 166–68, 184–85. *See also specific newspapers*
New York Times, 180, 185
noncombatants, 7, 81, 172–74
Nuevo Mundo (newspaper), 125, 128, 164
Núñez, Emilio, 180–81, 188
Núñez Florencio, Rafael, 125

Ochando, T., 57–60, 67, 85, 91
O'Donnell, Leopoldo, 28–29
O'Kelly, James, 57, 88, 95, 178
oppression, Cuban, 12–13, 16, 181
Oriente Province, Cuba, 10, 42–43, 54–55, 70, 93, 103–6, 181, 210n2; Baire, 98–100, 105; people of color in, 44, 72–73; property destruction in, 108–9
Ortiz, Antonio, 59
Ortiz, Francisco, 91
O'Ryan, Marcelo, 154
Ostend Manifesto, 32
Otero, Lisandro, 2
Otero y Pimentel, Luis, 109–10
Ovilo y Canales, Felipe, 139–40, 145

pacification, 53–54, 81–82, 128, 132, 164
pacífico population, 81, 150, 165, 174
Padilla Angulo, Fernando, 30–31
padrones (population surveys), 22
Palo Seco, 220n172
Paquette, Robert, 22
paramilitary forces, 6–7, 149, 181
pardo and *moreno* troops, 6, 24, 29–30, 34–35, 90–92
pardon, 91–92, 96, 163, 186
Partido Revolucionario Cubano, 53

Patria (publication), 189
patrimonio, 31, 37, 125, 127, 164, 174
patriots/patriotism, 167–68, 175, 189–90, 192–93, 194
peace/peacetime, 98, 170, 172, 176, 179–80, 183–84
peasants (*guajiros*), 10, 84, 89, 152, 164
Peña, Eduardo de la, 141
Penal Code, Republic in Arms, 157, 183
Penichet, Antonio, 192
peninsular/peninsulares, 4, 180, 208n116, 215n73, 257n42, 295n11; *criollos* and, 16–20, 45–46, 52–53; Cuerpo de Voluntarios made up of, 30–31, 51–52; as loyalists, 30–31, 48, 50; Spanish sovereignty and, 6–8, 176; troops, 24–25, 42–43, 54, 57, 68, 82, 94–95, 138
pensions, 24–25, 187
people/population of color, Cuban, 18, 27, 41, 44, 172, 177, 212n24; *criollos* and, 23; de la Concha on, 32; free, 3–4, 24, 28, 30, 35–36, 90, 204n72; in insurgent forces, 88–90, 99; *milicias de color*, 24–25, 29–30, 34, 91–92, 204n72. *See also pardo* and *moreno* troops
Pepper, Charles, 177, 179
Peral, Doroteo de, 8, 154–55
Peralejo, Oriente, 100
Pérez, Cresencio, 184
Pérez Abreu, Gustavo, 110, 131
Pérez Vento, Rafael, 164
Perinat, Santiago, 88
Perry, Horatio, 35, 38
peseta (currency), 124–25, 133, 176
Pezuela, Jacobo de la, 24–25, 43, 198n11
Pezuela, Juan, 34–36
physicians, army, 7, 62, 139–41, 240n214, 242n259
Piedra Martel, Manuel, 149, 156, 179
Pieltain, Cándido, 58–60, 83, 94–95, 225n254
Pierce, Franklin, 32, 35, 38
Pinar del Río, Cuba, 14, 108–9, 111, 128, 185
Pintó, Ramón, 32
Piqueras Causas, Enrique, 104, 135

Index   273

Pirala, Antonio, 68, 90
Pi y Margall, Francisco, 164
plantations, 13–14, 18, 28–29, 45, 56, 183–84, 217n100; *dotaciones* (enslaved plantation labor forces), 22, 25, 27, 41–42, 58, 90–91, 201n49
planters (class), 4, 13, 18–20, 24, 28, 41, 122, 206n99; property destruction and, 114, 132–33
Plumb, Edward, 51–52
Polavieja, Camilo, 42, 120, 174, 179
police, Cuban, 185, 188
political economy of colonialism, 14, 17, 41, 56, 58
Polk, James, 32
Ponte Domínguez, Francisco, 56
population, Cuban, 26, 32, 81, 99, 128, 131; Spanish, 51, 176–77, 180–81; white, 4, 11, 23, 26–27, 32, 35–37, 47, 177. *See also* people/population of color, Cuban; slaves/slavery
Porrua, Antonio, 50
Portell Vilá, Herminio, 10
Portuondo del Prado, Fernando, 10
postwar Cuba, 180, 183, 186
power, 23, 39, 46, 170, 177; Spanish colonial, 45, 108, 122–24, 175
Pozo, Alejandro del, 155
prácticos (Spanish military guides), 8, 70, 83, 85, 95, 97, 153–54, 184–85
Prendergas, Luis, 94
presentados (defectors), 8, 92, 94–95, 155, 163, 181
Price, Leopold, 222n206
price of sugar, 13, 18, 197n4
Prim, Juan, 59
prime minister, Spanish, 33, 37, 59, 124–25, 162–63
privilege, 3–4, 9, 24–25, 45, 46, 170–72
producing classes, 15–17, 29–30, 36–37, 170–72, 176; property destruction impacting, 115, 117; slavery and, 3–4, 18, 39; Spanish colonial administration and, 19–20, 41–43, 123, 133, 176; Spanish sovereignty and, 19–20, 31, 34, 45, 123

property destruction, 27, 57–59, 107–17, 119–20, 123–24, 172–75; under Weyler, 128–34
property/land, 14–15, 19–20, 21, 42, 56–57, 112, 132; owners, 11, 19, 36–37, 132–33, 149. *See also* agriculture; fires/burning
public office, Cuban, 175, 186–89
Puerto Príncipe, Cuba, 26, 32–33, 35, 92, 216n97

race/race relations, 10, 21–22, 66–67, 110–13, 147–48, 174, 254n9; hierarchies, 3–4, 16–20, 45, 89, 99, 171; *milicias de color* and, 24–25, 29–30, 34, 91–92, 204n72; racial fear in, 32–39, 89–90, 117–22, 172; slavery and, 2–4, 15, 18; white population in Cuba and, 23, 26–27, 32, 35–37, 47, 177. *See also* Black Cubans/Cubans of African descent; *criollos/criollidad* (creoles); *mambí/mambises*; people/population of color, Cuban
race war, 4, 20, 28–30, 44, 46–47, 90, 122, 164, 172; *independentista* project and, 117; Spanish colonial administration on, 89
Radillo, Luis de, 181
railroads/trains, 22, 57–58, 114, 116, 123, 150; property damage impacting, 61, 108, 124
Ramón y Cajal, Santiago, 222n213, 223n228
Rawson, James, 204n72
rebellions/revolts, 6, 17, 27–29, 41, 98–103, 117–18, 121–22
Rebello, Carlos, 198n11
Recio, Manuel Antonio, 132
Recio, Ramón, 8
reconcentration camps/policy, 81, 128–31, 156–57, 173–74, 178, 237n171; guerrilla units and, 150, 153; suspension of, 163, 165
reconciliation, 181, 193
reconnaissance, 83, 85, 94, 131
Redondo Díaz, Fernando, 23, 93

Reina y Massa, Cristóbal, 102–3
Remington, Frederic, 181
Renan, Ernest, 9
Reparaz, Gonzalo, 40, 59–60, 69, 101, 107, 128, 138; on climate, 74; on marches, 71; on property destruction, 108–9, 115
repatriation to Spain (*repatriados*), 142–45, 181, 186, 243n277, 243n280
repression, 3, 10, 109, 127
Republic in Arms, 55, 100, 157, 183
revenues, colonial, 15, 20, 31, 56
Reverter Delmas, Emilio, 99, 102, 104 119, 127, 129, 132, 140–41, 162
Revista Bimestre Cubana (newspaper), 15, 21
Rey, Santiago, 1, 155, 176
Reyes Zamora, Antonio, 53
rights, 4, 12, 28, 97, 176; *milicias de color* and, 24–25, 204n72
riots, 168, 185
Riquelme, José, 71, 84
Riva, Armando de J., 190
Roa, Ramón, 95
roads, 21–22, 59–60, 104–6, 218n119, 221n198
Robertson, William, 34–35, 39
Rodríguez, Alejandro, 149–50
Rodríguez, Antonio, 185
Rodríguez, Celestino, 185
Rodríguez, Emilio, 248n377
Roig de Leuchsenring, Emilio, 10, 172, 189
Romero Quiñones, Ubaldo, 134
Roncali, Federico, 31, 33, 37–38
Rosal, Antonio del, 64–66, 83, 89
Rosell, Eduardo, 131
Rosell, Francisco, 132
Rosende, Angel, 156, 188
Royal Exchequer, 15, 43
Ruiz, Ramón, 134
runaway/fugitive slaves (*cimarrones*), 34, 59, 70
rural Cuba, 25–27, 54–55, 57 61, 100; economy of, 42, 81; population in, 81, 99, 128, 131. See also *manigua* (rural interior)

Saco, José Antonio, 16–18, 24–25, 29
Sáenz, Eusebio, 88
Sagasta, Práxedes Mateo, 125, 160, 163
Sagra, Ramón de la, 14, 21, 198n11
Saint-Domingue, 13, 15, 18–19
Salas y Quiroga, Jacinto de, 13, 15, 18–19
Salazar, Martín, 120
Salcedo Montillo, Juan, 121–22
Samalea, Rafael, 188
San Antonio de los Baños, Cuba, 184–85
Sánchez, Diego, 185
Sánchez, Julián, 156, 158, 178
Sánchez-Boudy, José, 190
Sanguily, Julio, 8
Sanguily, Manuel, 178
Sanjenis, Avelino, 155, 157, 183
San Juan y Martínez, Cuba, 188
Santa Clara, Cuba, 110–11, 180–81, 183–84
Santa Isabel de Las Lajas, Cuba, 188
Santiago de Cuba, Cuba, 26, 35, 67, 179–80, 185
Santiago de Las Vegas, Cuba, 188
Santiesteban, Argelio, 190
Santo Domingo, Dominican Republic, 18, 26, 29, 35–36, 89, 122
Sarmiento Ramírez, Ismael, 173–74
Sartorius, David, 163
Schweyer Lamar, Guillermo, 192
Scott, Rebecca, 45, 90
Secades Japón, Manuel, 136–37, 154, 169, 175, 181–82
security under Spanish colonial administration, 20–27, 29–30, 41
self-government/home rule, 1 7, 5, 12, 17, 19, 48, 163, 167
separatists, 5–6, 53, 121, 134, 160–61, 164–66; Cánovas del Castillo on, 126; Méndez Capote on, 93; race and, 119
Serra Orts, Antonio, 71, 93, 142–43, 167, 181
Shafter, William, 170, 181
Sickles, Daniel, 43, 57, 59, 214n52, 254n9
Sierra Maestra mountains, 193–94
Silva, Francisco, 175
Silvela, Francisco, 160

slaves/slavery, 32, 56, 92, 96, 99; abolition of, 4, 16, 27, 37–38, 45, 90; chattel, 3–4, 16, 20, 31, 36, 117, 171; *dotaciones* (enslaved plantation labor forces) as, 22, 25, 27, 41–43, 58, 90–91, 201n49; emancipation of, 4, 19, 28, 34–35, 37–39 122; internal security and, 25–27, 29–30; producing classes and, 3–4, 18, 39; rebellions, 6, 17, 27–29, 41, 117–18; sugar production and, 15, 20–23, 25, 41; uprisings, 4, 18, 27–28. *See also* labor, slave
Sobrado, Juan Jorge, 174, 184
Sola, José Sixto de, 185–86
Sol y Ortega, Juan, 144
Soravilla, Lesbia, 191–92
Soulère, Emilio, 44, 55, 63, 70, 88, 95–96
South America, 15–16, 30, 58–59
sovereignty/sovereign, 4–5, 170, 172; colonial, 6, 10, 171; nation, 2, 12, 14, 49
sovereignty/sovereign, Spanish, 6–8, 41, 132, 170–72, 176, 254n9, 259n66; collapse of, 76, 122–23, 168; *criollos* defending, 23, 36–37, 123; insurgent forces impacting, 56–57; people of color defending, 34–36; producing classes and, 19–20, 31, 34, 45, 123; sugar production and, 23, 42; *la tea incendiaria* countering, 107–10, 112–17, 119, 130; Weyler seeking to restore, 125
Spain/Spaniards, 6, 31, 229n25, 253n2, 260n80; *los buenos españoles* as, 50–53, 126, 162–64, 167–68, 176–77; prime minister, 33, 37, 59, 124–25, 162–63; repatriation to, 142–45, 181, 186, 243n277, 243n280; United States and, 170–273, 253n1. *See also la madre patria*
Spanish army, 42–43, 98, 211n9, 212n13, 229n25, 234n106, 243n277, 243n280, 251n444; age of, 141–42; casualties, 7, 57, 65, 70, 138–44, 218n128, 220n172; defeats of, 100–101; diseases impacting the, 222n206, 222n213; *El Heraldo de Madrid* on, 234n108; evacuation/withdrawal of, 100, 110–11, 186; guerrilla units and, 93–95; *manigua* impacting, 59–60, 62–71, 96–97, 104, 113–14; morale

of, 70, 80, 127–28, 134–35, 161; peace arrangements by, 95–96, 126–27; reconcentration camps/policy, 81, 128–31, 150, 153, 156–57, 163, 165, 173–74, 178, 237n171; reinforcements for, 101–3, 128, 138, 144–46, 160–61; tactical methods of, 7, 25, 56–60, 90–92, 129–30; in Ten Years' War, 58–59; total war waged by, 173–74. *See also* convoys, military; *guerrillas/guerrilleros*; *pardo* and *moreno* troops; *prácticos* (Spanish military guides); Voluntarios; war-with-war policy
status, social, 24–25, 41, 45, 90–91
Suárez y Romero, Anselmo, 74
subsistence, 19, 129–30, 153, 260n83
sugar/sugar estates, 17, 131, 149–50, 234n108; harvests, 57, 108, 114, 116, 132, 234n108, 245n312; mills, 14, 33, 57, 89, 110, 123–24, 130, 198n11; plantations, 13–14, 56, 217n100; price of, 13, 18, 197n4, 297n4; production, 14–16, 20–23, 25, 41–42, 57–58, 113–15; property destruction/fires at, 107–8, 110, 112–16; slavery and, 4, 15, 23, 25
supplies: ammunition as, 22–23, 33, 43–44, 61–62, 74, 81–82, 107, 115; infrastructure and, 21–22, 57–60, 91, 105–6, 218n119, 221n198. *See also* convoys, military
surrender, 167–68, 183, 240n226; by *presentados* (defectors), 8, 92, 94–95 155, 163, 181
surveillance, 83, 85
survivors, 173, 186–87
Sydenham, T., 6

Tacón, Miguel, 27
Tanco, Félix, 12–13
telegraph communication, 67, 84, 216n97
Ten Years' War, 3, 9–10, 40–41, 58–59, 133, 194, 244n297
Thomas, Hugh, 41
tobacco/tobacco fields, 14, 108, 114, 130
Togores Sánchez, Luis Eugenio, 96
Tomás, Isidoro, 153
Tone, John, 174

276   Index

topography, 7, 21, 41, 70, 76–77, 83–84, 109–10, 147–48; Spanish colonial administration and, 61, 67–68
Torrente, Mariano, 12, 33
Torres Cuevas, Eduardo, 10
Torres y González, Vicente, 120
Torriente, Cosme de la, 188
total war, 15–16, 81, 129, 150, 172–74
trains/railroads, 22, 57–58, 61, 108, 114, 116, 123, 124, 150
traitors, 65–66, 94, 194; expulsion of, 187–90, 263n124; guerrillas as, 157–58, 183–93, 263n124; patriots and, 175 189–90; *prácticos* as, 8, 70, 83, 85, 95, 154, 184–85. *See also* insurgent Cuban forces (*insurrectos*)
transportation, 23–24, 42, 59–61, 67, 104, 108, 110
treason, 94, 129, 157–58, 163–64, 183, 190, 192, 194, 252n460
trenches, fortified (*trochas*), 57–58, 91, 100, 116, 128
Trinidad, Cuba, 27, 33, 35
trochas (fortified trenches), 57–58, 91, 100, 116, 128, 223n228
tropical climate, 43, 62, 74, 83, 134–36
Trouillot, Michel-Rolph, 2–3
tuberculosis, 143, 222n213
Turnbull, David, 36

Ubieta, Enrique, 130–31
Unión de Reyes, Cuba, 185
United States, 123, 168; annexation of Cuba to, 3, 5, 31–34, 38, 194. *See also* military occupation, US
University of Havana, 53, 179
Uraga, Esteban, 141
urban Cuba, 25, 41, 54–55, 60, 99, 102, 110–11
Urquiza, Alejandro, 95
Usatorres Perdomo, Ernesto, 137

Valdés, Andrés, 260n80
Valdés Domínguez, Fermín, 108, 159, 173, 178, 190
Valle, Miguel del, 157

Valmaseda, Conde de, 10, 53–54, 59, 61, 81, 180–81
Van Ness, Cornelius P., 208n117, 209n134
Varela, Félix, 4, 11, 20, 23, 30
Varona, Enrique José, 172
Varona, Ramón, 112
Varona Guerrero, Miguel, 10, 149, 154–55, 158–59, 245n311
Vázquez, Andrés Clemente, 109, 114, 159–60, 167, 174
Vázquez Queipo, Vicente, 24, 26
Vega, Armando de la, 190
Vesa, Antonio, 115
Veteranos (veterans), 186–90, 263n124
violence, 3, 7, 16–17, 154–57, 184–86; against civilians, 173–74
"*viva España con honra*" (dictum), 53, 132, 176
Vives, Francisco Dionisio, 19, 27, 36–37
Voluntarios, 53, 71, 101–2, 128, 207n109, 214n60, 215n73, 259n66; Cuerpo de, 30–31, 51–52; murder of, 180; not repatriated to Spain, 181; during US military occupation, 176–77, 186

wages/payment, 24, 90–91, 224n254, 260n83; for guerrillas, 87, 152–53, 183–84, 187–88
war for independence, Cuban, 3, 6, 170–73, 188, 192, 207n109
war/s, 6, 12, 30, 33–34, 58–59, 109, 183; civil, 8–9, 16, 48, 54, 152–53, 160–61; colonial, 7–8, 151; costs of, 16, 94–96, 107–8, 124–25, 161–62; of extermination, 53, 126–33, 173–74, 184, 187; irregular, 83–84, 146; total, 15–16, 81, 129, 150, 172–74. *See also* race war; *specific wars*
"war without quarter," 15–16, 81, 126, 129, 131, 178–79
war-with-war policy, 124–26, 128, 131–32, 166–68, 174, 176; guerrillas in, 151–57; Weyler enacting, 145–46
wealth/wealthy, 16, 18–19, 24, 39, 46, 52, 108, 177; property destruction impacting, 113–17, 130
Weightman, Richard, 164

Index 277

western jurisdictions, Cuban, 25, 56, 107, 112, 149, 221n9
Weyler, Valeriano, 106, 116–17, 144–48, 158, 160–63, 177, 189, 242n262, 252n452; cruelty of, 125, 128, 130–34, 180–81; extermination pursued by, 126–34, 174, 184
white population in Cuba, 4, 11, 16–19, 23, 28, 35–37, 47, 177; in the Centro jurisdiction, 32–33; internal security and, 26–27, 29–30
Wilson, James, 177, 180
Wilson, Richard, 183
withdrawal/evacuation of Spanish army, 100, 109–11, 186
women, 29, 49, 81, 93, 99, 130–31, 155–56, 173

Wood, Leonard, 179, 254n9
Woodford, Stewart, 254n9
woodlands (*monte*), 54–55, 64–65, 68, 95, 260n83
Wurdemann, John, 25

Ximeno, Dolores María de, 52

Yara, Cuba, 42–44, 52–54, 92, 114
yellow fever, 136–38, 141, 144–45
Yriondo de la Vara, Florentino, 129
Yznaga, Fernando, 122

Zanetti, Oscar, 22
Zaragoza, Justo, 54
Zaragoza, Ramiro, 184
Zea, Pedro de, 65–66

www.ingramcontent.com/pod-product-compliance
Lightning Source LLC
Chambersburg PA
CBHW030734250426
43671CB00035B/352